THE NATIONAL QUESTION AND THE QUESTION OF CRISIS

RESEARCH IN POLITICAL ECONOMY

Series Editor: Paul Zarembka
State University of New York at Buffalo, USA

Recent Volumes:

Volume 21: Neoliberalism in Crisis, Accumulation, and Rosa Luxemburg's Legacy – Edited by P. Zarembka and S. Soederberg

Volume 22: The Capitalist State and Its Economy: Democracy in Socialism – Edited by P. Zarembka

Volume 23: The Hidden History of 9-11-2001 – Edited by P. Zarembka

Volume 24: Transitions in Latin America and in Poland and Syria – Edited by P. Zarembka

Volume 25: Why Capitalism Survives Crises: The Shock Absorbers – Edited by P. Zarembka

RESEARCH IN POLITICAL ECONOMY VOLUME 26

THE NATIONAL QUESTION AND THE QUESTION OF CRISIS

EDITED BY

PAUL ZAREMBKA

State University of New York at Buffalo, USA

United Kingdom – North America – Japan
India – Malaysia – China

Emerald Group Publishing Limited
Howard House, Wagon Lane, Bingley BD16 1WA, UK

First edition 2010

Reprints and permission service
Contact: booksandseries@emeraldinsight.com

British Library Cataloguing in Publication Data
A catalogue record for this book is available from the British Library

ISBN: 978-0-85724-493-2
ISSN: 0161-7230 (Series)

CONTENTS

LIST OF CONTRIBUTORS *vii*

PART I: THE NATIONAL QUESTION

IS THE NATIONAL QUESTION AN APORIA FOR HUMANITY? HOW TO READ ROSA LUXEMBURG'S "THE NATIONAL QUESTION AND AUTONOMY"
Narihiko Ito *3*

IRAN: ISLAMIC REPUBLIC OR GOD'S KINGDOM? THE ELECTION, PROTEST, AND PROSPECTS FOR CHANGE
Farhang Morady *69*

PART II: CRISIS EMPIRICALLY AND THEORETICALLY UNDERSTOOD

CONSUMPTION DEMAND IN MARX AND IN THE CURRENT CRISIS
Radhika Desai *101*

LOW SURPLUS VALUE HISTORICALLY REQUIRED FOR ACCUMULATION, SEEN IN A MODEL DERIVED FROM MARX
Paul Zarembka *145*

WORLD MONEY: FROM THE EURODOLLAR TO THE SINODOLLAR
Karen Helveg Petersen 173

CRISIS AND "LAW OF MOTION" IN ECONOMICS: A CRITIQUE OF POSITIVIST MARXISM
Alan Freeman 211

PART III: A SCIENCE OF CAPITAL

FUNDAMENTALS OF A SCIENCE OF CAPITAL AND BOURGEOIS SOCIETY: MARXIAN NOTIONS OF VALUE, PRICES, AND THE STRUCTURE OF TIME
Jørgen Sandemose 253

LIST OF CONTRIBUTORS

Radhika Desai	Department of Political Studies, University of Manitoba, Winnipeg, Manitoba, Canada
Alan Freeman	Association for Heterodox Economics, London, UK
Narihiko Ito	Emeritus, Chuo University, Tokyo, Japan
Farhang Morady	Department of Social and Historical Studies, University of Westminster, London, UK
Karen Helveg Petersen	Radi-Consult, Copenhagen, Denmark
Jørgen Sandemose	Department of Philosophy, Classics, History of Art and Ideas, University of Oslo, Norway
Paul Zarembka	Department of Economics, State University of New York at Buffalo, Buffalo, NY, USA

IS THE NATIONAL QUESTION AN APORIA FOR HUMANITY? HOW TO READ ROSA LUXEMBURG'S "THE NATIONAL QUESTION AND AUTONOMY"

Narihiko Ito

> The historical mission of the bourgeoisie is the creation of a modern 'national' state; but the historical task of the proletariat is the abolition of this state as a political form of capitalism, in which they themselves, as a conscious class, come into existence to establish the socialist system.[1]
>
> (Rosa Luxemburg "The National question and Autonomy" Chapter 2)

> Only such a self-government will make it possible to unite various nationalities to jointly take care of the local economic and social interests, and on the other hand, to take into consideration in a natural way the different proportion of the nationalities in each country and each commune.[2]
>
> (Rosa Luxemburg "The National question and Autonomy" Chapter 5)

The National Question and the Question of Crisis
Research in Political Economy, Volume 26, 3–68

ISSN: 0161-7230/doi:10.1108/S0161-7230(2010)0000026003

1. PROLOGUE: THE END OF COLD WAR, COLLAPSE OF THE SOCIALIST SYSTEM, AND THE RISE OF THE NATIONAL QUESTION

In the second half of the 1980s, together with Perestroika in the Soviet Union, a process took place to end the Cold War as a confrontation between the United States of America and the Soviet Union. At the same time, this process caused the collapse of the Soviet Union and socialist system and thereafter the separation and independence of the many nationalities that constituted the Soviet socialist system in the East and South Europe. However to our regret, such nationalities could not enjoy freedom by independence, but went to brutal wars between separated nationalities. Even after many local wars and brutalities we cannot yet find the final solution through peace and justice for peoples.

Regarding my own nationality Japan as a "member of the West" entirely pursued the economic profit and enjoyed the illusion of a "Rich Big State" and yet fell into depression after the end of the Cold War and the collapse of the bubble economy. Notwithstanding, Japan is still believing in the illusion of a "Rich Big State" and going into ultranationalism by refusing the responsibility of invasion and war in its past and by militarization of the state and society against the Japanese Peace Constitution. Therefore, the Asian countries that were victimized by Japanese aggression are looking at Japan as a new threat.

Today, the appearance of nationalism shows diversity, but it seems to me that there is no theoretical viewpoint to observe nationalism in totality. This might be a reason why nationalism can be called as an "Aporia," even in the study of history and social science. But if we call nationalism as an "Aporia" of humanity, does it not mean that we cannot solve the struggle caused by nationalism? If we scientists give up on considering nationalism by calling it an "Aporia," how can we contribute to create a world with peace and justice?

Those who theoretically and comprehensively studied nationalism were the colonialists and the Marxists. Colonialists studied it from the viewpoint of imperialism ruling colonies, how effectively to invade and to dominate the colonies. Its purpose was not to solve the national question. Marxists studied it from the standpoint of the internationalism: "Let's unite workers in the world!" To create socialism internationally, first of all, it was necessary to solve the national question. Today, I think it is useful to consider the national question in the legacy of Marxist study.

For example: The works of Otto Bauer (1881–1938), Austrian Social Democrat, of Karl Kautsky (1854–1938), German Social Democrat, of Rosa Luxemburg (1870–1919), Polish, German, and Russian Social Democrat, and of Vladimir Ilyich Lenin (1870–1924), Russian Social Democrat. Among these Marxists, I would like to read here Luxemburg's main work on nationalism, "The National Question and Autonomy" (1908–1909)[3] and to consider the essence and solution of the national question.

2. THE FEATURES OF LUXEMBURG'S THEORY ON THE NATIONAL QUESTION

The first feature of Luxemburg's theory in "The National Question and Autonomy" is the absolute negation of the "right of nations to self-determination."

She criticized article 9 in the program of the Russian Democratic Labour Party: "The formula of article 9 which admits the right of national self-determination to all nations constituting the state does not give practical guideline for the day-to-day politics of the proletariat, nor any practical solution of national problems."[4] "In a word, the formula is essentially not a political and problematic guideline to the nationality question, but only a means of avoiding that question."[5]

She asks: "The 'nation' should have the 'right' to self-determination. But who is that 'nation' and who has authority and the 'right' to speak for the 'nation' and express its will?"[6] She asks further: "Does there exist even one political party which would not claim that it alone, among all others, truly expresses the will of the 'nation', whereas all other parties give only perverted and false expressions of the national will? All the bourgeois, liberal parties consider themselves the incarnation of the will of the people and claim the exclusive monopoly to represent the 'nation'."[7]

And then she indicates the reality of the "nation" according to the Polish example: "In Poland, the party of the Black Hundreds, National Democracy, had a claim to be the will of the people, and in the name of 'the self-determination of the nation' incited 'national' workers to assassinate socialist workers."[8]

She indicates: "Such a concept of the 'nation' is one of those categories of bourgeois ideology."[9] "In a class society, 'the nation' as a homogeneous sociopolitical entity does not exist."[10]

Indeed, "the nation" is an abstract and vague concept. But it is sure that the national question exists. Therefore, what does she think is the essence of the "national question"?

To explain it, she says, "For Social Democracy, the national question is, like all other social and political questions, primarily a question of class interests."[11] Therefore, "'The right of nations to self-determination' stops being a cliche only in a social regime where the 'right to work' has stopped being an empty phrase."[12]

In other words, "'the right of nations to self-determination' is only a metaphysical formulation of an idea which in bourgeois society is completely nonexistent and can be realized only on the basis of a socialist regime."[13] Therefore, the historical task of the social democracy is "called upon to realize not the right of nations to self-determination but only the right of the working class, which is exploited and oppressed, of the proletariat, to self-determination."[14] Here is expressed her fundamental idea that unless the right to self-determination of the working class cannot be realized, the right of nations to self-determination is meaningless.

From such a fundamental viewpoint she opposed consistently the restoration of the Polish independent state.

Why did she oppose so strongly the restoration of the Polish state? We have to think at least of two reasons. The first is her strong distrust in the modern nation-state in general. For her, the modern nation-state was an imperialist state that domestically oppresses and exploits the working class and ethnical minorities, and internationally invades and dominates the minor nations and weak states. She described the reality of the modern "nation-state" as following:

> The substance and essence of the modern state consists not in freedom and independence of the 'nation', but only the class dominance of the bourgeoisie, protectionist policy, indirect taxation, militarisms, war, and conquest. The bourgeoisie uses the obvious technique of trying to cover it up by offering the purely negative happiness of 'independence and national freedom'.[15]

> The struggle to stay in the world market, to play international politics, and to have overseas territories is both a necessity and a condition of development for capitalist world power. The form that best serves the interests of exploitation in the contemporary world is not the 'national' state, as Kautsky thinks, but a state bent on conquest.[16]

As an example of such a "state bent on conquest," Luxemburg pointed out the British and German states which are "based on national oppression in Europe" and indicated the United States of America as "a state which keeps in its bosom like a gaping wound the oppression of the Negro people, and seeks to conquest the Asiatic peoples."[17]

At the same time, she indicated that the Polish people are seeking independence as an oppressed nation, and that there is a possibility that they would oppress other nations after the establishment of the Polish state:

> We do not have to go far for an example, Polish bourgeois nationalism is directed as much against the Ruthenians as against the Lithuanians. The very nationality which had to endure the bitter policy of extermination by the partitioning powers – Prussia and Russia – now refuses the right of independent existence to other nationalities.[18]

This was her observation on the "right of the national self-determination" and independent nation state. At the same time, it was a historically accumulated observation regarding the Polish labor movement.

3. THE BACKGROUND FOR LUXEMBURG'S THEORY ON THE NATIONAL QUESTION[19]

3.1. Nationalism or Internationalism? Two Streams in the Movement of Polish Socialism

The Polish Kingdom was divided three times (1772, 1792, and 1795) by three countries – Russia, Austria, and Prussia. Furthermore, after the Napoleonic war, Poland was divided again by the Vienna Conference. Therefore, the Polish people tried repeatedly to recover their national independence since the November uprising of the 1830. In such a manner the national movement in Poland made a tradition and even became a legend.

In 1861, the Russian serfs were liberated (in Poland under the Russian rule, the serfs were liberated 1864) and the capitalism started to develop. At the same time, the socialist movement was born beside the nationalist movement.

Polish youth such as Ludwik Warynski (1856–1889) and Stanislaw Mendelson (1857–1913) were expelled from Russia in 1876 and came to Warsaw to establish a socialist society. Warynski published the "Brussel Program" in 1878 and insisted on socialism through international proletarian solidarity. In 1879, he established together with Mendelson a newspaper "Rownosc" (Equality) for exiled Poles and, on November 29, 1880, in Geneva, he held the 50th anniversary meeting of the November uprising. For this meeting, Warynski made two international slogans: "For the sake of the International Socialist Revolution" and "For the sake of the World Socialist Republic of Proletariats," but omitted the slogan for the Polish national independence. Boleslaw Limanowski (1835–1935) and the nationalists criticized Warynski's internationalism and organized a group "Lud Polski" (People of Poland) and published a pamphlet titled "Patriotyzm i socjalizm" (Patriotism and Socialism) to insist upon the connection between the socialist and nationalist movements.

Warynski went back to Warsaw at the end of 1881 and in August 1882 established "The International Socialist Party of Proletariat" (The Great Party of the Proletariat or the 1st Party of the Proletariat). On September 1, he published an Appeal of the "Workers' Committee of Socialist Party of Proletariat" in which he declared that there are more miserable people than the Polish. They are the proletariat. He made solidarity with the Russian group "People's Will" that assassinated Russian Czar Alexander II. In this way, two streams were formed in the Polish socialist movement: one aimed at the international solidarity of proletarian movement and other aimed at the Polish nationalist movement. The confrontation was deepened.

The Socialist Party of Proletariat signed the Cooperation treaty with the Russian group of the People's Will in 1884 in Paris. But in August 1884, the leaders of the Party of the Proletariat were arrested. Twenty-nine members were found guilty and sentenced at the military court. In January 1886, gallows were built in the Warsaw prison for the first time since 1864. Four leaders were executed by hanging. Warynski was sentenced for life and died 1889 in the notorious Schlüsselberg prison in St. Petersburg.

Although the Party of Proletariat was oppressed very sharply, Marcin Kasprzak (1860–1905) already began to reorganize the party in 1887 and established the 2nd Party of the Proletariat in 1888. Luxemburg already had contact with the Kasprzak group in 1887 as a school girl and joined to the establishment of the 2nd Party of the Proletariat as she finished the second girls' school in Warsaw. In 1889, as she faced danger of arrest, Kasprzak recommended to her to emigrate from Poland to Switzerland. She went to Zürich and visited the University of Zürich where women could study.

In the summer of 1889, in Poland, young socialists Julian Marchlewski (1866–1925), Adolf Warszawski (Warski) (1868–1937), Bronislaw Wesolowski (1870–1919), and others organized the Union of Polish Workers (Zwiazek Robotnikow Polskich – ZRP) as a legal organization for a strike fund. On May 1, 1890, ten thousand Polish workers celebrated May Day for the first time. In May 1892, eighty thousand workers gathered in Lodz. They struck for four days against hard oppression from the Russian government.

In Germany, where the 1890 notorious law against socialists was abolished, with the support of German Social-Democratic Party, the Polish

Socialist League was organized. In Lwow of Austria 1892, the Galician Social-Democratic Party (Galicyjska Partia Socjalno-Demokratyczna) was organized by Ignacy Daszynski (1866–1930) and others as a part of the Austrian Social-Democratic Party.

On November 17, 1892, eighteen Polish socialists met together in Paris at the invitation of Limanowski and Mendelson and established the Union of Polish Socialists Abroad (Zwiazek Zagraniczny Socjalistow Polskich – ZZSP). Limanowski became chairperson. Mendelson drafted its program for the Independent Democratic Republic of Poland. In January 1893, he went to Warsaw in order to establish the Polish Socialist Party (Polska Partia Socjalistyczna – PPS). In February and March, he talked with the members of the Party of Proletariat and the Union of Polish Workers. They organized the PPS.

However, thereafter, the people of Warsaw knew that Mendelson defamed, in his nationalist organ, Marcin Kasprzak as a Russian spy. Kasprzak was respected among the Polish workers. Therefore, they became angry and developed deep distrust for Mendelson. The nationalist group rejected the program drafted by him.

The Mendelson group sent another member Tadeusz Wojciechowski (1838–1919) to Josef Pilsudski (1867–1935) in Wilno to hold the 1st Party Congress of the PPS and decided to give the mandate for the 3rd Congress of the Socialist International to the delegation of the Limanowski–Mendelson nationalist group.

In July of the same year, the newspaper of the nationalist group "Przedswit" (Before the Dawn) reported the Wilno Congress and so the decision of the mandate for the 3rd Socialist International Congress arrived in Warsaw. The PPS group in Warsaw held a conference at once and decided to give the mandate for the 3rd Socialist International Congress to Marchlewski, emigrated to Zürich.

In Zürich, Marchlewski together with Luxemburg and Leon Jogiches (1867–1919) organized the Group of Social Democrats Abroad from the former kingdom of Poland (Socjaldemokracja Krolestwa Polskiego – SDKP) and started publication of its organ "Sprawa Robotnicza" (The Workers Problem) in July in Paris. Then on July 30, Mrs. Warszawski visited Warsaw and reported on it to the PPS group in Warsaw. At that conference, it was decided that the PPS group in Warsaw change its name to SDKP (Social-Democratic Party of the former kingdom of Poland) and adapted "Sprawa Robotnicza" as its formal organ. Furthermore, in August, as they made formal contract with Luxemburg and other editors of the "Sprawa Robotnicza," they used "SDKP" as the name of their party for the first time and also decided to give mandate for the 3rd Socialist International Congress to Luxemburg.

As a result, on August 6, 1893, she made her debut as a 23-year-old woman on the international stage of the music hall in Zürich.

3.2. Antagonism at the 3rd Congress of the Socialist International in Zürich

From this debut, Luxemburg consistently represented the standpoint of the internationalism, which is the tradition in the Polish socialist movement since the 1st Party of the Proletariat.

At the Congress, she had to fight against nine Polish nationalists such as Mendelson and Daszynski representing ZZSP. They were supported by Karl Marx's and Friedlich Engels' conceptions and had old and good contacts with the leaders of the Socialist International. Mendelson particularly had personal acquaintance with Russian Georgii V. Plekhanov and Daszynski with Viktor Adler of the Austrian Social-Democratic Party. Compare them with Luxemburg who was unknown and had no contact with the leaders of the Socialist International.

Paul Frölich quoted in his book "Rosa Luxemburg: Her Life and Work" the recollection of Emile Vandervelde (Belgian socialist leader, 1866–1938) at the Congress in Zürich:

> Rosa, 23 years old at the time, was quite unknown except in a few socialist circles in Germany and Poland. ...Her opponent had a great deal of trouble in holding their ground against her. I can see her now; how she sprang to her feet out of the sea of delegates and jumped onto a chair to make herself better heard. Small, delicate and dainty in a summer dress which cleverly concealed her physical defects, she advocated her cause with such magnetism in her eyes and with such fiery words that she enthralled and won over the great majority of the congress, who raised their hands in favour of the acceptance of her mandate.[20]

His recollection was not exact because she did not win the vote (9 against to 7 in favor, abstentions 3).[21] Nevertheless, that was a great outcome at her first international stage.

The following is the last part of her report to be read at the Congress. She showed here very clearly her position to the national question.

> This program for the restoration of Polish independence will not be able to create the political activity corresponding to the need of proletariat because it does not consider the reality. A common minimal political program of the working class in the three Polish countries of today is practically impossible, because one country has relative wide political freedom with general voting right, the second must fight for the general voting

right because the political rights of the people is very miserable, and the third is completely under the yoke of absolutism. The political activity of the worker's party must always engage the given political forms.

The political action standing on the real situation today is as follows. For the Galician Polish proletariat, it is their task to fight for the general voting rights together with all Austrian proletariats. For the Polish proletariat in Poznan and Silesia, their political program is to organize together with German Social Democrat. For the Polish proletariat in Russian-Poland, their task, according to their real living condition and together with the whole proletariat in the Russian Empire, is to cry the common slogan – down with absolutism.

This program will finally lead the working class straight away to the triumph of the socialism and at the same time bring them near to the moment in which all suppression and subjugation of Poles will be stopped definitively and will remove the ground of all cultural oppression.[22]

Against the argument of nationalist ZZSP that the restoration of independent Poland is the absolute condition to solve the social problem in Poland and bring socialism, Luxemburg showed a road for the SDKP: Through the cooperation of the Polish proletariats of the three countries (Austria, Prussia, and Russia) with the worker's movement of the each country, the Polish people can obtain their political freedom and national liberation.

At the Congress of the Socialist International in August 1893, Luxemburg's mandate was rejected by the Polish nationalist group. It was, however, an opening of the struggle between the Polish internationalist and nationalist. Although her mandate was rejected, her debut gave a strong impression not only on Vanderverde, but also on other attendees, particularly on Karl Kautsky, chief editor of the magazine for the theory of German Social-Democratic Party "Die Neue Zeit" (The New Age).[23]

4. CONFRONTATION WITH MARX'S AND ENGELS' ARGUMENTS IN SUPPORT OF THE MOVEMENT FOR POLISH NATIONAL INDEPENDENCE

4.1. Controversy over Polish Question

After the debut in Zürich, Luxemburg contributed two articles on the Polish national question to "Die Neue Zeit" edited by Karl Kautsky. She wrote these articles toward the 4th Congress of the Socialist International to be held in July 1896 in London. But before the London Congress, she ignited the controversy on the Polish question among members of the Socialist International. I pick up articles constituting the polemic as following:

- Rosa Luxemburg, "Neue Strömungen in der polnischen sozialistischen Bewegung in Deutschland und Österreich" (New Streams in the Polish Socialist Movement in Germany and Austria, *Die Neue Zeit*, Jg.14. Bd.2. 1895/96, Nr.32–33.)
- S. Häcker, "Der Sozialismus in Polen. Eine Entgegnung" (Socialism in Poland. A Reply), *Die Neue Zeit*, Jg.14. Bd.2. 1895/96, Nr.37.
- S. G., "Ein Beitrag zur Geschichte der Agrarpolitik Russlands in dessen polnischen Provinzen" (A Contribution to the History of Russian Agricultural Policy in its Polish Province), *Die Neue Zeit*, Jg.14. Bd.2. 1895/96, Nr.40.
- Rosa Luxemburg,"Sozialpatriotismus in Polen" (Socialpatriotism in Poland), *Die Neue Zeit*, Jg.14. Bd.2. 1895/96, Nr.41.
- Karl Kautsky,"Finis Poloniae?" (Will Finish the Polonaise?), *Die Neue Zeit*, Jg.14. Bd.2. 1895/96, Nr.42.
- S. G., "Die finanzielle Politik Russlands in dessen polnischen Provinzen" (The Financial Policy of Russia in its Polish Province), *Die Neue Zeit*, Jg.15. Bd.2. 1896/97, Nr.44.

Through these polemics, I focus on the points of the issue among them.

In her first article "New Streams in the Polish socialist movement in Germany and Austria," Luxemburg pointed out that, if the way to the independent Polish state was not through the socialistic change but only in the framework of the existing order, it only aims toward an independent capitalist class state that has nothing to do with social democratic thinking. Then she studied the practical possibility of their program and its result after its practice as follows.

First, the common interest of the bourgeoisie in the three parts of the former Polish Kingdom divided by three countries (Russia, Austria, and Prussia) is weakening because the economy of these three parts is developing in different ways. Particularly, the bourgeoisie in the Russian part is not interested in the reconstruction of Poland. Rather they are enthusiastic for the economic exploitation under the favorable conditions that are caused by the integration to the Russian Empire. Therefore, the reconstruction of Poland comes into conflict with the ongoing result of social and economic development.

If the Polish proletariat had the possibility to reconstruct Poland, then it does mean that it is also possible to begin to change the Polish society into socialism against the will of the three dominating states and against the

Polish bourgeoisie. But if their struggle for liberation were to succeed, it is not necessary to construct the independent state for the Polish workers.

If the Polish workers demanded within the German and Austrian labor movements the reconstruction of Poland, that demand would disturb the cooperation of the class struggle because reconstruction of independent Poland cannot become a common demand in the labor movement of Germany and Austria. Polish labor movement should, therefore, abandon the utopia of constructing the Polish class state with the force of the proletariats. The only way forward for the Polish workers in Germany and Austria are activities based on the common programs of the German and Austrian Social-Democratic Party.

The great difficulty before Luxemburg was not Polish nationalists, such as Dashinski and Mendelson who were not rooted in Poland, but Marx and Engels who supported consistently the Polish independent national movement. Hence, she also had to confront Marx and Engels in her article "New Streams in the Polish socialist movement in Germany and Austria."

4.2. The Polish Question and Marx and Engels

Marx and Engels, already before the Cracow uprising of January 1846, expressed their remarks on the Polish question. Here, I pick up some of their arguments.

1. Meeting in London on November 29, 1847, to mark the 17th anniversary of the Polish insurrection of 1830.

   After the rout of the November insurrection of 1830, many Polish democrats emigrated to Western Europe. Marx and Engels met with famous historian Joachim Lelewel (1786–1861) who was a leader of the November insurrection and emigrated to Brussels in 1845 for the first time. In January 1846, in Cracow, the Polish national government was declared. But there was no uprising in other districts. General Ludwik Mieroslawski (1814–1878) who organized the Cracow insurrection was arrested in Poznan. The insurrection was lost and the Cracow Free Republic was integrated into the Austrian Empire. But after the Cracow insurrection, the reconstruction of Poland was put in the basic foreign policy of the Western labor movement, especially in Britain, Germany, and France.[24]

   In November 1847, Lelewel established "La asociation democratique" in Brussels. Marx was elected Vice President of this association. On November 29, 1847, the "Society of Fraternal Democrats" organized the meeting to mark the 17th anniversary of the Polish insurrection of 1830 in London. Marx and Engels joined this meeting and made official speeches for the first time.

According to the report of "The Northern Star," Marx was introduced as following:

> Dr. Marx, the delegate from Brussels, then came forward, and was greeted with every demonstration of welcome, and delivered an energetic oration in the German language; The middle classes, the Free Traders, had held a congress, but fraternity was one-sided, and the moment they found that such congress was likely to benefit workingmen, that moment their fraternity would cease, and their congress be dissolved. The Democrats of Belgium felt that the Chartists of England were real Democrats, and the moment they carried the six points of their Charter, the road to liberty would be opened to the whole world. "Effect this grand object, then, you working men of England. You will be hailed as the saviours of the whole human race." [25]

Citizen Engels (from Paris):

> Fellow Citizens, the commemoration of the Polish Revolution is not only an advantage to Poland, but to the whole world, as it causes the principles of democracy to be spread far and wide. He, as German, had great interest in Polish success, as it would much hasten liberty in Germany, and freedom was resolved to be obtained sooner or later. And he firmly believed that no one nation could become free without benefitting all others. He had resided for some time in England, and was proud to boast himself a Chartist in 'name and all'. Who were now their chief oppressors? Not the aristocracy, but the wealth takers and scrapers, the middle classes. Hence, it was the duty of the working classes of all nations to unite and establish freedom for all.[26]

2. From the *Communist Manifest* (February 1848)

> In Poland they support the party that insists on an agrarian revolution as the prime condition for national emancipation, that party which fomented the insurrection of Cracow in 1846.[27]

3. K. Marx. Speech at the Polish Meeting in London, January 22, 1867.

> There is only one alternative left for Europe. The barbarism under the leadership of Moscow must fall over Europe's head like an avalanche, or she must restore Poland, thus placing between herself and Asia 20 million heroes, and gaining breathing time for the accomplishment of her social regeneration.[28]

4. K. Marx gave 10 Instructions to the Delegates of the Provisional General Council of the First International. The 9th Instruction was on the Polish question (February 20, 1867). He said as follows:

> "Why do we the workmen of Europe take up this question?

> In the present changed state of central Europe, and especially German, it is more than ever necessary to have a democratic Poland. Without it, Germany will become the outwork of the Holy Alliance, with it, the cooperator with republican France. The working-class movement will continuously be interrupted, checked, and retarded, until this great Europe question be set at rest:
>
> It is especially the duty of German working class to take the initiative in this matter, because Germany is one of the partitioners of Poland."[29]

5. K. Marx and F. Engels. To the Meeting in Geneva held to Commemorate the 50th Anniversary of the Polish Revolution of 1830, November 27, 1880, they sent a message to Geneva. The following is one paragraph from it.

> The cry 'Long live Poland!' which resounded throughout Western Europe was not merely an expression of sympathy and admiration for the patriotic fighters who were crushed with brutal force – with this cry, men hailed those people whose revolts ended so unhappily for itself yet always halted the advance of the counter-revolution, the people whose best sons never ceased to fight the struggle of resistance by everywhere going into battle under the banner of the popular revolutions. On the other hand, the partition of Poland consolidated the Holy Alliance, which served as a disguise for the Czar's hegemony over all the governments of Europe. Thus, the cry 'Long live Poland!' has really meant: Death to the Holy Alliance, death to the military despotism of Russia and Austria, Prussia, death to Mongole rule over modern society.[30]

Marx and Engels wrote and spoken many times on the Polish question. Their expressions shifted according to the situation. Around 1848, they emphasized "revolution" of the Polish movement from the standpoint of class solidarity. After 1863, their support to Polish nationalism, rather than to the solidarity of the class struggle, came to the fore. There were two elements. One is the sympathy to the Polish people who were deprived of the national independence and democracy. The other side was the Polish role as a seawall to protect the Western democracy from the Russian barbarism. They looked at the Polish national movement as an important buffer zone between East and West Europe.

4.3. Criticism against Social Patriotism

Against Marx's and Engels' support for an independent Poland, Luxemburg insisted in her article that the arguments of Marx and Engels belong to the beautiful time where "Pole and Revolution" – at least in the national sense – were identical.

> But now memory of all national uprisings belong to the forgotten past, because since that time, in the Russian-Polish sector, in the Polish heart and the stove of all national rising, nothing has happened except the total repeal of the bondage and the development of the big industries of capitalism through which the Polish social relations now also stand completely on its head. The Polish 'Revolutionaries' of the revolution 1848 – aristocracy – was bankrupted economically and politically. A new figure, bourgeois, appeared on the stage and is playing first violin, not the Polish national song "Pole is not yet lost" but the Russian national anthem "God save our Czar."[31]

She quoted Engels' analysis of Russia in his article "Can Europe Disarm?," which he published in Berlin *SPD*'s newspaper *Vorwärz* in March 1893:

> The internal situation in Russia is almost desperate at the moment. The emancipation of the serfs in 1861 and the development of large-scale capitalist industry related to it, partly as cause and partly as effect, have hurled this, the stablest of all countries, this European China, into an economical and social revolution which is now proceeding inexorably on its way; and its progress is, for the time being, overwhelmingly devastating.[32]

After this quotation she wrote:

> Today, Russia is no more Russia of Nicholas I. We no more need to protect ourselves against invasion by a physical wall. Now in her womb a strong upheaval is taking place, which will soon grow up and topple dawn the absolutism, unless it knew a timely concession. So, Russia is now in danger like 'a chicken-coop in the earthquake'.[33]

She quoted again from Engels' article.

> If it comes to war, ... The moment Russia loses a couple of battles the battlefield will be pushed back from the Vistula to the Dvina and the Dnieper; in the rear of the German army, under its the protection, an army of Polish allies will be formed; and it will be a just punishment for Prussia if it is then compelled to restore a strong Poland to ensure its own safety.[34]

Then she criticized the expectation of war as the reason to support the independent Poland:

> Those who think the independent Poland is necessary for Europe, expect the war. But first of all, even if it is spoken by Marx and Engels, war is against the principles of Social Democracy. Secondly, we cannot put the result of a future war as the basis of our program, unless the Socialist program accords to the war and the socialist is satisfied by war.[35]

Furthermore, in the beginning of her second article "Social patriotism in Poland," contributed to *Die Neue Zeit*, she criticized Häcker's argument that he did not insist upon the realization of Polish independence before "grossen Kladerradatsch" (crash, such as war or revolution): "It is nonsense that the Polish independence as a class state will be realized after the 'grossen Kladerradatsch'. The national liberation of Poland after the 'grossen Kladerradatsch' is obvious. It cannot form today the special postulate in our agitation."[36]

She criticized further the draft of the resolution which the Polish nationalist (PPS) made public before the London Congress of the Socialist International to be held in London in July 1896. It wrote: "The independence of Poland is for the international labor movement as well as for the Polish proletariat a necessary political demand." Against this she insisted, "This will disperse the united political struggle of all proletariats into the fruitless national struggle in each country."[37]

Against Häcker's other argument that the antagonism between the Russian government and Polish bourgeoisie makes a ground for the independence of Poland, she pointed out that the Polish aristocracy that formed the center of the Polish independence movement lost their economical and social basis after the liberation of the serfs in 1864 and "the era of the national struggle" was finished. So, she wrote, "There is now in Poland no social class which has an interest in the Polish reconstruction, and at the same time, there are no forces which can bring their interest in the reality."

After she studied all possibilities of each social class – bourgeoisie, petit-bourgeoisie, farmer, and intellectual, she concluded, "Today in Poland, a social stratum which has an interest in Polish independence has no power, and the stratum which has power has no interest in the Polish independence."[38]

As another important reason why the position toward Polish independence has no reality, she pointed to the formation of the Russian proletariat and its growth as a result of "change of Russia":

> Now the young mole is digging the foundation of capitalism and that is a guarantee from inside for the defeat of the absolutism. Russia now shows not only the bayonet but also the fighting proletariat and this is the natural guarantee for Europe to be liberated from the nightmare of Petersburg's autocracy. On the other hand, it is also the guarantee for the Polish proletariat that they are a partner of the Russian proletariat in the daily struggle to get their political freedom in their common 'Zwingburg'. Therefore, now the interest of the international movement for the Polish as well as the Russian is not to pursuit practically unrealistic reconstruction of the Polish class state, but, on the contrary, to unify all proletarian powers in the Russian Empire toward the overthrow of Czarism.[39]

She closed her article with the following words: "The struggle for the political freedom in Russia offers the Polish proletariat the possibility not only to gain their interest as workers, but also, in the only effective way, to obtain the autonomous freedom in Poland as the protector of the threatening Polish nationality." She used here for the first time the words "autonomous freedom in Poland (autonome Freiheiten in Polen)."[40]

4.4. Karl Kautsky's Theory in Support of Polish Independence and the 4th Congress of the Socialist International in London (1896)

The real opponent against Luxemburg who fought the Polish polemic on *Die Neue Zeit* against Polish nationalism was not Polish people but Karl Kautsky, its chief editor and the successor to Marx's thought. He published his article "Finis Poloniae?,"[41] and commented on Luxemburg's arguments. We can classify his comment into three parts: (1) The position of the Polish independence movement in the Western socialist movement, (2) criticism of Luxemburg's negative attitude against the Polish independence movement, and (3) the treatment of this issue at the London Congress of the Socialist International.

At the beginning of his article, Karl Kautsky pointed out: "It was not accidental that the 1st International was born from the big conference which was held in the hall of the St. Martin as an international solidarity to the January uprising of 1863 in Poland in September 1864."[42] Then he explained two reasons why the Western socialist movement had supported the Polish independent movement.

First, the Russian Czar's domination and intention to expand to the West and South are internationally dangerous to the Western democracy and civilization. The Polish people are the only Slavs opposing Russian Czar. Therefore, the reconstruction of the Polish state is important as a defensive wall against the Russian expansion.

Second, the Pole is the only resisting element in the Russian Empire and the Polish aristocracy that fought in the battlefield of the European revolution is always standing on the side of democracy. Looking back on such a history of the relationship between the Polish independence movement and the Western socialist movement, Kautsky explained that "Support to the Polish independent movement was the international duty of the Western revolution parties."[43]

Then he wrote, "It happened unexpectedly. An objection appeared from the Polish social democracy that the international labor movement should not support the Polish independent movement." He summarized Luxemburg's arguments in three points.

(1) The demand for Polish independence will not be achieved in the present society.

(2) The demand for Polish independence does not accord with the economic development that is aiming at the organic integration into Russia.
(3) The demand for Polish independence will divide the Polish social democracy into three parts and isolated from the practical task.[44]

After this summary, Karl Kautsky accepted many points of Luxemburg's arguments. He wrote: (1) Surely the Polish situation has changed widely. (2) The Polish aristocracy is defeated. The rump is asking for peace with Czar. (3) Poland is no more in a revolution state. Hence, the reconstruction of Poland has lost its meaning as a defensive wall against the Russian absolutism. (4) St. Petersburg is today more important as a revolution center than Warsaw. The Russian revolution movement is today more important as an international movement than the Polish.

But he opposed her position of the total negation of the Polish independent movement; "She goes too much forward. She denies not only the international meaning of the Polish question. She criticizes the Polish Social Democrats who demand the independence of Poland.

Then he asks her, "Is there no chance of the independence of Poland as Miss Rosa Luxemburg thinks?"[45] Admitting the big changes in the political, economic, and social situation in Russia and Poland, at the same time, he pointed out that there is still oppression of the Pole by the Russian. Hence, the Polish capitalists have the feeling that they are second-class citizens under the Russians. He pointed out, as a result of such a situation, that there is still a possibility that the antipathy against such discrimination could give power to the Polish national movement.

Furthermore, he insisted on the importance of language and that the society and language are closely connecting to each other. On the one hand, a closely connected community necessarily creates a certain language-community. On the other hand, the formation of society without a common language is very difficult. The Polish proletariat can find only in the Polish independent state their necessary basis to push their influence on the state. Therefore, the demand for Polish independence is not a meaningless play, but the greatest practical demand with the highest value. There is no reason to follow the Polish socialist who cries "Finis Poloniae."[46]

Third, he supported the slogan of the Polish nationalist as useful to the independent movement. But, on the other hand, he did not support their draft of the resolution which emphasized that "Independent Poland is a necessary demand for the whole international labor movement as well as for the Polish proletariat." Regarding this demand, he wrote of the Polish nationalist; "In the beginning of 1860 it was possible to make such a resolution against Russian Czar by demanding only Polish independence. But today, if we mentioned in the International Congress, only the Polish problem without a declaration on the Russian problem, it might be looked unfair to the Russian proletariat." Also Kautsky thought, if the resolution took up the concrete problem such as the Polish question, the people of Romania, Tirol/Trieste, Czechoslovakia, etc. will also demand the confirmation of their national right. So, he insisted that the principle of the resolution should be to limit the support to the right of the national self-determination and to the protest against the colonial domination.[47]

The International Congress in London voted the resolution as following:

> The Congress declares itself in favour of the complete right of all nations to self-determination, and express its sympathy for the workers of every country now suffering under the yoke of military, national, or other despotism; the Congress calls on the workers of all these countries to join the ranks of the class-conscious workers of the whole world in order to fight together with them for the defeat of international capitalism and for the achievement of the aims of international Social Democracy.[48]

5. NATIONAL INDEPENDENCE AS STATE OR AS PEOPLE'S AUTONOMY – THEORETICAL ANTAGONISM AGAINST LENIN

5.1. From Switzerland to Germany

At the beginning of her article "The National Question and Autonomy," Luxemburg evaluated in 1908 the resolution at the Congress of the Socialist International in London (1896): "The London Resolution replaces the exclusive consideration of the Polish question by the generalization of the question of all suppressed nationalities, transferring the question from a national basis onto an international one, and instead of a definite, completely concrete demand of practical politics, which the motion of the PPS demanded – the reconstruction of independent Poland – the resolution expresses a general socialist principle: sympathy for the proletariat of all suppressed nationalities and the recognition of their right to self-determination."[49] She wrote in the same place: "(it) signified a rejection of the motion for the reconstruction of Poland."[50] But that was not her complete victory because the right of nations to self-determination was recognized in general by this resolution.

What finally decides this problem was not the resolution at the Congress but activity at the point of the workers' movement. Therefore, after the London Congress, as soon as she completed her dissertation "The Industrial Development in Poland," she migrated from Zürich to Berlin in order to enter into the Social-Democratic Party of Germany to work in the labor movement.

Her participation in the German Social-Democratic Party had double aims. The first was to have an influence upon the international labor and social movements through the biggest and strongest socialist party in the world, i.e., German Social-Democratic Party. The second was to have an influence through the German party among the Polish people in the area ruled by Prussia. The first aim was to have an influence toward the West and the second aim was to have that toward the East.

In fact, as soon as she moved to Berlin on May 16, 1898, she joined the German Social-Democratic Party; in June, she went to the Upper-Silesia (Gorno-Slaska) in order to join to the election campaign for the candidate of the German Social-Democratic Party among the Polish voters. She had a strong impression from the daily life of the Polish people in that area and sent a letter dated June 9, 1898 to her lover Leon Jogiches-Tyszka as following.

> What has given me the strongest impression was the landscape of this area: cornfields, meadows, forests, wide planes and the Polish language, Polish farmers everywhere. You cannot understand how all these make me happy. I feel as if I was new-born and as if I found again the ground under my foots. I am satisfied to hear their talks and satisfied to smell the air of this area! Yesterday I had to wait for one hour for a train to go back to Leibnitz. How I walked around there in the grain field and picked up corn flowers and corn poppy. For my happiness I was missing only *one*. I have already decided that I would not go to Switzerland in next vacation but you should come here (the same cost), and we will quarter in somewhere in the Silesien village. For I strongly believe that you will here revive and feel the same satisfaction as me, if you looked at so huge a corn field as far your eye can hard reach (the stalk now already stand higher than you!). A meadow with cows, which a six-years-old barefoot boy is taking care, and our pine-forest! And also our farmers, emaciate, dirty but a splendid race! In Kandzin I saw three families. Two farmer's families and a Jewish. They were going to America! What poorness! I almost drop a tear, but at the same time I was so happy to see them that I could not break away my eyes from them.[51]

This was her first impression when she looked at the life of Polish farmers in the area under the Prussian rule. It seems to me that this impression made a basis for her activities thereafter.

Thus, on the one hand, Luxemburg found a site of her new activity among Polish farmers and workers in the Prussian area. At the same time, on the other hand, from autumn 1898 till winter 1899, she criticized Edward

Bernstein's works in her series of articles "Social Reform or Revolution?" and she started the revisionist debate, through which she appeared as a young and sharp theoretician criticizing Bernstein, an authority in the German Social-Democratic Party as well as in the Socialist International movement.

5.2. New Phase of the National Question (1898–1903)

Almost at the same time as Luxemburg moved to Berlin, the new Socialist movements appeared in Eastern Europe. Russian Jewish workers in 1897 established their organizational "Bund" in Vilunius in Lithuania. In 1898, the Russian Social-Democratic Labour Party (RSDLP) was established. The leaders of the Russian socialists such as Georgii V. Plekhanov and Vladimir I. Lenin lived in exile in Switzerland. But finally the Russian Social-Democratic Labour Party (RSDLP) was established inside Russia.

Stimulated by such a new movement in Russia, the Lithuanian Social-Democratic group guided by Feliks E. Dzerzhinski (1877–1926) wanted to unite with the Social-Democratic Party in the former Polish Kingdom (SDKO), and guided Luxemburg and others. They did unite in December 1899 and developed into the Social-Democratic Party in the former Polish Kingdom and Lithuania (Socjaldemokracja Krolestwa Polskiego i Litwy – SDKPiL).

The development from SDKP to SDKPiL brought about its organizational enlargement and strengthened the position of Luxemburg and others in the Polish socialist movement. At the same time, they faced with a new problem in how they would constitute a new relationship with Bund and the RSDLP.

Until this time, the "National Question" for Luxemburg was according to her words in the "Struggle against Social-Patriotism in the PPS" which aimed at the reconstruction of the Polish independent state. She fought against Social-Patriotism and Social-Chauvinism by counterposing them to internationalism. In the 20th century, she faced new antagonism with Lenin over the problem as to how to fundamentally solve the national question.

The time between 1898 when Luxemburg moved to Berlin and 1903 when the new antagonism with Lenin appeared was, for her, the time of transition from domestic struggle to the international.

We should remark on her next four articles on national question written in this period:

1. "For the Protection of the Nationality" (1900, published as a pamphlet in *Posen*)

2. "Acrobatics of the Social-Patriotism's Program" (*Review of Social-Democracy*, 1902, No. 3)
3. "For the Remembrance of the (Party) Proletariat" (*Review of Social-Democracy*, 1903, No. 1)
4. "Relationship between Polish and Russian Socialism" (1903, manuscript, unpublished)

1. "For the protection of the nationality"

This article was published as a pamphlet in Polish in Posen under the Prussian rule. Its contents were (1) The system of de-nationalization, (2) Whose sin? (3) Our Allies, (4) Aristocrat, citizen, and the people in Posen.

At the beginning, Luxemburg pointed out that a Prussian culture minister ordered the schools in Posen to change the lesson on the religion in Polish language to German language and she wrote: "Our children living half day in the school from now on cannot hear their national language, the language of their father and mother." "The Prussian government excluded the Polish language step by step from school in Posen in past 20 years and also excluded the Polish elements from the public life in order to colonize this area, while German farmers and workers were migrated into this area."[52]

She asked what is its purpose? And she answers: "To erase the Polish language and Polish nationality from Prussia. To allow 3 million Pole to forget that they were born as Pole." And she called out to the Pole: "Now Polish people should express their anger! It is time to stand up against Germanization to protect the Polish nationality."[53]

> "How should we protect the Polish nationality?" She answered to it: by solidarity with the German Social-democratic party because *SPD* is only party which would help Polish people in Germany and solve the national oppression from the standpoint of class struggle. So she finished her article: "By alliance with German workers we stand against the exploitation of German and Polish ruling class and against oppression of the Prussian government: That is our slogan!"[54]

Thus, she insisted upon the protection of Polish nationality from the standpoint of the alliance with German Social-Democratic Party and German working class.

2. "Acrobatics of the Social-Patriotism's Program"

Luxemburg had criticized the nationalism of the PPS since 1893 as "Social-Patriotism." In 1903, she criticized the "Social-Patriotism" of the PPS once again and comprehensively: The international situation around the Polish independence movement had changed from the time when Marx and Engels supported it and a revolutionary movement now appeared inside Russia. So, she pointed out that, if PPS would stand on the standpoint of the political demands of the Polish proletariat, the right solution to the national question of the Polish people should be "National Autonomy," but leaders of the PPS still insisted upon armed struggle without perspective to the success in the future.[55]

In fact, this article foresaw the armed uprising of the right wing of the PPS guided by Josef Pilsudski (1867–1935). As a result, the PPS left wing that insisted upon mass struggle against Pilsudski split from its right wing and joined the SDKPiL in the 1905–1906 Russian revolution.

3. "For the Remembrance of the (Party) Proletariat"

In this article, Luxemburg analyzed and described the character and history of the Proletariat (the party) in the 1880s. Together with her unpublished article "Relationship between Polish and Russian Socialism" (1903–1906), this article has a very important meaning in the development of her idea on the national question.[56]

She first emphasized here that Proletariat (the party) established by Ludwik Warynski (1856–1889) and others in 1882 consistently stood against the Polish nationalism and the reconstruction of the Polish state from the standpoint of the struggle against class rule and for the socialism as symbolized by his famous word: "There is more poor nation than Pole. There is the proletariat."

Second, she clarified that the Proletariat (the party) theoretically stood on the standpoint of the social democracy according to Marx but practically they were under the influence of the Russian "Narodnaya Volya (People's Will)," especially in 1884 when they made an agreement with Narodnaya Volya on cooperation in Paris. Therefore, the Proletariat was faced with a dilemma as to whether to go on the road of social-democratic mass strategy or to the secret terrorist group strategy of Blanquism.

Why did Luxemburg write such an article for "Social-Democratic Review" in 1903? Because, it seems to me, she wished to show a desirable relationship between Polish and Russian parties by reflecting on the past relations – in the 1880s – just before the Congress of the RSDLP which was scheduled in July 1903 in Brussels. That is, she wrote her Russian manuscript just before the Congress, which seems to me to indicate that it should be her proposal to the RSDLP.

This manuscript was written between May and July 1903 in ink and was written in serial numbers from page 1 to page 116. Why was this manuscript was not finished? It may be that the plan for the unification of both the parties was canceled before the Congress of RSDLP.

In her letter to Luise Kautsky dated January 2, 1906, Luxemburg requested Luise Kautsky to send her Russian manuscript in her room in Berlin to Warsaw.[57] When she was arrested by Russian police on March 4, 1906, in Warsaw, the seized manuscript was composed of 129 pages. Perhaps she wrote 13 more pages in Warsaw.

The content of her article "Relationship between Polish and Russian Socialism" overlaps in many parts with her Polish article "For the Remembrance of the (Party) Proletariat." The characteristics of this manuscript are that (1) she emphasizes her negation of Polish nationalism by writing: "the negative attitude toward Polish nationalism is a red thread through all steps of the Polish Socialist movement," and "the Polish nationalism of the PPS divided the Polish revolutionary movement from the Russian movement and supported indirectly the despotic rule of the Czars," and that (2) she, at the same time, implicitly criticizes the remnant of Blanquism in the RSDLP by writing "Polish social-democracy cannot be strengthened unless the RSDLP strengthen its social-democracy."

Thus, she was writing her manuscript with the hope and expectation to unify with RSDLP at the 2nd Congress of the RSDLP scheduled in July–August 1903 in Brussels.

5.3. Luxemburg vs. Lenin – The First Confrontation

The SDKPiL held the 4th Party Congress on July 24–29, 1903, in Berlin and decided on the unification with the RSDLP under seven conditions, which included "the complete autonomy of the Polish Social Democrats regarding their internal problem such as Party Congresses, committee and documents related to their propaganda and organizational activity," "change in the description of article 7 in the program of the RSDLP to more exact wording to avoid the misunderstanding regarding support to Polish nationalism," and "to adopt a resolution by the RSDLP against the Polish Social-Patriotism according to the spirit of the Polish Social-Democracy."[58]

On July 30, 1903, Adolf Warszawski (Warski), representing the SDKPiL, went to Brussels and attended the Congress of the RSDLP. Lenin already proposed a resolution "to welcome a Polish comrade as a guest" and the Congress adapted it. But at the same time, Lenin's article "The National Question in Our Program" (*Iskra*, No. 44) arrived at Luxemburg's.

On the top of that article, Lenin wrote almost the same ideas as of Luxemburg: "Our unreserved recognition of the struggle for freedom of self-determination does not in any way commit us to supporting every demand for national self-determination. As the party of the proletariat, the Social-Democratic Party considers it to be its positive and principal task to further the self-determination of the proletariat in each nationality rather than that of peoples or nations."

As Lenin was criticized by the PPS, he answered based on Karl Kautsky's article "End of Polonaise?" (1896 in *Die Neue Zeit*) that the Russian situation had tremendously changed from the time of Marx and Engels who supported the Polish movement for the reconstruction of the independent state. "In those times Poland was indeed the bulwark of civilization against czarism and the vanguard of democracy." "Today the advanced representatives of Marxism in the neighboring country, while attentively watching the political evolution of Europe and fully sympathizing with the heroic struggle of the Poles, nevertheless frankly admit that at present St. Petersburg has become a much more important revolutionary center than Warsaw, and the Russian revolutionary movement is already of greater international significance than the Polish movement." This argument was almost same as of Luxemburg's. But, as he concluded his article, he explained article 7 of the program of the RSDLP based upon Karl Kautsky's standpoint and resolution at the London Congress of the Socialist International in the following manner:

> Russian Social-Democracy does not in the least intent to tie its own hand. By including in its program recognition of the right of nations to self-determination, it takes into account all possible, and even all conceivable, combinations.

Although Lenin wrote further: "The program merely demands that a genuinely socialist party shall not corrupt proletarian class-consciousness, nor slur over the class struggle, nor lure the working class with bourgeois-democratic phrases, nor break the unity of the proletariat's present-day political struggle. The reservation is the crux of the matter, for only with this reservation do we recognize self-determination."[59] But seen from the standpoint of Luxemburg and SDKPiL, Lenin nevertheless recognized the demand of the PPS for the Polish independence similar to Karl Kautsky and the London resolution.

Therefore, she immediately sent a letter to Adolf Warski in Brussels with a request to demand the RSDLP an amendment to the article 7 in its program and directed him, if Lenin rejected the amendment to the program, to stop negotiation with Russian.[60] Indeed, the plan for the unification of Polish and

Russian parties was canceled. The difference between both parties here appeared very clearly, although they were not aware of it at that time.

Plainly saying, Luxemburg insisted upon "National Autonomy" and Lenin insisted upon "National Self-determination" instead. What did this difference mean?

Lenin pointed out in his article "On the Manifest of the Armenian Social-Democrats" (*Iskra*, No. 33, February 1, 1903) following two principles as the lodestar for all Russian Social-Democrats on the national question:

1. No demand for national autonomy, but demand for the political and civil freedom as well as complete equal rights.
2. Demand for the right of self-determination of all nations forming part of the state.

Also, Lenin wrote: "It is not task of the proletariat to sermonize on the federal system or national autonomy."

Lenin also wrote in his article "Does the Jewish proletariat need an *independent political party*?" (*Iskra*, No. 34, February 15, 1903) regarding the decision of the Bund at their 4th Congress: "The Bund decided to change its name (without stipulating that it would like to hear the Russian comrades' opinion on the name the section of the RSDLP should bear) and to *introduce* new federal relations into the Rules of the RSDLP." And he criticized the Bund: "Having once demanded *federation* instead of autonomy in matters concerning the Jewish proletariat, you were compelled to proclaim the Bund an *independent political party* in order to carry out this principle of federation at all costs. However, by declaring the Bund an independent political party, you reduce to an absurdity your fundamental error on the national question; it will inescapably and inevitably be the starting point of a change in the views of the Jewish proletariat and of the Jewish Social-Democrats in general."

Lenin further pointed out that "*autonomy* under the Rules adapted in 1898 provides the Jewish working-class movement with all it needs: propaganda and agitation in Yiddish, its own literature and congress, the right to advance separate demands to supplement a single general Social-Democratic program and to satisfy local needs and requirements arising out of the special features of Jewish life."

The following conclusion of this article shows very clearly Lenin's idea at that time on the national question:

> In everything else there must be complete fusion with the Russian proletariat, in the interests of the struggle waged by the entire proletariat of Russia. As for the fear of being

> *steam-rollered* in the event of such fusion, the very nature of the case makes it groundless, since it is autonomy that is a guarantee against all *steam-rollering* in matters pertaining specifically to the Jewish moment, while in matters pertaining to the struggle against the autocracy, the struggle against the bourgeoisie of Russia as a whole, we must act as a single and centralized militant organization, have behind us the whole of the proletariat whose unity is cemented by the continual joint solution of the problem of theory and practice, of tactics and organization; and we must not set up an organization that would march separately, each along its own track; we must not weaken the force of our offensive by break up into numerous independent political parties.[61]

Lenin, according to Karl Kautsky's argument on the national question and resolution at the International London Congress, put "recognition of the right to self-determination for all nations forming part of the state" in the program of the RSDLP. But as the organizational principle inside of the RSDLP, he insisted "a single and centralized militant organization" against the right to national self-determination.

Luxemburg was, for the program of the SDKPiL, theoretically against the right to self-determination of the each nation. But as the organizational principle within the RSDLP, she demanded "the complete autonomy of the Polish Social-Democrats" within the RSDLP and practically demanded the "federal system," as Bund demanded.

Clearly, this says that the difference between Luxemburg and Lenin on the organizational question was, at this stage, "centralized organization beyond nationality" or "national autonomy against centralism." Hereafter, this difference will be the undercurrent of their antagonism on the national and organizational questions.

For instance, Luxemburg published her article "Organizational Question of Russian Social-Democracy" (1904, *Die Neue Zeit*) at the request of Potresov of the Russian Mensheviks. The motive why she wrote this article lay in her fear as she read Lenin's work "One Step Forward, Two Steps Back" in which he described the division of the RSDLP into Bolsheviks and Mensheviks in the 2nd Party Congress and explained: "A Jacobin who wholly identifies himself with the organization of the proletariat – a proletariat conscious of its class interest – is a revolutionary Social-Democrat."[62]

She felt that there was still remaining here the strong influence of the style of conspiracy and terrorism from the Nardnaya Wolya in the RSDLP. Therefore, she criticized Lenin's theory on organization as "ultracentralist tendency" and pointed out that:

> "The social-democratic movement is the first movement in the history of class society to be premised in its every aspect and in its whole development on the organization and the independent direct action of the masses.

In this sense, social democracy creates a completely different type of organization from earlier socialist movements, e.g., those of the Jacobin-Blanquist type."[63]

Through these arguments she very clearly showed her idea regarding democratic organization. At the same time, her criticism against Lenin connected with the plan for the unification of both the parties, a plan which failed in 1903 at the 2nd RSDLP Congress.

In his work "One Step Forward, Two Steps Back," Lenin criticized "the undoubted tendency to defend autonomism against centralism, which is a fundamental characteristic of opportunism in matters of organization."[64]

We can read Luxemburg's following words as her criticism of Lenin's "ultra-centralism," at the same time, as her argument to defend their autonomism when they joined the RSDLP.

The ultra-centralism that Lenin advocates seems to us, in its whole essence, to be imbued, not with a positive creative spirit, but with the sterile spirit of the night-watchman state. His line of thought is concerned principally with the control of party activity and not with its fertilization, with narrowing and not with broadening, with tying the movement up and not with drawing it together.[65]

6. RUNWAY TO "THE NATIONAL QUESTION AND AUTONOMY"

6.1. Runway (1): The Collection of Essays "The Polish Problem and Socialism"

In May and June 1905, Luxemburg published a collection of essays titled "The Polish Problem and Socialism," which contained 20 articles by many authors, such as "The New Trend of the Polish Socialist Movement in Germany and Austria" (R. Luxemburg in *Die Neue Zeit*, 1995/1996), "The End of Polonaise?" (K. Kautsky in *Die Neue Zeit*, 1995/1996), "Polish Problem" (Parvus (Helphand Aleksander) in *Sachsische Arbeiter Zeituung*, 1896), "Polish Problem" (F. Mehring, 1902), "The National Question in Our Program" (Lenin in *Iskra*, 1903), etc. She contributed a long preface for it.

In the preface, Luxemburg summarized her arguments on Polish question. She reflected upon Marx's and Engels' expectations for the movement for the restoration of Polish independence, the birth of the socialist movement in Poland, and antagonism against the Social-Patriotism at the International Congress in Zürich (1893) and in London (1896), her dissertation

"The Industrial Development in Poland" (1898), and debate with Karl Kautsky on the Polish question. She concluded her standpoint as follows:

> Our proletariat can and must fight for the defense of national identity as a cultural legacy that has its own right to exist and flourish. And today our national identity cannot be defended by national separatism; it can only be secured through the struggle to overthrow despotism.[66]

Her foreword had very important meaning for her: On the one hand, it aimed to give a conclusion to the debate on the Polish restoration that had lasted about 10 years since 1893, whereas on the other hand, she prepared herself for the association with the RSDLP. She was very much satisfied with its performance. So, as she sent the foreword to Jogiches in Krakow, she wrote her pride in her letter dated May 7, 1905:

> The foreword has performed splendidly. It will be useful for our readers. It will teach them and give them data to decide the conclusion. What I am worrying about is whether I emphasized too strongly our standpoint against Marx. I think it might borrow trouble. …Seen as a whole, eventually it is a song on the victory of the Marxism.[67]

I believe this foreword was the first runway to her "The National Question and Autonomy."

6.2. Runway (2): "What We Demand? Comments on the Program of the SDKPiL"

The second runway to the "The National Question and Autonomy" was her comments on the program of the SDKPiL which was titled "What Do We Want?," which she started to write just after she finished her foreword.

The SDKPiL did not yet have a program since its establishment in 1900. She selected Jogiches, Warszawski, and Marchlewski as members of the drafting committee of the Party Program at the 4th Party Congress held on July 1903 in Berlin. However, they did not draft the program, and Luxemburg published "Outline of the Program" for the general public on the "Przeglad Robotniczy" (Labor's Review), which was published in January 1904 by the SDKPiL. But it was not enough. Therefore, just after she finished the essay collection "Polish Problem and Socialism," she began to write "What Do Ee Want?: Comments on the program of the SDKPiL."

She wrote to Jogiches from Berlin in her letter dated October 20, 1905:

This is in hurry because I just got your letter with comments on "What do we want?" and at once sat down to work in order to send it back by return mail and let you breathe freely. I included all your comments except for two:

1. I cannot figure out whether such details as the bicameral system, the responsibility of ministers, and so on belong in here, and if so, where. Let's keep it for the pamphlet anyhow, and by then we will decide.
2. Concerning the Duma, you are absolutely wrong in insisting we must mention it here. Something is wrong with your head, my treasure. These are comments on the program of permanent and general importance, a statement of our constructive demands, not some article or campaign pamphlet meant to last but a few weeks or months. Everything about the Duma must be said in Marchlewski's pamphlet, and I am not going to mention it here.[68]

She wrote further her thought on the "Autonomy" in her letter dated October 26, 1905, to Jogiches. It is very important as a document showing the formation process of her argument for "autonomy," which constitutes the pivot of her argument on the national question. I introduce the following details of her idea.

When I received your telegram, I thought over your remarks carefully, and found one of them very pertinent: namely, that we cannot base self-administration on cultural interests. Here, too, we must above all take into account not the "economic peculiarity" – as you put it inexactly – but rather the class struggle which is becoming ever more localized in character (due to the decentralization of capital). That is why I have tried to make a correction! "Historical and economic peculiarity" is mechanically repeated by the Iskra people after the bourgeois politicians, the way children imitate grown-ups – that only proves their lack of a critical faculty; and we are under no obligation to accept their theories.

This type of formulation is good enough for Trubetzkoi and Piotr Struwe (1870–1944). We are the party of class struggle, and not of "historical law."

As to the other remarks, I stand by my exposition:

1. I give first priority to the abolition of special privileges and to equal rights for all nationalities; self-administration is only a detail and a consequence. That is precisely the crucial point which differentiates us from the PPS, etc. and their notion of autonomy. For us, the starting point is the general interest – that the solidarity sought within national identity equals the solidarity of the proletariat. For the PPS, the starting point is – Polish peculiarity, which for other nationalities, inverting their autonomy notion, they derive magnanimous pipe-dreams based on "federalist maxims" like "Do not do unto another what you would not have him do unto you," "Each is master in his own house," "Unleash the elemental forces." We must hold on to our logical proposal in our agitation too, and, among other things, I will try to develop it in a brochure or an article about autonomy.

2. That is why I will not title my paper "Self-Administration" as you suggest, but rather "Institutions of the State which, etc.," as we proposed to Muscovites as an item in the general program and on national autonomy. Remember that we, as Social Democrats, although active on the spot, in contrast to the PPS, still are not a local particular party, but a splinter of a national party, which is why our program must maintain its basic national character in all points.[69]
3. Regarding Lithuania, I don't know what I should demand for it, whether we should demand one self-administration or two? We thank Zalewski. I will dare to demand autonomy "also for Lithuania." We should do it. But I speak from now on as "our country" as one. I will leave you the decision, whether you put in a short phrase, in order to give understanding that we demand the second Seim (Parliament in Wilna).[70]

She added further to this long letter a PS as follows:

P.S. As to the title, a few doubts come to mind: the "assurance to all nationalities" is a pious wish rather than a programmatic formulation of a demand. In the program, one should demand specific, concrete institutions, or laws. From this viewpoint, that formulation of ours which we proposed to the Muscovites (State Institutes) seems to me to be equally inappropriate now. Speaking concretely, what shall we now demand for all of them? I suggest "civic equality of rights for all nationalities residing in the Russian state, with the guarantee of linguistic and cultural freedom, especially in the schools, and territorial self-government for Poland and Lithuania.[71]

Feliks Tych, editor of Luxemburg's letters to Jogiches, wrote a footnote to this letter to explain the meaning of this letter:

The point of the self-administration was not put into the part II of "What do we want?". The article in the "Labour's Review" (1905, No. 6) announced that some points in this article – for example, the self-administration of the municipality, city and village – will be missing from the article because of the desire to avoid lengthening it since "What do we want?" will be later published with supplement as a pamphlet.[72]

"What Do We Want?" which was drafted by Luxemburg, was published in 1906 as a pamphlet together with part I and part II. Although she wrote on the Lithuanian problem in her letter to Jogiches, "I will dare demand autonomy *also for Lithuania*. We should do it.", the Lithuanian self-administration was omitted in the pamphlet.

As she was writing the foreword to the essay collection "The Polish Problem and Socialism" and "What Do We Want?," the Russian revolution of 1905 had already begun. In the process of the revolution in Warsaw, the RSDLP and two Polish parties (SDKPiL and PPS-Left) came close to each other. On April 1905, August Bebel, chairperson of the German Social-Democratic Party, appealed to the German labors who worked in the former Polish area to join the Polish Party (SDKPiL) and to act together with Polish labors. On June 1905, the RSDLP and the Polish Party (SDKPiL) approached each other quickly and the two military committees of both parties signed the contract of cooperation.

In such a situation, in November 1905, the Party Congress of the SDKPiL was held for the first time in the former Congress Poland under Jogiches's leadership. The Congress adapted the Party Program that was drafted by Luxemburg and decided the conditions for joining the RSDLP as "Autonomous Local Organization."[73]

On November 4, 1905, Luxemburg sent a letter from Berlin to Jogiches in Warsaw:

> Today, Martow and Dan arrived here. They are going to Petersburg from Berlin. They say that also Parvus will come here and go together with them. Starower (Potressow) and Vera (Sassulich) will soon appear here with the same purpose. You can understand how these influence me especially and how my heart is longing to escape from this miserable twaddle in the "Vorwarz" to go somewhere. I just envy them! When do you come here?[74]

Luxemburg waited for Jogiches in Berlin. He arrived in Berlin on November 5 and stayed a few days. But he went back to Warsaw soon. In the next month, on December 28, 1905, she entered Warsaw with a false passport with a false name of Anna Matschke. She joined Jogiches in Warsaw and led the revolution struggle of the SDKPiL.

6.3. 1905 – In the Midst of the Russian Revolution

On December 31, 1905, Luxemburg arrived in Warsaw and together with Jogiches began to lead the revolutionary struggle. But they were soon traced by the Russian police and arrested on March 4, 1906, at their refuge in Warsaw.

In the next month, April 1906, at the 4th Congress of the RSDLP, which was held in Stockholm, the SDKPiL joined the RSDLP. The SDKPiL publicly released their contract with RSDLP. Their contract included the "Autonomous" item as a condition of the unity. But the Russian contract lacked this item. The Polish side assumed that the RSDLP (Russian Social-Democratic Labour Party) had changed their program according to the request from Polish Party. But the Russian side did not ever think about even a possibility of such modification.[75]

The content of the contract between the SDKPiL and the RSDLP that was released on April 1906 was as follows:

1. The SDKPiL is a local organization among the RSDLP. The SDKPiL can work among the proletariats of all nationalities in this area and unite the activities of the whole parties in this area.

   Note 1. The Polish socialist organization can join to the RSDLP only to enter into the SDKPiL. The contract between the RSDLP and these socialist organizations can be effective only with the agreement of the SDKPiL.

   Note 2. The relationship between the SDKPiL and the Bund will be decided only by the agreement with RSDLP. The SDKPiL can decide their cooperative activity with Bund on a case-by-case basis in this general framework.
2. The central committee of the RSDLP and the executive committee of the SDKPiL call a conference of all concerned organizations and decide that the Lithuanian will stay in the action field of the SDKPiL.
3. The SDKPiL decides independently everything relating to the place and form of its organization in its field of action and also decide independently the relationship of the other organization in its action field.
4. The SDKPiL holds its own Party Congress.
5. The SDKPiL maintains the right to decide independently all problems from the relationship between the SDKPiL and the trade unions.
6. The SDKPiL attends the Party Congress of the RSDLP together with the other organizations based on the same principles.
7. The SDKPiL sends a member to the editorial office of the central organ of the RSDLP. This member joins in the entire works of the editorial office with the same rights as other members and also leads the political section.
8. The SDKPiL maintains its own mandate as far as the Polish constitutes a separate section at the Congress of the Socialist International and its bureau.
9. The SDKPiL maintains its former name as a subtitle of the RSDLP.
10. At all national conferences, if the many Polish active parties participate there, the SDKPiL will attend representing the RSDLP; also, the special representative person of the SDKPiL is obliged to attend there with equal rights as the other participants. (The national conference of the RSDLP acknowledges the demand for the Polish autonomy.)[76]

George W. Strobel comments on the last phrase in the parenthesis as following:

> In the RSDLP's contract with the SDKPiL in Russian language which was released after the joint conference of the RSDLP, the last phrase was not included. Therefore, the executive committee of the SDKPiL protested to the editorial office of the Bolshevik's daily newspaper "Vperoed" by pointing out this defect and insisted upon printing the letter of the SDKPiL' executive committee in the Vperoed. The editor of the "Vperoed" did agree to this demand but it was not printed.[77]

The Bolshevik of the RSDLP knew the rightness of the SDKPiL but neglected it.

> "The demand for the Polish autonomy" was very important for the SDKPiL as a condition of their unification with the RSDLP because it was related to the Polish state in the Russian Democratic Republic or the Russian Socialist Republic after the overturn of the Czar-Regime by the Russian revolution. Therefore, in the "Summary of the Program of the SDKPiL" which was drafted by Rosa Luxemburg and was approved at the Party Congress of the SDKPiL which was held on November 1905, for the first time inside of the former Polish Kingdom, the following phrase was clearly written: "The Polish Autonomy," together with "The equal right of the whole nations in the Russian Empire and the guarantee of their cultural development, use of the national school and national languages."[78]

Why did Luxemburg and the SDKPiL want the unification with the RSDLP on the one hand, and on the other, they demanded so persistently the Polish autonomy in the RSDLP? We can think the answer to this question comes from two sides: The first side is that the SDKPiL had to design in advance the situation of the coexistence of the whole nations, including the Polish, in the Russian Republic after the Russian revolution. In other words, if the Polish party could not build a normal relationship with the RSDLP based on the equal right and solidarity in the revolution movement, they could not imagine the equal right and their autonomy in the Russian Republic after the revolution. Therefore, they wanted the equal right and autonomy to establish a normal relationship with the RSDLP before the success of the revolution in the revolution movement itself.

At the same time, the SDKPiL wanted the absolute Polish autonomy concept against the idea of the independent Poland of the PPS. Thus, Luxemburg wrote the following in the pamphlet "What Do We Want? – Comments to the Program of the SDKPiL," which published 20,000 copies in 1906:

> Overturn of the Czarist and the achievement of the freedom are the first need for the Polish as well as for the Russian proletariat. Hence, in the political struggle the Polish workers together with the Russian build an unit, a political class with a same political program.[79]

In this way, Luxemburg put the solidarity of the Russian and Polish labor class as the first task. But at the same time, she did not ignore the national difference and discrimination. So, she wrote further in the "Comment to the Program of the SDKPiL":

> The Polish people, it is true, have a different existence within the Russian Empire as far as they are under the government of a foreign nationality. But the Polish proletariat will be further exploited and oppressed class, if they lived in their own national government, as the Russian proletariat will be further exploited and oppressed under their own government.[80]

Thus, although Luxemburg and SDKPiL were aware of the national question under the foreign government, they thought that the solution of the class problem is the first task, even to solve the national question.

6.4. Cooperation with Lenin and Bolsheviks

On Mach 4, 1906, Luxemburg was again arrested together with Leon Jogiches in the city of Warsaw by the Russian military police. But she was released on June 28, 1906, due to her "health problem," and on August 10, she arrived in Kuokkala in Finland where she met with Lenin, Bogdanov, and other leaders of the Russian revolution and directly talked with them for the first time regarding the Russian revolution.

Annelies Laschitza writes on this first talk between Luxemburg and the Bolsheviks: "She felt in the talking with them a completely different impression from what she got by reading of their printed matters."[81]

Peter Nettl wrote in his book on Luxemburg:

> Rosa Luxemburg spent most her time with Lenin and his immediate Bolshevik circle. She had met him personally only once before, during 1901 in Munich. ...Evening after evening she sat in Lenin's ground-floor flat in the house of the Leiteisen family in Kuokkala and talked over the Russian revolution at length with Lenin, Zinoviev, Kamenev, and Bogdanov. She made a considerable impression on them; 'the first Marxist who was able to evaluate the Russian revolution correctly and as a whole'. A personal sympathy between Lenin and Rosa Luxemburg – based, like all Lenin's friendships, on mutual intellectual respect – was born at this time and was to survive for six years until party differences drown it once more in the froth of polemics.[82]

After Luxemburg had a personal sympathy with Lenin in Kuokkala, in the next year she visited London to attend to the Party Congress of the RSDLP, which was held on May 13–June 1, 1907, in London. At the Congress, she made a speech representing the SPD and SDKPiL that the Russian revolution is not the last bourgeois revolution of the series in the 19th century, but heralds the proletarian revolution in the future. She particularly encouraged the RSDLP by stating that the RSDLP had a historical role to lead this revolution. And she recommended an overcoming of the split of the RSDLP since 1904 by emphasizing that the unity of the RSDLP is the most important condition to achieve this historical role.[83]

After the London Congress she moved to Stuttgart and attended the Congress of the 2nd International held on August 18–24, 2007 and cooperated with Lenin to strengthen the Bebel's resolution against the militarism and imperialism by adding the following phrase: "Facing the threat of the war. ... we are obliged to stop it with our best efforts. ... Nevertheless, with the outbreak of the war, we do our best to accelerate the abolishment of the rule of capitalism."[84]

In January 1908, on the way from Stockholm to Geneva, Lenin together with his wife Krupskaya visited Luxemburg in Berlin.[85] Thus, Luxemburg and Lenin were in the most intimate relationship from August 1906 onward. Under such an atmosphere she planned and wrote her article "The National Question and Autonomy."

7. THE POSITION OF "THE NATIONAL QUESTION AND AUTONOMY"

7.1. The Writing Process for "The National Question and Autonomy" – From Her Letters to Jogiches

On June 6, or 7, 1908, Luxemburg sent her letter to Jogiches:

> I will go on Tuesday or Wednesday to the seashore with my sister. I will send from there the first part of the article about autonomy for the next issue of the "Social-Democratic Review." I cannot promise to write the editorial. If there is no alternative, my autonomy article may be used as an editorial.[86]

She sent this letter from Berlin but a postcard dated June 12 to the Kautsky's family was sent from Kolberg at the Baltic Sea. So, she might have stayed from June 12 at Kolberg – she came to Kolberg in order to take care of her sick sister and stayed for 4 weeks. Meanwhile, she wrote the articles on autonomy. On June 19, 1908, she wrote a letter to Kostia Zetkin regarding her article:

> I am working now with my big Polish article on the autonomy of Poland. I treat this problem theoretically. I am very much interested in it. It will be published in three or four issues of the magazine. Then, it will be published as a pamphlet in Polish and Russian. Now I must give two articles for the issues of June and July by July 1st. Then, I will be free for my vacation.[87]

In her message, which might have been written on June 20, 1908, and sent the next day to Jogiches, she writes: "I cannot write a letter, because I am completely occupied by the Autonomy which I am writing almost new."[88]

According to these letters, I suppose, Luxemburg believed that she could finish her completely rewritten new articles on autonomy in three or four issues. Indeed, her article "The National Question and Autonomy" was published in four chapters in serial in the "*Social-Democratic Review*" as follows:

Chapter 1. August 1908 (No. 6)
Chapter 2. September 1908 (No. 7)
Chapter 3. October–November 1908 (No. 8–9)
Chapter 4. December 1908 (No. 10)

However, Chapter 5 was published in June 1909 (No. 12). Meanwhile, she wrote a letter dated May 1, 1909, to Jogiches:

> At the same time, today I sent by registered letter the manuscript on autonomy to Julek (Marchlewski). It is 90 sheets. I have written 106 sheets. But the article should not be more than 30 print pages. So, I divided it and added to the last part (I must write it further. I did not write even its draft).[89]

In her letter dated around May 25, from Levanto in Italy: "It is impossible to promise that I will finish the last part of the 'Autonomy' by June 10. I must write this thing completely new and I can do it only after few days."[90] In her letter from Genoa dated June 2:

> "As I already wrote, I do not think that I will finish the article on Autonomy by June 10. I need more materials as following:
>
> 1. Our old statements with demands for Autonomy (old "Sprawa Robotnicza," pamphlet published by Maciej Rozga); I have the "Review" from Zalewski.
> 2. The documents of the program of the National Democrat from the time before the revolution (with the demands for restoration), their first officially adapted program of autonomy (it must be 1903); also their appeal for election-campaign of January or February 1906 which I criticized in the editorial of our "Red Flag" (Czerwony Sztandar) in Warsaw, at least the number of the "Red Flag" of that day.
> 3. All documents of the program of the Progressive Party (pamphlets, etc.). I have only the formulation of their autonomy-project and other articles of the "Prawda."
>
> In the "Przedswit" of January or February 1905, there is a report on the negotiation of the "Paris Block" (from December 1904), but I also need the report on the Congress of the Kadett, National-Democrat and Progressives in Moscow (1904?). They are maybe in the "Liberation."[91]

Further in August, she wrote "I am still working with Autonomy. This article will be put not in the first folio but in the third folio. But I don't know how I can do it. If I hurry up, it might become nothing."[92] And in her letter dated August 10, she wrote:

> The plan of the work on Autonomy is so: Until now I explained why this subject belongs to the central authority. Now I will go to the reason for the autonomy's justification. The latter is therefore essential, because otherwise, after writing at great length on the competence of the central Parliament, there would be an inevitable impression that there is nothing left for Sejm and for our *Autonomy* – which would be a lie and a deception. Therefore, in order to give concrete content to our demand for autonomy, I will obviously develop the positive content of the autonomy as far as possible. I must, therefore, speak twice on the school system. At first I explain the reason of the general basis of the whole state, and after that the realization and the application of these principles which must be autonomous.[93]

The last chapter of "The National Question and Autonomy," Chapter 6, was printed in the "*Social-Democratic Review*" No. 14–15.

7.2. Negation of the Right of National Self-Determination

"The National Question and Autonomy" consisted of six chapters. I think it is necessary to notice at first the fact that Luxemburg did often call this article in her letters an "article regarding the Polish autonomy," but because her article is titled "The National Question and Autonomy," it is often read as her general opinion on the "National Question." Still, the purpose of this article was not her general explanation of the "National Question." It had a special purpose with a polemical character. She clearly wished to put the "Polish autonomy" as a decisive solution against PPS's argument on the restoration of the independent Polish state and to finish with the fatal antagonism from 1893 when the Polish socialist movement was divided into the PPS and SDKPiL.

Why did Luxemburg put the first chapter as "The Right of Nations to Self-Determination"? Because "The Right" was, according to her and the SDKPiL, an ideology by which the big nationality composing the "Nation-State" oppressed, integrated, and assimilated the small nationalities, and the PPS was a party aimed at reconstructing the Polish independent state based on this ideology. Therefore, SDKPiL was against the ideology of the "Nation-State" and criticized PPS based on "The Right." The RSDLP, RSDLP, also admitted "The Right of Nations to Self-Determination" in their program. Therefore, when SDKPiL unified with RSDLP, they requested the RSDLP to eliminate article 9 from their program.

As I already wrote, Luxemburg and Lenin were at the time in a very friendly relationship. Her purpose of the writing and publication of "The National Question and Autonomy" was not to criticize Lenin, but to explain her and SDKPiL's standpoint as a comrade fighting together against the Tzarist rule. Therefore, she put "The Right of Nations to Self-Determination" as a first chapter to point out the theoretical error of the RSDLP.

Here, she explained – by showing many materials such as Bruen thesis of the Austrian Social-Democratic Party and the resolution at the Congress of the Socialist International 1896 in London – how the RSDLP made a mistake by keeping article 9 of "The Right of Nations to Self-Determination" in their program. The central point of her insistence was that "The Right" gives no practical guidelines for the day-to-day politics of the proletariat, not any practical solution of nationality problem.[94]

What we should notice here is that Luxemburg considered always "The Right" from the viewpoint of the "practical guidelines for the day to day politics of the proletariat." According to this viewpoint, "A *right of nation* which is valid for all countries and all times is nothing more than a metaphysical cliché of the type of *rights of man* and *rights of the citizen.*"[95]

Young Marx pointed out in his books such as "Introduction to the Criticism on Hegel's Philosophy" and "The Jewish Problem" that the legal guarantee of *equality before the law* and *rights of man* can only be the *political liberation* of the people and "nothing more than a metaphysical cliché" without the social condition to support and practically to assure the rights. And he went to the same road in the "Manifesto of the Communist Party." Luxemburg was not against the idea of the *right of the nation.* She was against the illusion of this slogan which cannot solve the national question, but, on the contrary, reproduces the class society by establishment of the *nation-state.*

Therefore, she wrote:

> Social Democracy is the class party of the proletariats. Its historical task is to express the class interests of the proletariat and also the revolutionary interests of the development of capitalist society toward realizing socialism. Thus, Social Democracy is called upon to realize not the right of nations to self-determination but only the right of the working class, which is exploited and oppressed, of the proletariat, to self-determination.[96]

At the same time, we have to notice here that she did not see the relation between the *right of nations* and the *right of the working class to self-determination* as an absolute antagonism. She writes, "The position of socialists with respect to the nationality problem depends primarily on the concrete circumstances of each case, which differ significantly among countries, and also changes in the course of time in each country."[97]

Therefore, it is also possible theoretically to have coincidence of the *right of nations* with the *right of the working class*. But as a precondition for it, the problem of the class must be solved. Chapter 2 titled "Nation-State and the Proletariat" treats this problem.

7.3. Abolition of the Nation-State

Luxemburg points out that Karl Kautsky enumerates in his article on the struggle of nationalities and the Social-Democratic program in Austria, published over 10 years ago, that there are "three factors, which, according to him, make up the *roots* of the modern national idea, as founded in the rise of the modern state in all of Europe. These factors are, first, the desire of the bourgeoisie to assure for itself an internal or domestic market for its own commodity production; second, the desire for political freedom – democracy; and finally, expansion of the national literature and culture to populace."[98]

Then, she insists against Kautsky, in relation to his first factor, i.e., *the desire of the bourgeoisie to assure for itself an internal or domestic market for its own commodity production*, that the bourgeoisie needs not only that but also "many other conditions for its proper development: a strong military, as a guarantee of the inviolability of this *fatherland*, as well as a tool to clear a path for itself in the world market; furthermore, it needs a suitable customs policy, suitable forms of administration in regard to communication, jurisdiction, school system, and financial policy." And she emphasizes: "In a word, capitalism demands for its proper development not only markets, but also the whole apparatus of a modern capitalistic state."

So, she indicates, "the specific form of national aspiration, the true class interest of the bourgeoisie, is state independence" and "the nation-state is also simultaneously that indispensable historical form in which the bourgeoisie passes over from national defensive to an offensive position, from protection and concentration of its own nationality to political conquest and domination over other nationalities."

Furthermore, she writes, "Without exception, all of today's *nation-states* fit this description, annexing neighbors or colonies, and completely oppressing the conquered nationalities."[99] And she looks at the Polish case: "We do not have to go far for an example; Polish bourgeois nationalism is directed as much against the Ruthenians as against the

Lithuanians. The very nationality that had to endure the bitter policy of extermination by the partitioning powers – Prussia and Russia – now refuses the right of independent existence to other nationalities."[100]

Based on such analysis she insists upon her core argument of Chapter 2:

> The historical mission of the bourgeoisie is the creation of a modern *national* state; but the historical task of the proletariat is the abolition of the state as a political form of capitalism, in which they themselves, as a conscious class, come into existence to establish the socialist system.[101]

Now I want to ask about the relation between the national question and the proletariat aiming for the abolition of the nation-state and establishment of socialism, because this problem connects strongly with the national autonomy of the proletariat, Luxemburg's central theme. After she insists that "the *nation-state*, as an apparatus of the domination and conquest of foreign nationalities and indispensable for the bourgeoisie, has no meaning for the class interests of the proletariat," she explains the method to resolve the national question after the abolition of the states:

> Therefore, of these *three roots of the modern national idea* which Kautsky enumerated, for the proletariat as a class only the last two are important: democratic organization, and education of the populace. Vital for the working class, as condition of its political and spiritual maturity, are the freedom in using its own national language, and the unchecked and unwrapped development of national culture (learning, literature, the arts) and normal education of the masses, unimpaired by the pressures of the nationalists – so far as these can be *normal* in the bourgeois system. It is indispensable for the working class to have the same equal national rights as other nationalities in the state enjoy. Political discrimination against a particular nationality is the strongest tool in the hands of the bourgeoisie, which is eager to mask class conflicts and mystify its own proletariat.[102]

7.4. Centralization or Local Autonomy

Luxemburg rejected in Chapter 1 of her article the establishment of the *nation-state* by denying the "right of nation to self-determination," and in Chapter 2, by insisting on the abolition of the *nation-state* from the standpoint of the "right of proletariat to self-determination." Thus, she imagined Polish autonomy beyond the modern nation-state. Her Chapter 3, "Federation, Centralization, and Particularism," and Chapter 4, "Centralization and Autonomy," have a role in introducing Chapter 5, "The National Question and Autonomy," and Chapter 6, "Autonomy of the Polish Kingdom." Therefore, I will consider here Chapter 3 and Chapter 4 together.

Among the three aspects in the title of Chapter 3, she rejects federation and particularism but supports centralization. It looks strange that she would support centralization against the other two since she is against the nation-state in her principle and insists on Polish autonomy. Why does she support centralization?

According to her concept, she thought federation and particularism are reactionary before the historical development of the capitalism and that only centralization accommodates the development of the capitalism. Hence she wrote:

> As capitalism develops, centralization increasingly pierces all obstacles and leads to a series of uniform institutions, not only within each major state, but in the entire capitalistic world, by means of international legislation.[103]

She saw that centralization is a necessary result of – in current terms – the globalization of capitalism's. She thought that this centralization as the result of the capitalism's development will make a basis of the socialism in the future. So, she writes:

> This central tendency of capitalistic development is one of the main bases of the future socialist system, because through the highest concentration of production and exchange, the ground is prepared for a socialized economy conducted on a worldwide scale according to uniform plan. On the other hand, only through consolidating and centralizing both the state power and the working class as militant force does it eventually become possible for the proletariat to grasp the state power in order to introduce the dictatorship of the proletariat, a socialist revolution.[104]

> Therefore, the modern socialist movement, legitimate child of capitalistic development, possesses the same eminently centralistic characteristic as the bourgeois society and state. Consequently, Social Democracy is, in all countries, a determined opponent of particularism as well as of federalism.[105]

Did she really think that centralization is the necessary tendency of the capitalistic development and that capitalistic centralization will change at its highest point to the socialist movement which also includes the centralistic tendency? If she really thought that of socialism, what does her criticism mean against Lenin's "Organizational Problem of the Russian Social Democracy"?

Luxemburg's answer for this question is Chapter 4, "Centralization and Autonomy." She begins to write Chapter 4, "We have noted the general centralizing tendency of capitalism in the bourgeois state. But local autonomy also grows simultaneously out of the objective development and out of the needs of bourgeois society."[106]

Why does capitalistic development that includes necessarily the centralizing tendency need local autonomy which seems to be against the centralizing tendency? Let us listen to Luxemburg's explanation: "The centralism of the modern states is of necessity connected with a bureaucratic system." But:

> Capitalist production and exchange are characterized by the highest sensitivity and elasticity, by the capacity and even the inclination for constant change in connection with thousands of social influences which cause constant fluctuations and undulations in market conditions, and in the conditions of production themselves. As a result of these fluctuations, the bourgeois economy requires subtle, perceptive administration of public services which the centralized bureaucracy, with its rigidity and routine is not able to afford. Hence, already as a corrective to the centralism of the modern state, there develops, in bourgeois society, along with legislation by representative assemblies, a natural tendency toward local autonomy, giving the possibility of a better adjustment of the state apparatus to social needs. For local autonomy takes into account the manifold variety of local conditions and also bring about a direct influence and cooperation of society through its public functions.[107]

The local autonomy appears "as a corrective to the centralism of the modern state," yet, at the same time, she did not overlook that "local autonomy originates in all modern states very early, above all in the form of transferring the material burden of a series of social functions to the population itself." Therefore, she notices that "modern autonomy in all these forms is by no means the abolition of state centralism but only its supplementation; together they constitute the characteristic form of the bourgeois state."[108]

While, on the one hand, Luxemburg looks at the relation between the centralization and the local autonomy, on the other hand, she notices the contradiction and conflict between them.[109]

The more capitalism enters into the period of imperialism, the more it needs a strong authority. "On the other hand, autonomy itself puts up barriers to legislative centralization, even narrowly outlined and purely local, and no self-government is possible." Therefore, "the power of issuing within a certain sphere, of its own initiative, laws binding for the population, and not merely supervising the execution of laws issued by the central legislative body, constitutes precisely the soul and core of self-government in the modern democratic sense."[110]

And she points out the role of the social democracy:

> Social Democracy defends the view that a commune, district, or province is a social body called upon to take care – in the local sphere – of a number of social matters and not only financial ones. The practical conclusion of those two theories is that the bourgeois parties insist that electoral rights to self-government bodies should be limited by a

> property qualification, while Social Democracy calls for a universal and equal electoral right for the whole population.[111]

And she concludes this Chapter 4: "Precisely from the same foundations upon which, in all capitalistic states, grows local self-government, there also grows in certain conditions national autonomy, with local legislation as an independent manifestation of modern social development, which has as little in common with medieval particularism as the present-day city council has to do with a parliament of the ancient Hanseatic republic."[112]

7.5. Conditions of "National Autonomy"

Luxemburg indicated that "there also grows in certain conditions national autonomy." Then what are the "certain conditions" for it? The role of Chapter 5 is to consider this problem.

From the end of the 19th century, especially in her dissertation "The Industrial Development in Poland," she insisted that the capitalistic development of Poland needed the integration with the Russian market and deprived thereby the possibility of the independence of Poland. Therefore, she emphasized the "National Autonomy" of Poland instead of the national independence of Poland. And she explained the "certain conditions" of the "National Autonomy" as follows:

> Capitalism annihilated Polish national independence but at the same time created modern Polish national culture. This national culture is a product indispensable within the framework of bourgeois Poland; its existence and development are a historical necessity, connected with the capitalistic development itself. The development of capitalism, which chained Poland to Russia by socioeconomic ties, undermined Russian absolutism, united and revolutionized the Russian and Polish proletariat as a class called upon to overthrow absolutism, and in this way created, under the Czars, the indispensable preconditions for achieving political freedom. But within the framework and against the background of this general tendency toward the democratization of the state, capitalism at the same time knit more closely the socioeconomic and cultural-national life of the Polish kingdom, thus preparing the objective conditions for realization of Polish national autonomy.[113]

Luxemburg insists here that the capitalistic development in Poland united Poland and Russia in socioeconomic ties and created solidarity between the Polish and Russian proletariat to undermine the Russian absolutism, and, at the same time, this general tendency toward the democratization of the state knit more closely the socioeconomic and cultural national life of the Polish

Kingdom and prepared the objective conditions for the realization of Polish national autonomy.

However, the national autonomy is not possible everywhere under the social and cultural national lives. Then what are "the objective conditions for realization of Polish national autonomy"? She insists further:

> Where inside a modern state there exists distinct nationality districts constituting at the same time territories with certain economic and social distinctions, the same requirements of the bourgeois economy make self-government on the highest, country-wide level, indispensable. On this level, local self-government is also transformed, as a result of a new factor – national-cultural distinctness – into a special type of democratic institution applicable only in quite specific conditions.[114]

What we must notice here is that according to the requirements of the bourgeois economy, the local self-government comes out indispensable, yet at the same time, Luxemburg emphasizes that the local government is not always democratic, thus it must be transformed into "a special type of democratic institution applicable only in quite specific conditions." She further writes:

> The national autonomy of the Kingdom of Poland is primarily necessary for the Polish bourgeoisie to strengthen its class rule and to develop its institutions in order to exploit and oppress with no restriction whatsoever. In the same way as the modern state-political parliamentary institutions, and as their corollary, the institutions of local self-government are at a certain level an indispensable tool of bourgeois rule and a close harmonization of all state and social functions with the interests of the bourgeoisie, in a narrower sense, national autonomy is an indispensable tool of the strict application of the social functions in a certain territory to the special bourgeois interests of that territory.[115]

Furthermore, while she considers the "national autonomy" as the "most mature political form of bourgeois rule in Poland," she points out that "precisely for this reason, autonomy is an indispensable class need of the Polish proletariat." This observation is her special dialectical logic.[116]

Hence, she insists, "National autonomy has the same aims as are contained in the political program of the Polish proletariat: the overthrow of absolutism and the achievement of political freedom in the country at large; this is but a part of the program resulting both from the progressive trends of capitalist development and from the class interests of the proletariat."[117]

According to Luxemburg the national autonomy in Poland will be established after the overthrow of the Czarist absolutism and birth of the Russian Democratic Republic, but socioeconomically it will still be within the capitalistic system. This kind of the "national autonomy" is more favorable for the "self-determination of proletariat" compared with PPS's independent Poland that will be established by avoiding the struggles against Czarist absolutism.

But why will it be possible only in the Polish Kingdom? She answers this question.

> Local autonomy in the sense of self-government of a certain nationality territory is only possible when the respective nationality possesses its own bourgeois development, urban life, intelligentsia, its own literary and scholarly life. The Congress Kingdom demonstrates all these conditions.[118]

From this point of view, Luxemburg considers the possibility of the national autonomy among Jew, Lithuanian, Byelorussian, Caucasus, etc. After her conclusion that there are no conditions for the national autonomy except Poland, she writes:

> Just as in Lithuania, the only method for settling the national question in the Caucasus, in the democratic spirit, securing to all nationalities freedom of cultural existence without any among them dominating the remaining ones, and at the same time meeting the recognized need for modern development, is to disregard ethnographic boundaries, and to introduce broad local self-government – communal, urban, district, and provincial – without a definite nationality character, that is, giving no privileges to any nationality. Only such a self-government will make it possible to unite various nationalities to jointly take care of the local economic and social interests and, on the other hand, to take into consideration in a natural way the different proportions of the nationalities in each country and each commune.[119]

Therefore, her solution to the national question was "broad local self-government without a definite nationality character giving no privileges to any nationality" and "only such a self-government will make it possible to unite various nationalities to jointly take care of the local economic and social interests."

7.6. The Domain of "Polish Autonomy"

At the beginning of Chapter 6, "Autonomy of Polish Kingdom," she summarizes her views. At first, she writes as follows on the nations and the area outside of the Polish Kingdom:

> "The national autonomy is not a political form which can be applied only to all national group, nor a purely free ideal which will be aimed by the socialist under any condition. As the case of Lithuania shows, there is a case in which the application of autonomy would go against the freedom and democracy."[120]

And she writes on the territory of the Polish Kingdom as follows:

> The social, cultural and historical conditions of our country demand autonomy in the Polish Kingdom as indispensable. Precisely from this reason, autonomy becomes a demand of the program for the Polish revolutionary proletariats[121,122]

Therefore, Luxemburg firmly insists that *national autonomy* in the Polish Kingdom be based on a ground that the capitalistic development there is higher compared to other nations and areas. What is the necessity and merit for it? Chapter 6 was written to answer these questions.

In order to answer this question, she divides the discussion which should not be separated from the whole Polish Republic from a discussion with which the *national autonomy* must especially grapple. She counts first trade and tariff. Then she counts the traffic and communication. She sees, if these issues were separated by the name of autonomy, that this policy would be against the capitalistic development and weaken labor's unity and unification.

As far as the military is concerned, she insists upon abolishing the standing army and proposes the militia as the armament of all people. As far as the taxation system is concerned, she insists on the abolition of all indirect taxes and explains the policy of the Social-Democratic Party as follows:

> The reform of the tax-system by the spirit of the social-democratic program is only possible in relations with reform of the militarism, tariff-trade and world policy. The general and fundamental legislation of the tax-system must belong to the domain of the central parliament from the nature of the capitalistic development as well as from the fundamental position of the Social-Democracy.[123]

She insists further that public education, civil law, and criminal procedure code as well as legislation to protect laborers should be united within the Republic.[124] And she writes: "Also in the domain in which the democracy should in general guarantee such rights as those of coalition, association, assembly as well as freedom of speech and press, it needs for the same reason central legislation." So, she was against the division and decentralization because the "remains of de-centralism is solely used by the reactionary as means of conspiracy in the Republic of Switzerland as well as in the Monarchy of Germany."[125]

If the fundamental part of the people's life would be decided by the central government and Parliament of the Republic, where is the originality of the *national autonomy*?

What Luxemburg indicates as a task of the *domestic autonomy* is creation and bringing up of the public education and other fields such as agriculture, forestry, mining industry, traffic on the sea, and land and public health.

First, she insists on public education:

> All tasks of the development and construction of the public education from the following two decisive reasons naturally belong to the competence within autonomy. First, the experiences of all cultural states in the long time prove that public education can not well exist, if it were not organized by the organization of autonomy under the positive participation of the interested inhabitants. Secondly, the problem of public education is indivisibly connected as a thread of national life, that is, with the original language and spiritual culture of the each nation.[126]

The situation for the education of Polish people under Russian domination since 1815, which Luxemburg shows as a reason and background for her insistence, was cruel. Each fact which she shows here overlaps with the facts of the Japanese domination of people of Ainu, Taiwan, and Korea. The feudalistic rule of the Polish aristocracy and Russian colonial rule deprived Polish people of public education and pushed them into spiritual poverty. Therefore, she writes:

> As far as public education is concerned, in our country the legislation and administration of autonomy – after removal of the characterized works by managers of the Czar – will stay total tabula rasa, on which we must now construct a whole new building of the public education system from the ground to top – with the direct participation of the mass of our people.
>
> Whole re-building of the public education system means not only that the general education and the elementary, middle and higher school especially must respond to the social request, but also all institutes of the spiritual culture which were neglected by the administration of the absolutism, that is, the institute for the scientific study and experiment, supporting funds for the scientific study, school for arts and museum, etc.[127]

Luxemburg wrote in 1900 an article in Polish "For Defense of Nationality" (W obronie narodwosci) to protest strongly against the abolition of the Polish lectures in the school in Posen under the Prussian rule.

She exactly criticized in "The National Question and Autonomy" the destruction of the national culture under the Russian rule. What she points out as the other role of Parliament for autonomy is agriculture, forestry, mine industry, traffic on the sea, and land and public health. She closes this long series of articles published from August 1908 until September 1909 on the organ of the SDKPiL "Przeglasad Socjaldmokratyczny" as follows:

> If we add to the above mentioned areas and to that concerning the legislation for public health by including hospitals and every kind of medical institutions, we arrive at the legislation and administration of autonomy, that is the original culture, that is the culture of economic, social and spiritual activities. This culture has the most local and national character and connects directly with the interests of all the local inhabitants.

> To arrange the vast interests of these material and spiritual culture as much as possible from the standpoint of revolution and social progress, and also from the standpoint of the working mass of people is the original task of our administration. The working class of the Kingdom of Poland must make solidarity with the proletariat in the whole country to consciously point out this task.[128]

7.7. Is "The National Question and Autonomy" an Unfinished Work?

There is a conception that Luxemburg's article series "The National Question and Autonomy" is an unfinished work. This originates from Walski's article "Documents on the 4th Congress of the SDKPiL and the 2nd Congress of the RSDLP," which he published in the Polish magazine "*Z Pola Walki*" (From Battle Field) in 1929. He explained as follows:

> Only by reading quickly the last chapter of her articles ("The National Question and Autonomy") we can see that she did not finish her work. She did not want to answer this point. She would not explain its reason. But anyway it looks me that she wanted to take this problem completely out from her memory. However, when we read from her letters the history of the demand for autonomy in Lithuania, her article "what we want" and other articles in the "Przeglad Socialdemoktyczny" (Social-Democratic Review), she arrived at a result that it lacks some element for solving completely the national question in the nations under the Czarist Empire.[129]

Feliks Tych, editor of Luxemburg's letters to Jogiches, introduced Walski's article in the footnote to her letter dated May 25, 1909. But the explanation regarding the unfinished part of "The National Question and Autonomy" is based on Walski's conjecture. Luxemburg herself did not explain it and also later would not add to it. This does not mean that "The National Question and Autonomy" is a completed work.[130]

As I already pointed out, Luxemburg wrote to Jogiches in her letter dated August 10, 1909:

> My plan of work on autonomy is the following: Till now I argued the area belonging to the central authority, now I argue the area of autonomy. The latter was essential because otherwise after highlighting the authority of the central parliament, an impression must be avoided that nothing was left for the Sejmu (local parliament) and our *autonomy* was lie.[131]

I suppose she wrote the last part of Chapter 6 (of "The National Question and Autonomy") with such anxiety. Nevertheless, her explanation on the question why *national autonomy* has a possibility only in Poland is not enough. Further, if the national question could be solved in other district composed of many nationalities, the following question will arises: why must only Poland persist in *national autonomy*?

I understand that "The National Question and Autonomy" is not an article that argued the national question in general, but explained the national question in Poland from the viewpoint of the *Autonomy in Poland.*

8. CRITICISM AND EVALUATION OF "THE NATIONAL QUESTION AND AUTONOMY"

8.1. Lenin's Criticism

Lenin was the first person who violently criticized Luxemburg's "The National Question and Autonomy." But Lenin wrote his criticism after October 1913, four years after the publication of her work in 1909.

As I have already written, the relationship between Lenin and Luxemburg was very good when she published her article. However, after 1910, many problems arose between them such as: (1) her party (SDKPiL) tried mediating the split and antagonism between Bolsheviks and Mensheviks; (2) the relationship between the German Social-Democratic Party and Lenin–Bolsheviks became worst because of the antagonism about the management of the Bolshevik's funds[132]; (3) as a result of Lenin's intervention into the antagonism within the SDKPiL, after 1912 the relations between them became poor; and (4) especially after the disclosure that Lenin met Pilsudski, Luxemburg's political enemy as a leader of PPS, the relationship between them became worse.

An article, in which Lenin criticized her "The National Question and Autonomy", was titled "Critical Remarks on the National Question" (written in October–December 1913). He might have read the Russian translation of her work in a village near by Krakow.[133] I would guess that Lenin read the Russian translation of her work after their relationship became poor.

A main subject of the "Critical Remarks on the National Question" was *Cultural-National Autonomy*, insisted upon by the Jewish Party Bund. He criticized Luxemburg's article at the end of this work. Lenin wrote that "Rosa Luxemburg admits – and being a Marxist she is of course bound to admit – that all the major and important economic and political questions of capitalist society must be dealt with exclusively by the central parliament of the whole country concerned, not by the autonomous Diet of the individual regions."[134] And here he stands on the same ground as Luxemburg. Then he criticizes her: "One cannot help smiling, when reading how our magnificent Rosa Luxemburg tries to prove, with a very serious air and *pure Marxist* phrases that the demand for autonomy is applicable to Poland and by way of exception!"[134]

Lenin had here clearly misread her text because my guess is that he read it in Russian translation which was not exact. She did not wish to prove that the demand of autonomy can be applied only in Poland as an exception. She separated the general *regional autonomy* and the *national autonomy* and tried to prove that *national autonomy* can be applied only in Poland. As I already mentioned in the previous section, this separation had no persuasiveness. Nevertheless, she persisted in this theory because she had to compete with the argument of PPS, the recovery of the independent Poland State. The basis of her argument that *national autonomy* can be applied only in Poland was as follows:

> Modern domestic autonomy in the meaning of autonomy of a certain national area is only possible in places where the nation possesses its own bourgeois development, own city life, own intelligence, the life of literature and science. The Kingdom of Poland fulfills these all conditions. The population is nationally uniform, because, except for the Suwalski prefecture where the Lithuanian has advantage, the Polish has great advantage against other nationalities in the whole area of the Kingdom of Poland.[135]

Therefore, Luxemburg insists that in the area of the Polish population the development of capitalism and culture is advantageous compared with another area and nationality, and the Polish population is uniform and overwhelming a majority except for two prefectures. "Except two prefectures the Polish population constitutes more than 70% in the whole country and this population became a firm element of the social-cultural development."[136]

If we look at another side of her explanation, less than 30% of the population in Poland is not Polish. They belong to another nationality. Then, must they live outside of the Polish national autonomy? No, they should live equally in Poland. How did she think about that? She writes on it:

> Just as in Lithuania, the only method of settlement of the nationality question in the Caucasus, in the democratic spirit, securing to all nationalities freedom of culture existence without any among them dominating the remaining ones, and at the same time meeting the recognized need for modern development, is to disregard ethnographic boundaries, and to introduce broad local self-government – communal, urban, district, and provincial – without a definite nationality character, that is, giving no privileges to any nationality. Only such self-government will make it possible to unite various nationalities to jointly take care of the local economic and social interests, and, on the other hand, to take into consideration in a natural way the different proportions of the nationalities in each country and each commune.[137]

This is a very interesting idea and observation on the community of Caucasus. Therefore, I wonder why she must apply the national autonomy only in Poland. I guess the reason she persisted on *national autonomy* in Poland was that she must oppose the recovery of independent Poland of the

PPS. But Lenin disregarded the difference between the *national autonomy* and *general autonomy* that Luxemburg made and denied *autonomy in general*, because he believed that *autonomy* fundamentally opposes the *self-determination of the nation.*

Lenin wrote his second long article "The Right of Nations to Self-Determination" (February–May 1914) to criticize again Luxemburg's "The National Question and Autonomy." Lenin wrote this article with a very emotional sentiment. This is not polemic, but almost abuse. Relation between her party (SDKPiL) and his party (RSDLP) was the worst and Lenin attacked Luxemburg extremely. Hence, this article by Lenin is at the lowest level among his works, and theoretical difference between them is very clear.

8.2. Nation-State vs. Autonomy

Lenin's theory of nationalism completely depends on Karl Kautsky's theory. In the first chapter of his article "What Is Meant by the Self-Determination of Nations," he was irritated that Luxemburg did not accept Kautsky's theory, and he intimidated her: "A precise formulation of this question, which no Marxist can avoid, would at once destroy nine-tenths of Rosa Luxemburg's arguments."[138]

I think that Lenin's argument in this article will be summarized in the following sentence: "Consequently, if we want to grasp the meaning of self-determination of nations, not by juggling it with a legal definition, or *inventing* abstract definitions, but by examining the historico-economic conditions of the national movement, we must inevitably reach the conclusion that the self-determination of nations means the political separation of these nations from alien national bodies, and the formation of an independent national state."[139]

If I would say here their antagonism in a word, that is *nation-state* (but there is no *pure national state*, therefore the *nation-state* in the ideological meaning) vs. *Autonomy*. Here we should not forget that her article "The National Question and Autonomy" does not deal the *national question* in general but the national question in Poland only from the standpoint of *autonomy*. Luxemburg opposed the PPS, which under the Russian rule insisted upon the recovery of the Polish State dominated earlier by Polish aristocracy (Szlachta). At the same time, she tried to make solidarity with the Russian labor party to fight together with them against the Russian rule. Therefore, she insisted upon not *national independence* but *autonomy*.

Lenin belongs to the ruling nationality and could not understand such a difficult position such as Luxemburg and SDKPiL. At the same, because he did not understand such a difficult position, he pushed all nationalities under Russian rule by his theory of the *national self-determination* in order to get out psychologically from his *national yoke* of the ruling nationality as quickly as possible. Besides, he made accusations against those who would not accept his national theory. For example, he accused Luxemburg:

> It is here that we come up against the weakest point in Rosa Luxemburg's arguments. With extraordinary zeal, she embellishes her article with a collection of hard words directed against article 9 of our Programme, which she declares to be *sweeping, a platitude, a metaphysical phrase*, and so on without end. It would be natural to expect an author who so admirably condemns metaphysics (in the Marxist sense, i.e. anti-dialectics) and empty abstractions to set us an example of how to make a concrete historical analysis of the question. The question at issue is the national program of the Marxists of a definite country-Russia, in a definite period-the beginning of the twentieth century. But does Rosa Luxemburg raise the question as to *what historical* period Russia is passing through, or *what are the concrete* features of the national question and the national movement of that *particular* country in that *particular* period? No, she does not! *She says absolutely nothing about it!* In her work you will not find even the shadow of an analysis of how the national question stands in *Russia* in the present historical period, or of the special features of *Russia* in this particular respect![140]

However, the subject of her article is the solution of the Polish question. Therefore, it is very natural that she deals with the Russian national problem only in the context in the Polish question. It is obvious that the way to deal the Russian problem belongs to Lenin. But Lenin further puts strange questions.

> When, in her anxiety not to *assist* the nationalist bourgeoisie of Poland, Rosa Luxemburg rejects the *right* to secession in the program of the Marxists *in Russia*, she is in fact assisting the Grant-Russian Black Hundreds.[141]

Luxemburg and the Polish Social Democrats of the SDKPiL fought against the Polish nationalists (PPS), and so they must reject *the right to secession in the programme of the RSDLP* because they cannot fight together with Russian comrades, if the RSDLP holds in their program *the right to secession*. Why must Luxemburg be accused that they are *assisting the Grant-Russian Black Hundred*? To fight against *Grant-Russian Black Hundred* is the task of Lenin and the Russian socialists, but not task of Luxemburg and the Polish Social Democrats. That is a preposterously unjust charge to make against Luxemburg and the Polish socialists.

In this article, Lenin is arrogant and would not cut off the "right of nations to self-determination" from the program of his party. His argument became no more logical in its last part. For example, he explains the right to secession compared with the right to divorce as follows: "To accuse those who support freedom of self-determination, i.e., freedom to secede, of encouraging separatism, is as foolish and hypocritical as accusing those who advocate freedom of divorce of encouraging the destruction of family ties."[142]

This is an absurd and unreasonable analogy. Luxemburg did not oppose absolutely the "right of nations to self-determination." Her opposition depends on the case. She writes that even in her "The National Question and Autonomy, on the basis of the general assumptions of historical materialism, the position of socialists with respect to nationality problems depends primarily on the concrete circumstances of each case, which differ significantly among countries, and also change in the course of time in each country."[143] But Lenin denounces Luxemburg for "her inability to see things from a viewpoint any deeper and broader than that of the Krakow anthill."[144]

This is a very discriminating attitude toward a Jewish woman born in Poland by Lenin who belongs to a big nation. What was important for her was to fight against the Polish national-chauvinism. It was necessary for her to cut off the *right on nations to self-determination* from the program of the RSDLP. Her policy stands on the Polish concrete situation at that time even from the *viewpoint of the Krakow anthill.*

At the end of this article, Lenin writes: "In 1906 the Polish Marxists joined the Party: *neither* upon joining *nor* afterwards (at the Congress of 1907, the conferences of 1907 and 1908, or the plenum of 1910) *did they introduce* a single proposal to amend the article 9 of the Russian Programme!"[145]

This is also a lie. At the time of the unity of two parties, on April 1906, I already pointed out that the Bolsheviks cut out one clause in the contract presented by SDKPiL but without agreement (see Section 5.3). And her long article "The National Question and Autonomy," which Lenin denounced harshly, was written to request Lenin to cut out article 9 from the Russian Program.

8.3. Theoretical Differences between Lenin and Luxemburg and Historical Reality

How was Lenin after he denounced Luxemburg? Lenin wrote in an article "Discussion on Self-Determination Summed Up" (July 1916) as follows:

> We do not want to haggle over words. If there is a party that says in its programme (or in a resolution binding on all – the form does not matter) that it is against annexation, against the forcible retention of oppressed nations within the frontiers of *its state*, we declare our complete agreement in principle with that party. It would be absurd to insist

> on the *word self-determination*. And if there are people in our Party who want to change *words* in this spirit, who want to amend Clause 9 of our Party Programme, we should consider our difference with *such* comrades to be anything but a matter of principle![146]

Why the difference in tone from 1914 when he accused Luxemburg regarding "her inability to see things from a viewpoint of the Krakow anthill" just because she wanted to take out article 9 from Lenin's Party Program. I wonder, did Lenin really write this article by himself?

If Lenin could reasonably decide in 1903 that the RSDLP and the SDKPiL could smoothly unite, in which Lenin writes like Luxemburg:

> Take Poland's *specific* conditions in place of these general arguments: its independence *today* is *impracticable* without wars or revolution. To be in favour of an all-European war merely for the sake of restoring Poland is to be a nationalist of the worst sort, and to place the interests of a small number of Poles above those of the hundred of millions of people who suffer from war. Such indeed, are the *Fracy* (the Right wing of the PPS) who are socialists only in word, and compared with whom the Polish Social-Democrats are a thousand times right. To raise the question of Poland's independence *today*, with the existing alignment of the neighbouring imperialist powers, is really to run after a will-o'-the-wisp, plunge into narrow-minded nationalism and forget the necessary premise of an all-European or at least a Russian and a German revolution.[147]

What here Lenin writes was precisely what Luxemburg and the Polish Social Democrats insisted. Then, did Luxemburg and Lenin theoretically complete match? Speaking plainly, the theoretical difference between them lay in the point whether they admitted the formation of the State or not. The reason why Lenin persisted to keep article 9 of their Party Program was because Lenin thought that the formation of the State, namely the division and independence, is inevitable in order to solve the national question of the oppressed nationalities. For example, Lenin writes in his *theses* "The Socialist Revolution and the Right of Nations to Self-Determination" (January–February 1916):

> Victorious socialism must necessarily establish a full democracy and, consequently, not only introduce full equality of nations but also realize the right of oppressed nations to self-determination, i.e., the right to free political separation. Socialist parties which did not show by all their activity, both now, during the revolution, and after its victory, that they would liberate the enslaved nations and build up relations with them on the basis of a free union – and free union is a false phrase without the right to secede – these parties would be betraying socialism.[148]

But at the same time, he writes: "The aim of socialism is not only to end the division of mankind into tiny states and the isolation of nations in any form, it is not only to bring the nations closer together but to integrate them."[149]

The difference between Lenin and Luxemburg lay in the issue that Lenin insisted upon the *right to free political separation* of oppressed nations as a precondition for *free union.* Luxemburg insisted what is important is not the *right to self-determination of the states* but rather the *right to self-determination of the people* and strongly rejected the *formation of the nation-state.* Why did Luxemburg put the right of *people* against the s*tate*? Because the state always includes a *minority* and constitutes the class society. Her fundamental principle was that the *state and socialism cannot coexist.*

What is important, on the other hand, is that Lenin and Luxemburg had the same aim, that is *free union of all the nationalities* albeit through different means.

After the collapse of the Russian Empire, Lenin designed the formation of many small independent states and Luxemburg wanted the Polish autonomy in the vast Russian Republic. What did history later show?

The collapse of the Russian Empire by the Russian revolution and the collapse of the German and Austrian Empires by the defeat in the World War I liberated at once the nationalities under the rule of these empires and began to move the dynamics of class struggle in each nation. That was the course what Luxemburg as well as Lenin did not forecast.

Poland got independence because of the defeat of the three dominated empires, against Luxemburg's expectation. Her hope to establish Polish autonomy in the Russian Republic vanished. Pilsudski, Luxemburg's political enemy, made an independent Republic of Poland and raised war against Lenin's Russia (1919–1921).

Among the nationalities under the rule of the Russian Empire, Poland, Finland, Estonia, Latvia, and Lithuania became independent states. Other nationalities such as Ukraine, Belarus, Caucasus, in 1922 after the end of the Civil War, gathered to build the Union of Soviet Socialist Republics (USSR) together with Russia. Later, in 1924 Uzbekistan and Turkmenistan, in 1929 Tadzikistan, and in 1936 Azerbaydzhan, Armenia, Gruzia, Kazakhstan, and Kirgiztan joined the USSR. In 1940 Estonia, Latvia, Lithuania, and a part of Finland were forced to integrate into USSR.

Lenin wrote in his article "The Right of Nations to Self-Determination" that a "Marxist cannot include the defense of federalism in general in their programme."[150] History showed another reality against Lenin's theory.

8.4. Luxemburg's Theory on the National Question

Paradoxically speaking, Luxemburg developed her theory on national question after her work "The National Question and Autonomy." As I have written several times, "The National Question and Autonomy" was written to solve the national question of Poland from the viewpoint of *autonomy*. She did not argue in it about the national question in general. Her argument on the national question in general was developed later as the argument on imperialism in her works such as "The Accumulation of Capital" (1913), "The Crisis in German Social-Democracy" (1914), and "Manuscript on Russian Revolution" (1918).

Lenin got irritated when Luxemburg did not accept Kautsky's theory on nationalism that "for the whole of Western European, nay, for the entire civilized world, the national state is *typical* and normal for the capitalist period." He abused her in his article "The Right of Nations to Self-Determination" when he wrote "A precise formulation of this question, which no Marxist can avoid, would at once destroy nine-tenths of Luxemburg's arguments."[151]

At that time, what Luxemburg put against the *national state* of Kautsky was the *imperial state*. She wrote as follows in her work "The National Question and Autonomy":

> The form that best serves the interests of exploitation in the contemporary world is not the *national* state, as Kautsky thinks, but a state bent on conquest.
>
> Do we look to the British and German states as models, for they are based on national oppression in Europe and the world at large – and to the United States of America, a state which keeps in its bosom like a gaping wound the oppression of the Negro people, and seeks to conquer the Asiatic people.[152]

She wrote this article in 1908. Later in her work "Accumulation of Capital," she described minutely using many documents and materials how the European states penetrated into the noncapitalist areas to invade and exploit and became the *conquering state*. After the publication of this book, Lenin accused her in his article "The Right of Nations to Self-Determination": "After reading such arguments, one cannot help marveling at the author's ability to misunderstand."[153]

This was Lenin's real level at the time of 1914. Sumio Takanashi, Japanese scholar, analyzed Lenin's argument as follows:

> As far as I read Lenin's *The Right of Nations to Self-Determination* the opinions of Lenin and Rosa Luxemburg clash each other and do not engage, because their standpoints are completely different. Lenin argues the national question from the standpoint of the

> bourgeois democratic revolution, but Rosa Luxemburg stands on the precondition of imperialism. More critically speaking of Lenin, in June 1914 he had not yet established his understanding of the imperialism. That was a reason why their debate was fruitless.[154]

This is a very sharp remark. He quotes at the same time from Luxemburg's work after the outbreak of World War I, "The Crisis in German Social Democracy" (Junis Pamphlet), and pointed out as follows: "The invasion of the big powers of imperialism into the Balkan countries changed the slogan for the national unity and the build up of the independent state."[155]

Indeed, Luxemburg wrote in her work "The Crisis in German Social Democracy" on imperialism:

> Imperialism, with all its brutal policy of force, with the incessant chain of social catastrophe that it itself provokes, is, to be sure, an historic necessary for the ruling classes of the present world. Yet nothing could be more detrimental than that the proletarians should derive, from the present war, the slightest hope or illusion of the possibility of an idyllic and peaceful development of capitalism.[156]

Luxemburg had already watched the rise of imperialism since the end of the 19th century, and after the publication of her work "The National Question and Autonomy," she analyzed in many facets imperialism in her works "Accumulation of Capital" (1913), "The Crisis in German Social Democracy" (1914), "Manuscript of Russian Revolution" (1918), "Fragment on War, National Question and Revolution" (1918), and "Fragment on the History of the 1st and 2nd International and for the Problems of the Postwar" (1918)[157]. In these works, she describes imperialism and nationalism as the front and the back. For instance, German imperialism organized German nationalism to build the war system including the German social democracy. But my task in this chapter is to focus on her work "The National Question and Autonomy." Therefore, I must deal with the problem of the imperialism and nationalism in my next work.

9. EPILOGUE

Let's go back to the question at the beginning of this essay.

1. For Luxemburg, was the National Question an Aporia – a problem which is impossible to solve?

She was born in a small Polish town Zamosc under the rule of the Russian Empire in a Jewish family. She grew up in Warsaw and studied in a girl's high school where she was forbidden to use the Polish language and entered into a socialist group.

As an 18-year-old girl, she had to exile to Switzerland where she studied at Zürich University and became a doctor. She established in 1893 a Polish Social-Democratic Party in the Polish Kingdom together with her young comrades.

From the time of being a school girl, as a young socialist, she stood consistently upon internationalism. On May 1898, she went to Germany to join to the German Social-Democratic Party. In Poland as well as in Germany, she always experienced national discriminations, even inside the German Social-Democratic Party.

In the year 1900, she belonged at the same time to three parties (Polish, German, and Russian) and also was very active in the 2nd International. Therefore, she was always in the maelstrom of nationalism and the national question. The national question was for Luxemburg, a daily affair and fundamental problem for all nationalities. For her, the national question should not be an Aporia.

2. On February 16, 1917, Luxemburg sent a letter to her friend Mathide Wurm from Wronke prison during the World War I and showing symbolically her thoughts on being Jewish.

> What do you want with particular suffering of the Jews? The poor victims on the rubber plantation in Putumayo, the Negros in Africa with whose bodies the Europeans play a game of catch, are just as near to me. Do you remember those words written on the work of Great General Staff about Trotha's campaign in the Kalahari desert? "And the death-rattles, the mad criers of those dying of thirst, faded away into the sublime silence of eternity.
>
> "Oh, this "sublime silence of eternity" in which so many screams have faded away unheard, It rings within me so strongly that I have no special corner of my heart reserved for the ghetto: I am at home wherever in the world there are clouds, birds and human tears ... Your R."[158]

3. Her internationalism is not only her political policy and philosophical ideology. It comes directly from her heart. How was this internationalism to be built?

My friend Professor Jack Jacobs of New York University studied her father Eriasz Luksenburg through Jewish documents and showed that he was a leader of the *Enlightenment movement* in the Jewish society in Poland and was respected as a *Maskilim*.[159] He was against Zionism. He protected Jewish religion, culture, and customs and, at the same time, he encouraged the Jewish people to make friendly relations with the Polish society. Therefore, his home was always opened for the Polish neighboring people.

Her father's open-minded, humanistic thinking based on the *Maskilim* should be understood against the national oppression and discrimination and environment of her family as they influenced Luxemburg and established the background for her internationalism.

Hence, she stands always on the side of the oppressed and discriminated. That might be the original point of her national question. For her, the nationalities are always a real existence and support and help each other, not an *illusion connected with powerful state.*

But the nationalists connect always with *states*. They wish to expand their *states* not only in their illusion but also in the world. Invasion, national struggle, and war take away the illusion of nationalism. Nationalists cover up their class contradiction in their society and put it on the other nation. As a result, the strong states oppress the weak states. The typical examples are invasions into Afghanistan by Soviet Union in the 1980s and by the United States of America, and also invasion into Iraq by the Bush administration.

Therefore, the solution of the national questions depends on the international democracy. We use often the phrase *democratic state.* But the *democratic state* originally cannot exist. As Luxemburg insisted, the state and democracy cannot coexist. The solution of the national question is not *Aporia.* It will be solved only by the people's power, mutual support, and help of the many people beyond the national border and the nation-states.

It depends on the people of the 21st century how and when they will be able to abolish the state from the Earth.

NOTES

1. Rosa Luxemburg: "Kwestja narodowosciowa i autonomja. 2. Panstwa narodowe a proletariat" (Przegland Socjaldemokratyczny, 1908, Nr. 7, p. 603). English translation: Horace B. Davis "The National Question: Selected Writings by Rosa Luxemburg" Monthly Review Press 1976, p. 167.

2. Ibid, 5. Narodowosc i autonomja. (Przegland Socjaldemokratyczny, 1908, Nr. 10. p. 813). Horace B. Davis Ibid, p. 270.

3. "The National Question and Autonomy"("Kwestja narodowosciowa i autonomja" 1908–1909) was printed in the magazine "Przegland Socjaldemokratyczny" (Social democratic Review, theoretical organ of the SDKP which was established 1893 by Rosa Luxemburg, Leon Jogiches, Julian Marchlevski etc.; in 1901, the SDKP developed into the SDKPiL by joining the Lithuanian Social Democratic party). It was published over 2 years as follows:

Chapter 1. The Right of Nations to Self-Determination (Prawo narodow do stanowienia o sobie), August 1908, No. 6.

Chapter 2. The Nation-State and the Proletariat (Panstwa narodowe a proletariat), September 1908, No. 7.

Chapter 3. Federation, Centralization and Particularism (Federacja, centralizacja i partykularyzm), October—November 1908. No. 8–9.

Chapter 4. Centralization and Autonomy (Centralizatja i samorzad), December 1908, No. 10.

Chapter 5. The Nationality and Autonomy (Narodowosc i autonomja), June 1909, No. 12.

Chapter 6. The Autonomy of the former Polish Kingdom (Autonomja Krolewstwa Polskiego) September 1909, No. 14–15.

These articles were printed separately and never published as a book in Poland. After World War II, the first chapter was printed in the 2nd volume of the Rosa Luxemburg's "Selected Works" (Rosa Luxemburg, Wybor Pism T. 1–2, 1959). In Germany, the first chapter was translated into German: Rosa Luxemburg, "Internationalismus und Klassenkampf. Herausgegeben und eingeleitet von Jürgen Hentze," Sammlung Luchterhand 41, 1971. In France, a part of the first chapter was summarized in the book (Georges Haupt, Michael Löwy, Claudie Weill, "Les marxistes et la question nationale 1848–1914," Francois Maspero, 1974).

In English, American socialist Horace B. Davis translated up to Chapter 5. ("The National Question, selected writing by Rosa Luxemburg, edited and with an introduction by Horace B. Davis". New York, Monthly Review Press, 1987).

In Japan, the whole was translated from Polish into Japanese and published in 1984 as a book. In China, the first chapter was translated into Chinese (2nd volume of Rosa Luxemburg's "Selected Works," 1990). In Spain, "La Cuestion Nacional" (Traduccion y prologo de Maria Jose Aubet, El viejo topo 1998) was published. Translation was based on Horace B. Davis' English edition. Therefore, it lacks chapter 6.

4. "Kwestja narodowosciowa i autonomja," 1. Prawo narodow do stanowienia o sobie. in: Rosa Luxemburg," Wybor Pism T. 2 (1959), p. 122. H. B. Davis, Ibid, p. 109.

5. ibid, p. 123. H. B. Davis, Ibid, p. 110.

6. ibid, p. 123. H. B. Davis, Ibid, p. 141.

7. Ibid, p. 153. H. B. Davis, Ibid, p. 141.

8. Ibid, pp. 153–154. H. B. Davis, Ibid, p. 142.

9. Ibid, p. 154. H. B. Davis, Ibid, p. 135.

10. Ibid, pp. 147–148. H. B. Davis, Ibid, p. 135.

11. Ibid, p. 150. H. B. Davis, Ibid, p. 138.

12. Ibid, p. 151. H. B. Davis, Ibid, p. 139.

13. Ibid, p. 152. H. B. Davis, Ibid, p. 140.

14. Ibid, p. 153. H. B. Davis, Ibid, p. 140.

15. Przegland Socjaldemokratyczny. 2. Panstwa narodowe a proletariat. Nr. 7, 1908, p. 606. H. B. Davis, Ibid, p. 170.

16. Rosa Luxemburg, "Kwestja narodowosciowa i autonomja," 1. Prawo narodow do stanowienia o sobie. in: "Wybor Pism" T. 2 (1959), p. 143. H. B. Davis, Ibid, p. 131.

17. Ibid, p. 143. H. B. Davis, Ibid, p. 131.

18. Przegland Socjaldemokratyczny. 2. Panstwa narodowe a proletariat. Nr. 7, 1908, p. 602. H. B. Davis, Ibid, p. 164.

19. I refer in this Section 3 to the following books and studies. I would like to express my considerable appreciation for these authors.

- "Socjaldemokracja Krolestwa Polskiego i Litwy. Materialy i Dokumenty," Tom I, 1893–1903, Wydali H. Buczek i F. Tych. Ksiazka i Wiedza, 1957.
- M.K. Dziewanowski, "The Communist Party of Poland. An Outline of History," Harvard University Press, 1959.
- Peter Nettl, "Rosa Luxemburg," Kiepenheuer & Witsch, 1968.
- Georg W. Strobel, "Quellen zur Geschichte des Kommunismus in Polen 1878–1918" Verlag Wissenschaft und Politik.
- Ulrich Haustein, "Sozialismus und nationale Frage in Polen," Böhlau Verlag, 1969.
- Stefan Kieniewicz, "Historia Polski 1795–1918," Panstwowe Wydawnictwo Naukowe, Warszwa, 1970.
- Paul Frölich, "Rosa Luxemburg; Her Life and Work," newly translated by Johanna Hoornweg, Monthly Review Press, 1972.
- Georg W. Strobel, "Die Partei Rosa Luxemburgs, Lenin und die SPD," Franz Steiner Verlag, 1974.
- "The History of Poland Since 1863," edited by R. F. Leslie, Cambridge University Press, 1980.
- Annelies Laschitza, "Im Lebensrausch, trotz alledem Rosa Luxemburg. Eine Biographie," Aufbau-Verlag, 1996.

20. Paul Frölich,"Rosa Luxemburg. Gedanke und Tat," Verlag Friedrich Oetinger, 1949, p. 53. Paul Frolich, "Rosa Luxemburg: Her Life and Work," translated by Johanna Hoornweg, Monthly Review Press, 1972, p. 34.

21. "Protokoll des Internationalen Sozialistischen Arbeiterkongresses in der Tonhalle," Zürich, vom 6. bis 12, August 1893, p. 15.

22. Rosa Luxemburg, "An den III. Internationale Sozialistischen Arbeiterkongress 1893," in: Gesammelte Werke Bd. 1/1. Dietz Verlag, 1970.

23. Annelies Laschitza, "Im Lebensrausch, alledem Rosa Luxemburg. Eine Biographie," Aufbau Verlag, 1996, p. 49.

24. N. Rjasanoff, "Karl Marx und Friedrich Engels über die Polenfrage," in: "Archiv fur die Geschichte des Sozialismus und der Arbeiterbewegung," VI, Jg. 1916, p. 178. I learned many things on this subject from Rjasanoff' work.

25. Karl Marx & Friedrich Engels, "Collected Works," Vol. 6, p. 619.

26. Ibid, pp. 620–621.

27. K. Marx & F. Engels, "The Communist Manifest: A Modern Edition, with an Introduction by Eric Hobsbawm," Verso, London and New York, 1998, p. 76.

28. K. Marx & F. Engels. "Collected Works," Vol. 20, p. 196.

29. Ibid, p. 193.
30. K. Marx & F. Engels. "Collected Works," Vol. 24, p. 343.
31. Rosa Luxemburg, "Neue Strömungen in der polnischen sozialistischen Bewegung in Deutschland und Österreich" in Gesammelte Werke, Bad. 1/1, p. 33.
32. F. Engels, "Can Europe Disarm?," Karl Marx & Fredrick Engels, "Collected Works," Progress Publishers, Moscow 1990 Vol. 27, p. 386.
33. Rosa Luxemburg, Ibid, p. 31.
34. F. Engels, "Can Europe Disarm?," Karl Marx & Fredrick Engels, "Collected Works," Progress Publishers, Moscow, 1990 Vol. 27, p. 385.
35. Rosa Luxemburg, Ibid, p. 32.
36. Rosa Luxemburg, Ibid, p. 37.
37. Rosa Luxemburg, Ibid, p. 41.
38. Rosa Luxemburg, Ibid, pp. 46–49.
39. Rosa Luxemburg, Ibid, p. 42.
40. Rosa Luxemburg, Ibid, p. 51.
41. Karl Kautsky, "Finis Poloniae?" in "Die Neue Zeit," Jg. 14, Bd. 2, 1895/96, Nr. 42–43.
42. Ibid, Nr. 42, p. 484.
43. Ibid, Nr. 42, pp. 485–488.
44. Ibid, Nr. 43, p. 513.
45. Ibid, Nr. 43, p. 515.
46. Ibid, Nr. 43, pp. 521–523.
47. Ibid, Nr. 43, pp. 524–525.
48. "Verhandlung und Beschlüsse des Internationalen Sozialistischen Arbeiter- und Gewerkschafts-Kongresses zu London vom 27. Juli bis 1. August 1896," p. 18, in: "Kongress-Protokolle der Zweiten Internationale," Bd. 1, Paris 1889-Amsterdam 1904, Verlag Detlev Auvermann KG. 1975.
49. Rosa Luxemburg, "Kwestia Narodowoscowa i Autonomia," in "Wybor Pism," 2. 1959. pp. 120–121. "The National Question," "Selected Writings by Rosa Luxemburg. Edited and with an Introduction by Horace B. Davis," Monthly Review Press 1976, p. 108.
50. Ibid, p. 107.
51. Rosa Luxemburg, "Listy do Leona Jogichesa-Tyszki. Tom 1 (1893–1899)," Warszawa, 1968, pp. 196–197. Rosa Luxemburg "Gesammelte Briefe," Bd. 1, p. 143.
52. Rosa Luxemburg, "Zur Verteidigung der Nationalitat," 1900, in: "Gesammelte Werke," Bd. 1/1, p. 810, 1970.
53. Ibid, p. 810.
54. Ibid, p. 810.
55. Rosa Luxemburg, "Sozialpatriotische Programmakrobatik," in Rosa Luxemburg: "Internationalismus und Klassenkampf," Sammlung Luchterhand, 1971, pp. 176–177.
56. Rosa Luxemburg, "Dem Andenken der "Proletariat," in "Gesammelte Werke," Bd. 1/2, p. 362.
57. Rosa Luxemburg, "Gesammelte Briefe," Bd. 2, p. 241.
58. "Socjaldemokracia Krolestwa Polskiego i Litwy-Materialy i Dokumenty," Pod, editor, Feliksa Tycha, Tom II, 1902–1903. Ksiazka i Wiedza, 1962, p. 354.

59. V. I. Lenin, "Collected Works," Vol. 6, pp. 458–460, Foreign Language Publishing House, Moscow 1961.

60. "Socjaldemokracia Krolestwa Polskiego i Litwy-Materialy i Dokumenty," pp. 368–369.

61. V. I. Lenin, "Does the Jewish Proletariat need an *Independent Political Party*?," "Collected Works," Vol. 6, pp. 330–335.

62. V. I. Lenin, "One Step Forward, Two Steps Back," "Collected Works," Vol. 7, Progress Publishers Moscow 1965, p. 383.

63. Rosa Luxemburg, "Organisationsfrage der russischen Sozialdemokratie," in: G.W. Bd. 1/2, p. 252. "The Rosa Luxemburg Reader," edited by Peter Hudis & Kevin B. Anderson. Monthly Review Press New York, p. 250.

64. Lenin, Ibid, p. 396.

65. Rosa Luxemburg, Ibid, pp. 433–434. "The Rosa Luxemburg Reader," p. 256.

66. Rosa Luxemburg, "Przedmowa do ksiazki "Kwestia polska a ruch socjalistyczny," in: Rosa Luxemburg, "Wybor Pism, T. 1.," pp. 407–408. The English translation in "*The National Question. Selected Writings* by Rosa Luxemburg. Edited and with an Introduction by Horace B. Davis." Monthly Review Press, New York and London, 1976, pp. 97–98.

67. Rosa Luxemburg, "Listy do Leona Jogichesa-Tyszki, T. 2. (1900–1905)," "Listy zebral, slowem wstepnym i przypisami opatrzyl," Feliks Tych, Ksiazka i Wiedza, 1968, p. 328.

68. Rosa Luxemburg, "Listy do Leona Jogichesa-Tyszki," ibid, p. 500. English: "Comrade and Lover. Rosa Luxemburg's letters to Leo Jogiches." Edited and translated by Elzbieta Ettinger. The MIT Press, 1979, p. 152.

69. Rosa Luxemburg, "Listy do Leona Jogichesa-Tyszki," Tom 2, pp. 513–514. English Translation; "The letters of Rosa Luxemburg. Edited and with an Introduction by Stephen Eric Bronner with a Foreword by Henry Pachter," Westview Press, 1978, pp. 104–105.

70. Ibid, p. 514.

71. Ibid, pp. 515–516. English Translation, Ibid, p. 105.

72. Ibid, p. 516.

73. George W. Strobel, "Quellen zur Geschichte des Kommunismus in Polen 1878–1918, Programme und Statuten," Verlag Wissenschaft und Politik, Koln, 1968, p. 63.

74. Ibid, p. 536.

75. George W. Strobel, Ibid, p. 64.

76. George W. Strobel, Ibid, pp. 248–249.

77. George W. Strobel, Ibid, p. 249.

78. George W. Strobel, Ibid, p. 249.

79. "Was Wollen Wir? Kommentar zum Programm der Sozialdemokratie des Konigreiches Polen und Litauens," in: Rosa Luxemburg, Internationalismus und Klassenkampf. Sammlung Luchterhand, 1971, p. 92.

80. Ibid.

81. Annelies Laschitza, "Im Lebensrausch, trotz alledem Rosa Luxemburg. Eine Biographie," Aufbau-Verlag, 1996, p. 249.

82. J. Peter Nttl, *Rosa Luxemuburg*, Oxford University Press, 1966, Vol. 1, pp. 356–357.

83. Rosa Luxemburg, "Gesammelte Werke," Bd. 2, Dietz Verlag, 1972, p. 213.
84. Ibid, p. 236.
85. Rosa Luxemburg, "Listy do Leona Jogichesa-Tyszki," Tom 3, 1971, p. 25.
86. Rosa Luxemburg, "Listy do Leona Jogichesa-Tyszki," T. 3, 1971. English translation, "Comrade and Lover. Rosa Luxemburg's Letters to Leo Jogiches," Edited and translated by Eliizbieta Ettinger, The MIT Press, 1979, p. 170.
87. Rosa Luxemburg, "Gesammelte Briefe," Bd. 2, Dietz Verlag, 1982, p. 350.
88. Ibid, p. 351.
89. Rosa Luxemburg, "Listy do Leona Jogichesa-Tyszki," T. 3, p. 18.
90. Ibid, p. 22.
91. Ibid, p. 27.
92. Ibid, p. 41.
93. Ibid, pp. 47–48.
94. Rosa Luxemburg, "Prawo narodow do stanowienia o sobie," in: "Wybor Pism," T. 2, p. 122. English translation: "The National Question. Selected writings by Rosa Luxemburg. Edited and with an Introduction by Horace B. Davis," Monthly Review Press, 1976, p. 109.
95. Ibid, p. 123, English, ibid, 110.
96. Ibid, pp. 152–153, English, p. 140.
97. Ibid, p. 125. English, p. 112.
98. Rosa Luxemburg, "Panstwa narodowe a proletariat," in: "Przeglad Sicjaldemokratyczny," 1908, Nr. 7, p. 600. English, ibid, p. 159.
99. Ibid. English, ibid. pp. 162–163.
100. Ibid, p. 602. English, p. 164.
101. Ibid, p. 603. English, p. 167.
102. Ibid, p. 606. English, ibid, p. 169.
103. Rosa Luxemburg, in: "Przeglad Sicjaldemokratyczny," 1908, Nr. 8–9. English, ibid, pp. 189–190.
104. Ibid, English ibid, p. 190.
105. Ibid, English, ibid.
106. Rosa Luxemburg, "Centrallzacja i Samorzad" in: Przeglad Sicjaldemokratyczny, 1908, Nr. 10, p. 687. English, ibid, p. 214.
107. Ibid, pp. 687–688. English, ibid, pp. 214–215.
108. Ibid, p. 690. English, ibid, pp. 217–218.
109. Rosa Luxemburg uses here the two terms, *Samorzad lokalny (local autonomy)* and *Samorzad miejscowy (provincial autonomy)* in almost the same meaning.
110. Ibid, p. 708. English ibid, pp. 247–248.
111. Ibid, p. 709. English, ibid, p. 249.
112. Ibid, p. 710. English, ibid, p. 250.
113. Rosa Luxemburg, "Narodowosc i autonomja" in: "Przeglad Sicjaldemokratyczny," 1909, Nr. 12, p. 798. English, Ibid, pp. 255–256.
114. Ibid. English, ibid, p. 256.
115. Ibid, p. 799. English, ibid, p. 258.
116. Ibid. English, ibid, pp. 258–259.
117. Ibid. English, ibid, p. 259.
118. Ibid, p. 804. English, ibid, p. 265.

119. Ibid, p. 813. English, ibid, p. 279.
120. Rosa Luxemburg, in: "Przeglad Sicjaldemokratyczny," 1909, Nr. 14–15, p. 136.
121. Ibid, p. 137.
122. Ibid, p. 141.
123. Ibid, p. 152.
124. Ibid, p. 351.
125. Ibid, p. 356.
126. Ibid, p. 356.
127. Ibid, pp. 370–371.
128. Rosa Luxemburg, "Listy do Leona Jogichesa-Tyszki," Tom 3, 1971, p. 24.
129. Adolf Warski's article "Documents on the 4th Congress of the SDKPiL and the 2nd Congress of the RSDLP in "Z Pola Walki" (From Battle Field" in 1929).
130. Rosa Luxemburg "Listy do Leona Jogiches-Tyszki" Tom 3. 1974. p. 24. see Feliks Tych's comment.
131. "Listy do Leons Jogiches-Tyszki" Tom 3. 1974. p. 45 (Dated August 10, 1909).
132. See Annelies Laschitza, "Im Lebensrausch trotz alledem Rosa Luxemburg," pp. 404–409. Dietrich Geyer, "Kautskys Russisches Dossier. Deutsche Sozialdemokraten als Treuhander des russischen Parteivermogens 1910–1915," Internationales Institut für Sozialgeschichte Amsterdam, Campus Verlag, 1981.
133. Lenin, "Note on the National problem (II)," 1912, in Krakow.
134. Lenin, "Collected Works," Vol. 20, "Critical Remarks on the National Question," p. 46.
135. "The National Question," "Selected Writings by Rosa Luxemburg," edited and with an Introduction by Horace B. Davis. Monthly Review Press, 1976, p. 265.
136. Ibid. p. 266.
137. Ibid. p. 279.
138. Lenin "The Right of Nations to Self-Determination," Vol. 20, p. 396.
139. Ibid. p. 397.
140. Ibid. p. 402.
141. Ibid. p. 412.
142. Ibid. p. 422.
143. "The National Question. Selected Writings by Rosa Luxemburg, edited with an Introduction by Horace B. Davis," p. 112.
144. Lenin, "The Right of Nations to Self-Determination," "Collected Works, Vol. 20, p. 426.
145. Ibid, p. 446.
146. Lenin, "Discussion on Self-Determination Summed Up," p. 329.
147. Ibid, p. 350.
148. Lenin, "The Socialist Revolution and the Right of Nations to Self-Determination" (January–February 1916), p. 143.
149. Ibid, p. 146.
150. Lenin, "The Right of Nations to Self-Determination," Vol. 20, p. 441.
151. Ibid, pp. 306–307.
152. "The National Question. Selected Writings by Rosa Luxemburg, edited and with an Introduction by Horace B. Davis," p. 131.

153. Lenin, Ibid, p. 398.

154. Sumio Takanashi, "The National Question and Lenin," BOC Publishing House, 1987, p. 47.

155. Ibid. Sumio Takanashi.

156. Rosa Luxemburg, "The Crisis in German Socialdemocracy" (Junis Pamphlet), "The Rosa Luxemburg Reader," edited by Peter Hudis and Kevin B. Anderson. Monthly Review Press, 2004, pp. 337–338.

157. "Fragment on the History of the First and Second International and for the Problems of the Postwar," 1918, published for the first time in Annelies Laschitza "Im Lebensrausch, trotz alledem Rosa Luxemburg. Eine Bibliographie" Aufbau-Verlag, 1996, p. 580.

158. The Letters of Rosa Luxemburg. Edited and with an Introduction by Stephen Erich Bronner with a Foreword by Henry Pachter. Westview Press, 1978, pp. 179–180.

159. Jack Jacobs. "On Socialists and *The Jewish Question* after Marx", New York University Press, 1992.

IRAN: ISLAMIC REPUBLIC OR GOD'S KINGDOM? THE ELECTION, PROTEST, AND PROSPECTS FOR CHANGE

Farhang Morady

ABSTRACT

Since the election of June 2009, the Islamic Republic of Iran has witnessed a huge crisis with the outburst of street protests and demonstrations, challenging its validity. Indeed, it has been so intense that it has shaken the whole Islamic Republic for the first time since the 1979 Iranian revolution. What has happened since the disputed election was an upheaval few had anticipated, an opening of Pandora's box, with millions daring to question the, Velayate Fagih, *the most important constituent of the Islamic Republic. This postelection period has created a "revolutionary"' potential that has so far been met with repressive force and violence on the part of the ruling elites leaving no leverage for compromise. Of course, in the 30 years since the revolution, the Islamic Republic's power structures have faced factionalism. These recent developments demonstrate how deeply rooted run the contradictions and differences between the various groups. This upheaval has thrown all sorts of questions into the air: could Iran remain as a Republic? Or would Iran turn into a God's Kingdom, ever more dictatorial in its approach? Or would the splits within the ruling elites*

The National Question and the Question of Crisis
Research in Political Economy, Volume 26, 69–97

ISSN: 0161-7230/doi:10.1108/S0161-7230(2010)0000026004

continue to crack the fabric of the regime? Will there be a similar schism to that which took place during the Constitutional Revolution in the early 20th century when a leading member of the clergy, Noori, was finally hanged in July 1909 for being openly against reform? Finally, what is the possibility of change beyond the Islamic Republic in Iran?

1. INTRODUCTION

The uproar in Iran since the June 2010 presidential election has seen the most significant sequence of events in the Islamic Republic since the 1979 revolution. The legitimacy of the state and its institutions, especially that of the supreme leader, Ayatollah Ali Khamenei, have been questioned more than ever before in the Islamic Republic's 30-year history.

Since the outcome of the election, when the victory of Mahmoud Ahmadinejad was announced with an astonishing 62% majority, Iran has witnessed continuous protest and unrest. Although the trigger for this movement were questions over the election's legitimacy, allegedly rigged by supporters of the combatant president, the underlying economic, political, and social aspects cannot be set aside in any analysis of its causes. Over a year after there is no doubt that the magnitude of this mass movement has widened further the existing split within the Iranian ruling elites. Although factionalism has been a common character of the Islamic Republic of Iran (IRI) since 1979, the recent developments highlighted and magnified the contradictions and differences between various factions. This coupled with the IRI's violence and repression in response to opposition forces has allowed no possibility of conciliation, as the so-called Islamist conservatives, *Osulgarayan* (principalist) led by Iran's spiritual leader, Ayatollah Khamenei and president Mahmoud Ahmadinejad, now want only to impose their supremacy. This has caused so much concern that it even forced the Grand Ayatollah Montazeri, one of the founders of the IRI to accuse the ruling coalition that they should, ... *at least have the courage to declare that this government is neither a republic nor Islamic, with nobody allowed to protest, comment or criticize.*[1]

This is now at the heart of what is happening in Iran. That is, the extent to which the regime is removing from its republican element and how they present Islam both nationally and internationally. How long can dictatorial tools be used to repress the street protest? And what would be the reactions from the grassroots in Iran?

This chapter attempts to look at the roots of the postelection unrest and political crisis in Iran. It seeks to do so by unraveling the ideological ambiguity of Islam, its populist message, and its relations to social classes. It will argue that the current regime is not a return to the past or a break from modern global capitalism. Rather, it functions within a modern nation state with a populist ideology. In the light of this we will assess the patterns of socioeconomic and political development since the 1979 revolution and the changes within Iranian society. It will examine the class formation and the social base of different factions within the regime with special attention paid to the role of oil in Iran's politics and society. Finally, it will assess the extent to which the factionalism within the ruling elites will intensify the instability and how the opposition may react to this.

2. ISLAM, RELIGION, IDEOLOGY, AND SOCIAL CLASSES

In 1979 the establishment of the Islamic Republic, a state led by clergy, was not anticipated and has caused difficulties and confusion ever since. This is because it is supposedly "traditionalist" and against "modernization." Similarly because of its rise to power through revolution against the imperialism of the United States and the west (who supported the Shah's regime) this has been a key pillar of the revolution. As a result, there has been much confusion over the use and misuse of a concept such as "Islamic fundamentalism." It has become difficult to analyze what is seen as obscure, supported by traditional forces, and some poor groups in society. Yet in the light of what has been happening in Iran recently, the regime is now associated with totalitarianism[2] rather than its historical characterization as "progressive," and "anti-imperialist" in its opposition to the world oppressors. It is naive to characterize Ahmadinejad and his supporters as inherently antimodernist and totalitarian, as the political power in Iran operates through the modern institutions of parliament, presidency, and an apparatus with limited or managed levels of democracy. As Zubaida points out,

> Current Islamic movements and ideas are not the product of some essential continuity with the past, but are basically "modern." Even when they explicitly reject all modern political models as alien imports from a hostile West, their various political ideas, organisations and aspirations are implicitly premised upon the models and assumptions of modern nation-state politics. (Zubaida, 1989, p. ix)

It is equally wrong to suggest that the Islamic Republic is "progressive" or anti-imperialist (Petras, 2009). What is missing in both approaches is their inability to locate the class character of modern Islamism or to see its relationship to capital and the state (See Moaddel, 1993, pp. 215–218).

Religion is a social phenomenon and, as such, does not exist independently of the outside world: rather it has evolved and changed with regard to the transformation of social conditions that have occurred within every society. Religious institutions and ideas play a role in history but this does not take place in isolation. Religion with its institutions of hierarchy and clergy, arose from and interacts with society. Islam dates back to the 7th century in the Middle East, where it grew up in a trading community with a society organized on a tribal basis, yet today it is the official ideology of the modern capitalist state that is Iran.

Islam in general and the IRI, in particular, has been able to survive because it has been able to adapt to differing class interests. It has had the financial support of tradesmen, the bazaar, landowners, industrialists, and bureaucrats of modern capitalism in order to consolidate its role through building seminaries and recruiting students. It has equally gained the support of the mass of the people by offering comfort to the poor and oppressed, promising the exploited class a degree of protection. It is these ambiguities that provide various interpretations and an appeal to different classes, especially in times of social revolt, even if these ideas are contradictory. This has been the case since the origin of Islam, with Mohammed's death in 632 AD, when discussion broke out between those who followed Abu Bakr, the first Caliph to succeed Mohammed as leader, and Ali, his cousin and the husband of the prophet's daughter, Fatima. Ali and his supporters believed that some of Abu Bakr's rulings were oppressive (Lapidus, 2002).

The desire to recreate an imaginary past involves a reshaping of existing society but this does not mean a return to 7th century Islam, since the Islamists in general and specifically the Islamists in Iran do not reject every feature of existing modern Iranian society and have incorporated aspects of pre-Islamic culture, notably one of the most important festivals in Iran, New Year (Norooz). Far from dying off, this has maintained its importance since the Iranian revolution of 1979. Therefore, it is wrong to assume that Islam is a homogenous set of beliefs. In fact Islam has been incorporated into different societies of people who fitted aspects of Islam into their old religious practices, even if these contradicted some of Islam's original tenets (Roy, 1980). As Abrahamian correctly suggests it is wrong to use the term "fundamentalism" because "Fundamentalism" implies rejection of the modern world. Islamism in Iran is about, "… *ideological adaptability and intellectual flexibility, with political protests against the established order, and with socio-economic issues that fuel mass opposition to the status quo*" (Abrahamian, 1993, p. 2).

The different interpretations naturally appeal to those from different social classes. Islamism has grown within societies feeling the impact of imperialism and capitalism, a transformation of social relations, the rise of a local capitalist class, and the formation of an independent capitalist state. Since the establishment of the Islamic Republic in 1979, there have been massive social changes: Iran's population has more than doubled to 70 million – of whom 80% are below the age of 40 years; 70% are under 35 years; and 50% are under 25 years. The literacy rate has also rocketed from 48% at the time of the revolution to 90% now, with 60% of young Iranians attending college or university; while the number of Iranian women attending university has risen to over 60% (Central Bank of Iran, 2007). It is this magnitude of social change that has now cornered the Iranian elite as they have to adapt to differing social aspirations and class interests, a process that is not easy or smooth as current social unrest testifies.

The class base of Islamism is mainly middle class with its supporters based in the traditional commercial and professional petty bourgeoisie. In general, they are also hostile to the left, women's rights and secularism, and in some ways similar to some Third World nationalism. It is wrong to see the Islamist movements simply as "anti-imperialist": rather, they express people's bitterness and anger by focusing on external forces in order to avoid dealing with the real enemies at home. This has been clearly expressed by Ahmadinejad who since his presidential election in June 2009 has not stopped blaming the United States and the United Kingdom for the protest going on at home. Abrahamian compares Islamism with Peronism and similar forms of "populism" suggesting Khomeini's radical adaptation during the 1979 revolution made him appear more radical than the Marxists. But he was all in favor of the protection of middle class property and, as Abrahamian points out, "This form of middle class radicalism made him akin to Latin American populists, especially the Peronists" (Abrahamian, 1993, p. 3).

Abrahamian describes "populism" as a movement of the propertied middle class which mobilizes the lower classes, especially the urban poor, with radical rhetoric directed against imperialism, foreign capitalism, and the political establishment:

> Populist movements promise to drastically raise the standard of living and make the country fully independent of outside powers. Even more important in attacking the

> status quo with radical rhetoric, they intentionally stop short of threatening the petty bourgeoisie and the whole principle of private property. Populist movements thus, inevitably, emphasise the importance, not of economic social revolution, but of cultural, national and political reconstruction. (*Ibid.*, p. 17)

The Iranian regime has at times expressed its anger against those classes and states that exploit and dominate the mass of people. Khomeini, for example, in 1979 attacked the previous regime by condemning the Shah and his government:

> … they have left the country devastated … the dispossessed and the poor are everywhere whilst their natural resources [oil] has been plundered and wasted. (Khomeini, 1986, p. 119)

These contradictions are expressed in different forms and subject to internal pressures. Khomeini's interpretation was represented as a break rather than continuity with Islamic political traditions of his processors or even the Prophet Mohammed. Such a break illustrates that Khomeini and his followers are operating ideologically and politically within the context of a modern nation state. Consequently, how they present their arguments are constrained by the social forces within that nation state and its relations to the modern world.

3. IRANIAN REVOLUTION OF 1979: THE CLERGY'S RESPONSE TO A MODERN MOVEMENT

The 1979 revolution was one of the most popular, widely based revolutions of the 20th century, as it included different social forces from students, women's movements to the working class who played a leading role in toppling the Shah's regime with the establishment of workers' councils (Bayat, 1987). Contrary to the argument to what it has characterized Iranian revolution of 1979 as being reactionary (See Amir, 1986 and Halliday, 1988) this was a political revolution against a dictatorial regime of the Shah. The prominent features of the revolution were its populist, anti-imperialist, and antimonarchical stance.

Islamist supporters of the Iranian revolution claim that the political upheaval of 1979 was an attempt to restore the rightful role of *Shia* Islam in Iranian society by rejecting the Western secular culture, and reclaiming a vision of Islamic purity (Algar, 1983). Indeed after the revolution Khomeini stated that "*the recent religious movement was one hundred percent Islamic and was founded by clerics alone*" (Khomeini, 1979, p. 33). Supporters of this view take both religion and anti-imperialism as their core argument to emphasize that because the majority of the Iranian people believed in *Shia* Islam, therefore they demanded the replacement of the secular, pro-American monarchy with rule by true Islam. Abrahamian sees it rather differently: "*The Iranian revolution was a mass movement against deep-seated economic, political and social grievances with the more anti-regime religious authorities acting as public spokesmen*" (Abrahamian, 1982, p. 3).

Thus the revolution was not a product of Islamism; it was rather about the huge contradictions that began in the second half of the 1970s as the economic crises generated increasing divisions between modern capital connected to the state and the more "traditional" sections linked to the bazaar. This was intensified with the mass discontent felt by the workers and rural migrants who had recently flooded to the cities. The protests begun by students and academics were joined by sections of the clergy, deepened with strikes, most significantly that of the oil workers' union which ultimately led to the collapse of the state. Factors affecting revolutionary change are rooted in economic, social, and political conditions and do not arise from religious feeling alone. The revolutionary process contains conflicting ideologies: the dominant rationale is called into question, so the ability of the new vision to appeal to the hopes and desires of those who make the revolution is tested, as well as the participation and activity of individuals who no longer accept a passive role in society. Under such conditions, no one region, group or individual has a monopoly of ideas over political issues. In Iran, political discourse covered diverse ideological interpretations, encompassing Islamic-left ideology, liberal-democratic Islam, and socialist guerrilla groups of both Islamic and secular variants, not forgetting secular constitutionalism in socialist and nationalist forms. These diverse forms are now loosely grouped around the two main factions.

In contrast, Khomeini presented a radical argument from his exile in France, which meant that although his social base was mostly in traditional sections of society (the bazaar and landowners) he was able to capitalize on the revolutionary fervor of mass protests and thereby widen his appeal to other sections of society including those members of the working and middle classes who originally had reservations. This gave the real possibility to compete with the left and secular organizations and win ever greater support throughout society. Without the backing of substantial numbers from major social classes, the revolution could not have succeeded, that is, the triumph of the revolution necessitated the coalition of several classes. It was clear that Khomeini understood this, as he stated on the eve of his taking power, at a time when the unity of forces was vital:

> I offer my thanks to all classes of the nation: to the religious scholars … to the students … to the merchants and traders … to the youth in the bazaars, universities, and madrasas of the country … to the professors, judges, and civil servants; to the workers and peasants. You have triumphed because of your extraordinary efforts and unity of purpose. (Khomeini, 1981, p. 252)

The ability to articulate class unity was only one factor in making the revolution successful. Revolutions arise as a result of class conflict, a crisis of hegemony, and the failure of the ruling blocs to continue to operate in the face of the strength of oppositional forces. These factors are only part of the reasons for the revolution; in order to succeed, the revolution must have effective organization, leadership, and ideology (DeFronzo, 1991).

The leadership of the revolution – led by Khomeini and supported by Rafsanjani and Khamenei – were aware that the demands of the people protesting on the streets in their millions in 1979 went beyond uprooting the dictator, to embrace a wider vision of democracy and social equality. These demands were raised by both strikers and demonstrators: the oil workers called for the release of all political prisoners, national control over the oil industry, an end to discrimination against women workers, and the dissolution of the secret police (Bayat, 1987, p. 80). Halliday asserts:

> The demonstrators of 1978–79 did not want the Shah, but nor did they want a dictatorship of ayatollahs either: they wanted … "independence" and "freedom. (Halliday, 2009)"

The clergy led by Khomeini had to take this into account in dealing with the reality of managing the capitalist state in the aftermath of the revolution, a period we shall now go on to explore.

4. ESTABLISHMENT OF THEOCRACY AND REMOVAL OF THE CHALLENGERS

It took Khomeini and his allies nearly 2 years to impose their authority. It was not an automatic takeover for the clergy as there were challenges, from secular nationalists to Marxists, and the Islamist left. These social divisions were mirrored in the postrevolutionary government: Mehdi Bazargan, a secular politician and the first Prime Minister after the revolution expressed his concern at the increasing role of Iran's clergy. He wanted to ensure that political openness and democracy were not threatened by the clergy. Supporters of Bazargan were "moderate" Islamists associated with the modern bourgeoisie, while Khomeini's social base was made up of clerics, with its roots in the bazaar. Bazargan favored a French type of political system but Iran's constitution became a hybrid between *Velayat-e Faqih* and that of the French Republic, a mixture: "*between divine rights and the rights of man; between theocracy and democracy; between vox dei and vox populi; and between clerical authority and popular sovereignty*" (Abrahamian, 2008, p. 163).

Khomeini cleverly used the concept of nation in order to direct attention away from specific class interests. He argued that the revolution was for the nation and Islam, and had to be protected against opposition: the revolution should also be exported to create an Islamic community, *umma*. He asked the Iranian people to "*strive to export the Iranian revolution throughout the world*" arguing that Islam does not recognize any difference between Muslim countries (Khomeini, 1981, p. 286). However, when it came to social classes, workers' strikes, and management of the political economy he used the concept of "revolutionary morality" and responsibility to God as a weapon in an attempt to bring the country back to "normality." Khomeini ordered workers to return to work and build their Islamic nation:

> Today any invitation to strike or slowdown of work is treason to the country and the Islamic Republic. Today is not like yesterday [during the revolution] when you were invited to strike. Those strikes were the determining factor in our destiny. We asked you to go on strike to get rid of plunderers from the country [which] you did. Today is contrary to then ... to invite anyone to go on strike is going against Islam and harming the country. Therefore you have to be aware ... Expel those workers who don't want you to work for your people. (Khomeini, 1986, p. 183)

Using Islamist language, Khomeini rallied sections of the poor and workers into gangs of *hezbollah*, many of whom later joined organizations such as the Islamic Revolutionary Guards Corp (IRGC) and *Basij*. As a military arm of the new state both IRGC and *Basij*, grew from a volunteer force formed to challenge any attack from the old state's army to very quickly become an important economic and political institution for the new regime. In the years since 1979 they have been mobilized to attack the left, impose Islamic "morality" against women refusing to wear the *hijab*, and join the army to defeat the separatist revolts. They oversaw the execution of hundreds of separatist minorities, defeated the peasants who had occupied land in those regions, returning some land to former landlords while the rest remained under state control (Najmabadi, 1987, p. 200).

The occupation of the American Embassy by the students in 1979, taking 444 hostages was manna from heaven for Khomeini and his supporters, echoing his populism even louder to the people. In 1980, the regime was able to use the invasion of Iran by Iraq to evade internal economic, political, and social difficulties. They turned the war into an ideological struggle against the "atheistic" regime in Iraq and, most importantly, it kept the army engaged in war rather than interfering in the political process.

Gradually they were able to push aside their competitors, and ensured that the role of Ayatollah as the Supreme Leader was written into the Constitution. As such, he was provided with wide-ranging authority to "supervise policy implementation" and mediate between executive, legislative, and judiciary sectors, with power to grant reprieves, dismiss the president, and vet candidates for that office. He was appointed Commander in Chief who could declare war and appoint army leaders. Significantly, he was granted the authority to appoint the top positions beyond the formal structure of the state, including the director of the radio and television networks, supervisors of *imam jumeh* office (the Friday prayer organization), and the heads of powerful foundations. The new state did not change the existing capitalist relations, but gave new names to the Pahlavi state foundations, the huge state-run industrial and charity organizations, renaming it *Bonyad-e Mostazafan*, "The Oppressed." This was another populist twist to win the support of the poor – a double edged sword as it switches blame from individuals but implies they cannot rebel against their oppression.

The constitution also created the Guardian Council, made up of expert clerics who can veto candidates for office as well as legislation in the parliament or *Majlis*. The Supreme Leader was given the power to appoint 6 of the 12 jurists in the Guardian Council, as well as the chief judge and the chief prosecutor, heads of the judiciary and legislative sectors respectively.

The clerical rulers removed the secular and left wing Islamist oppositional forces, preferring an alliance with different social classes such as the bazaar, combined with the use of nationalist, anti-imperialist rhetoric and populism, to justify their actions. They legitimized their attack on secular academics and students by claiming to impose "Islamic values" as part of the struggle against "cultural imperialism." This helped Khomeini and his allies to advance their control over the state.

The establishment and consolidation of the Islamic state was not inevitable nor were the regime totally against capitalism. It merely changed bourgeois rule from a monarchy to an Islamic Republic, a repressive, authoritarian, and one-party state. However, this was not a "medieval" state, but a theocratic state led by religious rulers.

5. FACTIONAL FIGHTS: FROM REVOLUTIONARY VANGUARD TO REFORMISM

While Khomeini was alive he was able to stand above the competing factions: the Islamist right (mainly conservative clergy) and a moderate, or pragmatic right led by Rafsanjani, representing big business interests. The Islamist left led by Mir Hussein Mousavi, who was Prime Minister during the 1980s, mixed religious slogans with nationalism. Crucially, during the early part of the revolution, the factions had managed to put aside their differences in order to outmaneuver their competitors, that is, the secular nationalists and the Marxists.

In order to maintain its support base under the premiership of the left Islamists, Mir Hossein Mousavi increased the state control of Iran's economy and imposed government rationing to feed the poor. He called this "Islamic social justice" and "preservation of the revolution" (echoed in Ahmadinejad's later policy of "justice share"). Although his policy worried sections of the Bazaar and clergy (Moslem, 2002, p. 120), Mousavi succeeded in providing economic assistance to both the rural and the urban poor. It was not religion alone that made up their stronghold: the regime's social programs were decisive factors in cementing popular support in the early years of the Islamic republic. Sections of the rural and urban poor did support the regime at least in the early part of the war because *Jahad Sazandegi*, Reconstruction Crusade, organized by the regime during the revolution, mobilized young Iranians to go to the rural areas to help the peasants. The state also provided food subsides and, at times, cheap housing to the poor in both rural and urban sectors. The IRGC and *Basij* also used the poor as a recruitment center for their organizations: in return they gained social status as well as economic necessities.

The industrial policy of the state also followed a populist approach, similar to that of the previous regime's import-substituting industrialization strategy (Morady, 1996). The language now took the form of pride that the country was trying to be self-sufficient rather than dependent on the "Western world." The state more or less controlled most of the economic areas such as trade, foreign exchange, and above all the oil industry, their prize asset.

The newly established Islamic regime's anti-Western rhetoric has echoes in its current nuclear policy: whether it is to be used only for civilian purposes as they profess or more radically by developing an "Islamic" atomic bomb, it may serve to reestablish their fragile state some 30 years since the heady days of the revolution. Both the fighting of a "Holy War" and the building and development of a nuclear reactor are played out in the modern world using modern technology and paid for by hard currency, earned from oil. Before the end of the war with Iraq, the price of oil fell dramatically from about $30 to $10 a barrel in 1986 and settled at around $18 in 1987 (Statistical Centre of Iran, 1991). In 1979, Iran was exporting around 3 million barrels of oil a day (b/d) which had declined to an average 1.2 million b/d in 1988.[3] Saudi Arabia, an important ally of both the West and Iraq, did not need its huge revenues from oil and therefore was able to use oil as a political weapon to flood the market and keep the price down.[4] The impact of this was a sharp drop in Iran's oil revenues by 59% in the first half of 1986, as compared to the first 6 months of the previous year. The comparative figures for oil revenues in the same period were a 30% fall in Iraq, 24% in Saudi Arabia, and only 8% in Kuwait (Michael, 1988). This external pressure was compounded by combining the United States continued support for Iraq[5] and the increased number of US fleets in the Persian Gulf. The continued economic crisis and the difficulty of mobilizing troops after 8 years of bitter fighting finally led Khomeini to accept UN Resolution 598 which implemented a cease-fire on July 18, 1988, an act he described as having to "drink from the poisoned chalice." Meanwhile the exhausted Iranian population was left with 300,000 dead and 700,000 injured (Hiro, 2005, p. 233).

Not long after the war Khomeini died in June 1989 and Ali Khamenei was appointed as the Supreme Leader, with strong support from Rafsanjani, and by the 25-man Constitutional Reform Council. As he was not an Ayatollah,[6] the council had to make constitutional amendments while Mousavi and his left wing allies lost their main source of support within the regime.[7] His differences with Khamenei and later Rafsanjani surfaced in 1988 when, during a heated debate in *Majlis*, Mousavi attacked Rafsanjani over his acceptance of Western countries' assistance in building postwar Iran. Finally, the position of Prime Minister was abolished and Mousavi did not reappear on the Iranian political scene until the 2009 presidential election.

Rafsanjani became President in 1989 with 94% of the vote but he did not rule alone: the Supreme Leader, Khamenei, was now running the state alongside the President. In an effort to respond to Iran's internal pressures and to maintain its political domination over the country, the regime began to advocate a reformulation of its economic and political strategy. Rafsanjani, seen as a radical at the time when he called for the export of revolution and cutting Iran's relations with the West would later admit to growing rifts among the ruling elites in Iran during his presidency in the late 1980s:

> We have not been able to clarify for people economic problems as they relate to Islam: we have differences of opinions among ourselves over these issues and we have not arrived at clear ideas for our foreign policy. We have not evolved any new policies regarding social and cultural issues, minorities, and debatable religious matters which differ vastly from the early era of Islam, as we live under new conditions. (*Ettelat*, 25th October, 1988)

The postwar reconstruction with reformist (*eslahat*) coloring was supposed to bring Iran closer to international capitalism, to reduce the state subsidies, promote free trade, promote privatization, and stimulate the stock exchange. While Khamenei had in the past denounced Western liberalism, he was in agreement with Rafsanjani of the need to end rationing, price controls, and to balance the budget, reducing both the level of inflation and the defence budget.

Rafsanjani's second term in office did not attract the same support as his first, evidenced by the fact that 13 million voters (50% of the electorate) did not bother to vote in 1993. The economic liberalization policies hit the poor with cuts in food subsidies and the rising rate of unemployment. By the mid-1990s, Rafsanjani's government faced huge economic difficulties as unemployment reached 30%, and prices rocketed especially for staples such as sugar, meat, butter, and rice. The young especially felt the socioeconomic problems of the country and grew to resent government restrictions on their civil liberties and freedom of speech. The problem was so severe that it resulted in a series of riots in April–May 1992, August 1994, and April 1995 (Bayat, 1994, p. 10).

In 1994, the *Majlis* rejected Rafsanjani's choice of finance minister, Mohsen Noorbakhsh.[8] Rafsanjani and Khamenei's marriage of convenience was coming to an end. Khamenei, the Guardian Council and the conservative clergy rejected his policies for fear that it may threaten their traditional supporters. Sections of the bazaar were concerned that Rafsanjani's policies were harming the traditional economy with the emergence of modern trading centers. Khamenei was anxious about the growth of discontent among the poor and the loss of traditional "Islamic values."

Khatami's candidacy for presidency generated much enthusiasm especially among Iranian youths. He won two elections in 1997 and 2001, promising on the eve of his presidency to improve economic, political, and social conditions at home. His view on the world order was to promote a "dialogue of civilizations" instead of a "clash of civilizations." He presented himself as a humble man, with an ordinary life, but with knowledge of the Western world: he had lived in Germany and studied Locke, Hume, and Kant. His victory in 1997 was an overwhelming 70% of the vote, on an 80% turnout, although this fell in his second term.

Khatami made alliances with two factions of the state, the "modern right," a liberal coalition promoting economic liberalism, and the "Islamist left." These two forces joined together to defeat the "traditional right." However, he did not have a clear economic policy and was constricted by fear of upsetting the various factions of his allies. He simply tried to appease everyone by having some kind of free market tempered by state control. He promised commitment to social justice and the equitable distribution of income, larger bank credit and adjustment to the exchange rate, more political freedom, transparency, and accountability. He hoped to diversify the economy through increasing in investment from the West and procuring Iran's membership of the World Trade Organization (WTO).

The new President became a symbol of Iran's reform movements with students, women, and intellectuals both within and outside Iran viewing his election as proof that the winds of change were at last stirring up a breeze inside Iran. Many observers on the Guardian Council, IRGC, and state-run foundations especially the conservative clergy led by Khamenei, believed that gradual liberalization and opening up the economy to the outside world would eventually lead to secularization. They could not challenge him directly as Khatami had huge popular support, but fearing reprisals he did not want to take them on either.

This period of relative political openness brought changes in the level of confidence in sections of society, notably trade unions and supporters of women's rights. As such, it was challenged by the conservative Islamists under Khamenei. The President did not control the judiciary, which was headed by Mohammed Yazdi, a prominent right wing conservative and ally of Khamenei. So, they arrested reformists (including Khatami's friend, Hojjat-ul-Islam Mohsen Kadivar) who were brought to trial in special courts. In 1998, several prominent intellectuals, journalist, and writers disappeared and were later found dead (Keddie, 2006, p. 275).

By the time Khatami ended his period in office he had lost the support of the young workers, students, intellectuals, and the unemployed who had hoped he would deliver their basic needs. Under his presidency wealthy Iranians continued to benefit as the top 10% of the population received 34% of the national income while the bottom 10% received only 2% (Rakel, 2009, p. 91). Many of his supporters thus became disillusioned by the failure of his economic, political, and social reforms. The US role in the region and inflammatory statements such as President George Bush's 2002 speech that included Iran in the "axis of evil," did not help the reformist case and created space for their conservative opponents to voice their displeasure.

6. FAILURE OF REFORM MOVEMENTS AND EMERGENCE OF AHMADINEJAD

When the July 2005 election took place, a large section of the population were let down by the failure of Khatami to deliver on his promised economic and political reforms. It was a time when Iranians experienced continuing unemployment, inflation, limited political freedom, closing down of newspapers, and imprisonment of journalists and student leaders.[9] While many Western and Iranian observers predicted ex-president Rafsanjani would emerge victorious, many Iranian voters blamed him for all their economic difficulties, not to mention great political and social injustices. Instead, then, they turned to his opponent: as a graduate living in a rural area explained to the author when giving his reason for supporting Ahmadinejad, "*He has been able to stand firm against Hashemi Rafsanjani, this is the key reason why I voted for him. He is fearless in criticising him!*"[10]

Rafsanjani, Moein, and the other reformists drew their support from the modern middle class, intellectuals, students, and progressive clergy in theological schools in Qom. Mahmoud Ahmadinejad's power base lay among the conservative clergy in the seminaries, the traditional middle class, and officials of the IRGC and *Basij*. Although he did not get directly involved, Khamenei clearly favored Ahmadinejad, who also gained the support of segments of the lower classes organized through right wing Islamic organizations such as *Ansar-e Hezbollah*. Therefore the conservative faction around Khamenei chose to promote Ahmadinejad as someone who could protect their interests.

Ahmadinejad cleverly revived the populist approach of the early days of the Islamic Republic, mixing religious slogans with nationalism and, at times, Marxist class analysis in order to present himself as the people's candidate. He called for an end to the misuse of oil revenues, hinting at Rafsanjani's failures, without naming individuals. In presenting a populist agenda he echoed other radical politicians and leaders such as Morales in

Bolivia, Castro in Cuba, and Chàvez in Venezuela. Slogans used during his first term in office included putting the petroleum income on people's tables, that is promising to redistribute Iran's oil profits among the poor. Such statements did not fall on deaf ears as they echoed Khomeini's 1980s accusation that the Shah had squandered Iran's resources by allowing the Western countries to take it away in return for very little: *Our oil is being plundered; and our country is being turned into a market for expensive unnecessary goods. (…) A number of foreign states carry off our oil (…) and the negligible sum they pay to the regime they have installed returns to their pockets (…) [and] God only knows what it is spent on* (Khomeini, 1981, p. 115).

Twenty-seven years later, the words of the new president, Ahmadinejad, are not so different when it comes to Iran's oil industry. However, this time the angle of criticism is not against the Shah but aimed at one of the founders of the Islamic republic, Hashemi-e Rafsanjani when he attacked him by pointing out that he will "*cut the hands off the mafias of powers and factions who have a grasp on our oil, I stake my life on this. People must see their share of oil money in their daily lives.*"[11]

Ahmadinejad praised the poor and dispossessed, as they were the ones who had saved the country from foreign invasion, and the ones who hold the correct values for preserving the "true Islamic revolution."[12] He appeared to favor state control of the economy or more state involvement in general, in a vague manner emphasizing "The Third Way," promoting ideas of Iranian independence and self-reliance.

Just like his predecessors, Ahmadinejad has brutally suppressed any strikes, nationalist movements in Kurdistan or Azerbaijan, and attempts for more freedom by women's movements. In 2005, 1 year into his presidency, the bus workers' union organized a successful strike of its 17,000 members in Tehran protesting against their poor working conditions; the result was the arrest and detention without charge of their leader, Mansour Osanlu.[13] As recently as April 2009, Iran's Teachers' Union went on strike for better pay despite suffering consequent harassment and imprisonment from the state security forces.[14]

During his first 4 years in office, Ahmadinejad used his patronage to reward his supporters with prominent positions of influence. His allies who make up the majority of the cabinet and more than a third of the current parliament wield real business and economic power, with control over huge oil and chemical industry projects. Under Ahmadinejad's presidency, the IRGC also benefited handsomely from his privatization policy and expanded their reach to the oil and gas industries (Mather, 2009, p. 73).

Ahmadinejad was committed to accommodate the interests of an emergent bourgeois class, fuelled by oil income and consolidated by skyrocketing oil prices of the time, reaching above $100 in early 2008. The increase in windfall revenues from oil empowered the conservatives under Ahmadinejad, which in turn served to intensify the competition over this resource. The IRGC have thus emerged as a central organization in this new class, which consists of a symbiosis of the clerical and Bazari classes, supplemented by the IRGC's military power and their auxiliaries, namely the Basij (Mottale, 2010).

It is believed the IRGC now controls 70% of Iran's state-run economy, ranging from dental and eye clinics to car factories and construction firms. According to the state-run media the IRGC has received at least $6 billion worth from the government budget in the last 2 years (Erdbrink, 2010). In 2006 alone, the IRGC received subsidies of $7 billion to develop gas and oil fields and to refurbish the metro in Tehran.[15] Bina suggests that Iran is now under what he refers to as "wholesale para-militarization of the economy, polity, and the social space" (Bina, 2009).

Ahmadinejad's rhetoric is to support the poor by introducing a "justice share" of stock in privatized state companies for the needy, but in reality it is the IRGC who is actually benefiting from this. His move to transfer shares from state-owned companies to the poor seems more like a boost to the cooperative sector whose management could be appointed by the state. In September, *Etemad-e Mobin*, an investment company linked to the IRGC bought a 51% share of the national telecommunications sector after it was privatized (Erdbrink, 2010). The success of the theocratic state in Iran was assisted by oil revenue, lubricating the machinery of government since the revolution, and this has been key to the continued alliance of Khamenei, Ahmadinejad, and the IRGC.

The period after the war marked by the transfer from Rafsanjani's presidency to Khatami's presented a new interpretation of Islam, a far more secular/liberal oriented explanation. This was developed by a faction of the dominant political elite including Abdul Karim Soroush, Ayatollah Mohammad Mojtahed Shabestari, Mohsen Kadivar, and Hasan Yousefi-Eshkevari. However, since Ahmadinejad rose to power with the support of Khamenie and the IRGC, this was to some extent a break, a move to a less republican, secular, and democratic element in Iranian politics. This current ruling faction rests on two pillars of power: the security forces and the oil industry. These two pillars form the main support base for the regime at the present time and which are not separable.

7. STATE, OIL, AND JUNE 2009 ELECTION: FACTION FIGHTS TO CONTROL THE PRIZE ASSET?

The importance of oil as political weapon cannot be dismissed, since its discovery in 1908, from Mossadeq's nationalization of oil in the 1950s during the anti-imperialist struggle against Britain and the United States, to the Iranian revolution of 1979. Khomeini's populism in 1979 included oil-related rhetoric, attacking imperialism, defending nationalism and Islam but crucially criticized the Shah.

Oil accounts for 80% of the country's foreign-exchange receipts, while oil and gas together make up about 70% of government revenue as a whole.[16] In the last 5 years, Iran's oil income varied from between $50 and $100 billion per year. The oil revenue has helped the state and its institutions by providing economic and political power, reducing its dependence on other revenue sources. In return, state institutions such as the IRGC and other foundations have provided political support for Khamenei and Ahmadinejad. Oil bestows a large spending power for these foundations and for religious organizations, providing finance to over 100 foundations or *Bonyads*, who are given tax exemptions and government subsidies. They receive special access to credit, foreign exchange, and are protected from private sector competition. They have a huge role in trade with claims that the *Bonyads* account for 33–40% of Iran's total GDP, and employ nearly 5 million people. These figures can only be estimates, because the foundations never publish accounts and report only to the Supreme Leader, Khamenei, who personally appoints their heads. These foundations are linked with the Bazaar merchants, who make their money in import–export trade, through the so-called Islamic Coalition Council led by Habibollah Asgar-Oladi, a business partner of Khamenei. Furthermore, the arms trade, worth some $4.5 billion a year, is almost completely controlled by the "Office of the Leader" in that it distributes contracts to those to whom it is closest, in this case, the IRGC.

The Supreme Leader gains religious legitimacy from some clerics in Qom, and of course the support of his clients in these organizations, which themselves are supported by oil money. *Bonyads* and their business partners in return represent a political constituency, able to build support for the Supreme Leader and Ahmadinejad among some of the poor and lower classes.[17] These groups have a common interest to support the state and will continue to give allegiance to Khamenei as long as their own benefits are protected. Thus, oil income gives the state enough power to be independent from civil society as it does not need to rely on high levels of public taxation. The army which is a major supporter of the rentier state (Morady, 1996, 2005) is singled out for special attention: with the huge oil income at its disposal, the state is able to increase its spending on arms to combat both internal political opposition and any external challenge which may arise. Inflated salaries and social positions are given to individuals, especially in the religious schools, in order to become part of a support base for the state. The expenditure on arms and regional security is directly linked to the geopolitics of the region, expressing the Iranian state's desire to have hegemony within a limited area.

The Supreme Leader, with the help of oil income, acts as a patron and his supporters, generals in the army and security service act as his clients (Randall & Theobald, 1998). What emerges clearly from this analysis is that the Patron's closest clients have managed to take over all the political institutions of the state including the parliamentary and presidential roles. However, this has not been achieved without dispute or conflict, sharpened through ideological shifts due to the economic, political, and social constraints faced by any ruling elite. For example, the *Majlis* conducted an investigation into oil "*baksheesh*" deals that concerned dozens of foreign personalities. Bizhan Namdar-Zangeneh, the Oil Minister in 2005, was asked to resign but refused, arguing that the favors had been distributed on orders from The Supreme Leader.

Iran's oil revenues act as public goods that assist the regime to carry through its populist policies and are used in the name of religion whereby those who hold the highest office inside Iran decide who should get what share of the cake. The oil revenue has assisted state-owned companies, the top 500 of which account for 76% of the national budget and two-thirds of Iran's GDP. Khamenei, Ahmadinejad, the IRGC, the *Basij,* and their security apparatus aim to benefit from these funds to reconstruct Iranian capitalism. The Islamist right and their supporters could well become the new industrialists as they are more involved in the economy over time.

This is certainly the case with Ahmadinejad continuously promoting his colleagues from the IRGC, *Basij*, and security services to top positions in the state. IRGC members hold important political posts with easier access to oil income. In fact, the IRGC is now challenging business tycoons such as Rafsanjani and his allies; therefore, it is not an accident when Ahmadinejad attacks Rafsanjani and his family, but rather a planned and calculated strategy: in the *name* of the poor, but in effect to line the pockets of his supporters.

8. ELECTION, PROTEST, CONFUSION, AND REVOLT

In the election, Ahmadinejad was challenged by Karoubi, Rezaie (the ex-commander of IRGC) and his main competitor Mousavi. In private, Ahmadinejad had the support of Khamenie, different state foundations, and a section of bazaar as well as right wing clergy in Qom, especially, his mentor Ayatollah Mesbah Yazdi. Rafsanjani backed the rest including Mousavi even though he did not agree with his program.

It was difficult to predict the outcome of the election in the early stages, especially as students, along with some of the working class had experienced economic and political hardship under Rafsanjani and Khatami. However, they have also witnessed the fake populism of Ahmadinejad for over 5 years, especially the youth in the major cities who have suffered from higher levels of unemployment and inflation, their lives made more difficult by social restrictions and constant harassment by religious police. Being well aware of this, Mousavi, used his election rallies in Tehran and other cities to promise liberalism on social questions. This was crucial for a country with such a young population: educated, aware of the modern world, and with more than 30 million Iranian internet users, a staggering increase from only 200,000 less than 10 years ago. There are computers in every university and internet cafes in all major cities. Of the two million blogs in cyberspace, over 700,000 are in Farsi (Persian), making it the fourth most popular language for bloggers.[18] Use of technology can have political consequences as a young Iranian blogger died under mysterious circumstances in jail in March 2009.[19] Nevertheless Mousavi's liberal stance was accepted positively by Iranian youth as the momentum for June's election increased.

Before the election a Washington-based NGO, Terror Free Tomorrow: The Centre for Public Opinion (see http://www.terrorfreetomorrow.org/), conducted a telephone poll in Iran from Turkey. This involved interviewing 1,001 Iranians with the following results: 34% favored Ahmadinejad, 14% Mousavi, but 50% had yet to make up their mind. The same poll showed that 80% wanted constitutional change for the Supreme Leader too. This poll has been used by the supporters of Ahmadinejad within and outside Iran to claim legitimacy for the outcome of the election. However, the name, location of the organization, and where they conducted the interviews was not mentioned when they presented their case. This poll also did not identify the support base of different candidates or differentiate between their policies.

While Ahmadinejad continued to have support from sections of the poor, especially in rural areas, he has lost some of his support in the last 6 years. As part of his national tour since his election in 2005, Ahmadinejad has visited various cities and towns but since the disputed 2009 election there are significantly less people attending. On his recent visit to Khorramshahr in the south of Iran (May 24, 2010), while Ahmadinejad was addressing a crowd in the port city voices were raised, chanting "Unemployment! Unemployment!," as local workers expressed their concerns about the local economy (see http://www.reuters.com/article/idUSLDE64N0LJ20100524).

The street debates and discussion in the last 4 weeks prior to the election opened a huge space, the likes of which had not been witnessed since 1979. With live televised presidential debates gripping the whole country, Ahmadinejad's claims about Iran's economic progress were backed up by misleading statistics, playing his populist card by a personal attack on Mousavi, Karoubi, and especially Rafsanjani and his family. This time, however, Ahmadinejad's appeal did not have the same resonance as in the 2005 election. He was losing more ground to the other candidates, Mousavi in particular.

Popular interest in the outcome of the election gathered momentum, bringing in wider social forces including the working class who have stopped short of strike action but actively participated in the demonstrations. The street debates and protests revealed Ahmadinejad's populism as fake and his support rapidly declined especially among those young Iranians facing acute economic difficulties: 1 million a year join a workforce with no guarantee of a job; a graduate may be lucky to find employment 3 years after graduating; unemployment among the youth has increased from 15% to nearly 25% in the last 20 years. This inability to find work coupled with the huge cost of rent (often over half a worker's wages), has forced many to delay marriage and, as a result, the number of unmarried men and women between the ages of 25 and 29 has more than doubled in the last 20 years. Add to this the social and religious restrictions on relationships outside marriage and you can begin to appreciate young people's sense of alienation and frustration (see http://www.huffingtonpost.com/navtej-dhillon/the-many-crises-of-irania_b_220897.html).

Daily demonstrations occurring in major cities began to shake the regime, particularly the IRGC who used their weekly magazine, *Sobhesadegh*, to threaten to "*destroy anyone who attempts to bring a velvet revolution*,"[20] a clear warning that Ahmadinejad's camp will not tolerate the reform movements.

By this time the possibility of the second round was the least likely outcome but the consequences of this would have been very serious for the regime, and likely to lead to yet more demonstrations. Furthermore, the regime and particularly Ahmadinejad would have lost more support. To stop this required drastic action which became possible with the intervention of the Interior Ministry when it announced the election result only a matter of hours after the ballot boxes were closed. So, in the early hours of the morning, while most were still sleep, Ahmadinejad's huge majority was announced (see www.chathamhouse.org.uk/files/14234_iranelection0609.pdf). His success was sealed when Khamenei declared Ahmadinejad victorious only a few days later.

Thus an attempt to curtail the demonstrations, political debates, and discussions provoked the opposite effect, forcing people into the street, to express their anger at the hasty election result and to share widespread feelings that the electorate had been cheated. The regime's response then served to make a bad situation worse. Ahmadinejad in his victory rally described those who were opposing his election as "specks of dirt." When Mousavi and Karroubi called for a peaceful rally to be held in Tehran on June 15, millions joined the protest. The demonstration included all sections of society: old, young, professionals, workers, bazaaris and students, women wearing headscarves alongside those in full length chadors. According to some estimates the protest stretched as long as 10 km, embracing both rich and poor parts of Tehran. The slogans on the banners varied from "What Happened to My Vote?" to "No to Dictator." As the protest was coming to an end skirmishes broke out with the intervention of Revolutionary Guards in a park nearby leading to some fatalities.

The regime felt threatened by the magnitude of the protest and so declared any protest illegal, threatening to execute anyone participating in or calling for further demonstrations. Revolutionary Guards and *Basijis* armed with weapons were sent onto the streets, as vigilante supporters of the regime poured into University dormitories. More than 4,000 associates of Mousavi and Karroubi, including journalists and campaigners were arrested. Some foreign journalists were ordered to leave, while the regime jammed foreign broadcasts, and shut down newspapers and websites.

The killings, imprisonment, and torture did not, however, stop the protest movement as people continued to take to the streets in numbers at every opportunity. *Quds* Day (the annual pro-Palestinian demonstration) fell on 18th of September meaning that a state-sponsored protest was cleverly hijacked by opposition forces to express their continued discontent with the regime. A few days before the demonstration IRGC and security forces warned they would arrest anybody shouting antigovernment slogans, or daring to wear the opposition's green armbands or scarves, yet despite this intimidation, thousands of protesters took to the streets of Tehran and major cities in Iran, with slogans including: "*Ahmadinejad's resignation*," "*independence*," "*freedom*," and "*no to Islamic Republic*!"[21]

Imaginative forms of protest continue, making use of the widespread popularity of football in Iran: live television coverage of a recent match was blacked-out because sections of the crowd were chanting antigovernment slogans and waving green emblems. The match was eventually shown nearly an hour late but minus sound and with close-up shots focusing only on the pitch thereby cutting out the 70,000 spectators!

Protest slogans have now been directed against The Supreme Leader himself, something unthinkable even 5 months before. Khamenei's actions since the June election mean that The Supreme Leader has lost its traditionally accepted role as a judge or neutral individual. The strategy of arresting protesters, ordinary people, students, and intellectuals and shutting down the remaining opposition newspaper, *Etamade Meli*, alongside the show trials has failed to resolve the political crisis.

The political turmoil was triggered by the death of Grand Ayatollah Montazeri during the sensitive festival of Ashura that commemorates the 7th century death of Imam Hussain, grandson of the Prophet Mohammed. who was martyred in Shia Islam. This offered yet another opportunity for the regime's opponents to evade the ban and they again poured onto the streets on 27th of December, which led to more deaths and arrests. Since then the situation has continued to be fluid, with the regime appearing to have the upper hand by using extremely repressive measures: any protest has been dealt with brutally and there have been many arrests of individuals ranging from academics, film makers, and students.[22]

9. FROM A SECULAR KING TO A GOD'S KING OR A SECULAR REPUBLIC?

Khamenie/Ahmadinejad and the IRGC coalition's continued attempt to eliminate the reformists from the center of power has consequences for the nature of the Islamic Republic. This political schism can be traced back to 1979 and continues to be at the forefront of debates and lies at the heart of the split between Khamenie and others such as Rafsanjani, Khatami, Karoubi, and Mousavi. The reformists including Rezaie are concerned about the survival of the regime but most notably the republican aspect of the political system, that is, the notion that absolute legitimacy to rule is given only by God to *Velayate Fagih*, that is, the Imams or the supreme theologian, the *Fagih*. This conflict rose to the surface on July 18, 2009 when Ayatollah Mohammed Yazdi, a conservative clergy, member of the

Guardian Council, supporter of Khamenie and Ahmadinejad chose to openly challenge Rafsanjani over his exaggeration of the role of democracy in Islamic government. Yazdi pointed out that, "*The vote of the people alone does not create legitimacy in government*" (Fars News Agency, July 18, 2009).

The debates over embedding democracy in religion have been going on for many years but what is apparent from Rafsanjani and Yazdi's speech is that it has increasing significance now and potentially has direct impact on control of Iran's considerable economic and political power. This goes back to Ayatollah Khomeini's idea of *hokoumat-e Eslāmi,* the rule of Jurist, in his book *Hokoumat-e Eslāmi* (1981). This was the notion that gave executive authority to the Supreme Leader, with huge power held in the hands of one man as a consequence. This blatantly emphasizes a return to a God's king rather than an Islamic Republic. However, there is opposition to this from different forces including conservative alliances such as the Speaker of Parliament, Javad Larijani, and his brother Sadegh Larijani, head of the judiciary who have distanced themselves from Ahmadinejad on many occasions. Both brothers were critical of Iran's reformist movement but have major differences too with the hard-line principalists headed by Ahmadinejad In fact, after Sadegh Larijani's appointment, Gholamhossein Mohseni-Erjei, the intelligence minister who had been sacked by Ahmadinejad, was given a new post as the Islamic Republic's top prosecutor, although he had been fired because of his disagreement with Ahmadinejad. Indeed others such as Ali Motahari, one of the principalist members of parliament, called in an interview for honesty, justice, and integrity within the regime. He demanded that Ahmadinejad should admit he made mistakes and ask for forgiveness.[23]

Whatever the maneuvering between different factions and the outcome of this movement, the ruling elites in Iran have not been able to remove economic, political, and social contradictions despite being in power since 1979 and as Moaddel points out:

> ... the ruling clerics, despite their intensive financial and organisational resources and consistent brutality in eliminating their secular opponents, have failed to create a religious order in the country. Iranians today appear to be less religious in comparison to ... other Islamic countries, and the trend in their value orientations is towards ... gender equality, democracy, and national identity. (Moaddel, 2009)

The opposition movement is now questioning the whole system of the Islamic Republic, not just Ahmadinejad as its elected leader but the roles of *valayate fagih* and the Supreme Leader, Ayatollah Khamenei.

Islamist conservatives are now in a quandary: to retreat will encourage more protests; to arrest more people may lead to further loss of religious legitimacy with Khameinei being seen as moving Iran toward a military state. The regime will continue to use the threat of intervention by the United States and its allies to avert internal crisis. The nuclear program is used as a political tool for hardline conservative politicians who have chosen a confrontational foreign policy. Whatever the legitimacy of having uranium enrichment in Iran this has supported the coalition forces of Kahmenie/Ahmadinejad and IRGC. It is not impossible to oppose both the repressive regime of Khamenie/Ahmadinejad and US imperialism abroad. Iran has a history of defiance and revolt against both dictatorship at home and imperialism. Therefore the only force that is capable of bringing progressive change in Iran is not the United States through direct intervention or by encouraging Israel to attack Iran. Rather, it is the Iranian people themselves, as they have shown in the wake of the 2009 election and no doubt will do so again.

10. PROSPECTS FOR CHANGE

The Green Movement[24] or *Jonbesh-e Sabz*, is a coalition of forces led by Karoubi and Mousavi during and after the election of 2009. It consists of groups with different interest who are from different social groups, modern middle class, and a section of the working class with varying ideas and aspirations. The core leadership includes reformists, clergy, and academics who claim that this is a nonviolent civil rights movement and that it is not revolutionary. They are still committed to Islam, Ayatollah Khomeini, the founder of the Islamic Republic and advocator of a theocracy (Dabashi, 2009). They believe the democratic process is only possible through the Islamic Republic and its constitution. Others however within the Green movement are against this, even wanting removal of *Velayate Fagih*. Mousavi and Karoubi are aware that this would have repercussions for them, as they were once part of the same system. Any radical changes would bring their position into question, alongside the current ruling elites. Mousavi and Karoubi's opposition within the Islamic republic also sends signals to those such as Larijani, the speaker of parliament, who are now in power but find themselves not in total agreement with Ahmadinejad. They portray themselves as a mediating force between the opposition and the government to ensure survival of the system. However, in order to keep pace with the movement from below, the Green leadership may find itself having to respond positively to different agendas such as national minorities and most importantly workers organization.

In sum, the Green coalition is not yet a revolutionary movement with a radical approach to change the political system and socioeconomic structures. The leadership of the movement is merely expressing anger against electoral fraud and the transfer of economic and political institutions to different groups led by IRGC. For the Green Movement to shift itself into a revolutionary force it would have to distance itself from the system and call for other social forces to join them. At the present time they do not want to take such a risk.

The Islamic Republic will continue with the process of state-led authoritarian modernization but this will not be a smooth process or without contradictions, as indeed the current social revolt shows. Although a revolutionary change in Iran is not impossible, it requires strong leadership with a clear ideology and a strong organization for mobilizing the different social groups. The regime will continue to use its coercive apparatus, backed by significant financial resources – oil and gas income – to avert the protest. This will not be easy as there is very little cohesion within the current political elites.

Whether the Green Movement can respond positively to these contradictions remains to be seen but the social movement can, through struggle, identify an alternative appealing ideology and perhaps strong leadership, capable of challenging Islamic Republic. This is neither impossible nor unimaginable as the events of the 1979 Iranian revolution clearly demonstrated.

NOTES

1. Agence France Presse, August 27, 2009.
2. The term is used by Khalaji to analyze the Islamic Republic in Iran. See Ayatollah Khamenei's Coup? – Interview with Mehdi Khalaji with Tehran Broadcast. Available at http://tehranbroadcast.com/Ayatollah-Khamenei-s-Coup.html
3. The bombing of oil fields and tankers had a significant impact on Iran's oil exports. See Chubin and Tripp.
4. Saudi Arabia was producing around 5 million b/d in 1986, an increase from 3.5 million b/d in 1985. See Central Bank of Iran (1987).
5. The United States intervened twice in the United Nations, first to prevent an emergency meeting to end the war of the cities and later to oppose a formal condemnation of Iraq for its use of chemical weapons. See Sick (1988).
6. Ayatollah is a high title given to major Shia clergy. Those who carry the title are experts in Islamic sciences such as jurisprudence, ethics, philosophy, and mysticism.

They normally become teachers in schools of Islamic theology (hawza). The title is granted by consensus through recognition of his written thesis and acceptance by existing Ayatollahs and popular acclamation.

7. See BBC in Farsi. Available at http://www.bbc.co.uk/persian/iran/2009/05/090521_og_ir88_mosavi.shtml

8. See *Tehran Times*, February 12, 1994.

9. The most well known being Akbar Ganji, journalist, and writer who has been in prison since 2000 after taking part in a political conference held in Berlin. He recently went on hunger strike for over a month and two leading member of "Green Movement."

10. Anonymous source, quoted in private interview in Iran, July 2009.

11. See ISNA: Iranian Students News Agency. Available at http://www.isna.ir/Main/

12. See his web site: http://www.mardomyar.com/indexnew.aspx

13. See International Transport Workers Federation. Available at http://www.itfglobal.org.

14. See International Trade Union Congress. Available at http://www.ituc-csi.org.

15. See Economist magazine, August 27, 2009.

16. See ISNA: Iranian Students News Agency. Available at http://www.isna.ir/Main/

17. See his speeches during and after the election on his web site, http://www.mardomyar.com/indexnew.aspx

18. The first blog was posted in November 2001 by a young Iranian journalist who now resides in Canada. For more details see Alavi (2005).

19. He was sentenced for 30 months in jail for allegedly insulting Iran's supreme leader and Ayatollah.

20. The name "velvet revolution" is given to Mir Hussain Mosavi's supporters who wear green armbands and the movement has become known as the green revolution. See Sobhesadegh, 8/05/2009, No. 402.

21. See BBC. Available at http://www.bbc.co.uk/persian/iran/2009/09/090920_ka_tavakoli_mosavi.shtml

22. The most well known of them was Jafar Panahi who was detained by security forces in early March and released in late May.

23. See BBC. Available at http://www.bbc.co.uk/persian/iran/2010/01/100108_l07_larijani_motahari_jalili.shtml

24. For Green Movement see http://www.rahesabz.net/

REFERENCES

Abrahamian, E. (1982). *Iran between two revolutions*. Princeton, NJ: Princeton University Press.

Abrahamian, E. (1993). *Khomeinism*. Cambridge: Cambridge University.

Abrahamian, E. (2008). *A history of modern Iran*. Cambridge: Cambridge University Press.

Alavi, N. (2005). *We are Iran: The Persian blogs*. New York: Soft Skull Press.

Algar, H. (1983). *The roots of the revolution*. The Open Press: London.

Bayat, A. (1987). *Workers and revolution in Iran*. London: Zed Press.

Bayat, A. (1994). *Squatters and the state: Back street politics in the islamic republic in Middle East*. Report no. 191. Iran's Revolutionary Impasse (Nov.–Dec., 1994), pp. 10–14.

Bina, S. (2009). Post 2009 election Iran: Crossroads of history and a critique of prevailing political perspectives. *Journal of Iranian Research and Analysis, 26*(2). Available at http://www.cira-jira.com/

Dabashi, H. (2009). Iran's younger, smarter revolution. *Daily beast coverage*. Available at http://www.thedailybeast.com/tag/hamid + dabashi + green + movement/?cid = bsa:related10

DeFronzo, J. (1991). *Revolution and revolutionary movements*. New York: Westview Press.

Erdbrink, T. (2010). Elite revolutionary guard's expanding role in Iran may limit U.S. options. *Washington Post*, January 10.

Halliday, F. (1988). The Iranian revolution: Uneven development and religious populism. In: F. Halliday & H. Alavi (Eds), *State and ideology in the Middle East and Pakistan*. New York: Monthly Review.

Halliday, F. (2009). Iran's tide of history: Counter-revolution and after. *Open Democracy*. Available at http://www.opendemocracy.net/article/iran-s-tide-of-history-counter-revolution-and-after. Retreived on July 17, 2009.

Hiro, D. (2005). *The Iranian labyrinth: Journeys through theocratic Iran and its furies*. New York: Nation Books.

Keddie, N. (2006). *Modern Iran: Roots and results of revolution*. New Haven, CT: Yale University Press.

Khomeini, R. (1979). *Payame Pishva Dar Sale Engelab* (*Leader's message in the first year of the revolution*). Qom: Faqr.

Khomeini, R. (1981). *Islam and revolution*. Berkeley, CA: Mizan Press.

Khomeini, R. (1986). *Rahnomoud Hai-e Eqhtesadi (Guidance to economy)*. A. Kabir, Trans., in two volumes. Tehran: Amir Kabir Publication.

Lapidus, L. (2002). *A history of Islamic societies*. Cambridge: Cambridge University Press.

Mather, Y. (2009). The latest economic crisis in Iran and the continued threat of war. *Critique, 37*(1), 67–79, Abingdon, Oxford, Taylor & Francis.

Michael, R. (1988). Determinants of the Islamic republic's oil policies: Iranian revenue needs, the Gulf War, and the transformation of the world oil market. In: E. Amirahmadi & E. Parvin (Eds), *Post-revolutionary Iran* (p. 194). Boulder, CO: Westview Press.

Moaddel, M. (1993). *Class, politics and ideology in the Iranian revolution*. Cambridge: Columbia University Press.

Moaddel, M. (2009). The Iranian revolution and its nemesis: The rise of liberal values among Iranians. *Comparative studies of South, Africa and the Middle East, The Thirtieth Anniversary of the Iranian Revolution, 29*(1), 126.

Morady, F. (1996). *Oil, the state and industrial development in post revolutionary Iran*. Amsterdam Middle East Paper. Amsterdam International Studies, Amsterdam.

Morady, F. (2005). *Oil, state and development in Iran*. Unpublished paper.

Moslem, M. (2002). *Factional politics in post-Khomeini Iran*. New York: Syracuse University Press.

Mottale, M. M. (2010) Focus: The birth of a new class. Aljazeera [online], April 22. Available at http://english.aljazeera.net/focus/2010/04/2010421104845169224.html

Najmabadi, A. (1987). *Land reform and social change in Iran*. Salt Lake City, UT: University of Utah Press.

Petras, J. (2009). Iranian elections: The 'Stolen Elections' hoax in global research. Available at http://www.globalresearch.ca/index.php?context=va&aid=14018

Rakel, P. E. (2009). *Power, Islam, and political elite in Iran: A study on the Iranian political elite from Khomeini to Ahmadinejad.* Herndon, VA: Brill Press.
Randall, V., & Theobald, R. (1998). *Political change and underdevelopment: A critical introduction to third world politics.* Durham, Duke: University Press.
Roy, O. (1980). *Islam and resistance in Afghanistan* (pp. 38–44). Cambridge: Cambridge University Press.
Sick, G. (1988). Trial by error: Reflection on the Iran–Iraq War. *Middle East Journal, 43*(2), 22.
Zubaida, S. (1989). *Islam, the people and the state: Political ideas and movements in the Middle East* (2nd ed.). London: I.B. Taurus.

WEB SITES

For information on Iranian newspapers, weekly and monthly journals. Available at http://www.magiran.com/
Bassij. Available at http://web.archive.org/web/20040803084837/http://bso.ir/BSO/Index.htm
Fars news Agency. Available at http://www.farsnews.net/
Central Bank of Iran. http://www.cbi.ir/
Central Bank of the Islamic Republic of Iran. (2009). [Online]. Iran: Central Bank of the Islamic Republic of Iran. Available at http://www.cbi.ir/default_en.aspx [accessed April 9, 2009].
Gooya News in Farsi. Available at http://news.gooya.com/
Majlis Report Center. (2009). A review of women, family and children laws after three decades of Islamic Revolution [online]. Iran: MRC. Available at http://www.majlis.ir/mhtml/modules.php?name=News&file=article&sid=2686 [accessed April 9, 2009].
Mehr News Agency. Available at http://www.mehrnews.com/en/
National Iranian Oil Company (2009). Brief history of Iran's oil nationalization [online]. Available at http://www.nioc.ir/portal/Home/Default.aspx?CategoryID=f398bd54-e170-44e9-a841-710c6c92b3a0&TabNo=1
Nikzad, S. (2010). Jonbesh-e kargari, mobarezeye madani dar zire khatte faqr (Workers' movement, a syndicate under the poverty line). BBC Persian [online] March 17. Available at http://www.bbc.co.uk/persian/iran/2010/03/100317_l15_labour_rw.shtml
Open Democracy. Available at http://www.opendemocracy.net/
Parliament News in Farsi. Available at http://parlemannews.com/
Press TV. Available at http://www.shiatv.net/view_video.php?viewkey=2578e5e627cd93ab0938
Publication of Revolutionary Guard, Sobehe Sadegh in Farsi. Available at http://www.sobhesadegh.ir/
Statistical Centre of Iran, http://www.amar.org.ir/Default.aspx/

PART II
CRISIS EMPIRICALLY AND THEORETICALLY UNDERSTOOD

CONSUMPTION DEMAND IN MARX AND IN THE CURRENT CRISIS

Radhika Desai

ABSTRACT

This chapter challenges the denial of "underconsumption" – the role of consumption demand in capitalist reproduction and its paucity in crises – in contemporary Marxism. At stake are better understandings not only of crisis theory but also, inter alia, of imperialism, "reformism," and Marx's intellectual legacy. The chapter shows how the centrality of consumption demand is underlined in the three volumes of Capital *and the* Grundrisse, *and goes on to discuss the origins, weaknesses, and persistence of this denial. The chapter also shows that Marx did not regard underconsumption as a moralistic argument about unfulfilled need. The denial originates not in Marx but in productionism, the idea that capitalism is a system of "production for production's sake."*

Originating in the overkill of Tugan Baranowski's refutation of the Russian populists' view that capitalist development was impossible in Russia due to lack of a home market, productionism is based on his attempt to force Marxism into the marginalist and the general equilibrium framework. Despite its antipathy with Marxism, most contemporary Marxist economics are based on it. Inevitably its adherence to Say's Law – the denial of the possibility of gluts in the market – infects

The National Question and the Question of Crisis
Research in Political Economy, Volume 26, 101–143

ISSN: 0161-7230/doi:10.1108/S0161-7230(2010)0000026005

the tendency to assume that capitalism's contradictions do not lie in circulation. Productionism's denial of the importance of consumption demand also rests on nonsequiturs, nondialectical thinking, and an underestimation of the contradictions in capitalism Marx identified, other than the tendency of the rate of profit to fall. The chapter ends by showing the centrality of demand in the recent historical evolution of capitalism as reconstructed by Robert Brenner, followed by a discussion of whether underconsumption is "reformist."

> The value of the old industry is preserved by the creation of a fund for a new [capitalist] one in which the relation of capital and labour posits itself in a *new* form. Hence exploration of all of nature in order to discover new, useful qualities in things; universal exchange of the products of all alien climates and lands; new (artificial) preparation of natural objects, by which they are given new use values; the exploration of the earth in all directions, to discover new things of use as well as new useful qualities of the old; such as new qualities of them as raw materials etc; the development, hence of the natural sciences to their highest point; likewise the discovery, creation, and satisfaction of new needs arising from society itself; *the cultivation of all the qualities of the social human being as the most total and universal possible social product*, for, in order to take gratification in a many-sided way, he must be capable of many pleasures [*genussfähig*], hence cultured to a high degree – is likewise a *condition of production founded on capital.*
>
> Marx, *Grundrisse* (p. 409, emphases added)

This chapter seeks to challenge the deep-seated and powerful tendency in contemporary Marxist economic thinking to deny the role of consumption demand in capitalist reproduction, and its paucity in crises.[1] Ideas about inadequate consumption demand, the bulk of which is workers' demand, in capitalism were practically contemporaneous with the rise of industrial capitalism (Bleaney, 1976, pp. 22–101). By the late 19th century they constituted a clearly identifiable strand of "underconsumption" theories and Marx had criticized their characteristic remedy, increasing wages, in *Capital I*. But a specifically Marxist debate on the role consumption demand in capitalism seems not to have arisen until Russian populists, *Narodniks*, took the view that capitalism could not develop in Russia. Not only was the home market limited, they reasoned, so was the possibility of acquiring other markets through imperialism because, as a latecomer, Russia faced a world already divided up among major powers. It was in contesting the populist argument that Russian Legal Marxists denied consumption demand a role in capitalist reproduction. Rosa Luxemburg strenuously contested this denial as excessive, surplus to the requirements of refuting the *Narodnik* case. However, her views were inexplicably, and certainly inexcusably, sidelined in the further development of Marxist thinking on capitalist reproduction and crisis (Zarembka, 2002). While Paul Sweezy read Marx in a Keynesian (rather than Keynes' – see below) spirit in which paucity of demand figured centrally (Sweezy, 1962); this account was distinctively Sweezy's own. In any case, the decline of Keynesianism was accompanied by vigorous revival of those earlier refutations among Marxists (Weeks, 1977). Today few argue overtly about the role of consumption demand. The case is closed. But the verdict is wrong and supports a cluster of widely and deeply held convictions that prevent cognizance of consumption's role in capitalist reproduction. It also permanently consigns the wrongfully convicted parties – preeminently Luxemburg – to an entirely undeserved intellectual disdain, while consumption's importance in the ideas of others – Marx, Keynes, or Kalecki – is denied or underemphasized.

Accounts that give consumption demand a role in capitalist reproduction and crises are dismissed as "underconsumptionist" – empirically and logically inadequate if well-meaning moral condemnations of capitalism that, "as we all know," Marx rejected. Worse, they are held to lead to the dead-end of reformism, as with the 19th century underconsumptionists Marx criticized, and, according to some, with Keynes. Such accounts are also faulty for focusing on the sphere of circulation when the "real" contradictions of capitalism lie in the sphere of production which, moreover, increases in importance as capitalism develops. This "productionism" originated in the denial of the role of consumption by Russian Legal Marxist, Michael von Tugan Baranowski.

> Technical progress is manifested in the increasing importance that the instruments of labor, and machines even more, acquire in relation to living labor, to the worker himself. The means of production play an ever-growing role in the process of production and on the commodity market. Facing the machine, the worker steps to a second place and, accordingly, the demand based on workers' consumption is relegated to a minor position in comparison to that originated from productive consumption. The whole activity of the capitalist economy assumes the character of a mechanism existing by itself, so to speak, in which human consumption appears to be a simple factor in the process of capital reproduction and circulation. (Tugan Baranowski, 2000a, p. 73)

Since famously paraphrased as the "factories that produce factories that produce factories," productionism not only sees capitalism as unconstrained by consumption demand, it has gone along with a tendency to identify a single, "fundamental" cause of capitalist crisis located in the sphere of production alone. For Tugan Baranowski, the favored cause was disproportion between sectors of capitalist production while contemporary Marxists favor the Tendency of the Rate of Profit to Fall (TRPF), in so far as they subscribe to any Marxist account of crises at all (more on this below). If members of this productionist tendency admit the possibility of crises also arising outside production, in circulation, they refer to the paucity of investment demand being a factor in crises. However, that would, in any case, be part of the sphere of production, strictly speaking.

This chapter does not seek to deny the relevance of either disproportion or TRPF. Indeed, it agrees, in opposition to many Marxist economists who hold that Marx was mistaken on this count, that the latter, in particular, was one of Marx's most important discoveries about capitalist accumulation and its contradictions. This chapter also goes a step further than some defenders of Marx on the TRPF by pointing out that in Marx's account of capitalist accumulation production and consumption or circulation are inseparable moments of a single process. It does, however, seek to reinstate the role of consumption demand as a major factor in capitalist reproduction.

In what follows, I begin with a discussion of the stakes in contesting productionism's sway in Marxist economic thinking: including, most importantly, an escape from the monomania that surrounds thinking about capitalist production and crises to comprehend the sheer variety of sources, forms, and mechanisms of crises in capitalism, of which the paucity of consumption demand is one. I go on to show that in the *Grundrisse* and the three volumes of *Capital* Marx takes the view that consumption demand has a critical role in capitalist reproduction and its paucity is a major cause of crisis. I then present my critique, discussing the main misconceptions that lie at the root of the rejection of the role of consumption demand and the two main ways in which it has been rejected – by Tugan Baranowski and by contemporary Marxists as evinced in a key and widely cited article by Anwar Shaikh (1978). As the work of a widely respected and sophisticated Marxist economist, it as good a representative of this view as one can get. Following this, we will be in a position to appreciate the full extent of the folly of denying consumption demand a role in capitalist reproduction as I show how central a role it has played in postwar capitalism using Robert Brenner's influential, and in my view largely correct, historical account of the pattern of world capitalist development of the last many decades and of the current crisis (1998, 2002, 2006, 2009).

While I hope these arguments will be independently persuasive, insofar as much of the animus behind the productionist case comes from the idea that affirming the role of demand might lead to "reformist" conclusions, the chapter ends with a plea not to see reforms and revolution as mutually exclusive. In a properly historical view, they emerge as having a "dialectical relationship" (Patnaik, 2009b). While the underconsumptionism that

Marx criticized did indeed assume, incorrectly, that increasing wages would overcome capitalism's problems, there is no absolute necessity for an insistence on the role of consumption demand to lead to such "reformism," that is, an assumption that capitalism's problems can be solved through measures falling far short of a fundamental change in the social order, of revolution. Such an insistence did not lead to "reformism" in Marx's case, or in Luxemburg's or Kalecki's. (Also Keynes, the only other writer to affirm the importance of the paucity of consumption demand on a radical understanding of capitalism's fundamental problems, was lead to propose changes to the capitalist order that amounted to such a radical transformation that it became moot whether, if Keynes' prescription were applied, capitalism could be said to exist. He may have continued to call it capitalism but, the meaning he invested in the term concerned individual freedom not private ownership of the means of production. While it is true that he was loath to align himself openly and consistently with Marxism, socialism, or the working class, and while there is no need to excuse his statements to this effect, his intellectual and even political affinities were considerably more complex than most Marxists and Keynesians have been willing to allow. On this see Desai, 2009; Desai & Freeman, 2009; Dostaler, 2007; Sardoni, 1997.)

1. BEYOND MONOMANIA: THE STAKES AND THE GAINS

Denying the role of consumption demand in capitalist reproduction and crisis seems incredible when we consider that the most fundamental contradiction of capitalism according to Marx is that between social labour and private appropriation. This was also caught in wider understandings such as Janos Kornai's. He distinguished "pure" socialist and capitalist systems as "supply constrained" and "demand constrained" respectively. In capitalism

> the effective constraint on production increase is the buyer's demand. Demand constraints are narrower than physical resource constraints. The available quantity of resources would allow a further increase of production. Yet producer firms do not avail themselves of this possibility, since they do not see the excess as saleable. Capitalism is, in its "classical" form, a demand-constrained system. This is the economy Marx treats in "Das Kapital" when he writes about the contradiction between the tendency of unlimited expansion of production and the limited purchasing potential of the market.' (Kornai, 1979, p. 804)

Reinstating the role of consumption demand can be expected to open a wide breach in the fortifications that protect contemporary Marxism's monomania about the causes of capitalist crises. It is an important reason why Marxists find themselves on the intellectual back foot in the midst of the greatest crisis of capitalism since the Great Depression, one that may yet turn out to be its greatest ever.

The broad range of crisis mechanisms are routinely seen at work in capitalism and were anticipated in Marx's analysis, some more fully than others because, tragically, that work remained uncompleted. Many Marxist scholars have pointed to the plurality of mechanisms of crises. Mandel believed that overproduction (or underconsumption: the two are, as we see below, hard to separate entirely), disproportionality, and the TRPF accounts of crises were all valid at different times and could be seen at play in different phases of the development of a particular crisis. Paul Sweezy (1970, pp. 145–146), for his part, classified Marxist accounts of crisis into two: those associated with falling rates of profit and those associated with realization. However, an even wider and more systematic view is possible. While both these views recognized that crises are possible in production as well as circulation, there are at least two other indispensable spheres of capitalist accumulation and reproduction – finance and the nation-state. Crises would then also be seen to arise from the financial structures without which capitalism cannot function and from the necessarily international geopolitical order that emerged from the imperial as capitalism developed, creating a world of national capitalisms rather than a single, unified, world capitalism (Desai, 2009).

Further, the wider and more systematic approach to crises might also take into account the fact that crises arising in each of these spheres of capitalism can take one of two forms – an intraclass, that is, intra-capitalist class, form arising from the mechanisms of competition and an interclass form, pitting capitalists and workers against each other, arising from the mechanisms of class struggle. Provisionally these four sources of crises and the two forms that crises originating in each of these sources may take give us at least eight different mechanisms of crises. Whether any of these are more fundamental than the others is not immediately clear and, as we shall see, accumulation and realization, at least, are intimately connected. Nor can "value" exist without money or capital without finance, and therefore credit is inevitably involved. Finally, geopolitical competition, which under capitalism necessarily involves a plurality of nation-states – whether a small number of these in imperial competition as in the late 19th and early 20th century or in the increasingly "geoeconomic" competition of today – is also endemic to capitalism.

So we may have the following eight mechanisms of crises: The first two – those of accumulation – would involve increasing organic composition of capital reducing the profit rate and rising wages reducing the rate of exploitation and having the same effect, the TRPF and profit-squeeze respectively. Considering that so many today consider the TRPF to be the quintessentially Marxist crisis it is noteworthy that until Henryk Grossman's work in the 1930s, no major Marxist linked the TRPF to crises and Marxists tended to neglect *Capital III* where this analysis was developed (Howard, 1989, p. 316). While the phenomenon was generally accepted, it was not considered important in explaining crises.

Intercapitalist crises of realization would be the crises of "disproportionality" between sectors or departments of production which Tugan Baranowski identified and which most Marxists refer to when they accept the possibility of shortfalls in investment demand. Crises of realization of the interclass sort would result from a paucity of consumption demand. Intracapitalist mechanisms of financial crises would be manifest as credit crunches – with banks unwilling to lend to each other or to businesses – of the sort that currently plagues so many advanced capitalist economies. The chief interclass financial mechanism of crisis would be the "mortgage crisis" – with high default rates in forms of credit extended for consumption, of which the recent "subprime crisis" in the United States was such an important instance. Geopolitical crises, finally, of the intracapitalist sort could arise out of imperial competition between organized national or imperial bourgeoisies of the sort that culminated in the First World War and which the first Marxist theorists of imperialism such as Bukharin, Hilferding, Lenin, and Luxemburg attempted to comprehend. Geopolitical crises could also emerge from Luxemburgian processes involving the role of the periphery in contributing to the stability of core capitalism – such as oil price increases of the 1970s or contemporary surges in commodity prices (on this see also Patnaik, 1997, 2009a).

Crises in Capitalism: By Source and Form.

Form	Source			
	Accumulation	Realization	Credit	Geopolitical
Intraclass	TRPF	Disproportionality	Credit Crunch	Imperial or International Geopolitical Competition
Interclass	Profit-Squeeze	Overproduction/ Underconsumption	Mortgage Crises	Centre-Periphery Exploitation and Resistance.

One can safely say that all these mechanisms involve fundamental processes of capitalist reproduction and malfunction of each has the capacity to culminate in crises. Every major crisis is a complex amalgam of more than one of these and they can also be seen successively in the development of any given crisis. If the argument of this chapter is accepted, it will have not only reinstated the role of consumption demand as a factor in capitalist reproduction and crises, it will also release Marxists from the productionism that screens the full complexity and difficulty of capitalist reproduction and the variety of its mechanisms of crises.

This wider vista will not be the only gain from reinstating the role of consumption demand. Where one stands on that question also has implications for two other important questions. First, it has never made any sense to lift Marx out of the context of the intellectual tradition in which he is so centrally located – breaking his relationship with the predecessors whose contradictions he resolved with such élan and the successors – not just Marxists – who dealt with his powerful legacy, with more or less grace and more or less fairness. To be sure, this isolating operation was and remains a bourgeois and Cold War one. However, there is no reason why Marxists should cooperate in it. Rather we should question it, overturn it, and restore to Marx his rightful place at the core of our intellectual traditions. He stands at the culmination of the social and economic thought that preceded him and is the fount of most of the important developments that followed, whether they supported or opposed him. While Marx's relation to his predecessors is better-studied, the links between him and later developments in understanding capitalism, particularly Keynes's, are rarely explored.

Secondly, I am critical of the view, closely associated with the dismissal of the consumption demand problem as the hobby horse of "reformist underconsumption" and the critique of Luxemburg that goes with it, that capitalism can be viewed either as a "pure" system or a self-contained one. Thinking of capitalism as a "pure" system forgets that Marx's representation of "pure" capitalism in *Capital* was a heuristic device, not to be equated with Actually Existing Capitalism (AEC) anywhere. Not only did the capitalism of *Capital* never refer to any real system, "pure" capitalism existed nowhere, as Engels pointed out, confidently predicting also that it would not be allowed to since revolutionaries would not "let it come to that" (Mandel, 1978, p. 68). Notwithstanding Marx's strictures to German comrades – *de te fabula narratur* and all that – it *especially* did not exist in England (Perry Anderson, 1987).

Capitalism is everywhere born amidst noncapitalist productive relations which it only slowly, and, until today at least, never completely, transforms.

AEC is everywhere "contaminated" not only with legacies of the precapitalist past – say patriarchy, slavery, or caste – which capitalism everywhere puts to good use, but also by modern systems which modify its workings – chiefly regulatory and welfare states which, Polanyi (1975) insisted, were unavoidable. If the spread of market relations prompted a countervailing effort of social protection, it needs to be taken into account. Kornai clarified his account of capitalism as a demand-constrained system: "Modern capitalism – mainly owing to the effect of active state interventions often undertaken *in the name of Keynes* – can no longer be qualified a 'pure' demand-constrained system." (Kornai, 1979, p. 804, emphasis added). The limitations of such "Keynesian reformism" – effectively expanding the home market by raising workers' purchasing power – are clear but it is all too often forgotten that it was based not on any "reformist" essence of Keynes' but, as Joan Robinson so well put it, on "bastard Keynesianism." While hardly revolutionizing capitalism, it was sufficiently effective, as we see in Section 4 below, to play a key role in both the Long Boom of the 1950s and 1960s and the Long Downturn that beset world capitalism in the 1970s, as Brenner terms these eras.

Analyses of "pure" capitalist dynamics decontextualized from the social, political, and cultural integuments in which they everywhere operate also tends to go with a never-fully-stated view that the only capitalisms that deserve the name, that are worth examining in order to understand capitalist dynamics, are those of the advanced industrial world. They are also, for all practical purposes, treated as the same. In reality, not only do both first and third world capitalisms feature inherited noncapitalist social forms interacting with the mechanisms which Marx identified in *Capital*, first world countries feature modern modifying welfare and regulatory forms that are considerably more powerful than their counterparts from the third world. The AECs of the advanced industrial world are, moreover, each distinct historical formations with distinct historical inheritances and modern regulatory and welfare structures as the literature on "varieties of capitalism" and "worlds of welfare" (Coates, 2002; Esping-Anderson, 1990) testifies.

Thinking of capitalism as a "self-contained" system usually involves focusing on the centres of advanced capitalism alone, leaving the rest of the world out of account. It takes us back to the question of the relationship between imperialism and capitalism. Is it inevitable as, from their different perspectives, Hobson (1965) and Luxemburg (1913/2003) saw it when they identified the search for markets to compensate for low demand within a capitalist country as the imperialism's chief motor? Or is it merely contingent, if also reprehensible, as so many Marxists aver today?

Is capitalism in the advanced world subject to no contradictions that spill over, on the one hand onto the noncommodified or decommodified realms of the developed world itself, say the family and the welfare states, and on the other on the developing world? As Prabhat Patnaik put it, capitalism is "a mode of production *that never exists in isolation*, that is necessarily linked with the surrounding precapitalist modes [and, one might add, noncapitalist contexts], and that continuously keeps itself viable by encroaching on [them]" (Patnaik, 2009a, p. 5). What is certainly clear in this chapter is that Luxemburg's arguments on this score were unfairly rejected while Hobson's vision of social reform as an alternative to imperialism, though rejected by Marxists as "reformism," was ironically vindicated in the deepening of national markets of the capitalist core's welfare capitalisms in the postwar period of decolonization. As our discussion of Brenner shows, neither the "Long Boom" nor the "Long Downturn" can be understood without taking this deepening into account.

2. MARX ON CONSUMPTION DEMAND

The importance of consumption demand in capitalist reproduction and its paucity as a factor in capitalist crisis can be traced throughout *Capital* and in it the preparatory thinking for it as revealed in the *Grundrisse* even though the attention of the completed and published parts of these works was focused away from this issue. What we have of *Capital* concentrates on the productive and bourgeois aspects of capitalism. *Capital I*, the only one finished by Marx and published in his lifetime, famously concentrates on the process of production where surplus value originates and workers appear in this volume primarily as producers, not consumers. When, in the posthumously published *Capital II*, the focus does shift to circulation, the emphasis is on attempting to show that capitalist reproduction on an expanded scale is possible, not on emphasizing its potential for crises. When we finally turn, in *Capital III*, to the totality of capitalist production, *and its potential for crises*, we find that precisely the elements of circulation, of "the world market, competition, the industrial cycle and the state" (Mandel, 1981, p. 10) remained to be written.

2.1. Grundrisse

In the *Grundrisse*, the clearest statement of the importance of workers' consumption is relegated to a footnote in which the matter is flagged for detailed treatment later. Marx notes clearly how, although capitalism imposed "a relative restriction on the sphere of workers' consumption (which is only quantitative not qualitative, or rather, only qualitative as posited through the quantitative)," workers have "as consumers (in the further development of capital the relation between consumption and production must, in general, be more closely examined) an entirely different importance as agents of production from that which they possessed, e.g., in antiquity or in the Middle Ages, or now possess in Asia" (Marx, 1973, p. 283). For Marx, then, a key aspect in which capitalism was distinct from precapitalist societies was in the economic importance of workers' consumption. This phenomenon, historically specific to capitalism, was the chief anchor of the idea that capitalism laid the basis for the transition to socialism in part by increasing productive powers so as to enable humanity to transcend the realm of necessity, of scarcity, and enter that of freedom and plenty. This was also the meaning of the epigraph of this chapter: capitalism would prepare the groundwork, albeit in a contradictory manner, for the many-sided person to emerge.

One might discount these ideas, particularly the last, as well-meaning but mistaken philosophies flourish, especially at a time when the many-sided consumption of the few rests, often fairly directly, on the all-sided deprivation of most. And they would be, were it not for the fact that, in critical ways, the reliance of capitalism on popular consumption, on (at least some) workers' consumption, is underlined in Marx's critique of political economy, from the *Grundrisse* onwards. Levels of workers' consumption higher than hitherto known in the history of class society are, as we have seen, the other side of the coin of increasing accumulation, increases in the means of production and productive capacity, creating the "more massive and more colossal productive forces than have all preceding generations together" such that no "earlier century had even a presentiment that such productive forces slumbered in the lap of social labour" (Marx & Engels, p. 1848). It is precisely because of workers' consumption demand, the bulk of consumption demand in capitalist society, looms large that it can act, when it is insufficient, as a limit and constraint in capitalist production in a way that was inconceivable in precapitalist class societies.

2.2. *Capital I*

Although *Capital I* clearly shows that the sphere of circulation cannot create value, and thus surplus-value, that these can only arise in production, the importance of realization and consumption is underscored in the very foundation for the analysis of *Capital* that is laid in its opening pages – the contradictory unity of use value and value which is the commodity. This contradictory unity is the basis of Marx's critique of Say's Law – the idea that "every seller brings his own buyer to market with him and that, therefore, there can never be gluts" – that is, crises arising out of paucity of demand in relation to production.

> Nothing could be more foolish than the dogma that because every sale is a purchase, and every purchase a sale, the circulation of commodities necessarily implies an equilibrium between sales and purchases. ... its real intention is to show that every seller brings his own buyer to market with him ... No one can sell unless someone else purchases. *But no one directly needs to purchase just because he has just sold.* Circulation bursts through all the temporal, spatial and personal barriers imposed by the direct exchange of products, and it does this by splitting up the direct identity present in this case between the exchange of one's own product and the acquisition of someone else's into *two antithetical segments of sale and purchase*. ... The two processes lack internal independence because they complement each other. Hence, if the assertion of their external independence [*äusserliche Verselbständigung*] proceeds to a certain critical point, their unity violently makes itself felt by producing – a crisis. There is an antithesis, immanent in the commodity, between use-value and value, between private labour which must simultaneously manifest itself as directly social labour, and a particular concrete kind of labour which simultaneously counts as merely abstract universal labour, between the conversion of things into persons and the conversion of persons into things; the antithetical phases of the metamorphosis of the commodity are the developed forms of motion of this immanent contradiction. These forms therefore imply the possibility of crises. ... (Marx, 1867/1977, pp. 208–209, Emphasis added.)

Not only was Say's Law a dogma, which assumed "that overproduction is not possible or at least that no general glut of the market is possible" (Marx, 1867/1977, p. 210n), the market was a critical factor in the core process of capitalism – in the creation of value. Value could be determined *only* when commodities were sold, that is, socially validated. Only then did the labour embodied in them become abstract and thus the basis of value. The multitude of private and concrete labors could only be validated as social and abstract value through the mediation of the market, by commodities finding buyers who wanted them for their use value. And value is what competition, including competitive cost-cutting, determines is the "socially necessary" amount of labour needed to produce any given product. It was the market, therefore, that determined whether, and to what extent, the various concrete labors successfully realized themselves as abstract labour. It translated the private into the social, the concrete into the abstract. It was only because use value and exchange value, concrete labour and abstract labour were not immediately identical that they required the mediation of the market which, in turn, "implied the possibility of crises." Capital or surplus value did not arise in circulation, nevertheless "it is equally impossible for it to arise apart from circulation. It must have its origin both in circulation and not in circulation" (Marx, 1867/1977, p. 268).

In distinguishing use value and value in the first pages of *Capital*, Marx had meant neither to discount the first, nor to imply that the latter could be self-sustaining as in accounts which one-sidedly view capitalism as merely "production for production's sake": "nothing can be a value without being an object of utility" (Marx, 1867/1977, p. 131). His point was rather more complex: Value was condemned to seek fulfillment as the satisfaction of individual and concrete human needs, to become a use-value, however real or fan/phan-tastical, in order to realize itself as abstract and social. As for the heroes of yore faced with similar "missions," for the ever-growing mass of commodities let loose on the market by the grotesque-Promethean productive powers of capital, there might be numerous detours in the fulfillment of their mission of realization as a use value, including becoming producers' goods, but the ultimate test of human utility could never be foregone. In order to be sold, commodities had to have use value – whether directly as an object of consumption or indirectly as objects that were used to produce objects of consumption. If in the process of valorization capital appears to be "value which can perform its own valorization process, an animated monster which begins to 'work,' 'as if its body were by love possessed,'" the animus that drives it is the search for realization as use value (Marx, 1867/1977, p. 302).

2.3. *Capital II*

In Volume II, Marx specifically treats the circulation of capital and its realization. Although his main focus is on demonstrating realization's possibility, rather than its difficulty, he nevertheless registers the latter.

> The maximum limit of the capitalist's demand is $C = c+v$, but his supply is $c+v+s$; ... the greater the percentage of s produced (the rate of profit), the smaller his demand in relation to his supply. Although, as production advances, the capitalist's demand for labour power, and hence indirectly for necessary means of subsistence, becomes progressively smaller than his demand for means of production, it should not be forgotten that his demand for *mp* is always smaller than his capital, considering this day by day. (Marx, 1884/1978, pp. 197–198)

Marx goes on to add, "That many capitalists are involved here, and not just one, in no way affects the matter" (Marx, 1884/1978, p. 198), clearly dismissing arguments that capitalists buying producers' goods from each other was the solution. Nor does he dismiss the role of foreign trade in alleviating overproduction in both Department I and Department II, remarking that it "only shifts the contradictions to a broader sphere, and gives them a wider orbit" (Marx, 1884/1978, p. 544). However, the problems created by the limits on workers' demand are noted only in a footnote, and postponed, once again, for proper discussion to a later volume:

> The workers are important for the market as buyers of commodities. But, as sellers of their commodity – labour-power – capitalist society has the tendency to restrict them to their minimum price. ... the periods in which capitalist production exerts all its forces regularly show themselves to be periods of over-production; because the limit to the application of the productive powers is not simply the production of value, but also its realization. However, the sale of commodities, the realization of commodity capital, and thus of surplus-value as well, is restricted not by the consumer needs of society in general, but by the consumer needs of a society in which the great majority are always poor and must always remain poor. (Marx, 1978, p. 391n)

2.4. *Capital III*

In Volume III, while Marx notes that "Capitalist production ... is not ... production whose immediate purpose is consumption, or the production of means of enjoyment for the capitalist" (Marx, 1894/1981, p. 352), he goes on to clarify that the "production of surplus-value is only the first act in the capitalist production process, and its completion only brings to an end the immediate production process itself. ... [In] ... the second act ... The total mass of commodities, the total product, must be sold, both that portion which replaces constant and variable capital and that which represents surplus-value."

> The conditions for immediate exploitation and for the realization of that exploitation are not identical. Not only are they separate in time and space, they are also separate in theory. The former is restricted only by the society's productive forces, the latter by the proportionality between the different branches of production and *by society's power of consumption*. And this is determined ... by the power of consumption within a given framework of antagonistic conditions of distribution, which reduce the consumption of the vast majority of society to a minimum level, only capable of varying within more or less narrow limits ... The *more productivity develops, the more it comes into conflict with the narrow basis on which the* relations *of consumption must rest*. (Marx, 1981, pp. 352–353, emphasis added)

This is how "excess capital coexists with a growing surplus population" (Marx, 1981, p. 353). Marx concludes that section by saying:

> The *true barrier* to capitalist production is *capital itself*. It is that capital and its self-valorisation appear as the starting and finishing point, as the motive and purpose of production; production is production only for *capital*, and not the reverse, i.e. the means of production are not simply means for a steadily expanding pattern of life for the *society* of producers. The barriers within which the maintenance and valorisation of the capital-value has necessarily to move – and this in turn depends on the dispossession and impoverishment of the great mass of the producers – therefore come constantly into contradiction with the methods of production that capital must apply to its purpose and which set its course towards an unlimited expansion of production, to production as an end in itself, to an unrestricted development of the social productive power of labour. (Marx, 1981, p. 358)

He repeats later on, "The ultimate reason for all real crises remains the poverty and restricted consumption of the masses" (Marx, 1981, p. 615), frontally challenging any idea that the "fundamental" cause of capitalist crises lay in some separate sphere of production. That Marx's views directly contradict productionist views is hardly surprising, given the constitutive nature of Marx's distinction between the use value and value *sans phrase* which lies at the root of the commodity, the primary unit of capital. Production and circulation are equally necessary – "The circulation of commodities is the starting point of capital" – to the reproduction of capital and therefore equally problematic in its reproduction and productive of crises.

3. HOW TO DENY THE OBVIOUS: LET US COUNT THE WAYS

Underconsumption, as Anwar Shaikh's influential 1978 "Introduction to the History of Crisis Theories" put it, is the view that "if left to itself, capitalism is incapable of generating sufficient effective [consumption] demand to support accumulation" (Shaikh, 1978, p. 222). Two distinct arguments are made in rejecting this view (a rejection that is all the more relished because the view is so intuitive for so many). One is that it is a sort of moralistic argument about human needs left unfulfilled by capitalism which takes no cognizance of Marx's clear recognition that "effective demand," backed by the ability to pay, is the only sort of demand that matters in capitalist society. We deal with this in Section 3.1. The second argument is productionist. It takes the view that capitalism is a system of "production for production's sake," that for Marx only investment demand matters in capitalism, not consumption demand. Productionism comes in two variants according to the particular mechanism of crisis each deems as the fundamental one. In Tugan Baranowski's original version the favored mechanism of crisis was disproportional production between sectors while in productionism's more modern versions it is the TRPF that is the fundamental crisis mechanism. While the first dismisses consumption problems on the basis of an outright adherence to Say's Law, the second argues that only investment demand matters in capitalist reproduction and crisis or that consumption demand is merely a part of investment demand in that it is the variable capital set in motion in any period (Shaikh, p. 227). Both variations on this view too are, as we shall see, remarkably like "every seller bringing his own buyers to market," like Say's Law. Section 3.2 deals with four general problems of productionism before Sections 3.3 and 3.4 deal with each of its chief forms.

3.1. What's Really Wrong with Underconsumptionism?

The dismissal of underconsumption as a problem claims to derive from Marx's own discussion of underconsumptionism in which he famously said that

> It is a pure tautology to say that crises are provoked by a lack of effective demand or effective consumption. The capitalist system does not recognise any forms of consumer other than those who can pay, if we exclude the consumption of paupers and swindlers. The fact that commodities are unsalable means no more than that that no effective buyers can be found for them, i.e. no consumers (no matter whether the commodities are ultimately sold to meet the needs of productive or individual consumption). (Marx, 1978, 486–487)

However, those who take this to be Marx's refutation of underconsumptionism miss an important point. What is wrong with tautologies is merely that they go no further than themselves, that they have no further implication. Statements only become tautologies when there is an attempt to draw implications which cannot be drawn. But they are not, thereby, wrong. As we have already seen, Marx emphasized repeatedly the difficulties of realization thanks to the restriction of workers' consumption.

The real problem was, as Marx pointed out, that the classic underconsumptionist remedy – increasing wages – would not avoid crises.

> [W]e need only note that crises are always prepared by a period in which wages generally rise, and the working class actually does receive a greater share in the part of the annual product destined for consumption. From the standpoint of these advocates of sound and "simple" (!) common sense, such periods should rather avert the crisis. (Marx, 1978, pp. 486–487)

Two things cry out for notice. First, while underconsumptionists were certainly wrong in thinking that crises could be avoided through increases in workers' incomes, this did not mean that rising wages would make no material difference to patterns of accumulation and reproduction. Section 4 elaborates on how they did during the "Long Boom" and how the stagnant wages played out in the "Long Downturn." Secondly, on the one hand increasing wages could contribute to stabilizing capitalism by increasing demand, not to mention improving the lives of workers and their families, but that could be at the cost of a squeeze on profits and another kind of crisis, as Marx pointed out in the passage quoted above and Kalecki (1943) also recognized. On the other, on their own, rising wages would not solve the fundamental problem that the workers receive only a portion of their product under capitalism, only postponing the problem at the price of making it greater in the future. While increasing wages can, under certain circumstances, squeeze profits, leading to crises of profitability, rising wages do not have this effect when productivity is rising faster than wages are and wage increases constitute a less than proportional share of the rising product. In this scenario, however, they can, despite creating greater consumption demand than before the productivity-led wage increases, lead to a still-greater disproportion between consumption and production thanks to the increases in productivity and therefore, eventually, to an even greater paucity of demand.

One may note in concluding this part of our argument that Bleaney's well-known Marxist study of underconsumption theories, widely cited though it is by those wishing to dismiss the role of consumption demand, does nothing of the sort. He only dismisses as underconsumptionist theories which, unlike Marx and Keynes, consider only the role of consumption demand, leaving out investment demand. However, he does not dismiss the role of consumption demand and nor does he argue that Marx and Keynes do. Moreover, Bleaney is sufficiently careful to note that while most underconsumption theories hitherto were deeply flawed, they did not have to be:

> Underconsumption theories can be constructed free of elementary mistakes, and therefore the whole tradition of thought cannot be rejected on these grounds alone. In skeletal form they can be presented as follows: the consumption of the working class always falls substantially short of the total productive capacity of the community, while capitalists will always only absorb a limited portion of the surplus value in personal consumption. On average, there is a tendency for capitalists not to plan to invest sufficiently to fill this gap between production and consumption, so that the economy is being pressed down towards stagnation because of inadequate effective demand. (Bleaney, 1976, p. 237)

This is no more than a summary of Marx's views, and, one might add, Luxemburg's, Keynes' and Kalecki's.

3.2. Productionism and its Problems

There are four distinct general problems with productionism which need to be understood before we can go on to discuss the two specific arguments against consumption demand.

3.2.1. Nonsequitur

First, productionists infer a *nonsequitur*. Engels had counted the discovery of surplus value to be one of Marx's two key discoveries, the other being the historical materialist interpretation of history (Engels, 1998). It is true that the most critical departure on the way to this discovery was going from the sphere of circulation, where labour power is merely bought and sold, into the hitherto-neglected sphere of production, where it is (productively) consumed, going, as Marx picturesquely put it, from "the noisy sphere [of the market], where everything takes place on the surface and in full view of everyone ... into the hidden abode of production on whose threshold there hangs the notice 'No admittance except on business.' Here we ... see, not only how capital produces, but how capital is itself produced." (Marx, 1977/1867, pp. 279–280).

It is also true that in doing this Marx corrected the "astounding" error in political economy hitherto – including Smith's and Ricardo's – of presenting "accumulation as nothing more than the consumption of the surplus product by productive workers" (1977/1867, p. 736), nothing more than the wages of productive workers alone (a doctrine that "political economy has not failed to exploit in the interests of the capitalist class" Marx, 1977/1867, p. 738). Accumulation may be resolved into wages alone in some infinite regression, Marx argued. Indeed this must be so if labour power was the source of value. But that did not help us understand the instabilities that drove capitalism. The real issue was to understand the accumulation process within a reasonable time-frame, say a year (perhaps this was Marx's version of "In the long run we are all dead!"). Within such a time-frame, without the infinite regression that permitted Smith and Ricardo to dissolve all capital outlay into workers' wages, any outlay of capital consisted, in addition to variable capital that purchased living labour, of constant capital that purchased dead labour. This was, in turn, composed of circulating and fixed capitals.

It is further true that this is where Marx's analysis finally got on the path to demonstrating the TRPF. With only part of constant capital's value being transferred to the product in any given year, a necessary gap emerged between the outlay of capital and the portion of it which was transferred to the value of the product of any given year. On this gap rested the critical distinction between the rate of surplus value and that of profit: the former was the ratio between the surplus and variable capital (wages) while the latter was that between the surplus and constant capital (with significant increases being possible in the outlay on fixed constant capital) as well as variable capital. If the value of fixed capital rose sufficiently relative to other components, rates of profit could decline even as rates of surplus value rose. It was the tendency of constant capital, particularly of its fixed portion, to go up which accounted for the TRPF, a phenomenon widely lamented but unexplained until Marx's *Capital*.

All of this is true but the nonsequitur lies in assuming that any of it implies that circulation does not matter, that demand, particularly consumption demand, particularly still workers' consumption demand, is not a factor in capitalist reproduction and its paucity, a cause of crisis. None of the above means that capitalism, as generalized *commodity* production, was, in Marx's view, anything other than the *contradictory unity* of its production and circulation processes. Both words are important. On the one hand, the contradiction that was the TRPF could not operate, could not manifest itself, without the intervention of circulation. Profits could only be had upon realization, upon sale, and only through sales of any product could the level of the "socially necessary labour" required to produce it be determined. This was necessary before the higher-cost, lower-profit firms could be separated from the lower-cost, higher-profit firms. This constituted the benchmark that more dynamic firms attempted to undershoot in order to gain cost advantages, thereby setting off the processes that typically brought down the rate of profit across any sector. On the other hand, a critical determinant of this process is the level of demand: without demand constraints limiting the market, the whole process would be quite unnecessary. This is clearly reflected in Brenner's account, as we shall see, where the level of demand is among the parameters that determine the behavior of the rate of profit. Brenner's own rejection of the TRPF (whose problems are discussed in the third section) notwithstanding, there is no reason to believe that this is incompatible with Marx's understanding of the operation of the capitalist economy.

3.2.2. Leaving Out Dialectics

If the first problem is in one sense an unwarranted inference, the second is undialectical reading. Marx may have insisted that accumulation was capital's one and only commandment – "Accumulate, accumulate, that is Moses and the Prophets! ... Accumulation for the sake of accumulation, production for the sake of production" (Marx, 1867/1977, p. 742). However, he regarded this as a *contradiction* – both imperative and (near) impossible – indeed the fundamental one within which capitalism lived out its tortured existence, not an accomplished and self-perpetuating fact as it appeared in the flatly one-sided understandings of all-too-many, including its probable originator, Tugan Baranowski:

> Not consumption, but production is the determining factor in capitalism. The capitalist entrepreneur seeks to realize the largest feasible profit, but not to create the largest possible amount of means of consumption. In fact, the laws of capitalist competition enforce the capitalization of an important part of profit, its transformation, to a greater or lesser extent, into means of production, not apt for human consumption at all. Hence, one could say that the aim of capitalist production is not consumption but the growth of capital itself. (Tugan Baranowski, 1901/2000a, p. 72)

Such separation of production and consumption is simply alien to Marx's reasoning in *Capital*, as we have already seen. What is particularly ironic about this flat reading is that the enforcement of the "capitalization of an important part of profit, its transformation, to a greater or lesser extent into means of production" was precisely what Marx held responsible, as is clear from the passage from the *Grundrisse* which forms the epigraph for this chapter, for the historical peculiarity of capitalism as a class society – that, unlike all others, and without intending it, it was capable of, and rested on, advancing (at least some) ordinary workers' consumption to previously unimaginable levels.

3.2.3. How Many Key Discoveries?

A third remarkable aspect of the rejection of the role of consumption demand is a partial understanding of how Marx advanced our understanding of capitalism. While Engels may have deemed the discovery of the source of surplus value the key discovery of Marx's economic analysis of capitalism, it is far from clear that there were not other equally weighty aspects to his understanding of capitalism. If the TRPF was based on Marx's understanding of the role of fixed capital in accumulation which was built, in turn, on the foundation of his discovery of the origin of surplus value in production, Marx's understanding of the paucity of consumption demand as a source of crisis also equally rested on his discovery of the source of surplus value. It was the difference between the value of labour power and the value of what it was capable of producing which accounted for the gap between the goods produced and the goods demanded, a gap which could not always be filled by capitalist consumption demand, however gluttonous, or investment demand, however prodigious. Along with his clear understanding that in a monetary economy such as capitalism, money could also be hoarded, the paucity of consumption demand was also the basis of his unprecedented critique of Say's law (Marx, 1867/1977, p. 210).

This insight links Marx, who died in March 1883 to Keynes, who was born three months later. Exploration of this nexus has been blocked by the majority of Marxists who are only interested in rejecting Keynes as a "mere reformist" and the majority of Keynesians who never read Marx. Contrary of the image of mutual repulsion between a rigidly productionist Marx and an anti-Marxist, antisocialist, antiworking class Keynes, Keynes' oft-quoted expressions of disdain for Marx, socialism, and the working class were part of a more complex set of attitudes which included the rarely noted strong, and acknowledged, intellectual affinities with Marx (Desai, 2009; Desai & Freeman, 2009; Dostaler, 2007; Sardoni, 1997). In particular, Keynes' distinction between the neoclassical "real exchange economy" and his own conception of a "monetary economy" on which he built his whole approach in the *General Theory* is derived from Marx's foundational distinction between the circuit of commodities – C–M–C – and the circuit of capital – M–C–M' which opens *Capital.*

> The distinction between a co-operative economy and an entrepreneur economy bears some relation to a pregnant observation made by Karl Marx, though the subsequent use to which he put was highly illogical. He pointed out that the nature of production in the actual world is not, as economists seem often to suppose, a case of *C–M–C'* i.e., of exchanging commodity (or effort). That may be the standpoint of the private consumer. But it is not the attitude of *business*, which is the case of *M–C–M'*, i.e., of parting with money for commodity (or effort) in order to obtain more money. (Keynes, 1979, p. 81)

These foundational similarities are hardly surprising: both needed to reject Say's Law before they could proceed with their respective critiques of capitalism and the classical tradition of legitimizing it that each inherited.

While Keynes misunderstood Marx in many ways, partly because he seemed to take his Marx second-hand from unreliable accounts, he understood enough to see that he stood with Marx and against the classical tradition on some fundamental issues (Keynes, 1979, pp. 81-2n). As Claudio

Sardoni has shown, an early draft of the *General Theory* was formulated in terms close to, and derived from, Marx's. Keynes only

> abandoned his 1933 approach and, in *The General Theory*, ... formulated the critique of orthodox economics in a different way from Marx ... [because] ... the economic theory criticised by Keynes was significantly different from the Ricardian theory to which Marx referred. In particular, a satisfactory criticism of the marginalist version of Say's Law and its implications required the development of some theoretical issues that Marx was not compelled to take into consideration. (Sardoni, 1997, p. 261)

Marx had criticized Say's Law in its classical Ricardian version but it remained for Keynes to take it on in the form it took in the wake of Marx. The legitimation of capitalism now required that its central category – value – be shifted from the objective basis it had in classical political economy onto an entirely subjective basis. This move broke, and was meant to break, the contradictory unity of value and use value on whose foundation Marx exposed the limitations of classical political economy and its understanding of value. Marx's critique of Say's Law and his understanding of the workings of a monetary economy may not have received the fuller treatment that the source of surplus value or the TRPF did in the incomplete work that was *Capital*. Whether this makes them less important discoveries is, in my view at least, moot.

3.2.4. Productionism's Neoclassical, Marginalist, and Anti-Marxist Origins

This brings us to the final general feature of the rejection of consumption demand as a factor in capitalist reproduction and crisis. It not only antedates Marx, lying in the Russian Legal Marxists', particularly Tugan Baranowski's, overzealous rejection of the populists' arguments, the theoretical foundation of these arguments are noteworthy. While Shaikh rightly traces the rejection of the role of consumption demand to Tugan Baranowski and points out that the target of Tugan Baranowski's critique was the Narodnik idea that capitalism could not develop in Russia, there are four critical things he does not mention.

First, the paucity of consumption as a source of reproduction problems and crisis was not merely the product of Narodnik misunderstanding of Marx's theories, but was a widely held understanding among Europe's social democratic leaders. Kautsky, for instance, had been a target of Tugan Baranowski's original critique and, in turn, the former pointed out in a 1902 review of Tugan Baranowski's work that while markets would indeed grow with the development of capitalism, thanks to the commodification it relentlessly wreaked, they could only grow

> less rapidly than the accumulation of capital and the rise in the productivity of labor. Capitalist industry must, therefore, seek an additional market outside of its domain in non-capitalist nations and strata of the population. Such a market it finds and expands more and more, but not fast enough'. (Kautsky cited in Zarembka, 2000, p. 217)

Secondly, Shaikh elides important differences between Lenin and Tugan Baranowski and simply assimilates the two positions as antipopulist. However, Lenin concentrated on processes of commodification in the rural economy while Tugan Baranowski focused on the industrial economy (Howard, 1989/I, pp. 168–176). While Lenin's *The Development of Capitalism in Russia* (1899/1967) had refuted the Narodnik argument by showing how the commodification that came with capitalism would expand markets and that, in that sense, the development of capitalism in Russia was not impossible, he nowhere assumed that the market would be sufficient, or that consumption demand did not matter and that capitalism would not suffer from problems and contradictions on this front. Indeed, when later confronted by Tugan Baranowski's argument to this effect, Lenin gave it an interpretation which "subsumed consumption conditions under proportionalities" (Zarembka, 2003, p. 290), that is, considered the paucity of consumption demand to be an instance of disproportionality. Tugan Baranowski, however seems to have at least partially accepted this subsumption (Zarembka, 2003, p. 291) raising questions about the seriousness of his commitment to the view that capitalist contradictions were to be located in the sphere of production alone and that realization problems could be solved by the infinite production of producers' goods.

Thirdly, Shaikh does not inform us that, as a marginalist, Tugan Baranowski operated with a conceptual apparatus considerably at variance from Marxism. Most seriously, it differed on the central idea of value, rejecting classical political economy's objective value in favor of a subjective idea of value, based on utility and individual preferences (Clarke, 1991). The resulting chasm between the two ways of thinking can be illustrated with a brief passage in which Tugan reflects on profit, price, and value.

> the problem of profit has nothing in common with the problem of value. It is clear that, from the point of view of the individual firm, profit is a phenomenon of trade and can only be clarified through the laws of the formation of price and, consequently, of value. In a society in which the division of labor prevails, a good produced by a particular entrepreneur, considered as a thing, as a use-value, has nothing in common with the

> goods which make up its production costs. For example, a piece of cloth as a thing, as a use-value, is something completely different from the machines, the factory buildings, the workers' means of consumption, the raw material, the fuel and the other things which were needed to produce it. Only in its characteristic as exchange value is the produced good – the piece of cloth – greater than the goods that were necessary for its production. ... [S]ocial wealth is independent of prices. This wealth can only be expressed in terms of use-values. (Tugan Baranowski, 1901/2000b, pp. 98–99)

Not only is profit no longer a function of the extraction of surplus value, but a "phenomenon of trade," not only does price exhaust the meaning of value, not only is social wealth thought of only in terms of use-value, Tugan Baranowski has no use for the complex social alchemy of objective value through which alone concrete labour becomes abstract and socially necessary labour the basis of value. Tugan Baranowski's Marxism, if it so be called at all, is drained of all Marx's critical and analytical power. It is hardly surprising then that, in line with most marginalists, Tugan Baranowski also considered himself an adherent of Say's law whose rejection lay at the heart of Marx's understanding of capitalism as a contradictory system.

> Tugan considers himself a supporter of the doctrine he ascribes to Say, James Mill, John Stuart Mill, and Ricardo that "given a proportional distribution of social production, supply and demand must coincide." ... For Tugan, therefore, "when Marx opposes the lack of proportionality to the efficiency of social consumption as two independent causes of stagnation, he acknowledges being a follower of Sismondi's underconsumptionist theory." (Zarembka, 2003, p. 291)

Tugan Baranowski's "disproportionality" theory of crises arises precisely from this rejection of Marx's value analysis and his fundamental assumption of Say's Law. Since there can be no general "excess of social product" (Tugan Baranowski, 2000a, p. 78), and since value is only price – a matter of supply and demand – there can only be disproportions arising from the unplanned nature of capitalist production. These can give rise to crises, for in Tugan Baranowski's view, they can have no other origin.

> We have seen that capitalist production itself creates its own market – consumption being only one of the elements of capitalist production. If social production were planned, if the directors of production had a perfect *knowledge* of demand, and the *power* for transferring labor and capital from one branch of production into another, then, commodity supply could not exceed demand, however low social consumption might be. Yet, given the complete lack of planning of social production and the anarchy that reigns over the market, the accumulation of capital leads inexorably to crises. (Tugan Baranowski, 1901/2000a, p. 77)

3.3. Productionism Against Populism

In insisting that capitalism was not a system of production for need or consumption, productionists forget that this was only one side of a contradiction whose other side was value's existential imperative to realize itself as a use value. While becoming a use-value in the production of further value was a detour, and indeed an increasingly frequent one as capitalism developed, the ultimate prize for all values produced was to be realized in the consumption as final use values. However, productionist arguments, which Mandel labels "neo-harmonicist," locate the problems of capitalism in the sphere of production alone, and assume, like J. B. Say, that "there is no specific problem of value realization, only one of surplus-value production." (Mandel, 1981, p. 40). Both versions of productionism assume an expansion of the production of producers' goods to an extent and in a way that would obviate any potential for paucity of workers consumption to cause crisis. While it is certainly true that the production of producers' goods can be expected to become a growing portion of any capitalist economy as it develops, these two arguments envisage a phantasmagorically one-sided "production for production's sake" that was neither envisaged by Marx nor experienced in any capitalist society.

As we have seen Tugan Baranowski, productionism's originator, saw crises as originating in the anarchy of capitalist production. More specifically, disproportions arise between the production of Department I, producing investment goods and Department II, producing consumption goods. These could be averted by organizing investment through cartels or the state. In Tugan Baranowski's view, which he illustrated mathematically, "department I could develop completely independently from department II, to the point where the output of consumer goods would tend to fall towards zero, without such a development causing any crisis whatsoever" (Mandel, 1981, pp. 43–44). Thus discounted, consumption played no independent role: shortfalls in consumption demand could be made up by increases in investment demand, provided "disproportionality" between sectors could be avoided.

Tugan Baranowski's resulting conception of capitalism as an endless production of producers' goods is easily contradicted. As Mandel rightly points out, "unlimited growth of department I leads to an ever faster growth of the productive capacity of department II (although not necessarily in the same proportion); in other words, that under capitalist *commodity* relations production can never fully emancipate itself from sales to the final consumer" (Mandel, 1978, p. 72). What needs accounting, however, is the enduring attraction of this view.

As mentioned earlier, Tugan Baranowski and other Russian Legal Marxists developed this view in the course of their debates with the Russian Populists. As Rosa Luxemburg pointed out in her critique of their views, the result was overkill.

> There can be no doubt that the "legalist" Russian Marxists achieved a victory over their opponents, the "populists," but that victory was rather too thorough. In the heat of battle, all three – Struve, Bulgakov and Tugan Baranowski – overstated their case. The question was whether capitalism in general, and Russian capitalism in particular, is capable of development; these Marxists, however, proved this capacity to the extent of even offering theoretical proof that capitalism can go on without limits, one has obviously proved the unlimited capacity of capitalism to survive! (Luxemburg, 1913/2003, p. 304)

Tugan Baranowski developed this view of capitalism on the basis of his reading of Marx's reproduction schemas at the end of Volume II of *Capital*, schemas whose relation to the rest of *Capital* was problematic, going, as Rosa Luxemburg showed, directly against its grain. They particularly contradicted "the conception of the capitalist total social process and its course as laid down by Marx in *Capital*, volume III ... based on the inherent contradiction between the unlimited expansive capacity of the productive forces and the limited expansive capacity of social consumption under conditions of capitalist distribution" (Luxemburg, 1913/2003, p. 323).

As we have also noted, the insufficiency of consumption demand, and its centrality to capitalist reproduction, is a theme that runs through all the volumes of capital, including volume II. It is only the incompleteness of *Capital* that prevents this theme from being developed more fully in its own right. Against this, in the reproduction schemas at the end of volume II, Marx sought to show merely the *possibility* of capitalist reproduction, simple or expanded, abstracting from capital's contradictions, and the possibilities for crises, whether they arose from accumulation or from realization. Indeed, as Rosa Luxemburg showed, in these schemas Marx also abstracted from technical progress and increasing labour productivity and the account of crisis most associated with this, the TRPF, is not developed until volume III. Moreover, the abstraction of the schemas was reinforced, in Tugan Baranowski's case at least, by his marginalism and adherence to Say's Law. What is interesting is that this adherence was not unconnected with his rejection of the TRPF in terms similar to those which would be invoked by Okishio many decades later. Tugan Baranowski argued that Marx ignored the fact that increased investment, increased organic composition of capital, also increased productivity.

> The error of the whole argument lies, however, in that we cannot suppose that all the rest remains constant. Marx himself has noted that the elevation of the composition of capital is only a capitalist expression of an increase in labor productivity. As variable capital is a smaller proportion of total capital, the productivity of labor rises. The effect of both factors on the rate of profit – and Marx ignored this – is balanced out, and the profit rate cannot fall, in spite of the modification of capital composition. (Tugan Baranowski, 1901/2000b, p. 91)

Having first shown that it could offset increases in the organic composition of capital, leading to no fall in the rate of profit, he then went on to show that actually, increased investment would increase productivity to such an extent that

> The total mass of product undergoes a strong increase. So, the rise in the productivity of labor is much higher than we have supposed. Hence, this implies a modification in our conclusions: We have concluded that the replacement of manual labor by mechanical work does not reduce the rate of profit. This would be correct under the supposition that the introduction of machines does not imply an increase in the mass of goods. But, since actually the mechanical work generates a greater amount of product than the manual labor, the rate of profit must increase as a consequence of the relative rise in the constant capital. This is, exactly the opposite of Marx's theory. *On the basis of the theory of labor-value, we reach the conclusion that the replacement of workers by machines, in itself and for itself, not only does not imply a tendency for the rate of profit to fall; rather, it implies a rising tendency of this rate.* (Tugan Baranowski, 1901/2000b, pp. 95–96)

We take up the matter of this "disproof" of the TRPF in the next section. What is relevant in explaining the endurance of productionism is that though Rosa Luxemburg brilliantly exposed this position and insisted on the reality of the problem of consumption demand in *The Accumulation of Capital*, this work remains was unjustifiably dismissed. In that work, which is regularly dismissed as flawed with the appellation "brilliant" attached, one suspects, as a consolation prize, she had posed a very simple question: for successful accumulation to take place

> the desire to accumulate plus the technical prerequisites of accumulation is not enough in a capitalist economy of commodity production. A further condition is required to ensure that accumulation can in fact proceed and production expand: the effective demand for commodities must also increase. Where is this continually increasing demand to come from which in Marx's diagram forms the basis of reproduction on an ever rising scale? (Luxemburg, 1913/2003, p. 104)

Luxemburg comes, via a process of elimination, to the answer that in the "pure" capitalist economy consisting of only workers and capitalist, the sources of demand inevitably remained inadequate and therefore capitalism had to either reach beyond itself to non-capitalist formations or seek in other ways to deepen and broaden the home market. This was in line with

Marx's emphases all along and only corrected the smoothing out of contradictions in the schemas of reproduction.

But, as Paul Zarembka shows, Luxemburg's work has been subject to some of the most irresponsible critiques in the history of Marxism. Among the most important critiques of *The Accumulation of Capital*

> made after her 1919 murder, Nikolai Bukharin's [was] the most well-known and most instrumental in putting her down. These critiques carry differing political agenda – some pro-Soviet, some anti-Soviet, some "independent," some Hegelian-based, some not so – but are not more cogent for their diversity. Typically they choose a secondary issue, raise it to front-line status, and criticize that. The result is often either an error or a distortion. But confronting Luxemburg's theory in its full integrity is a rarity. (Zarembka, 2002, pp. 4–5)

Diverse as these critiques were, one point emerges, perhaps, as a very widely shared criticism of Luxemburg: that the penetration by capitalism of noncapitalist formations "can and does happen and it does aid capitalist accumulation when it does happen, but it is not *required* by the logic of capitalism" (Zarembka, 2003, p. 8). However, it is only by dismissing the necessity of consumption demand falling short that this can be asserted.

The impact of these unjustified dismissals of Luxemburg's arguments by Marxists can be seen, ironically, in Mandel's defence of Luxemburg. Mandel is, of course, not among those who dismiss consumption demand. But even he ends up conceding something to the dismissal of Luxemburg. Luxemburg had indeed erred, he avers, in thinking of capital in general rather than of capitalism as the competition of many capitals in which "capitalists can indeed grow richer by buying one another's surplus product" (Mandel, 1978, p. 64) and where "the surplus-value created at one point requires the creation of surplus-value at another point, for which it may be exchanged" (Grundrisse, p. 407). Her working out of the "interrelated variables of the reproduction schemas" (Mandel, 1978, p. 67) did not make her case fully, at the level of the actual historical process of capital accumulation. Nevertheless,

> Luxemburg seems fundamentally correct. Capitalism was born essentially in a non-capitalist milieu; it has immensely enriched itself by plundering that milieu, and the same value transferring metabolism has continued to this very day. (Mandel, 1978, p. 68)

But does Mandel really need to put Luxemburg in the position of being theoretically wrong but historically correct, as though she was, though logically deficient, at least that lesser thing, a better observer? Surely not, given his agreement with her on the relevance of consumption demand.

Luxemburg is one of the few Marxists of her generation, and for that matter, of all Marxists since Marx, to refer to the critical link between paucity of demand and crisis on which Marx's understanding clearly rested even if he did not have the time to develop it. Among commentators on Luxemburg it was left to Joan Robinson, by no means immune from the general condescension toward, and tendentious reading of, Luxemburg, to note this. Perhaps it had to be Robinson. For this theme also links Marx and Luxemburg to Keynes and Robinson was one of the few scholars to know Marx and Luxemburg as well as Keynes. Luxemburg, Robinson says, "appears to be concerned with the inducement to invest. What motive have the capitalists for enlarging their stock of real capital? How do they know that there will be demand for the increased output of goods which the new capital will produce, so that they can 'capitalize' their surplus in a profitable form?" (Robinson, 2003, p. xxix). Robinson believed Luxemburg to be incognizant of the "savings and investment problem, for she takes it for granted that each individual act of saving out of surplus is accompanied by a corresponding amount of real investment, and that every piece of investment is financed out of surplus of the same capitalist who makes it." Thus, Robinson held, Luxemburg had greater affinities to Hobson than to Keynes. But the passages to which she refers us merely state the assumption that Luxemburg believes Marx makes in his reproduction schemas and are neither a statement of her belief about capitalism in general nor, considering that Luxemburg regarded these schemas as out of joint with the rest of the analysis of *Capital*, are they a statement about Marx's beliefs. In any case, any assumption of an identity of saving and real investment flies in the face of Robinson's own understanding of Luxemburg as being concerned about the inducement to invest – what else might a lack of inducement refer to but a difference between surplus and investment, a hoard?

As Prabhat Patnaik notes, Marx always insisted that in any monetary economy there was always the possibility of a "hoard" (Marx, 1867/1977, p. 736), an uninvested portion of the profit which implies that Say's Law cannot possibly hold and which, therefore, implies the possibility of generalized overproduction.

> But neither Marx nor his followers pursued this fundamental contribution of Marx any further; they preferred instead to follow exclusively the other major theoretical discovery of Marx, namely, the one relating to his theory of surplus value. This is why three quarters of a century had to elapse before the same themes surfaced again during the Keynesian revolution through the writings *inter alia* of Kalecki and Keynes … .(Patnaik, 2009a, pp. 3–4)

Part of this difficulty here is, of course, the mutual ignorance and antagonism between the partisans of Keynes and of Marx, not to mention the systematic distortion of the work of each by his own followers. This link points to another implication of the role of consumption demand in capitalist reproduction and crises. As we have seen, Rosa Luxemburg had already noted how the paucity of consumption demand required either that capitalism reach beyond itself to noncapitalist formations to find markets, in short engage in imperialism, or it must seek ways to deepen and broaden the home market. This link was also underscored by Hobson in his case against imperialism.

In Hobson's view, since it was the paucity of home demand that was a major driver of imperialism, government action could overcome the problem of overproduction and underconsumption in better, universally beneficial, ways through social reforms and the redistribution of income. As he put it,

> If the consuming public in this country raises its standard of consumption to keep pace with every rise of productive powers, there could not no excess of goods or capital clamorous to use Imperialism in order to find markets: foreign trade would indeed exist, but there would be no difficulty in exchanging a small surplus of our manufactures for the food and raw material we annually absorbed, and all the savings we made could find employment, if we choose, in home industries. (Hobson, 1965, p. 81)

One might say here that Hobson was subject to the same criticism that Marx made of the underconsumptionists of his time. One might also recognise that the nonimperialist national social order envisaged by Hobson, which was essentially no different from the one envisaged by Keynes (1933, 1936/1967), required not reform but a change in the nature and dynamics of capitalism, in particular in its class structure, that amounted to a revolution. Marxist critics of imperialism of the time were simply more conscious of the political implications of their critique.

3.4. Investment Against Consumption

The contemporary Marxist productionism views not disproportion but the TRPF as the chief cause of crisis, that is, provided they agree that the TRPF is a valid theory. Many Marxist economists do not. It is well-known that Marxist economists in the postwar period believed they could demonstrate a rise in the rate of profit (e.g., Sweezy, 1970). While assessing this argument, though issues of data and the suitability of the statistical measures used would take us too far away from the main concerns of this chapter, one may safely say that this demonstration did not necessitate to a rejection of the TRPF. The TRPF is just that, a tendency, which can be, and often has been, counteracted by other tendencies – including that held responsible for the postwar rise in the rate of profit – the cheapening, reduction in value, of capital equipment. However, some Marxist economists reject Marx's account of the TRPF on stronger, theoretical, grounds. They believe, first, that Marx could not solve the "transformation problem" of how values were transformed into prices (Steedman, 1981) and second that, as the famous "Okishio Theorem" had "proved," Marx was wrong about the TRPF and that instead of falling, the rate of profit necessarily rose.

In the wake of these arguments Marxist economists who are interested in these issues are broadly divided into those who seek to give, like Shaikh, what they consider is better account of capitalist reproduction in which they have solved the "transformation problem" and the rate of profit does fall, logically and empirically, and those who reject Marxist accounts of reproduction and crises entirely. However, scholars adhering to what they call the Temporal Single System Interpretation (TSSI) (Kliman, 2007, Freeman in Freeman & Carchedi, 1996) have recently shown, correctly in my view, that the transformation problem exists only for those who attempt to fit Marx's economic analysis in a neoclassical equilibrium format, assume that prices and values are determined by two independent systems, and refuse to see that input and output prices are not determined simultaneously but in circumstances that change with the time that elapses between the moment of input and the moment of output.

We have already seen that Tugan Baranowski dismissed the TRPF by simply assuming that because increased investment lead to increased productivity, the rate of profit must rise. Part of the problem here was the necessitarian assumption: the rate of profit in Marx's account *tends* to fall, though it can be counteracted by opposing tendencies. However, at least some contemporary Marxists, following the famous Okishio Theorem which 'refuted' the TRPF, seem think that according to Marx the rate of profit should rise because capitalists would not "adopt new techniques that *decrease their own rate of profit* – and ... end up reducing overall profitability" (Brenner, 1998, p. 12n, citing Okishio, 1961 and Roemer, 1978). This seems to imply a relation between capitalists' intentions and the effects of their actions that flies in the face of Marx's careful explication of the operation of the TRPF.

> No capitalist voluntarily applies a new method of production, no matter how much more productive it may be or how much it might raise the rate of surplus value, if it reduces the rate of profit. But every new method of production of this kind makes commodities

> cheaper. At first, therefore, he can sell them above their price of production, perhaps above their value. He pockets the difference between their costs of production and the market price of the other commodities, which are produced at higher production costs. This is possible because the average socially necessary labour-time required to produce these latter commodities is greater than the labour-time required with the new method of production. This production procedure is ahead of the social average. But competition makes the new procedure universal and subjects it to the general law. A fall in the profit rate then ensues – firstly perhaps in this sphere of production, and subsequently equalised with the others – *a fall that is completely independent of the capitalists' will.* (Marx, 1981/1894, pp. 373–4)

Andrew Kliman's account of TSSI puts the problem down to the simultaneous valuation of inputs and outputs, equalizing them in a way that "spirits away the disinflationary or deflationary effect of technological change" (Kliman, 2007, p. 117). It is not merely that these Marxist economists are, like Tugan Baranowski, mesmerized by the increase in the volume of output which results from productivity increasing, cost-diminishing investment. Rather, they are theoretically constrained from taking into account the price declines which also ensue in the process of equalization because they value inputs and outputs simultaneously:

> That physical output rises in relation to physical input as a result of increasing productivity is undeniable, as is the fact that this tends to boost profitability. Yet these same increases in productivity also tend to reduce the rate of increase in the *price* of the output relative to the price of the input. (Kliman, 2007, p. 114)

Marx's version of the TRPF can only be rejected on the basis of erroneous neoclassical equilibrium methods, a trend of which Tugan Baranowski was a pioneer, as we have seen, in which prices and values are determined by separate systems and time plays no role, and by the most tendentious readings of his careful explanations. On may note in passing here that the question of exactly how the TRPF or, for that matter, paucity of demand, lead to crises is a separate one (Itoh, 1978).

While Shaikh does believe there is a "transformation problem," he is not a partisan of Okishio. The detail of his reconstruction of the TRPF that most concerns us here is that Shaikh assimilates workers' consumption demand, that is, the bulk of consumption demand in any society, into investment since it consists of constant capital (fixed and circulating capital) and variable capital, that is, wages. Having done that he merely seeks to "prove" that it was *possible* that consumption demand would pose no problem. As he sees it,

> if capitalists did undertake the appropriate amount of investment, then they would indeed be able to sell their produce and make the anticipated profits. If this success spurs

> them to reinvest once again in anticipation of yet more profits, they would be rewarded once again, and so on. All the while, consumption would expand due to the growing employment of workers and the growing wealth of capitalists. (Shaikh, 1978, p. 229)

In such a reading, paucity of demand can only be a symptom of a deeper, more fundamental, problem – the decline in the rate of profit that reduces the willingness of capitalists to invest. However, there are at least two reasons why this argument is not successful in relegating consumption demand to the margins as a cause of crisis. First, both Marx's own analysis and the historical experience of capitalism over recent decades show that while investment demand, when it is robust, can and does often offset the paucity of consumption demand by increasing employment and therefore consumption demand (as in the classic "Keynesian" prescription), the conditions of existence of capitalism ensure that it can never keep pace with the ever-increasing scale of production. Secondly, capitalists' desire to invest is negatively affected by perceptible shortfalls in demand, as both Marx and Keynes recognized.

In Shaikh's scenario, investment demand, defined as including constant and variable capital, could keep growing in a way such that the expansion in each period produced adequate demand for the value, including surplus value, produced in the previous period. Such "balanced growth."

> implies that productive power and effective demand *can* grow at roughly the same rate. Taken by itself, however, it does not necessarily imply that capitalism achieves anything remotely like that. Nor does it tell us anything about the way the causation might run if such growth was indeed possible on the average. *Nonetheless*, the fact that expanding reproduction is possible poses a distinct threat to underconsumption theories. (Shaikh, 227, emphasis added – RD)

Shaikh spends no time on whether such "balanced growth," now proved theoretically possible, can be actually realized, or why capitalism does not "achieve anything remotely like that." Instead he moves swiftly on to talking as though this mere *possibility* is enough to dismiss "underconsumption." The problems with this maneuver should be obvious to anyone. First, if the possibility of "balanced growth" is to serve as the refutation of the relevance of consumption demand, Shaikh would have to demonstrate that the conditions of expanded accumulation he stipulates would be normally, or at least fairly regularly, exist to the extent necessary to undo the effects of the extraction of surplus value on the income, and therefore consumption capacity, of workers. Though by his own admission, they do not, Shaikh is not thereby led to wonder what effect such imbalances might have on capitalists' inclination to hoard, rather than invest. Second, deriving workers' consumption from investment as "variable capital" overlooks the fact, continuously emphasized by Marx, that the laws of competition tend, over time, to *reduce* the labour necessary for capitalist production and therefore the amount of variable capital. Can constant capital take up the slack?

Here there are two scenarios. One is where the increased production of Department I goods is realized in sales to Department II firms. In that case,

> The only thing this analysis proves is the fact that consumption … grows as long as accumulation grows. But it does not prove that consumption grows in the same proportion as does the productive capacity of Department II. Indeed, the combined operation of the increasing organic composition of capital in department II and the increase in the rate of surplus-value in the overall economy makes it rather probable that (at least periodically) consumption, while growing, will grow less than productive capacity in department II. In which case, a glut of consumer goods can indeed occur before accumulation has slowed down in the economy taken as a whole. (Mandel, 1981, p. 47)

However, some raise a second Tuganesque possibility: that the increased production of Department I is realized through sales to other Department I firms, and not to Department II firms. This would indeed be the ultimate phantasy of noncontradictory, self-perpetuating capitalist accumulation, production for productions's sake gone bonkers. However, the conditions under which it would take place would have to be specified – what would the relevant demand conditions have to look like? Where would demand for more and more producer goods which did not produce consumer goods come from? Why would it occur? Has it ever occurred? Certainly no historical examples can be mustered for this (the Chinese economy of recent years, where investment has accounted for nearly a third of total annual product, and the Soviet economy of the 1930s might be the closest examples. But given the degree of state involvement in the first and the noncapitalist nature of the second, they do not apply since the argument in question concerns a competitive private capitalist economy explicitly).

Contrary to the reproduction schemas of volume II, where we begin with the production of goods in Department I, with the production of producers' goods, the analysis of the rest of capital clearly demonstrates that capitalism developed originally by taking over existing precapitalist production for need, subsuming workers only formally. It triumphed over these precapitalist producers, *manufacturers*, by the efficiency of its production which it continually increased by producing producers' goods. However complex and sophisticated, this production of producers' goods has got over the decades and centuries, it does not seem to me to have broken its *ultimate* link to human need (albeit expressed through *effective* demand alone). If a case is to be made that this link was indeed broken, the point in the historical development of capitalism where it was broken would need to be clearly specified. It is hardly surprising that no one has done this. It cannot be done. There has been no such break.

4. THE DEMAND PROBLEM IN THE CURRENT CRISIS

Indeed, the career of capitalism in the latter 20th century shows that the link between capitalist production and consumption remains alive and well. Robert Brenner's account of the political economy of postwar capitalism, in particular its "Long Boom" and "Long Downturn" (1998, 2002, 2006, 2009) foresaw the present crisis and is, to my mind, the only properly historical Marxist account of capitalism in the latter part of the 20th century. It has elicited considerable critique. Debate revolves around his focus on manufacturing to the exclusion of other sectors of the economy, his use of the triad of United States, Germany, and Japan as a stand-in for the world capitalism, as well as other issues (*Historical Materialism*, 1999; Arrighi, 2003). From our point of view, however, the work's most germane aspect is its view of capitalist crises: his theoretical dismissal of the TRPF and his subsequent historical reconstruction of the same. The matter is complex.

On the one hand, Brenner misunderstands, or at least misrepresents, the TRPF. In criticizing what he calls "Fundamentalist Marxist theory" he says that "The rate of profit falls, from this perspective, because with the real wage assumed constant, investment in mechanization cannot but result in an increase in labour productivity (output–labour ratio) that is more than cancelled out by a decrease in capital productivity (real output–capital ratio)" (Brenner, 1998, p. 11n). Here Brenner, like other critics of the TRPF forgets that the proposition in question is a tendency not an iron law as he portrays it. He seems, further, to assume that the paradox that "capitalists adopt new techniques that *decrease their own rate of profit*" (Brenner, 1998, p. 12n) simply cannot be obtained. We have already seen, on the contrary, that this is precisely the paradox that underlies the TRPF. Marx would not deny that in increasing the organic composition of capital the individual capitalist is motivated by a desire to increase his rate of profit both absolutely and relatively to others, an increase which would last until the new technology became generalized in the sector. Nor would Marx deny that when certain technologies raise productivity particularly high, and other circumstances prevent wage increases in line with productivity increases and price decreases in line with lower costs, conditions for continuing high profit rates may exist even after a given technology is generalized.

On the other hand, Brenner's dismissal of the TRPF is, in any case, rather gratuitous – it is not necessary for his essentially historical argument. If that were not enough, he re-establishes the same tendency out of the facts he encounters! His explanation of the "Long Downturn" turns on falling profitability in manufacturing and it is hard to distinguish from Marx's account of the TRPF as outlined in this chapter. Indeed, one might say, having rightly dismissed his own wrong understanding of Marx's TRPF, Brenner is more or less forced to recreate a TRPF in historical form in the course of his explanation which is essentially the same as Marx's original and correct understanding. Brenner's recreation of the TRPF vindicates the TSSI view that only assuming away the product price declines that follow the generalization of a technology across a sector allows the critics of the TRPF to make their case that profit rates necessarily rise. It also reveals the profound link between demand and the mechanisms of the falling rate of profit. Brenner's

> account of the long downturn ... finds its source of the profitability decline ... in the tendency of producers to develop the productive forces and increase economic productiveness by means of the installation of increasingly cheap and effective methods of production, *without regard for existing investments and their requirements for realization*, with the result that aggregate profitability is *squeezed by reduced prices in the face of downwardly inflexible costs*. (Brenner, 1998, pp. 23–24, emphases added)

In Brenner's empirical account, then, not only do profit rates fall, not only do they fall because price decreases follow increasing productivity, the rise and fall of profit rates is inextricably tied up with the problem of realization, of demand, including, as will become clear, consumption demand.

Brenner's explanation of the Long Boom and Long Downturn has two further virtues which, however, have not hitherto been pointed out. First, it puts the political economy of our time in its historical context, seeing capitalism not as an unchanging and self-contained system but one which has evolved over time – whether through the critical role of national economic management or the postwar recovery of Europe and Japan and the entry of new industrial competitors. Second, it is an essentially geopolitical account of capitalism, putting the economic role of states – both domestically and in their geoeconomic competition – within a wider perspective on capitalism's uneven and combined development. Thus formulated, his account features demand centrally.

How so? First, the ordinary processes of capitalist competition – investment to increase productivity, cost-cutting, and later price-cutting to expand market share – lead to a situation in which "the cost-cutters' rate of profit remains the same as before and ... the higher cost firms' rates of profit are reduced, the outcome is an aggregate reduction in the rate of profit in the line." This constitutes "over-capacity and over-production" "in the sense that – *there is insufficient demand* to allow the higher cost forms to maintain their former rates of profit; they have been obliged to cease using some of their means of production and can make use of the rest only by lowering their price and thus their profitability." (Brenner, 1998, pp. 25–26, emphasis added). Moreover, over-capacity and over-production further exacerbate the problem of demand: "the slowed growth of demand that is the unavoidable expression of the reduced growth of investment and of wages that inevitably result from falling profit rates makes it increasingly difficult to reallocate to new lines" (Brenner, 1998, p. 33).

Demand is also central to the geopolitical aspect of the story. It was important in the Long Boom, though in ways distinct from the usual "Keynesian" understandings. On the one hand, while the Long Boom was not, according to Brenner, rooted in favorable demand conditions created by Keynesian welfare states, they "must have helped endow these economies with greater stability than in the past" (Brenner, 1999, p. 91). On the other, though all major capitalist states featured Keynesian demand management, the bulk of the Long Boom's growth took place in the recovering economies, while the United States stagnated relative to the other fast-growing centres of capitalist accumulation in the 1950s and enjoyed only a brief and highly inflationary boom in the 1960s. This pattern of growth could only be attributed to supply-side factors. However,

> *Where the autonomous growth of demand did operate powerfully to augment investment and growth, it appears to have done so, paradoxically, less within national boundaries than across them.* German and Japanese manufacturers derived much of their dynamism by means of appropriating large segments of the fast-growing world market from the US and the UK. This redistribution of market share ... gave a powerful boost to their investment and output, while detracting somewhat from the growth prospects of the US and the UK. The resulting pattern of development was extremely uneven, but it made for a boom of historic proportions. (Brenner, 1998, p. 91, emphasis added)

Moreover, demand and demand management were critical to Brenner's account of why, once it had set in, the downturn was so prolonged. The "insufficient exit" of firms which prolonged the downturn was partly because of their "intangible assets" (Brenner, 1998, p. 147) and partly because of "barriers against their entering new lines." It was also because, critically, "With the growth of profits – and thus of investment and wages – suppressed, *aggregate demand grew more slowly*" (Brenner, 1998, p. 148, emphasis added). Demand management – taking the perverse form of tax-cuts and a credit boom in the neoliberal decades that followed – was also critical to easing the series of recessions that nevertheless occurred. And they prolonged the Downturn.

> In 1974–75, 1979–82, and in the early 1990s, the advanced capitalist world did indeed sustain a series of recessions more severe than any since the 1930s, after each of which the level of unemployment was generally higher and the rate of growth of output lower than following the previous ones. Had it not been for the *unprecedented expansion of both public and private debt in response to these recessions*, the world economy could not easily have avoided a depression. Yet, the same expansion of credit which ensured a modicum of stability also held back recovery. For, by cutting recessions short – and more generally making possible the survival of those high-cost, low-profit firms which perpetuated over-capacity and over-production, and prevented the average rate of profit from recovering – the subsidy to demand through Keynesian debt creation prolonged the downturn. Keynesianism made the downturn both milder and longer. (Brenner, 1998, pp. 150–151)

Of course though Brenner calls the stimuli to demand "Keynesian," they were so only in a perverse sense. In the anti-Keynesian neoliberal times, demand was stimulated first by expansion of government military spending (military Keynesianism) rather than an expansion social and working class consumption. Later, when consumption demand did expand, thanks to wage stagnation, it had to take the form of unsustainable forms of consumption credit – the famous wealth effect, first of the stock market boom and then the house price boom – and was skewed towards higher income groups ("credit Keynesianism") (Needless to say, the extension of this demand creation farther down the social scale to the hapless "subprime" borrowers laid the basis of the now infamous "subprime" crisis a few years later).

Brenner's analysis captures the central irony of neoliberalism: its attempt to restrict working class wages and consumption forced it into perverse forms of demand expansion which soon came up against their own limitations, most spectacularly in the present crisis. But perversely produced or not, expanded private and public consumption via debt, particularly in the United States, sustained both investment and consumption demand in the United States and in the parts of the world economy reliant on the US market. The extent of the stimulus the United States thus provided was so great that consumption came to account for about 70% of US GDP and, as the United States emerged as the world's "consumer of last resort," it produced approximately 6% less than it consumed (i.e., the US trade deficit was about 6% of its GDP). And, one might add, some expect that the prospect of the United States ceasing to be able to perform the "consumer-of-last resort" function, thanks to the current economic and financial crisis, will result in a brutal interruption of growth worldwide. Others expect a major reorientation of growth patterns in the emerging economies, with the reliance on export demand of recent decades giving way to one on domestic or inter-emerging economy demand.

Marxists who discount the role of consumption demand in capitalist reproduction and crisis would have to deny all this: the role, so clearly brought out by Brenner, of demand in the Long Boom, the Long Downturn; the role of fiscal and monetary measures in mitigating the potential severity of recessions by putting a floor under demand, including consumption demand; and neoliberalism's own perverse ways of generating demand. They would also have to deny that the severity of the present crisis, the most severe since the Great Depression of the 1930s, has been mitigated, if not resolved, by government stimulus policies. And they would be unable to understand how the search for new sources of demand by the emerging economies in the current crisis, and its success or failure, will shape the outcome of the present crisis in a fundamental way.

5. REFORMS AND REVOLUTION

Part of the unpopularity of underconsumptionism arises from the taint of "reformism." However, reformism – the belief that capitalism's problems are limited and can be resolved without questioning its fundamental basis in private property in the means of production – is one thing, and reforms quite another. A reform may not be attached to any wider idea of whether capitalism needs to be transformed, or it may be attached to a quite opposite belief – that achieving it would require the overthrow of capitalism. The same demand – say for a radical form of income equality – would be called a reform in one case and a revolutionary demand in another. Calling does not make things so. What *makes* a given demand a reform and another a revolutionary demand is not the labels this or that band of self-styled revolutionaries deem to apply to them but the wider political situation that determines the historical outcome of any struggle whether it be styled reforming or revolutionary. The most modest demand – say for cheap bread – might turn out to be revolutionary if the ruling order is unable or unwilling to fulfill it and the political energy and organization exist behind it to inspire people to believe that if it is not going to be fulfilled it is time for people to remove the ruling order and fulfill it for themselves. "Merely reformist" demands for higher wages may become revolutionary and apparently more radical demands may become "granted" reforms. Labels can also be misleading in another sense. As has been pointed out above, there may be some writers who, like Keynes or Hobson, for whatever reason, alight on critiques of capitalism that are pretty thoroughgoing and whose implications for "reform," modestly though they may be couched, are such as to require a fundamental transformation of capitalism.

Moreover, if the ruling class does concede a given reform it is likely to increase the ability of working people to advance further demands. This is why reforms and welfare measures are opposed by capitalists, as should surely be clear after three decades of neoliberal attacks on welfare states. They are, for all the complexity of their history – Bismarck and all – direct or indirect achievements working class struggle. Attacks on them have only been possible in an era of historic working class retreat. As Prabhat Patnaik notes, the capitalist classes oppose the welfare states for several reasons: because "it militates against the basic ethics of the bourgeois system ... that the distribution of rewards by the spontaneous working of the capitalist system is 'fair'; because, therefore, "the acceptance of welfarism amounted to 'no confidence' in the bourgeois system" and, most importantly, because

> Welfare State measures improve the bargaining strength of the proletariat and other segments of the working people. The maintenance of near-full employment conditions improves the bargaining strength of the trade unions; the provision of unemployment assistance likewise stiffens the resistance of the workers. The "sack" which is the weapon dangled by the "bosses" over the heads of the workers loses its effectiveness in an economy which is both close to full employment and has a system of reasonable unemployment allowances and other forms of social security. (Patnaik, 2009b)

In this sense, as Patnaik notes socialism and welfarism, revolution and reform, are "dialectically linked." "Socialists must support Welfare State measures, not just because such measures are humane, not just because such measures benefit the working people, but above all because such measures stiffen the will of the people to resist, help the process of changing them from objects to subjects, and hence contribute to the process of sharpening of class struggle" (Patnaik, 2009b). Kalecki had identified much the same logic in his analysis of the political implication of full employment – it was because full employment as a reform would have this effect that he recognized that it would be politically difficult for the bourgeoisie to accept.

How reforms and revolution can be linked dialectically was illustrated in the case of Sweden where a long history of working class gains led, at its culmination, in "reforms" which entailed the gradual transfer of the ownership of the means of production to workers (Korpi, 1983). If this failed it had more to do with the political conditions – of ruling class capacity to fight back and of fissures within working class solidarity – and less to do with any "inherently" reformist or revolutionary character of the demand.

This complex relationship between reform and revolution is especially important to understand because no one, not even the citizens of the most advanced capitalist country, lives in a "pure" capitalism. Actually existing capitalism everywhere necessarily (and not least because they are not abstract capitalisms but national ones) rely on a number of political, social, and cultural structures and practices – both traditional and modern – to intensify oppression and exploitation. But other structures of the same sort also furnish the second aspect of Karl Polanyi's "double movement" – the movement of social protection. These measures constitute, especially in the advanced capitalist world, a dense network of structures and practices – from city zoning restrictions to national regulatory and welfare structures – that modify the dynamics of capitalism quite thoroughly (Elson, 2000). The further extension of such modifications in ways that favor working people and strengthen their organizations would be reforms worthy of achievement in their own right. If undertaken with sufficient organization, seriousness of purpose and political will to take on the inevitable opposition to them, there is no telling at what point in the struggle for their extension capitalism might be modified beyond recognition. The problems will certainly not be the reforms themselves but how ambitious we are in conceiving them and how seriously we mean to achieve them.

NOTE

1. I have learned much from Makoto Itoh, Andrew Kliman, and John Weeks' comments on earlier drafts, not least about the virtues of intellectual generosity towards work which attempts a critique of one's long-held positions. My debt to Paul Zarembka's careful argumentation on related matters is evidenced in the references and his editorial suggestions have greatly improved this chapter. Alan Freeman's careful comments on two drafts sharpened the argument and many parts of it are simply strands of our on-going conversations. Unresolved problems remain my responsibility.

REFERENCES

Anderson, P. (1987). Figures of descent. *New Left Review, I/161*(January–Feburary), 20–77.

Arrighi, G. (2003). The social and political economy of global turbulence. *New Left Review, 20*(March–April), 5–71.

Bleaney, M. (1976). *Under-consumption theories: A history and critical analysis*. London: Lawrence and Wishart.

Brenner, R. (1998). *The economics of global turbulence: A special report on the world economy, 1950–98*. London: New Left Review.

Brenner, R. (1999). The economics of global turbulence. *New Left Review I/229*, May–June, pp. 1–265.

Brenner, R. (2002). *The boom and the bubble: The US in the world economy*. London: Verso.

Brenner, R. (2006). *The economics of global turbulence: The advanced capitalist economies from long boom to long downturn, 1945–2005*. London: Verso.

Brenner, R. (2009). What is good for goldman sachs is good for America. Prologue to the Spanish Translation of *The Economics of Global Turbulence*. Madrid (?): Akal. Available at http://escholarship.org/uc/item/0sg0782h

Clarke, S. (1991). *Marxism, marginalism and modern sociology: From Adam Smith to Max Weber*. Basingstoke, England: Macmillan.

Coates, D. (Ed.) (2002). *Models of capitalism: Debating strengths and weaknesses*. Northampton, MA: Elgar Reference Collection.

Desai, R. (2009). Keynes redux: World money after the 2008 crisis. In: W. Anthony & J. Guard (Eds), *Bailouts and bankruptcies*. Winnipeg: Fernwood Press.

Desai, R., & Freeman, A. (2009). Keynes and the crisis: A case of mistaken identity. *Canadian Dimension*, July.

Dostaler, G. (2007). *Keynes and his battles*. Cheltenham, England: Edward Elgar.

Engels, F. (1998). Speech at the grave of Karl Marx. Available at http://www.marxists.org/archive/marx/works/1883/death/burial.htm.

Esping-Andersen, G. (1990). *The three worlds of welfare capitalism*. Cambridge, UK: Polity Press.

Elson, D. (2000). Socializing markets, not market socialism. In: *Socialist register*. London: Merlin.

Historical Materialism (1999). *4*(1).

Hobson, J. A. (1965). *Imperialism, a study*. Ann Arbor, MI: University of Michigan Press.

Howard, M. C. (1989). *A history of Marxian economics*. Basingstoke: Macmillan Education.

Itoh, M. (1978). The formation of Marx's theory of crisis. *Science and Society, XLII/2*(Summer), 129–155.

Kalecki, M. (1943). Political aspects of full employment. *Political Quarterly, 14*(4), 322–331.

Keynes, J. M. (1933). National self-sufficiency. *The Yale Review, 22*(4), 755–769.

Keynes, J. M. (1967). *The general theory of employment, interest and money* (first published 1936). London: Macmillan.

Keynes, J. M. (1979). *The collected writings of John Maynard Keynes, Volume XXIX. The general theory and after: A supplement*. London and Basingstoke: MacMillan and Cambridge University Press for the Royal Economic Society.

Kliman, A. (2007). *Reclaiming Marx's capital: A refutation of the myth of Inconsistency*. Lanham, MD: Lexington Books.

Kornai, J. (1979). Resource-constrained versus demand-constrained systems. *Econometrica, 47*(4), 801–819.

Korpi, W. (1983). *The democratic class struggle*. London: Routledge & Kegan Paul.

Luxemburg, R. (1913/2003). *The accumulation of capital*. London: Routledge.

Mandel, E. (1978). *Introduction. Karl Marx, Capital* (Vol. II). London: Penguin.

Mandel, E. (1981). *Introduction. Karl Marx, Capital* (Vol. III). London: Penguin.

Marx, K. (1848/1973). *Grundrisse*. London: Penguin.

Marx, K. (1867/1977). *Capital* (Vol. I). London: Penguin.

Marx, K. (1884/1978). *Capital* (Vol. II). London: Penguin.

Marx, K. (1894/1981). *Capital* (Vol. III). London: Penguin.

Okishio, N. (1961). Technical change and the rate of profit. *Kobe University Economic Review, 7*, 85–99.

Patnaik, P. (1997). *Accumulation and stability under capitalism*. Oxford: Clarendon Press.

Patnaik, P. (2009a). *The value of money*. New York: Columbia University Press.

Patnaik, P. (2009b). Socialism and welfarism. International Development Economics Associates. Available at http://www.networkideas.org/news/aug2009/print/prnt250809_Socialism.htm.

Polanyi, K. (1975). *The great transformation*. New York: Octagon Books.

Robinson, J. (2003). 'Introduction' to Luxemburg 1913/2003.

Roemer, J. (1978). 'Technical change' and the 'tendency of the rate of profit to fall'. *Journal of Economic Theory*, *ii*(March).

Sardoni, C. (1997). Keynes and Marx. In: G. C. Harcourt & P. Riach (Eds), *A 'second edition' of the general theory* (pp. 180–261). London: Routledge.

Shaikh, A. (1978). An introduction to the history of crisis theories. *U.S. capitalism in crisis*. New York: U.R.P.E.

Steedman, I. (Ed.) (1981). *The value controversey*. London: Verso Editions & NLB.

Sweezy, P. (1962). *A theory of capitalist development*. New York: Monthly Review Press.

Sweezy, P. M. (1970). *The theory of capitalist development: Principles of Marxian political theory*. New York: Monthly Review Press.

Tugan-Baranowski, M. (1901/2000a). 'Chapter 1: The fundamental causes of crises in the capitalist economy' Tr. Alejandro Ramos-Martíez. Value, Capitalist Dynamics and Money. *Research in Political Economy, 18*, 53–80.

Tugan-Baranowski, M. (1901/2000b). 'Chapter 7: Marx's theory of crises' Tr. Alejandro Ramos-Martíez. Value, Capitalist Dynamics and Money. *Research in Political Economy, 18*, 53–80.

Weeks, J. (1977). The sphere of production and the analysis of crisis in capitalism. *Science and Society*, *XLI*(3 Fall), 281–302. Available at http://jweeks.org/Political_Economy.html.

Zarembka, P. (2000). Accumulation of capital, its definition: A century after Lenin and Luxemburg. *Value, Capitalist Dynamics and Money, 18,* Research in Political Economy, pp. 183–241.

Zarembka, P. (2002). Rosa Luxemburg's *Accumulation of Capital*: Critics try to bury the message. *Bringing Capitalism Back for Critique by Social Theory, 21*, 3–45.

Zarembka, P. (2003). Lenin as economist of production: A Ricardian step backwards. *Science and Society, 67*(3), 276–302.

LOW SURPLUS VALUE HISTORICALLY REQUIRED FOR ACCUMULATION, SEEN IN A MODEL DERIVED FROM MARX

Paul Zarembka

ABSTRACT

In Volume I of Capital, *Marx offers actual data from a Manchester spinning factory describing that business. In Volume II, he offers schemes of reproduction to help understand accumulation of capital while mentioning numbers that actually suggest correlation to the spinning factory data. Nevertheless, Marx seems to slide over the costs of new machinery when analyzing accumulation, instead focusing on wear and tear (depreciation). In this chapter, we offer a modeling of accumulation that takes account of modern estimates of the composition of capital, that is, the relation of labor time invested in constant capital compared to the labor time employed with that constant capital, relying principally upon U.S. and Canadian estimates.*

We find empirically that the composition of capital fluctuates but does not show much trend. We also consider levels of the rate of exploitation and of utilization of surplus value required for achieving actual historical levels of accumulation of capital, and include consideration of the turnover of capital. We find that only a small portion of surplus value,

The National Question and the Question of Crisis
Research in Political Economy, Volume 26, 145–172

ISSN: 0161-7230/doi:10.1108/S0161-7230(2010)0000026006

perhaps 10%, is required for actually achieved accumulation. This suggests that a focus on the utilization of surplus value for the accumulation of capital misses vast other terrains for the utilization of surplus value.

Our result is suggestive of an overemphasis within Marxist political economy on accumulation of capital.

1. MARX ESTIMATING CONSTANT AND VARIABLE CAPITAL CONSUMPTION IN COTTON SPINNING

There has not been a lot of attention to empirical observations of Marx, but in *Capital, Volume I*, Chapter 9, he offers actual data from a Manchester spinning factory that is directly relevant to his discussion of accumulation of capital and to his schemes of reproduction. From his data, Marx reports a consumption of constant capital of £378 weekly, compared to a variable capital of £52 weekly, which implies a ratio of 7.3 (Marx, 1867, p. 211).[1] Most of the constant capital consumed in his textile example is for cotton, that is, £342 out of £378. Marx lists an additional £20 for wear and tear (depreciation) of spindles, £6 for building rental, and £10 for auxiliary materials. Marx suggests £10,000 as the outlay for the fixed constant capital in the 10,000 spindle factory for which he is providing data; therefore, his weekly depreciation of £20 corresponds to £1,000 annually, that is, a depreciation rate of 10%. Surplus value is £80 so that the rate of surplus value is $80/52 = 1.54$.

In Chapter 24, as he begins his well-known discussion of converting surplus value into capital, Marx suggests for cotton spinning a money advance of constant capital equal to £8,000 for "cotton, machinery, &c." and of variable capital equal to £2,000 for wages paid (Marx, 1867, p. 543). The ratio of the consumption of constant capital to variable capital is 4, less than the 7.3 empirical ratio implied in Chapter 9. (Did Marx perhaps believe his particular spinning manufacturer to be unrepresentative?) In neither case does Marx label the ratio of consumed constant capital to variable as a composition of capital, perhaps on the reasonable grounds that the constant capital here refers to its *consumption*, not its level, while a composition of capital (yet undefined by him) should have reference to the level, the *stock*, of constant capital being utilized by workers. As we shall see shortly, this distinction is born out by Engels when he does discuss composition of capital. Nevertheless, the focus of Marx's Chapter 24 is upon expanding the business by converting surplus value into capital; thus, there must be investment in *new* machinery. It would be costly.

In his next chapter (p. 574), Marx defines a *technical composition of capital* as the "relation between the mass of the means of production employed, on the one hand, and the mass of labor necessary for their employment on the other." The *value composition* is determined, however, by the ratio of "constant capital or value of the means of production, and variable capital, or value of labor-power." He goes on to claim a "strict correlation" between these two and defines the *organic composition of capital* as "the value composition of capital, insofar as it is determined by its technical composition and mirrors the changes of the latter." That claim of "strict correlation" is rather unfortunate as the value of the constant capital can change with technological improvements in the production of means of production while the value of the value-composition ratio can also change with the value of labor power.

In *Volume 2*, Marx suggests levels of 2, 4, or 5 for the ratio of consumed constant capital to variable capital in his well-known schemes of reproduction. For spinning specifically, and also much earlier in this same volume, he notes a consumption of constant capital of £372 and a variable capital of £50 (Marx, 1885, pp. 27 and 38ff), very close to the *Volume 1* data in Chapter 9 mentioned above.

Volume 3 refers to the same spinning manufacturer's data that is presented in *Volume 1*, but the text (Marx, 1894, pp. 75–76) is by Engels, drafted when editing Marx's manuscript in the context of discussing the turnover of capital. Engels repeats the data Marx reported in *Volume 1*, including the installation cost for machinery consisting of 10,000 spindles at an "assumed" £1 for each spindle, a total cost of £10,000. Wear and tear is at £20 weekly (implying £1,040 yearly, or about 10%). Building rent is £6 weekly (£312 yearly), along with £10 auxiliary materials costs weekly (£520 yearly). Engels offers his own assumption that the unreported yearly level of circulating capital (constant and variable) is one-quarter of the level of £10,000 for the spindle machinery, that is, £2,500. He calculates £12,182 in constant capital: £10,000 for the stock of fixed capital, as well as £2,182 circulating, that is, £2,500 yearly total circulating capital, variable included, less £318 as the portion of the circulating capital which is for wages (£318 obtained by using the same proportion of circulating capital which variable capital represents in Marx's data, while applying it to Engels' own total circulating capital of £2,500). Note that the £52 weekly wage cost Marx provided and the £318 annual outlay for wages implies a turnover – a recirculation of wages costs – of 8.5 times in the year (52 × £52/£318 = 8.5).

Referring explicitly to "composition of capital," Engels obtains a remarkably high level of £12,182/£318 = 38.3 with the £10,000 in fixed constant capital being much larger than the £2,182 for circulating constant capital (Marx, 1894, p. 76). Given the high rate of wage cost turnover, Engels calculates a rate of surplus value of 13.1. Modern estimates, as we shall see, are not remotely close to such numbers.

There is a significant puzzle surrounding that £10,000 cost of the spindle factory: Why does not Marx pay more attention to the cost of the machinery, the cost of fixed constant capital, the cost which he explicitly states as early as Chapter 9 of *Volume 1* in his empirical example of cotton spinning? When he discusses the conversion of surplus value into capital beginning on p. 543 of Chapter 24, Marx does include costs of wear and tear of the machinery as part of constant capital consumption, but he slides over the required investment in the machinery itself? How is it possible to convert, in this later chapter, a £2,000 level of surplus value for the year into £1,600 constant capital and £400 variable capital? That is, a £400 expenditure for new variable capital would seem to require the purchase of new machinery totaling £15,320 to be able to successfully employ those workers (following Engels' calculation for the composition of capital). Where are the resources when surplus value totals only £2,000 for the year?[2] (If one should slip into thinking of borrowing the money for this spinning factory, do not forget that this problem would renew on an increasing scale every year thereafter! Furthermore, truly, we are discussing the entire economy, not just the spinning example.)

Engels asserts (Marx, 1894, p. 76) that the data of April 1871 used by Marx were particularly favorable for capitalist profits as cotton prices were particularly low and yarn prices particularly high.[3] Should the market price of yarn drop to the level in which surplus value is just £52, instead of £80, surplus value would equal variable capital and the rate of surplus value becomes unity, as Marx assumes in Chapter 24. Since annual surplus value now equals £2,704 instead of £4,160, growth falls from 33% to 22%. Alternatively, if yarn prices had not dropped, but cotton prices had risen enough to raise cotton costs from £342 weekly to £370, then surplus value would still drop to £52 weekly. Growth would be somewhat less than 22% as somewhat more costs are drawn toward cotton. These levels of accumulation do contrast favorably with Marx's illustration of 20% growth when converting surplus value into capital. Nevertheless, the key question to ask is what sense can we make of Marx's spinning illustration in Chapter 24 in which the substantial fixed capital costs for new spindles are not even identified, let alone numerically incorporated into his illustration? While constant capital consumption relative to variable capital is less in Chapter 24 than in Chapter 9 (four times greater, instead of seven times), still this is insufficient as an explanation for the similarity of the growth rates. The larger reason is that Chapter 24, by ignoring turnover of capital, leads the reader to understand a turnover of unity. The significantly higher ratio of consumed constant capital to variable capital in Chapter 9 is "compensated" by the high annual turnover of 8.5 for the circulating capital as compared to the illustration in Chapter 24. At best, Chapter 24 makes a theoretical point on an inadequate empirical base. More reasonably, the illustration in Chapter 24 can be considered to be simply misleading. While the actual illustration by Marx in his Chapter 24 is intended for theoretical understanding and not intended to duplicate the actual data provided in the earlier chapter, still, it is too far off the marker of his empirical work.

2. MODERN ESTIMATES OF THE COMPOSITION OF CAPITAL

Now that we have explored Marx's empirical representations, we can turn to modern estimates of the composition of capital. These are typically undertaken as part of a project to determine the behavior of the rate of profit, rather than for a purpose such as ours of comprehending the level of accumulation of capital. The level of the composition of capital is necessary in order to ascertain how much of the surplus value used for accumulation must go into constant capital as compared to variable capital. Major lines of demarcation for such empirical work include the conceptualization of constant capital in its fixed as well as its circulating component, turnover, the relation of values to prices, and whether unproductive labor needs to be distinguished from productive labor in the overall calculations leading up to the composition of capital. Although turnover of capital is important for accurate discussion of the accumulation of capital, some modern authors ignore turnover altogether. Webber and Rigby (1986, pp. 37–38) offer the clearest exposition of turnover we have seen and include calculations of the level involved.

As a first step, note that it is rather easy to confuse the consumption of constant capital, which is a *flow* of used up constant capital, with its level, which is a stock and reflective of the labor time required for producing means of production. Only if the stock is turned over once a year would the two magnitudes be the same. In order to keep the distinction clear, we distinguish the flow from the level by referring to the level as the *outlay*. For example, an annual flow of circulating constant capital totaling four million dollars, with a turnover of circulating constant capital equal to four, would require an outlay of one million dollars – once each quarter the products are sold and receipts used to renew that capital. In order to avoid confusion, from here on we will denote the stock of constant capital as C. Retaining c for the annual flow of constant capital consumed, the organic composition is represented by C/v.

Secondly, recall that the organic composition confounds two factors – technological requirements and the portion of the working day returned to workers captured in the rate of surplus value. That is, technology could remain unchanged, but the organic composition C/v rises as v falls when capital achieves a higher s/v. Clarity is therefore aided if we reformulate our empirical question in terms of the ratio of labor time invested in constant capital to the total labor time of workers working that constant capital (not simply the paid portion of the working day), that is, $C/(v+s)$. Shaikh (1987, p. 304) labels this ratio as the *materialized composition of capital* and we will follow that language below. As such, the organic composition $C/v = (1+s/v)\,C/(v+s)$, and is of course greater in magnitude than the materialized composition.

Alberro-Semerena and Nieto-Ituarte's (1986) work on Mexico illustrates the importance of the distinction between the organic composition and the materialized composition of capital. They calculate an organic composition C/v of 5.40 in 1970, rising to 7.02 in 1976 (p. 37). However, with their calculated rate of surplus value rising from 2.17 to 2.92 in the same period, the materialized composition $C/(v+s)$ is almost unchanged, moving only from 1.70 to 1.79. A focus on the organic composition would lead to discussion of the rise, while a focus on the materialized composition would not! We will focus on the materialized composition since it abstracts from the rate of surplus value.

Thirdly, constant capital includes two basic components, fixed capital, lasting more than one year and representing the stock of equipment and buildings required for the production process, and circulating capital, representing the needs for raw materials, energy requirements, and maintenance/depreciation requirements of fixed capital. Fixed capital can last for decades, maintenance being undertaken and included in the consumption of constant capital. Circulating constant capital, however, can turn over much more quickly than one year, meaning that the outlay on it would be much less than the annual needed flow of circulating constant capital.[4]

There are quite a number of estimates of the composition of capital, often for the United States, but also for other countries. In Table 2, we report three U.S. estimates and one Canadian. To help investigate the differing estimates, in Table 1 we report the manner by which these authors we cite differ in incorporating fixed and circulating capital in the calculation of constant capital. Shaikh and Tonak (pp. 120–121) do have a separate calculation of the flow of circulating capital relative to variable capital, but it is not included in the values along with their calculations for fixed capital. If we were to divide their circulating capital flows (which moves from 2.35 in 1948 to 2.89 in 1989) by a measure of turnover, we could get a measure of outlay on circulating capital which could be added to their measure of fixed capital. Moseley, as we shall discuss, does provide an estimate of the ratio of the outlay of circulating constant capital to fixed capital over the time period and the results suggest an economizing process on the outlay on circulating constant capital and so suggesting more stability in the compositions of capital than Shaikh and Tonak suggest.

Table 1. Methodologies Used for Estimates of Constant Capital.

	Constant Capital	Fixed Capital	Circulating Capital
Wolff	= fixed + circulating	"total capital stock owned by each input–output sector"	"intermediate inputs in the input–output tables"
Moseley	= fixed + circulating	"net stock of fixed nonresidential private capital" – "net stock of unproductive fixed capital" + "net stock of fixed capital of government enterprises"	"value of total business inventories (current cost)"
Shaikh and Tonak	= fixed only (adjusted for utilization)	"fixed nonresidential gross private capital"	(absent – see text)
Webber and Rigby	= fixed + circulating	"midyear net capital stock"	"constant capital share of the owned inventory"

Sources: Wolff (1986, p. 105, fn. 6, and 1987, pp. 186–188, utilizing Bureau of Labor Statistics, Bulletin 2034, *Capital Stock Estimates for Input–Output Industries: Methods and Data,*1979), Moseley (1991, pp. 175–176, utilizing Department of Commerce, *Fixed Reproducible Tangible Wealth in the United States, 1929–85*, 1987), Shaikh and Tonak (1994, p. 125, same data source as Moseley), and Webber and Rigby (1986, pp. 43 and 54, who note: "the measure of owned inventory includes both variable capital and circulating portion of constant capital").

Since inclusion or exclusion of the level of unproductive labor is a basic distinction in undertaking these estimates, it is so indicated. Please note that Simon Mohun (2005) has offered a correction and updating of Shaikh and Tonak's work suggesting a faster rise in s/v between 1967 and 1989 (the only overlapping years of data) and suggesting, with an appropriate calculation, virtually no change in the materialized composition of capital for the same period, that is, about 1.68 to 1.74 (p. 812, Figure 4).

First, it is important to acknowledge the turnover of circulating constant capital because, as we have indicated, the invested outlay is distinct from the total annual costs; the outlay is much less. As displayed in Table 2, Webber and Rigby (1986, p. 50) calculate turnover for Canadian manufacturing at approximately four times annually between 1950 and 1981, trending upward, calculated as the ratio of annual costs of circulating constant capital to inventories of such capital.[5] For the U.S. economy as a whole, Moseley used some of his own data and some from Wolff to calculate turnover rates rising from 3.27 in 1947 to 4.32 in 1976. In his work with such data, Wolff (1988, p. 305) defers to Moseley's calculations as "preferable" to his own. Wolff notes that, compared to his use of interindustry flows for estimating such flow costs, only if turnover were one year would his estimates for circulating constant capital be "identical" with Moseley's; otherwise, he defers to Moseley's.[6] As described methodologically in Table 2's footnote a, we adjusted Wolff's figures on materialized composition reported in the table with calculations by Moseley regarding turnover. This correction suggests 1.89 as the composition for 1947 and 2.06 for 1976, with unproductive labor included.

Webber and Rigby (p. 42) state that the fixed capital costs are about three times greater than outlay on circulating constant capital costs, but they do not display the behavior over time. Moseley does and Table 3 displays two calculations based upon estimates he has made, one based upon current dollars and the other adjusted for price changes (price changes for fixed capital are growing more rapidly than for circulating constant capital). Note the increasing relative importance of fixed capital for this period in the United States. But also note that if we multiply the outlay on circulating constant capital costs by the turnover to obtain the flow, fixed capital costs are, in fact, similar to annual circulating constant capital costs, that is, $C \sim c$.

Table 3 also indicates the relation of the outlay on circulating constant capital costs to the flow of $v+s$, citing data from Moseley. However, none of our cited authors include depreciation within their calculations of circulating constant capital costs. If depreciation were roughly 10%, as in Marx's own example, its annual flow would be 0.1 C, so that for a

Table 2. Estimates of Organic and Materialized Compositions of Capital, C/v and $C/(v+s)$.

	Unproductive Labor Absent				Unproductive Labor Incorporated				S&T + Moseley
	C/v	Turnover	s/v	$C/(v+s)$	C/v	Turnover	s/v	$C/(v+s)$	$C/(v+s)$ Moseley table C(2) added to S&T
U.S. (Wolff)	circ. as flow			circ. as flow	circ. as flow (or as outlay[a])			circ. as flow (or as outlay[a])	
1947	5.61		0.96	2.86	8.30 (5.88)		2.11	2.67 (1.89)	
1958	5.98		1.01	2.98			2.60		
1967	5.38		1.08	2.58			2.72		
1976	5.16		0.75	2.95	9.22 (6.94)		2.27	2.82 (2.06)	
U.S. (Moseley)					circ. as outlay			circ. as outlay	
1947					3.58	3.27	1.40	1.49	
1958					4.33	4.14	1.59	1.67	
1967					4.03	4.29	1.72	1.48	
1976					5.15	4.32	1.66	1.94	
1981					5.76		1.81	2.05	
1985					5.47		2.15	1.74	
1989					5.03		2.28	1.53	
1994					4.61		2.33	1.38	
U.S. (S&T)					no circ.; adj.[b] (or no adj.)			no circ.; adj.[b] (or no adj.)	cir. from Moseley adj.[b] (or no adj.)
1948					3.27 (4.36)		1.70	1.21 (1.61)	
1958					4.27 (5.55)		2.01	1.42 (1.84)	1.70 (2.13)
1967					5.00 (5.05)		2.10	1.61 (1.62)	1.91 (1.92)
1976					5.27 (6.35)		2.11	1.70 (2.05)	1.96 (2.30)
1981					5.95 (7.08)		2.16	1.88 (2.24)	2.11 (2.46)
1985					6.19 (6.96)		2.33	1.86 (2.09)	2.06 (2.29)
1989					6.20 (6.97)		2.44	1.80 (2.02)	

Table 2. (*Continued*)

	Unproductive Labor Absent				Unproductive Labor Incorporated				S&T + Moseley
	C/v	Turnover	s/v	$C/(v+s)$	C/v	Turnover	s/v	$C/(v+s)$	$C/(v+s)$ Moseley table C(2) added to S&T
Canada – mfg. only (W&R)	circ. as outlay; v as outlay		v as flow	circ. as outlay; v as flow					
1950	14	3.9	1.7	1.3					
1958	18	4.1	1.8	1.6					
1967	20	4.4	1.6	1.7					
1976	22	4.7	1.4	1.9					
1981	26	4.8	1.6	2.1					

Sources: Wolff (1986, p. 95; 1987, p.133, Table 6.6, line 4 – to calculate s/v required for $C/v = (1 + s/v)\ C/(v+s)$; and 1988, p. 306), Moseley (1991, p. 74 for turnover, and 1997, pp. 25 and 33, for other data), Shaikh and Tonak (1994, pp. 125–127 and commentary on 200–202), and Webber and Rigby (1986, pp. 45 – in which $s/v = (1\text{–value of labor power}) \div (\text{value of labor power})$, 47, 50; in which $C/(v+s) = C/v \div \text{turnover} \div (1 + s/v)$). Conceptually, Moseley's C/v, the traditional concept utilized also by Wolff and Shaikh and Tonak, is Webber and Rigby's $C/v \div$ turnover, itself a measure of the ratio of constant capital to variable capital advanced (turned over enough times to imply a substantially lower measure than for variable capital costs).

Note: As indicated, circulating constant capital is either the annual flow or the outlay. Except C/v for Canada, variable capital is always the annual flow. Depreciation costs are not included.

[a]Wolff (1988, p. 306) reports that the materialized compositions $C/(v+s)$, when only fixed capital is included, were 1.54 for 1947 and 1.83 for 1976. Noting his circulating constant capital flows as 1.13 and 0.99, respectively, and dividing the resulting numbers by Moseley's (1991, p. 74) calculated turnovers for those years, that is, 3.27 and 4.32, then the outlays on the circulating constant capital are obtained as 0.35 for 1947 and 0.23 for 1976. These are added to the fixed capital figures and provide the 1.89 and 2.06 figures in the table. The numbers for the organic composition C/v were similarly obtained.

[b]Shaikh and Tonak adjust for the utilization levels of equipment to obtain operating fixed constant capital. They multiply capital stock figures by the following utilization figures: 1948 – 0.75, 1958 – 0.77, 1967 – 0.99, 1976 – 0.83, 1981 – 0.84, 1985 – 0.89, and 1989 – 0.89. For comparability to the other estimates, the parenthetical figures remove this adjustment for utilization.

Table 3. Cost Ratios.

	Fixed Capital Relative to Outlay on Circulating Constant Capital		Outlay on Circulating Constant Capital Relative to the Flow of $v+s$
	(1) Current dollars	(2) 1972 dollars	(3) Current dollars
1947	2.07	3.14	0.49
1958	3.06	3.47	0.41
1967	3.08	3.28	0.36
1976	3.51	3.91	0.43
1981	3.72	4.37	
1985	4.15	4.89	
1987	4.18	4.88	

Source: Derived from Moseley (1991, pp. 51 and 163–164, noting that his FC for 1976 in Table A.3 has a typo and should be 1662, not 662).

$C/(v+s)=2$, the required flow for depreciation would be 0.2 $(v+s)$. A turnover of four would thus imply an outlay of $0.05(v+s)$ for depreciation. In other words, the last column ratio in Table 3 would be increased somewhat to account for depreciation.

Wolff's work for the United States, based upon input–output techniques, shows only a small increase over time in the materialized composition, but does report higher estimates for the materialized compositions than do Moseley or Shaikh and Tonak. Moseley's work, based upon national accounts, does not exhibit a trend. Shaikh and Tonak's work, based also upon national accounts, does show a trend upward.[7] Shaikh and Tonak adjust for utilization levels which lowers the calculation of C for all the years listed except 1967; without that adjustment Shaikh and Tonak's estimates of the materialized composition of capital would be 1.61 in 1948 and rise to 2.02 in 1989, thus, uniformly exceeding Moseley's. This is all the more surprising in that Shaikh and Tonak exclude circulating constant capital altogether, while Moseley includes circulating constant capital, representing as much as 33% of his measure of constant capital in 1947, albeit down to 19% in 1985 (1991, p. 163). The origin of the significantly higher estimates by Shaikh and Tonak must be that Moseley utilizes net stock data while Shaikh and Tonak utilize gross stock.[8] If Moseley is correct that circulating capital becomes less important over time as a proportion, its inclusion in calculations similar to Shaikh and Tonak would imply that the reported rise of the materialized composition of capital in Shaikh and Tonak would be less than above and would likely disappear altogether by the end of Moseley's data in 1994. Furthermore, we have already mentioned Mohun's work correcting Shaikh and Tonak's and suggesting no rise in the materialized composition of capital.

Our empirical conclusion from analyzing Wolff's, Moseley's, and Shaikh and Tonak's work for the U.S. economy is *the absence of much support for a rising materialized composition of capital.* A rising rate of surplus value, on the other hand, does seem supportable and would suggest some rise in the organic composition of capital.

Webber and Rigby use net stock and do report a rising materialized composition of capital for Canadian manufacturing in the postwar period, at least up to 1981. If the U.S. economy is indicative and represented well enough by Moseley's work for which the composition peaked around that year, we would expect a falling off after 1981. In any case, we note that Webber and Rigby's calculation of constant capital relative to the outlay on variable capital is similar in form of calculation to Engels' calculation of 38 for the composition of capital in cotton spinning, examined in Section 1 above.

3. AN IMPROVED MODEL OF CAPITAL ACCUMULATION, CORRECTING MARX'S

We have seen how the *stock* of fixed constant capital is quite distinct from the *consumption* of constant capital used in Marx's schemes of reproduction. Marx himself had been quite explicit at the beginning of his discussion of schemes of simple reproduction regarding how he delimits his study:

> *Constant Capital.* This is the value of all the means of production employed for productive purposes in this branch. These, again, are divided into *fixed* capital, such as machines, instruments of labor, buildings, laboring animals, etc., and *circulating* constant capital, such as materials of production: raw and auxiliary materials, semifinished products, etc. ....
>
> Portion *c* of the value, representing the constant capital *consumed* in production, does not coincide with the value of the constant capital *employed* in production. True, the materials of production are entirely consumed and their values completely transferred to the product. But only a portion of the employed *fixed* capital is wholly consumed and its value thus transferred to the product. Another part of the fixed capital, such as machines, buildings, etc., continues to exist and function the same as before, though depreciated to the extent of the annual wear and tear. ... At this point in the study of the total social product and of its value, however, we are compelled, at least for the present, to leave out of account that portion of value which is transferred from the fixed capital to the annual product by wear and tear, unless fixed capital is replaced in kind during the year. (Marx, 1885, p. 400).

In other words, Marx side-stepped depreciation. As he goes on into his discussion of simple reproduction he does have an extended discussion of the "Replacement of the Fixed Capital" (pp. 453–473). But when he gets to his schemes of extended reproduction in the next chapter, he ignores the outlay for *additional* fixed capital needed for accumulation represented by machinery and equipment.

We now develop a model that does incorporate the need for the production of new fixed constant capital in order to implement an accumulation of capital. This model will follow the long-run nature of Marx's exposition and will follow Marx's schemes of reproduction insofar as they suggest a stable composition of capital that our empirical survey suggests is approximately the case. We depart, however, from Marx's modeling by taking the *materialized* composition as stable, rather than the *organic* composition; as we have mentioned, the latter would be influenced by the behavior of the rate of surplus value.[9]

After an introductory discussion, Marx (1885) had developed two arithmetical "illustrations" for schemes of extended reproduction. Both have the rate of surplus value as having a unit value. Both begin with one-half of surplus value in Department I used for accumulation of capital (additional labor power as well as additional constant capital), with the other half used for consumption of capitalists. Both keep the ratio of consumed constant capital c to variable capital v in each department as unchanging as extended reproduction takes place. The First Illustration (pp. 514–517) takes this ratio in means-of-production Department I to be 4:1, while in consumption-goods Department II it is taken to be 2:1. In the Second Illustration (pp. 518–523) both departments have the ratio of 5:1. Marx's two illustrations begin from the following numerical examples:

Marx's First Illustration

Department I: $4000\ c + 1000\ v + 1000\ s = 6000$

Department II: $1500\ c + 750\ v + 750\ s = 3000$

Marx's Second Illustration

Department I: $5000\ c + 1000\ v + 1000\ s = 7000$

Department II: $1430\ c + 285\ v + 285\ s = 2000$

Pannekoek's (1934, pp. 63–64) work is useful in this regard. He was interested in Marx's second illustration, the one with the same ratios of c to

v in the two departments, but used different numerical values which are easier to deal with. Taking the ratio as 4:1 in both departments, with k indicating consumption by capitalists at one half of surplus value in each department – the other half being used for accumulation, Pannekoek's illustration for the first period is

Pannekoek's Illustration for Marx's Second Illustration

Department I: $4400\ c + 1100\ v + 1100\ s = 6600$,
with $1100\ s = 550\ k + (440\ c + 110\ v)$

Department II: $1600\ c + 400\ v + 400\ s = 2400$,
with $400\ s = 200\ k + (160\ c + 40\ v)$

Given one half of surplus value being used for accumulation – 550 + 200 for the two departments and so totaling 750, after one period the accumulation of 750 is divided between 600 additional means of production (440 + 160 for the two departments) and 150 additional means of subsistence for newly hired workers (110 + 40 for the two departments). The other half of surplus value is used for capitalist consumption k ($550 + 200 = 750$). Note that Department I needs 4,400 + 440 means of production to begin the next period and thus has 1,760 to sell from its 6,600 total production. Department II needs 400 + 200 + 40 for its own consumption needs to begin the next period and thus has 1,760 to sell from its total production.[10] The relevant numbers for Pannekoek's second period now become:

Pannekoek: Second Period

Department I: $4840\ c + 1210\ v + 1210\ s = 7260$,
with $1210\ s = 605\ k + (484\ c + 121\ v)$

Department II: $1760\ c + 440\ v + 440\ s = 2640$,
with $440\ s = 220\ k + (176\ c + 44\ v)$

In other words, the total value of production has grown 10% from 9,000 to 9,900, with 10% more workers hired and 10% more means of production being used in addition to the 6,000 which were originally required. Pannekoek goes on to comment that either allowing for differing organic compositions (he is referring to c/v, not our C/v) or rates of accumulation in the two departments, or allowing for organic compositions to grow, would bring the schemes closer to reality, but would not change basic results since the proportion of Department I to II could always be adjusted as needed to establish equilibrium (at least in theory, if not always in reality). Although Pannekoek does not write it down, the next period would be

Pannekoek: Third Period

Department I: $5324\ c + 1331\ v + 1331\ s = 7986$,
with $1331\ s = 665.5\ k + (532.4\ c + 133.1\ v)$

Department II: $1936\ c + 484\ v + 484\ s = 2904$,
with $484\ s = 242\ k + (193.6\ c + 48.4\ v)$

Let us return to the Pannekoek's first period, that is,

Department I: $4400\ c + 1100\ v + 1100\ s = 6600$,
with $1100\ s = 550\ k + (440\ c + 110\ v)$

Department II: $1600\ c + 400\ v + 400\ s = 2400$,
with $400\ s = 200\ k + (160\ c + 40\ v)$

Were the c above to refer to the stock of fixed constant and the outlay on circulating constant capital, the materialized composition of capital would be two – 4,400/(1,100 + 1,100) or 1,600/(400 + 400) – quite in line with the empirical work we have summarized. In fact, however, in Pannekoek, as in Marx, c seems to refer only to the outlay on circulating constant capital with its turnover not indicated to be anything other than unity so that its flow has the same magnitude.

Removing Marx's delimitation regarding fixed capital, we must reformulate Pannekoek's equations equations to include the need for additional fixed capital with which the laborers will work under extended reproduction (capital accumulation), along with the circulating capital to be needed. If we follow the suggestion of Shaikh and Tonak's empirical work utilizing gross, rather than net, estimates of fixed stock (see Tables 1 and 2) and maintain materialized compositions of capital at two in both departments, with C the stock of means of production, then the portion of surplus value to be used for accumulation is allocated in the ratio of $C{:}(v + s) = 2$ for fixed capital in each department. The surplus value allocated for additional fixed capital can be represented by i. Additional circulating constant capital to be consumed at the higher level of production will be needed as well, and Moseley's work suggests an upper limit of one-half of newly created value, $v + s$, as its outlay. Introducing a turnover of four, then, $c{:}(v + s) = 2$. This, in turn, requires additional subsistence needs for additional workers to be engaged in new production. (Investment of circulating constant capital – at least represented in Moseley's calculations, pp. 161 and 163 – is roughly equal to variable capital. If we multiply that level by the turnover, the resulting annual consumption of circulating constant capital would be some four times larger than variable capital and quite in line with Marx's numbers more than a century earlier.)

With the rate of surplus value at unity and one-half of surplus value used for accumulation (the other half used for capitalist consumption k), the representation, although absent in Marx and in Pannekoek, must include the *surplus value used for production of new items of fixed capital.* In the following illustration, we illustrate this additional requirement i for additional fixed capital, in addition to requirements for additional circulating constant capital and variable capital to be in place as the next period begins. We assume a turnover of circulating constant capital of four, while the gestation for the new fixed capital is one year. Only one turnover of c and v is needed to put into place the raw materials, etc., which must be ready for the expanded reproduction of the next year, this turnover presumably in the last quarter.

Illustration 1a. Accumulation with $s/v = 1$, $k = 1/2\ s$, $C/(v+s) = 2$, and $c/(v+s) = 2$

Department I: $4476\ c + 1119\ v + 1119\ s = 6714$,
with $1119\ s = 559.5\ k + (426.3\ i + 106.6\ c + 26.6\ v)$

Department II: $1524\ c + 381\ v + 381\ s = 2286$,
with $381\ s = 190.5\ k + (145.1\ i + 36.3\ c + 9.1\ v)$

Growth of 9.5% has occurred. Employment represented by variable capital also increases by 9.5% during the expansion. The next period will then read

Department I: $4901\ c + 1225\ v + 1225\ s = 7352$

Department II: $1668\ c + 417\ v + 417\ s = 2503$

Were the process to continue, the following allocation would obtain for the use of surplus value in the next period:

Allocation of surplus value in Department I: $1225\ s = 612.5\ k + (466.7\ i + 116.7\ c + 29.2\ v)$

Allocation of surplus value in Department II: $417\ s = 208.5\ k + (158.9\ i + 39.7\ c + 9.9\ v)$

Another 9.5% growth would then occur.

In order to drive home the importance of the level of surplus value which is accumulated, as opposed to being consumed by capitalists, the next illustration presumes no capitalist consumption and all surplus value is used for accumulation. Note that, compared to the previous illustration, Department I expands and Department II contracts in order that the exchange between the departments balance.

Illustration 1b. Accumulation with $s/v = 1$, $k = 0$ (only accumulation), $C/(v+s) = 2$, and $c/(v+s) = 2$

Department I:	$4952\ c + 1238\ v + 1238\ s = 7428$, with $1238\ s = (943.2\ i + 235.8\ c + 59.0\ v)$
Department II:	$1048\ c + 262\ v + 262\ s = 1572$, with $262\ s = (199.6\ i + 49.9\ c + 12.5\ v)$

Growth of 19.1% has occurred. The next period will read

Department I:	$5898\ c + 1474\ v + 1474\ s = 8847$,
Department II:	$1248\ c + 312\ v + 312\ s = 1872$

The following illustration presumes no accumulation and all of surplus value being used for capitalist consumption. This is nothing other than simple reproduction and Department I is relatively less important compared to Department II as compared to our two preceding cases.

Illustration 1c. Accumulation with $s/v = 1$, $k = s$ (no accumulation), $C/(v+s) = 2$, and $c/(v+s) = 2$

Department I:	$4000\ c + 1000\ v + 1000\ s = 6000$, with $1000\ s = 1000\ k$
Department II:	$2000\ c + 500\ v + 500\ s = 3000$s, with $500\ s = 500\ k$

No growth has occurred and the next period will read the same.

Table 4 displays these illustrations. They have been designed to help understand the impact of the proportion of surplus value being used for accumulation versus being used for consumption by capitalists.

Table 4. Illustrations Allocating Surplus Value to Accumulation when $s/v = 1$, $C/(v+s) = 2$, $c/(v+s) = 2$, and Turnover of Annual Circulating Capital Costs = 4.

		s Only for Accumulation	$s = 1/2$ Consumption, 1/2 Accumulation	*s* Only for Consumption
Department I				
Value of output		7428	6714	6000
C and *c*		4952	4476	4000
v		1238	1119	1000
s		1238	1119	1000
k, that is, *s* for consumption		0	559.5	1000
s for accumulation		1238	559.5	0
of which	*i* for fixed capital	943.2	426.3	
	c for circ. capital	235.8	106.6	
	v for circ. capital	59.0	26.6	
Next period output value		8847	7352	6000
Department II				
Value of output		1572	2286	3000
C and *c*		1048	1524	2000
v		262	381	500
s		262	381	500
k, that is, *s* for consumption		0	190.5	500
s for accumulation		262	190.5	0
of which	*i* for fixed capital	199.6	145.1	
	c for circ. capital	49.9	36.3	
	v for circ. capital	12.5	9.1	
Next period output value		1872	2503	3000
Sales between departments		1297	1705	2000
Growth		19.1%	9.5%	0%

These limited presentations encourage us to develop a rather more general model. That is, we permit:

(a) The rate of surplus value s/v to be other than unity.
(b) The allocation of surplus value between capitalist consumption and accumulation to be parameterized, with α representing the proportion of surplus value devoted to accumulation so that $1-\alpha$ is the proportion consumed by capitalists. We have already defined k as the level of capitalist consumption, and so $k = (1-\alpha)s$.
(c) We retain the suggestion from empirical evidence that $C/(v+s) = 2$.
(d) We permit circulating constant capital to be a constant fraction f of new value created, that is, $f = c/(v+s)$. (In Marx's Chapter 9 discussed in our introduction, f would be £378/£132 = 2.86, after noting that the denominator £132 is obtained from $v =$ £52 plus $s =$ £80. Table 3, column (3), here would suggest an f near to 2, if turnover is 4).
(e) We maintain the turnover of circulating capital equal to four times yearly.

Accumulation $\alpha \cdot s$ requires investment in new fixed capital, new circulating constant capital, and new variable capital. We are taking the gestation of new fixed capital as the full year, that is, it takes a year to construct and put into place the new fixed capital. However, new circulating constant capital (much of which is raw materials) and new variable capital requires only one turnover period, that is, the last quarter, given turnover to be quarterly. Now recall that variable capital v always represents yearly flow, as does circulating constant capital c. Therefore, accumulation, in each department, is the *additional* $C + c/4 + v/4$. Dividing by v, we obtain the additional constant plus variable capital relative to variable capital as

$$C/v + \tfrac{1}{4}c/v + \tfrac{1}{4}$$

Given that we accept the empirical approximation that $C/(v+s) = 2$, then $C/v = 2(1+s/v)$. Also, since $c = f(v+s)$, then $c/v = f(1+s/v)$. Therefore, the expression for additional constant plus variable capital relative to variable capital in either department can be restated as

$$2(1+s/v) + \tfrac{1}{4}f(1+s/v) + \tfrac{1}{4} = (2+\tfrac{1}{4}f)(1+s/v) + \tfrac{1}{4}$$

For convenience, let this expression, applicable to either department, be labeled D, that is,

$$\mathrm{D} = (2+\tfrac{1}{4}f)(1+s/v) + \tfrac{1}{4}$$

Both fixed and circulating constant capital come from Department I. Compared to the total of both constant and variable capital, the proportion of new capital needs coming from Department I is therefore

$$(2 + \tfrac{1}{4}f)(1 + s/v) \div \mathrm{D}$$

and the proportion coming from Department II is

$$\tfrac{1}{4} \div \mathrm{D}$$

The following second illustration can therefore be demonstrated.

Illustration 2. Accumulation with s/v variable, capital accumulation $= \alpha s$ and $k = (1-\alpha)s$, $C/(v+s) = 2$, and $c/(v+s) = f$.

The value of the output levels (measured in labor hours) for Department II *relative to* Department I is

$$\{1 + s/v[1 - \alpha(2 + \tfrac{1}{4}f)(1 + s/v)]/\mathrm{D}\} \div \{2(1 + s/v) + \alpha s/v - \tfrac{1}{4}\alpha s/v/\mathrm{D}\}$$

In other words, balance between the departments requires that the ratio of Department II output to Department I output be given by the formula above.[11]

The growth rate of the value of outputs and employment can also be shown[12] to be

$$\text{output growth rate} = \alpha s/v \div \mathrm{D}$$

For example, if one half of surplus value is used for accumulation so that α is one-half, the rate of surplus value is one, and f, the ratio of flow of circulating constant capital to new value created, is two, then the growth rate is 9.5%, that is, the value in our Illustration 1a. But if the rate of surplus value were two, that is, the value suggested by the empirical work summarized in Table 2, then the growth rate would rise to 12.9%.

Table 5 provides growth rates in the two departments under our representation of balance between the departments being maintained. We have not introduced any discussion of technological changes, which would only increase output growth rates, but not necessarily for the labor force requirements. Indeed, since our interest is primarily on accumulation of capital as it affects the labor-power requirements, it is perhaps more useful as presented. We learn, even with only 10% of surplus value being allocated for accumulation, the growth rates still exceed the recent high levels of population growth worldwide. Such employment growth could only be sustained over a longer period by the penetration of noncapitalist modes of

Table 5. Sample Growth Rates Under Differing Values for α, s/v, and f.

	$\alpha = 0.40$		$\alpha = 0.20$		$\alpha = 0.10$		$\alpha = 0.05$	
s/v	$f = 2$	$f = 1$	$f = 2$	$f = 1$	$f = 2$	$f = 1$	$f = 2$	$f = 1$
1	7.6%	8.4%	3.8%	4.2%	1.9%	2.1%	0.9%	1.1%
2	10.3%	11.4%	5.2%	5.7%	2.6%	2.8%	1.3%	1.4%
4	12.5%	13.9%	6.3%	7.0%	3.1%	3.5%	1.6%	1.7%

production and conversion of populations into wage laborers. As Rosa Luxemburg had already been aware a century ago, this potential source declines as the very result of capitalist expansion continues. Capitalist accumulation is ever more difficult. Therefore, the rate of accumulation α must decline and alternative uses of surplus value employed.

4. POPULATION INCREASE AND ACCUMULATION

Let us examine how much of accumulation is associated with population increase. According to United Nations figures, in 1850, of the total world population of 1,262 million, 64.1% was in Asia, 21.9% in Europe, 8.8% in Africa, 3.0% in Latin America and the Caribbean, 2.1% in Northern America, and 0.2% in Oceania (Population Division of the Department of Economic and Social Affairs of the United Nations Secretariat, "The World at Six Billion." (ESA/P/WP.154), October 12, 1999, Table 2. www.un.org/esa/population/publications/sixbillion/sixbilpart1.pdf). In that year of 1850, only Europe with its 276 million persons had a significant working class of wage-laborers.

By 1900 the world is estimated to have had 1,650 million persons, representing an annual growth rate of 0.54% since 1850. And, by 1999, the world is estimated to have arrived at 6 billion persons, an overall growth rate since 1850 of 1.05%, but 0.85% annually between 1900 and 1950, and 1.78% between 1950 and 1999. Thus, Marx was writing at a time of lower levels of world population growth, albeit above 1% in England (including net migration).[13]

If the world in 1850 had 3% of its population as working class – that is, 38 million – and in 1900 had 10% its population of 1650 million as working class, the growth rate of the working class from 38 million to 165 million is 3.0% annually. This could represent accumulation of capital if all of the working class were producing value and surplus value, unproductive wage-labor not involved (the issue of unproductive labor does not seem to be a substantial phenomenon until the 20th century). We can see from our previous section that such a 3% growth rate could correspond to merely 10–15% of surplus value being utilized by capitalists for accumulation of constant and variable capital (see Table 5, interpolating between 10% and 20%). The balance of surplus value at a 85–90% level being used for consumption would be much too high and higher rates of surplus value would only suggest a more severe problem for the utilization of surplus value.

The difficulty can also be illustrated by focusing upon the United States where data are available and the United States became the leading industrial power by the 20th century. The decade of 1860 to 1870 represents conversion of slaves into share croppers, tenant farmers, or wage laborers. The period thereafter includes massive immigration into the country. The U.S. census population in 1870 was 38.6 million, and was 106.0 million in 1920, a 2.0% annual rate of increase, net immigration of course included (www.census.gov/population/www/censusdata/files/table-4.pdf). As reported by Weinberg (2002, p. 185), the number of wage laborers increased from 5,600,000 to 23,300,000 from 1870 to 1920, representing a growth rate of 2.9% annually. These figures do not include "clerical" workers which moved from 260,000 to 3,715,000. If the clerical were included, the growth rate would be somewhat higher at 3.1%. On the other hand, if reduction in hours in the workweek were included, the increase in produced value would be less and the growth rate of total work hours, and thus value produced, would be somewhat lower.

Even with a fast developing capitalist economy, represented by U.S. history, only approximately 15% of surplus value would be needed to sustain the employment rise. We are therefore compelled to ask as to the destination of a major portion of surplus, the portion neither used for capitalist consumption nor accumulation of capital. This is the third, yet very large, portion of surplus value which Marx did not focus upon. In other words, we are drawn to ask at what level does the accumulation of capital play a role in the dynamics of the capitalist mode of production. Has it been over-played?

NOTES

1. Wages for a spinner were less than £1 per week, according to Marx's 1865 lecture (Marx, 1865, p. 21), a spinner being a rather skilled occupation, although here it could be averaging the spinner with an assistant. A very comprehensive study of

British wages indicates 160 (old) pence or only £2/3 weekly for cotton factory operatives in 1871 (Wood, 1910, p. 587), which would imply 78 operatives earning £52 total on the 10,000 spindles. Robson (1957, p. 342) suggests about 150 spindles per operative around 1871, implying 67 operatives on 10,000 spindles.

Incidentally, Marx indicates in the footnote on the following page that he assumes prices = values for this calculation. He calculates the rate of surplus value as 1.54.

2. We can ask, if the composition of capital is 38.3 as reported by Engels, why did not Marx begin his Chapter 24 something along the following lines:

[What Marx could have written in Chapter 24:]

Recalling our data for mule spinning of cotton presented in Chapter 9, our capitalist receives £80 of surplus value weekly, which amounts to £4,160 for the year. If expanded production is desired, we need first to note the fixed capital cost of £10,000 for spindles, since our capitalist is going to need to buy more spindles. In addition, let us assume £2,500 as the level of circulating capital costs for the year, divided up into the same proportion which we described in Chapter 9, that is, 6.9 to 1 (being £358/£52, weekly, before expansion). Then, the £2,500 circulating costs are £2,182 for the cotton, auxiliary materials, and building rent, and £318 for variable capital. The composition of capital is then (£10,000 + £2,182)/£318 = 38.3. Note that £318 of variable capital over the year actually commands £2,704 wage payments – there are £52 wages weekly for 52 weeks. Products are being sold after about six weeks in the production cycle, so that the "turnover" is 8.5 times per year (more on turnover in *Volumes 2* and *3*). Our composition of capital is thus calculated on a ratio of the fixed capital plus flow of circulating constant capital to outlay on variable capital.

Without any allocation for capitalist consumption and focusing only upon expanded reproduction, the sum of £4,160 in surplus value can be utilized during the next year as follows: £3,324 buys new spindles on January 1 for the year's expanded operations. This represents 33% more spindles. During the year £730 is invested for the additional circulating portion of constant capital consumption needed (wear and tear of fixed capital ignored for the initial year) and £106 is invested for additional variable capital needed. Note that the composition of capital for the expanded production remains at 38, that is, (£3,324 + £730)/£106. The ratio of circulating portion of constant capital consumption to variable capital remains at 6.9, that is, £730/£106. In our calculation, the rate of surplus value remains at 1.54.

Since the turnover of wages, as described above, is 8.5 annually, the £109 yearly committed to variable capital actually represents an additional command over labor power of £901 compared to the £2,704 before expansion which we have mentioned. We now have £3,605 in wages paid annually. In other words, our capitalist friend has expanded the labor force also by 33%, even with the high relative cost of spindles.

3. This would call into question whether prices = values but we leave this point aside.

4. When calculating a composition of capital, an issue could arise as to whether the flow of circulating capital over the year or the outlay (a stock variable) should be considered.

5. Webber and Rigby are studying Canadian manufacturing only, not the entire economy, and calculate turnover of circulating capital – both its variable and constant components. In the process, they explain turnover quite well, including how

wage payments and circulating constant capital payments stretched out over time implies higher turnover.

6. A year earlier, Wolff (1987, p. 82–83, fn. 21) had focused on the issue, and had estimated turnover rates to average just about one year from 1947 to 1976, that is, 1.08, based the economywide estimate of the *sales*-to-inventory ratio. Rather than annual costs of only circulating capital, Wolff's attempted use of sales in the numeraire included also fixed capital costs, wage costs, and profits. He reports a ratio moving from 0.89 in 1947 to 1.19 in 1972, back to 1.04 in 1976, basing his numbers upon the inverse of the average yearly level of inventories (averaged from end-of-quarter data) to what he thought was annual sales. However, when he added the four quarterly numbers to obtain sales, he thought these were quarterly sales when in fact they were at "monthly rate" (same citation as his, p. 226, fn. 3). Thus, Wolff's calculated figures must be multiplied by a factor of three and become thereby not dissimilar to Moseley's or Webber and Rigby's.

We might add that the inverse of the "nonfarm inventories to final sales of goods and structures" data provided may be a better representation of turnover, of course corrected from the monthly rate to the annual. This inverse ratio is fairly stable from 1947 to 1997 as can be determined from *National Income and Product Accounts of the United States, 1929–97*, Volume 1, U.S. Department of Commerce, 2001, Tables 5.12 and 5.13, pp. 309–320. That inverse ratio, using current dollar data, trends only somewhat downward from 3.52 for the first quarter of 1947 to 3.26 for the last quarter of 1997 (jumping down as far as 2.59 in the second quarter of 1980).

7. Curiously, Shaikh and Tonak (1994) discuss the book by Wolff (1987), but not the follow-up article by Wolff (1988). Discussion of the latter would have given them an opportunity to explain the differing estimates for the materialized compositions of capital provided by Wolff in his 1988 article. Shaikh and Tonak do cite an earlier work of Moseley (1985) in which Moseley had used the same methodology as for his estimates reported in the table. However, the lack of a trend was not yet apparent in those estimates by Moseley, in that the article went only to 1977.

8. Wolff refers to "capital coefficient matrix," yet, unclear as to meaning.

9. Although fixed capital has been included in the calculations of constant capital, the problems of identifying it are rarely described in the conceptual detail that is in the work of Swanson (1986). Shaikh and Tonak, for example, devote little attention to the problem. In any case, we will overlook Swanson in this discussion.

10. As described in Zarembka (2002, pp. 44–45) and reproduced here (please check the 2002 publication for references other that for Bukharin and Luxemburg), Bukharin (1924, pp. 154–159) formulated the schemes algebraically, and concluded with the same conditions for extended reproduction as had Luxemburg (1913, p. 127), albeit Luxemburg's condition refers to *increases* in constant capital in Department II equaling increases for variable capital plus increases for capitalist consumption in Department I, while Bukharin's condition refers to the *level* of the new constant capital in Department II equaling the level of the new variable capital and the capitalist consumption in Department I (p. 159).

For Pannekoek's example above, Bukharin's condition (at the end of the first period ready for use at the beginning of the second period) is that constant capital for

Department II, that is, 1,760 (= 1,600 + 160), must equal variable capital for Department I, that is, 1,210 (= 1,100 + 110), plus the capitalist consumption during the first period, that is, 550. In fact, this obtains, 1,760 = 1,210 + 550. For the following period, Bukharin's figures are 1,936 = 1,331 + 605. Luxemburg's condition, on the other hand, refers to the corresponding *changes* in each of the magnitudes. In other words, 176 (= 1,936–1,760) must equal the sum of 121 (= 1,331 − 1,100) + 55 (= 605 − 550). In the example, it does.

Although he does not mention conditions for extended reproduction, Tarbuck lays out Marx's second scheme showing the process step-by-step and may aid in understanding. Kuehne does lay out both Bukharin's and Luxemburg's conditions for extended reproduction and seems to prefer the greater simplicity of Luxemburg's.

Bukharin's algebraic formulation was criticized by Sweezy who thought that Bukharin had not included increasing capitalist consumption during accumulation. Sweezy added a term for that increase. Sweezy's point is difficult to understand, however, since Bukharin's condition refers to levels, not changes in levels. Furthermore, Marx had assumed that the rate of surplus value as well as the proportion of surplus value used for capitalist consumption remain fixed so that capitalist consumption does necessarily increase over time. Kuehne ignores Sweezy's criticism of Bukharin, while Tarbuck defends Bukharin, saying that the latter had only excluded increasing capitalist consumption in the first period, not for later periods. Tarbuck goes on to say that if changes in levels of capitalist consumption are to be included, other changes in levels should also be included and he modifies Sweezy accordingly. Such a defense of Bukharin seems unnecessary as Bukharin was discussing levels, and levels can increase over time.

With the help of a statistician H. Chester, Rosdolsky elaborates on the equilibrium condition offered by Bukharin to include the case in which the organic compositions in the two departments are distinct (although remaining unchanged). Tarbuck does not indicate that he had seen Rosdolsky's work (perhaps because the English translation was not to appear until 1977). Kuehne seems unimpressed by Rosdolsky's equilibrium condition and provides an alternative interpretation. In any case, on his following page Rosdolsky indicates that he accepts Sweezy's criticism of Bukharin even if, for Rosdolsky, the problem does not seem to involve Bukharin's basic condition for equilibrium under extended reproduction, but rather two derived conditions. To this reader the relevant passage in Bukharin does not in fact pose such supposedly derived conditions that Rosdolsky lists. This controversy does not seem worth further discussion.

We should note that in Appendix I to Sweezy's work, Shigeto Tsuru offers his own explanation of Marx's reproduction schemes and indicates their relationship to Keynesian categories.

11. In order to demonstrate this relationship, first note that the flows between Department I and Department II must match. Now, the value of production in either department can be reformulated as follows:

$$c + v + s = c + c/(c/v) + (s/v)c/(c/v)$$

Since $c/(v+s) = 2$ with the approximate empirical finding we are adopting, then

$c/v = 2(1 + s/v)$ and we have

$$c + c/(2(1 + s/v)) + (s/v)c/(2(1 + s/v))$$

an expression applicable for both departments. In order to ascertain the portion for sale to the other department, we must subtract from this sum the amount which is retained within either department. For Department I, this subtraction is the consumed constant capital c needing to be replaced, along with the proportion of surplus value – that is, $(s/v)\ c/(2(1 + s/v))$ – used for accumulation, that is, α, along with the proportion of that accumulation allocated to Department I, that is, $(2 + (1/4)f)(1 + s/v)/\mathrm{D}$. We are recalling the definition of D from the text. The latter subtraction is, therefore,

$$\alpha(s/v)[c/(2(1 + s/v))] \cdot (2 + \tfrac{1}{4}f)(1 + s/v)/\mathrm{D}$$

Department I therefore sells its net output of means of production as follows:

$$c + c/(2(1 + s/v)) + (s/v)c/(2(1 + s/v)) - c$$
$$- \alpha(s/v)[c/(2(1 + s/v))] \cdot (2 + \tfrac{1}{4}f)(1 + s/v)/\mathrm{D}$$

After simple algebra and now adding the departmental subscript, Department I sells,

$$[c_I/(2(1 + s/v))] \cdot \{1 + s/v[1 - \alpha(2 + \tfrac{1}{4}f)(1 + s/v)]/\mathrm{D}\}$$

For Department II consumption goods, starting from $c + v + (s/v)c/(2(1 + s/v))$ and subtracting away v as well as consumption of its capitalists and the proportion of Department II accumulation needing new variable capital — thus providing sales to Department I, we similarly obtain

$$[c_{II}/(2(1 + s/v))] \cdot \{2(1 + s/v) + \alpha s/v - \tfrac{1}{4}\alpha s/v/\mathrm{D}\}$$

Equate the flows between Departments I and II to obtain:

$$[c_I/(2(1 + s/v))] \cdot \{1 + s/v[1 - \alpha(2 + \tfrac{1}{4}f)(1 + s/v)]/\mathrm{D}\}$$
$$= [c_{II}/(2(1 + s/v))] \cdot \{2(1 + s/v) + \alpha s/v - \tfrac{1}{4}\alpha s/v/\mathrm{D}\}$$

Through another simple algebra, c_{II}/c_I is represented by the relationship in the text. That relationship also obtains for the relative departmental sizes of v and s – since all are proportional – and, therefore, additionally represents the relative sizes of production levels for Department II compared to Department I.

12. Growth rates are the same in the two departments and so it does not matter which is chosen. Taking Department II, the rate of growth can be calculated as the allocation to its accumulation of variable capital for itself, relative to the level of its variable capital, adjusted for turnover of 4. This is

$$\alpha(s/v)v(\tfrac{1}{4})/\mathrm{D} \div v/4$$

which is $\alpha\ s/v \div \mathrm{D}$ – as provided in the text.

13. Based upon census data, "the population of England had more than doubled from 8.3 million in 1801 to 16.8 million in 1851 and, by 1901, had nearly doubled again to 30.5 million" (www.statistics.gov.uk/downloads/theme_compendia/

fom2005/01_FOPM_Population.pdf), implying 1.4% and 1.2% population growth rates, in the respective half centuries.

REFERENCES

Alberro-Semerena, J. L., & Nieto-Ituarte, M. D. (1986). Empirical estimates of Marxian categories in Mexico: 1970–1975. *Review of Radical Political Economics, 18*(4), 32–46.

Bukharin, N. I. (1924). *Imperialism and the accumulation of capital* (1972). New York: Monthly Review Press.

Luxemburg, R. (1913). *The accumulation of capital* (1951) (Translated by A. Schwarzschild with an introduction by J. Robinson). New York: Monthly Review Press.

Marx, K. (1865). Value, price and profit (abridged): An introduction to the theory of capitalism. (edited by E. M. Aveling, abridged and prefaced by P. Zarembka). In: P. Zarembka (Ed.), *Value, capitalist dynamics and money. Research in political economy* (Vol. 18, pp. 3–39). New York: JAI/Elsevier Press.

Marx, K. (1867). *Capital: A critical analysis of capitalist production, Volume 1*, translated by Samuel Moore and Edward Aveling from the third German edition as edited by Frederick Engels in 1883, Progress Publishers, Moscow, 1954, and Lawrence and Wishart, London, 767 pages. Also, translated by Ben Fowkes, Vintage Books, New York, 1977. Pagination is to the Moore-Aveling edition.

Marx, K. (1885). F. Engels (Eds.), *Capital: A critical analysis of capitalist production* (Vol. 2). Moscow: Progress Publishers, 1956, Lawrence and Wishart, London, 1974, 551 pp

Marx, K. (1894). F. Engels (Eds.), *Capital: A critical analysis of capitalist production* (Vol. 3). Moscow: Progress Publishers, 1959, Lawrence and Wishart, London, 1974, 948 pp

Mohun, S. (2005). On measuring the wealth of nations: The US economy, 1964–2001. *Cambridge Journal of Economics, 29*, 799–815.

Moseley, F. (1985). The rate of surplus value in the postwar U.S. economy: A critique of Weisskopf's estimates. *Cambridge Journal of Economics, 9*(1), 57–79.

Moseley, F. (1991). *The falling rate of profit in the postwar United States economy*. New York: St. Martin's Press.

Moseley, F. (1997). The rate of surplus value and the future of capitalism. *Review of Radical Political Economics, 29*(4), 23–41.

Pannekoek, A. (1934). The theory of the collapse of capitalism (A. Buick, Trans.). *Capital and Class*. No. 1, Spring 1977, pp. 59–81.

Robson, R. (1957). *The cotton industry of Britain*. London: Macmillan.

Shaikh, A. (1987). Organic composition of capital. In: J. Eatwell, M. Milgate & P. Newman (Eds), *The New Palgrave: Marxian economics* (pp. 304–309). London: Macmillan.

Shaikh, A., & Tonak, E. (1994). *Measuring the wealth of nations. The political economy of national accounts*. Cambridge: Cambridge University Press.

Swanson, P. A. (1986). The labor theory of value and fixed capital. *Review of Radical Political Economics, 18*(3), 44–64.

Webber, M. J., & Rigby, D. L. (1986). The rate of profit in Canadian manufacturing, 1950–81. *Review of Radical Political Economics, 18*(1&2), 33–55.

Weinberg, M. (2002). *A short history of American capitalism.* Available at www.newhistory.org

Wolff, E. N. (1986). The productivity slowdown and the fall in the U.S. rate of profit, 1947–76. *Review of Radical Political Economics, 18*(1 & 2), 87–109.

Wolff, E. N. (1987). *Growth, accumulation, and unproductive activity: An analysis of the postwar U.S. economy.* Cambridge: Cambridge University Press.

Wolff, E. N. (1988). The rate of surplus value, the organic composition of capital and the general rate of profit in the U.S. economy, 1947–1967: Reply. *American Economic Review, 78*(1), 304–306.

Wood, G. H. (1910). The statistics of wages in the nineteenth century. Part XIX – The cotton industry. Section V. Changes in the average wage of all employed, with some account of the forces operating to accelerate or retard the progress of the industry. *Journal of the Royal Statistical Society, 73*, Part IV, 585–633.

Zarembka, P. (2002). Rosa Luxemburg's *Accumulation of Capital*: Critics try to bury the message. In: J. Lehmann (Ed.), *Bringing capitalism back for critique by social theory, Current perspectives in social theory* (Vol. 21, pp. 3–45). New York: JAI/Elsevier Press.

WORLD MONEY: FROM THE EURODOLLAR TO THE SINODOLLAR

Karen Helveg Petersen

ABSTRACT

The chapter presents an overview of major currency and international capital market movements after World War II, showing that the movements brought about by US investments in the fifties and sixties that created the offshore Eurodollar bear resemblance to what is now taking place between the United States as the world's investor and China. International money is created in a triangular process of long and short lending intermediated by short borrowing. The imbalances often recorded on US current account are to some extent counterbalanced by the huge returns accruing to businesses of the west. This follows the "dark matter" theory but with the twist that real value is extracted through foreign direct investment in line with the rationale of Eurodollar flows. However, threats are also created in this way. Rather than in superficial notions of instability in currency markets, the high returns on capital abroad have been instrumental both in the deindustrialization of the west and the maintenance of a high rate of consumption through the financialization of

The National Question and the Question of Crisis
Research in Political Economy, Volume 26, 173–209

ISSN: 0161-7230/doi:10.1108/S0161-7230(2010)0000026007

the housing market. The eventual overdrive precipitated the crisis starting in 2007, but the dollar relationship with China continues unabatedly.

1. INTRODUCTION

Money unfolds its properties *par excellence* in the international setting where it is registered as more than a vehicle for spending people's income or storing their wealth. Sometimes the foreign-exchange market is at the forefront of attention, at other times it plays in the background. One currency has come to dominate, the dollar, but there is speculation that the dollar is losing out as an international vehicle of trade and capital while a bipolar system is emerging for the currency in which reserves are held, prices quoted, and assets denominated and traded. There are fewer important currencies now with the advent of the euro, but what is the euro? Does it diverge from other currencies in its mode of functioning? What is its backing?

The analysis of the monetary developments after the Second World War justifies the contention that money is created in the capital accumulation process. Keynes in *The General Theory* (1970) latently saw the "value" of money as deriving from the money/capital markets through the interest rate and the interaction of the latter with the "marginal efficiency of capital," viz. the return on real assets. He thus approached the view that money is created endogenously through the demand for it. However, he did not develop a consistent monetary theory in his own *General* one. His different motives (transactions, speculative, and precautionary) for liquidity preference do not constitute a complete theory since the motives for holding money do not indicate the genesis and substance of money. They are just a derivative phenomenon superimposed back onto money itself.

Mainstream economists tend to think that the institutions set to defend the value of the currency, the central banks, are what matters. Hard-core monetarists hold that central banks should interfere as little as possible or be completely predictable. It shall here be argued that although central banks have a role in regulating markets, "new" money results from the process of capital accumulation as the manifestation of surplus value creation in accordance with Marx who also thought that its value was basically determined via one particular commodity, gold. But Marx did not seem to recognize that these two "functions," money as standard and as a vehicle of the capital accumulation process, would eventually collide.

The chapter proposes a review of the mechanisms and official reforms of international money in order to detect its form developments in the interplay between official central-bank action and financial market responses. It highlights key structures in the Bretton Woods system, its breakdown, and the surprising developments since the seventies by going into balance-of-payments (BOP) metrics, exchange-rate determination mechanisms, new currency developments (the euro), and the persistent survival of the dollar in a dynamic interaction with investments in China.

2. BRETTON WOODS

The Bretton Woods Agreement of 1944 institutionalized the par value principle for currencies. During the reign of the predecessor "classical" gold standard there was no official, internationally agreed-upon par value, so actually Bretton Woods constituted a more rigid approach to exchange rates (fixed) than before. The pound had, with interruption 1919–1925, been international money until 1931, but other countries had decided on the principles they wanted to adopt around the general acceptance of gold as the central value that currencies were mirrored in. By 1914, Britain had been on gold *de jure* for 70 years. The pound was the reference currency of trade because such a large part of world trade was in British hands. Since gold was not used in market transactions, only as reserves, it is a bit naïve to imagine that its stock should be of a particular size. In the nineteenth century, David Ricardo sided with the Bullionists reclaiming convertibility of paper money into gold. But in actual fact, Bank of England tended to raise Bank rate when gold outflow threatened because of paper money losing its value. This was meant to prevent the outflow from taking place, and the exchange parities were reestablished and so gold stock became unimportant. This debate was resuscitated in the 1960s/1970s.

The US Congress enshrined by the Bretton Woods Agreements Act in 1945 stated that only Congress could change the gold content of the dollar. In 1949 major currencies became arranged around par values on the basis of the already prevailing ratio of $35 for one troy ounce of gold. The gold-exchange standard or gold-dollar standard took off (Gilbert, 1968). However, pars were not actually rigid. Currencies could move 1% up or down in the free market before intervention. Concomitantly the United States decided to sell and buy gold freely, a decision that exempted it from pegging or defending exchange rates of other countries to keep them within 1% of their par value with the dollar. In addition, adjustments could take place after market development indicators in the form of official devaluations. This part of the system came to be known as the "adjustable peg." It was not until 1959, however, that the dollar became key currency by a by-law allowing a single convertible currency to be pegged to gold in lieu of that of every other member. Still, the United States should not actively defend its currency, an obligation incumbent on other countries. This is often termed the $n-1$ (*n* minus one) problem. The dollar was not an asset for the US Federal Reserve System, only a liability. The United States did not hold other currencies as reserves either, only gold. This was at the root of the asymmetry between the dollar and other currencies that emerged as a problem in the beginning of the 1970s. Official devaluations did take place under Bretton Woods, the pound was for example devalued in 1967.

In August 1971, President Richard Nixon announced the discarding of market convertibility of dollars into gold. The giving-up of convertibility did not mean that there was no international monetary significance to gold anymore. It only meant that the official price became meaningless for all other purposes than transactions among central banks. And it did mean that the official price could be considerably at odds with the market price, which had been timidly allowed already in 1968 through the acceptance of a two-tiered pricing system for gold. After the Smithsonian Agreement of December 1971 the dollar was devalued for the first time since 1934. One ounce of gold was to cost $38 officially. In February 1973, the Smithsonian Agreement broke down and the most important exchange rates started floating. In Kingston, Jamaica, floating exchange rates were condoned officially by the IMF (1976), but at the same time it was stated that "a stable system of exchange rates" should be aimed at. Central banks were henceforth allowed to buy and sell gold freely.

At the turn of the year 1975/1976 the average price of an ounce of gold was $140 on the important exchanges. However, this was an improvement for the dollar relative to its status a year earlier when gold sold for up to $198 (December 1974).

The Kingston agreement abolished not only the gold standard, but also an officially agreed-upon standard altogether. Despite the fears experienced at the time, the international system survived. Had a *de facto* standard been developing behind the back of the gold-exchange standard in the sixties and beginning of the 1970s so that it was ready to fly when the formal system had finally caved in? But behind the back of gold another reality had emerged, the dollar standard.

In the beginning of the 1920s there was a similar situation, that is, there was no internationally agreed-upon standard. However, neither was there a *de facto* standard, and some exchange rates were totally flexible or floating.[1] At that time the historical tendency away from gold and toward a dollar standard was articulated by Keynes in pregnant form,

> The theory on which the Federal Reserve Board is supposed to govern its discount policy, by reference to the influx and efflux of gold and the proportion of gold to liabilities, is as dead as mutton. It perished, and perished justly, as soon as the Federal Reserve Board began to ignore its ratio and to accept gold without allowing it to exercise its full influence,[.] merely because an expansion of credit and prices seemed at that moment undesirable. From that day gold was demonetised by almost the last country which still continued to do it lip-service, and a dollar standard was set up on the pedestal of the Golden Calf. For the past two years the United States has *pretended* to maintain a gold standard. *In fact* it has established a dollar standard; and, instead of ensuring that the value of the dollar shall conform to that of gold, it makes provision, at great expense, that the value of gold shall conform to that of the dollar. This is the way by which a rich country is able to combine new wisdom with old prejudice. (Keynes, 2000, p. 198)

This prophecy came true only after the Second World War. Dollars came to substitute for gold, rather than to follow its moves. The monetary management became independent of the underlying gold base. Not allowing reserve inflows to exert full influence on credit later on became known as "sterilization" and grew into an instrument cherished by a number of economists. During the Bretton Woods era a development took place from a quasi gold standard to a dollar standard, but with a period of overlapping or, rather, the dollar standard lay dormant in a prolonged chrysalis stage before it could finally fly. Contrary to the twenties, nobody has seriously looked back or tried to go back to gold ever since.[2]

3. AN INTERNATIONAL STANDARD

The textbook definition of an international monetary "standard" is a currency/commodity with the properties ascribed to money generally, (1) of numeraire (which, to echo Marx's criticism in the beginning of the *Capital* (1976, pp. 192–195) is used for both the substance and the arbitrary units of the measuring rod), (2) of medium of exchange, (3) of store of value. Essential for Marx was that money is the general equivalent of the exchange value of commodities. Internationally, this has proven a more difficult proposition.

Derived from gold as standard, in the Bretton Woods days the dollar became the unit of account measuring the more or less of something of value, viz. the substance of the standard. It took 35 units of dollars to buy an ounce of gold. As it required, for example, 7 Danish kroners to buy a dollar in the Bretton Woods parity days, through the dollar it could be calculated how many kroners it would take to buy one ounce of gold, 245 kroners logically. A krone was worth 1/245 ounce of gold and, by extension, 1/7 dollar. In that sense the dollar could also become the substitute "substance" standard for all currencies. As numeraire it often is "just one," that is other currencies are stated in the numerator: 7 kroners to 1 dollar. But the pound is normally quoted in the denominator when it is part of a ratio, even vis-à-vis the dollar. This can be seen to be for practical and probably also historical reasons. Gold was the store of value, and dollars came to be the reference unit. Through its role as derived standard of value the dollar slowly assumed the "store of value" function, which it could at first only do in a metaphorical sense by representing gold in a fixed proportion. Subsequently, the dollar transformed itself, not into a commodity store of value like gold, which would obviously be impossible, but into a store of value in an asset sense through its easy use in investments to command a rate of return. By being a roving vehicle of surplus extraction, it was as if the dollar in itself carried a yield.[3]

The dollar has for many years been the most-used medium of exchange in the world. It is also the means of borrowing and settlement of debt, of quoting prices of international commodities and trading in them (oil, cotton, coffee,...). Consequently, all types of capital market instruments are issued and traded in dollars, and the US stock market is still by far the most important one in the world.

Keynes saw the dollar standard in terms of control of the price level and of monetary policy by the United States. But the important point is that, Keynes or no Keynes, the dollar standard in the sense of its locking-out gold as "value" in fact came about through the Eurodollar market that developed after convertibility of currencies was allowed after the Second World War, that is, in trades combined with a gradual liberalization of capital account transactions. It was based not on price levels and official monetary policy by any central bank but on market developments. In *The General Theory* Keynes (1970) intuited this direction, but did not concern himself with such details as the finer mechanisms of the monetary system. He saw money creation in terms of "demand" associated with more or less subjective motives. At any rate, the dollar could only become a reserve because it carried a premium of sorts, that is, a reliable rate of interest, and this was perfected via the Eurodollar market, which also consolidated its role as international money that could escape the US money supply. The massive holding of US Treasury bills as reserves only developed later.

4. THE EURODOLLAR AND INTERNATIONAL FINANCIAL INTERMEDIATION

The claim that the full-blown dollar standard was created through the Eurodollar market calls for an explanation. This market developed around 1960 as short-term deposits held with first of all British and, to a lesser degree, continental banks, but expressed in dollars instead of local currency. Holding dollars was not considered risky. Therefore the question is whether dollars had or came to have a special advantage, and how this came about.

In the first place, dollars seeped into Europe through the Marshall Plan. Altogether USD 13.3 billion were donated. The Plan itself consisted of shipment of US goods, but American private interests followed[4] by Americans starting to invest in Europe because of the higher returns on long-term capital.[5] Some of this investment may simply have started as a complement of the reconstruction.[6] The second precondition of the Eurodollar market was convertibility of currencies that was reinstated in 1958 for the first time since World War II. Given convertibility and fixed exchange rates, there was no perceived exchange risk. The foreign-exchange departments in London could busy themselves with exploiting interest-rate differentials.

Financial intermediation is often shortened to the formula of lending long and borrowing short, that is, short-term deposits are converted to long-time lending.[7] Translated to international financial intermediation (IFI), it denotes international (mutual) lending where one party borrows short, the other lends long. In normal definitions this only concerns financial assets. Short-term funds would flow to the United States in return for the long-term investments overseas and be redeposited in the US commercial system or come back to the Fed if foreigners wanted to exchange dollars for their own currency. Long-term rates were higher in Europe after the war than in the United States. If the United States should be the other pole in IFI as normally perceived, short-term rates should be higher in the United States than in England, but this was not the case. Nevertheless, IFI did take place, but in a roundabout way through the dollar market that developed in

Europe. A Keynesian "theoretical" explanation for this type of IFI would be based on different liquidity preference schedules meaning that a lower short-term rate is accepted where liquidity preference is high (i.e., money holders require a premium on long-term instruments). Therefore liquidity preference as a function of the different "motives" should be higher in Europe than in the United States corresponding to lower short-term rates in Europe. However, this was not the case in England where the short rate was an average of 1.35 percentage points above the American rate in the period 1961–1971 (Aliber, 1974, p. 119). In the strictest sense, Eurodollars could be defined as short-term deposits held with British or Continental banks, but expressed in dollars instead of national currency. Maybe a fanatical disciple of the low liquidity preference/high short-term interest rate relation could show that the ex-colonial British had acquired such fortunes overseas that liquidity preference was quite low! At least that would be correct in terms of the relative level of the comparable interest rates on each side of the Atlantic.[8]

But this would be another sad case of bungling reality into a lame theory. Money rates in the United States were not very favorable, in the first place because of the famous Regulation Q forbidding, since 1933, Federal Reserve member banks to offer interest on demand deposits. Furthermore, when analyzing rates one should also look at reserve requirements, deposit insurance, etc. Thirdly, Europeans had confidence in the dollar. European money markets did develop but with the higher rates offered in England and the fact that foreigners had free access to London banks and could get higher rates also on dollars, funds that were paid to Europeans for long-term investments were not converted into local currency but kept in dollars. These dollars exited from the US money supply by becoming private deposits in overseas foreign banks.

When the United States money supply (M_1: cash and demand deposits) was counted, deposits by foreigners in the US Federal Reserve banks were included. M_3 comprised dollar deposits of US residents at foreign branches of US banks and banking offices in Canada and the United Kingdom, but not foreign banks' deposits (Meulendyke, 1998, p. 10). The English concept of the money supply, on the other hand, excluded deposits by all foreigners in English banks and British deposits in foreign banks. The exclusion of deposits by foreigners from the money supply could then be seen as further ground for a special Eurodollar market in England (Yeager, 1966, pp. 467–471). And true enough, although US investments tended to go to other European countries than the United Kingdom, the postwar money market developed in London. So both short and long-term rates were higher in the United Kingdom/Europe than in the United States with long-term rates favorable on the continent, short-term rates high in the United Kingdom.

A Marxian explanation could handle this (investments are made where profits are higher and basically money rates are lower than profits) while the Keynesian one on different liquidity preference was limping. A Keynesian could then retort that the reason was that Regulation Q "distorted" the market. Particularly faulty has been the contention that rates would eventually be unified because liquidity preferences would cross and the schedule would become the same in both markets, as per the broken line below.[9] The Eurodollar market exploited differences. When long-term rates started falling, this had nothing to do with liquidity preference but with a falling "marginal efficiency of capital."

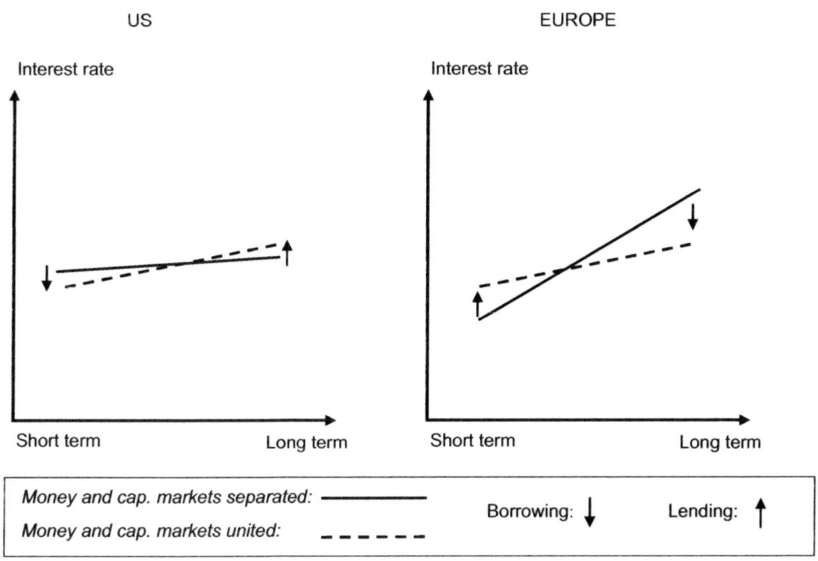

When a dollar became a Eurodollar it was not missed. This of course could only happen because there was a triangular relationship where something was created without countermovement but rather based on layering in a banking sense, surplus value creation in a "real" sense.

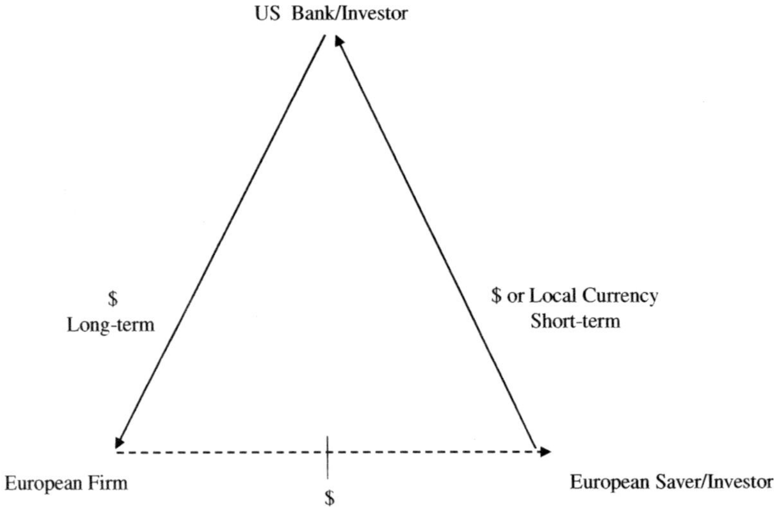

Starting from the top, a US bank/investor sought investment abroad.[10] The bank acquired a European asset, matched by an outflow of dollars transferred to a European-owned account (the solid arrow starting from the US bank). The bank could then borrow short in Europe (the other solid arrow). This represented, technically, a liability where the inflow equilibrated the outflow. The European firm could simply maintain its proceeds in the United States as working balances. If, instead, a European saver would borrow this money, this would be the case of pure IFI. In this case no international money would be created, only circulated. In order for money creation to take place, a financial asset would have to be transferred from Europe, which was the case through the titles acquired to European businesses. The international money creation thus became the *quid pro quo* between the European firm and the saver by first converting long to short-term lending. The firm would hold its dollars in the Eurodollar market. On the other hand, the US bank could take a short-term loan in Europe to fund its long-term investments. This might be helped by European savers acquiring dollars by selling own currency, adding to the pressure to get dollars, and this represented the element of international money. In fact, Americans both borrowed and put money into the Eurodollar market, partly because it is difficult to have one without the other, a further reason that Kindleberger's prediction of a tendency toward unification of rates did not have much to it. If one divergence is disappearing, new ones will emerge.

Long-term lending will of course ultimately be related to real investments. It is difficult to imagine how money can be created without some real counterpart, just because it turns over.

The Eurodollar market represented a blow-up on a larger scale of two of the sides in the above triangle: the lending from Europe to the United States, and the lending from European to European (the dotted line). This explains two contentions by Helmut Mayer (1970), (1) the Eurodollar market grew with growth in claims on American banks, and (2) the growth was stimulated by placement of American deposits in the market generated through the long-term lending. The first was the basis, the second the outlet. An interesting difference must be noted between the treatment of foreigners and foreign banks holding money in the United States, with the former being part of the American money supply.

5. BALANCE OF PAYMENTS CONCEPTS

In order to understand these problems better, it is necessary to look at BOP concepts and measures. The following is built upon the first chapter of Charles P. Kindleberger's book, *Europe and the Dollar*, quoted from earlier.

If there were no capital transfers, BOP would look as follows in the good old days of gold clearance between central banks:

Exports of goods and services
  less imports of goods and services
equals net inflow of gold

The sum of the elements above the solid line indicates a surplus (if positive) or deficit (if negative) on the balance of payments which must be reflected in below-the-line opposite, accommodating moves. If the value of exports is larger than import value in a given time period, then gold should flow into the country in this primitive schedule. The below-the-line items are the passive flows. If they are not needed for further flows, they get stuck as reserves.

With capital, short-term and long-term, this became:

Exports of goods and services
  less imports of goods and services } current account
equals net outflow of long-term capital
  plus net outflow of short-term capital } capital account
- -
  plus net inflow of gold.

This way of positing the problem suggests that if capital and current account cancelled each other, then the desired equilibrium would obtain, that is, if the surplus of goods and services corresponded to a capital account deficit (the current account surplus was converted to capital outflow), no gold would have to flow. In fact, many economists have thought that way (Johnson, 1969). It is worth remarking that long-term capital flowing out of a country is a negative. However, the outflow for investment may turn around immediately and flow into the capital exporting country again, either to buy goods or to deposit the funds in the outflow country. This creates endless confusion, even accusations of corruption.

Realizing that outflow of long-term capital signifies a transfer of the same impact as imports, that is, both having corresponding money outflows, the *basic balance* of Nurkse can be explained.[11] Net outflow of long-term capital was moved up above the line with a negative sign and short-term capital flows were treated as a measure (with gold) of surplus or deficit:

Exports of goods and services
less imports of goods and services
less net outflow of long-term capital
equals net inflow of short-term capital
plus net outflow of gold.

A surplus or deficit is still read above the solid balance line. If the items listed there sum to a negative number, this amounts to a deficit on the balance of payments. Therefore the below-the-line items must be positive to obtain the balance. There is a duality here: it is often seen not only as a question of definition but as a condition of stability or a quasi-automatic phenomenon.

The *liquidity balance* or the Department of Commerce definition (also attributed to Walther Lederer (1963)[12]) divided short-term capital movements. Net outflow of short-term capital through increase in foreign assets was allowed to figure above the line together with net outflow of long-term capital (and with the same sign). As balancing items were thus only kept – in this crude framework – net inflow of short-term capital through increase in foreign liabilities together with net outflow of gold.

The liquidity balance could be stated as *gross* or *net*. The *gross liquidity balance* was:

Exports of goods and services
less imports of goods and services
less net outflow of long-term capital

less net outflow of short-term capital (increase in foreign assets)
equals net inflow of short-term capital (increase in foreign liabilities)
and sometimes also purchases of Treasury securities
plus net outflow of gold.

Appearing at the same time as the Eurodollar market, the liquidity balance had to do with the "triangular" problem. However, in fact it represents the European *quid pro quo* in the form of counting the basis for liquidity creation in addition to the liquid liabilities themselves. The European might hold his dollar acquisitions in liquid form; at the same time an American might borrow on the market to acquire the asset, and the ensuing liability would also be considered to be liquid. Patricia H. Kuwayama (1975) wrote about the absurd results. And so did Charles Kindleberger (1966, p. 2) who lamented that the difficulty with this measure was that it was asymmetrical. The liquid liabilities to foreigners in fact grew so excessively that the measure lost meaning (Kuwayama, 1975, p. 188). This question emerged if the balance was read from below the line. The *net liquidity balance* tried to sort out if a short-term liability was truly "liquid" or not. Some loans were not considered to be liquid and thus moved above the line, but this distinction can also be shown to be arbitrary.

The *official settlement* balance (or the Bernstein Committee concept) pushed the net inflow of short-term capital above the line where it figured with a positive sign like exports, but this was only if it represented liabilities to foreign private creditors; the balancing item was – apart from gold – net inflow of short-term capital through increase in foreign liabilities to foreign official creditors.

Exports of goods and services
less imports of goods and services
less net outflow of long-term capital
plus net inflow of short-term capital (foreign private creditors)
equals net inflow of short-term capital (foreign official creditors)
plus net outflow of gold.[13]

Kuwayama thought that the underlying assumption of this balance was that central banks gained or lost reserves in accordance with their direct foreign-exchange market intervention. But this was not the only case for losing official reserves. If foreign official authorities placed dollar holdings with for instance Eurodollar banks, this would be counted as an addition to short-term liabilities to private foreigners for the United States and be credited above the line. Hence the sum of official settlements would not necessarily sum to zero when all countries added their corresponding balances (Kuwayama, 1975, p. 190). Nevertheless this concept seems to have become the official measure.

Kindleberger brought a discussion of one or two additional concepts or variants of BOP measures, but one of them mixed motives of "liquidity preference" as justification to put flows above or below the line, and that is too immaterial and psychological to have any practical significance (Kindleberger, 1966). Finding out motives can be difficult enough in a court of law. Here it would take far too many resources to use such concepts for statistical purposes. Conversely, it shows that easy measures and intuitive categories may not have the significance normally ascribed to them.

A contention of Kindleberger's was that both the liquidity and official settlements concepts were obsessed with liabilities, not with assets. One could sympathize with the complaint, but would have to point out that it was based on the fact that the dollar, basically, was a liability only to one party, the US Fed.

These BOP statistics became highly debatable, particularly for the "world money" country. In the end, the United States gave up publishing full balance of payments statistics, concentrating on current account and the stock of capital held abroad by US citizens and businesses and by foreigners in the United States.

6. THE END OF THE EURODOLLAR

The interest in the balance of payments was first of all the direction it gave for pressure on exchange rates. This was the underlying concern in the majority and minority views that formed around the strength or weakness of the dollar subsequent to the enormous growth of overseas dollar holdings vis-à-vis its base in gold, the majority being worried, the minority less so. The latter position was taken by Keynesians.

Under fixed exchange rates capital movements were not induced by exchange-rate speculation, except that some movements around par were allowed and devaluation or revaluation was possible. However, once capital flows were allowed below the line as a balancing item along with gold and other traditional reserves, the balance of payments got out of whack because of the particular interest-bearing character of the dollar and the less-than-clear distinction between advantages and disadvantages related to flows. As was seen above, theory had difficulty determining where capital movements should be recorded, and even if theory could agree on the categories, in practice it was impossible to make a clean cut between them. The more fundamental question could then be put: why this concept of *balance* or *equality with opposite signs* between below-the-line and above-the-line items? The concept of balance corresponded to a situation in which there was either no growth or the reserves were growing symmetrically. This means that the reserve should not be a liability for one country and an asset for another at the same time as was the case. By the dual role of the dollar, there was no real clearing, only a blow-up of the monetary base. It might also be said that the reserve should preferably have the ability of falling home whenever it was moved. Why was this a problem?

On the official settlement balance outstanding dollar liabilities were counted in the same way as outflow of gold. They were substitutes. However, if dollars were sold to the United States for other currencies, they were repatriated. If a country repurchased its own currency holdings with the Fed, nothing would be changed in the balance of payments. A liability would be mutually cancelled. If dollars were used abroad for intervention purposes, nothing happened to the balance. But if Eurodollar funds were sold for European currency, this would augment the deficit of the United States. No official holdings were involved previously, implying that it would then be a pure drain on American gold or currency reserves, to take the extreme case. This, then, was the danger of the Eurodollar market from an American point of view: the Eurodollar market could create or seriously augment the "deficit" without any genuine moves above the line. The hidden money came out in the open, going from international to national money. In a way, the liquidity balance best took this threat into account.

A high proportion of the operations against the dollar in 1971 was financed by the Eurodollar market. The flight was into D-Mark and yen. The American borrowing did not help. The dollar depreciated, gold was abandoned in three stages and flexible rates substituted for fixed in at least *duo tempi*, through stages of allowed floating. However, other currencies fared worse than the dollar or, rather, the dollar showed ability to sustain itself. Those that fared better were the D-Mark and the yen. The dollar standard was limping (McKinnon, 1974). But it survived.

In the beginning of the seventies the United States initiated a monetary expansion. Lower borrowing rates enabled American banks to repay their Eurodollar debt; concomitantly, the American part in the Eurodollar market was reduced.

Under the Bretton Woods system, once parities were established, imbalances required adjustments, particularly for the n–1 countries but in actual fact also for the core country if its currency was threatened. As exchange rates were fixed, albeit only by *fiat*, imbalances should be averted. But disturbances were as ever inbuilt, and the Eurodollar market did represent a threat-momentarily. In hindsight it represented a way of getting out of the narrow confines of a system, which was imposed by people living in the past and which hampered international cross-border growth in investments and financial flows.

It is ironical, at any rate, that at the same time that the Bretton Woods system collapsed, the Eurodollar market also retrenched. Keynes had been worried about London losing out. In fact, it barely did. After the Eurodollar market had peaked, it maintained its role as the prime partner of Wall St. The Libor (London interbank offered rate) is still a benchmark and may be seen as a later offspring of the Eurodollar market. It started as a dollar rate for corporate borrowers. However, it is not identical with the Eurodollar deposit rate.

7. THE ROUTE TO FLEXIBLE EXCHANGE RATES

The breakdown of Bretton Woods meant that fixed exchange rates were abandoned. But this did not solve the perceived problem of the lack of international reserve assets. Already before the Kingston agreement abolished the gold standard in the form of an official gold price and thereby the last shade of official pegging of exchange rates, the IMF had created the Special Drawing Rights (1969), purportedly as an additional reserve and standard. It never took off as a standard, though, since its "value" in turn was a weighted average of the 16 most important currencies. It started out at SDR 35 to 1 ounce of gold, that is, at par with the dollar. After the abolition of the gold-exchange standard, it came to measure the weighted average devaluation or revaluation of the dollar because all other currencies were measured in the dollar. The SDR thus also expressed the importance of other currencies for the dollar, or the economies of other countries for the United States. The common devaluation of most currencies was not measured. Now it only consists of four currencies, the dollar, the euro, the yen, and the pound. The SDR as "measure" is only for IMF and World Bank use. It is basically accounting money. Its role as reserve has also remained limited since its manifestation is IMF quotas, which can be dissolved into underlying currencies. Instead the reserve function of the US dollar was reinforced. The outcome of the breakdown of Bretton Woods was therefore first of all flexible exchange rates, later regrouped around centers of common currencies with fixed rates or altogether new currencies, such as the euro.

The unfettered market for foreign exchange exploded after the fixed parities were given up, but there were precedents in earlier history, which also started to develop the mechanisms to manage the movements. Keynes wrote that forward rates for the dollar were quoted already before the First War, but they did not really gain momentum until after the "unpegging" of the leading currencies in 1919 (Keynes, 2000, p. 121).

The mechanism of spot and forward rates was laid out by Keynes. If dollars would be cheaper forward (the current price of the currency delivered at a future date) than spot, this would show a preference for holding dollars (in the English notion of cheaper, i.e., at lower pound costs). A buyer of pounds would, by selling dollars spot and buying them back forward, earn in dollars. If he did not gain (or think he would not gain), the transaction would not be performed, that is, he would think that the dollar was somehow more safe and would stay put. The premium was the same as the opportunity cost of not holding dollars during the time elapsing before the forward contract matured. The market's preference for holding dollars is determined by the interest-rate differential, presumably. But only if there are no other factors to take into account, and interest-rate differentials are not primarily products of international exchange rates.

There are two variables in the equation for forward exchange, one being the interest-rate differential, the other the spot/forward ratio for two different currencies. If the premium or discount equaled the interest-rate differential, there would be no transaction. It is noteworthy that the spot and forward rates were taken as exogenous and obvious that they could "flex" (as well as the exchange rates themselves in a world of flexible exchange rates). The market for spot and forward exchange developed such that the interest-rate differential was used for calculating the premium as a way of hedging against exchange risks. The reason was that interest-rate differentials were much more stable than exchange rates, at least in the short run. Or, the other way around, exploitation of interest-rate differentials could not thrive within a span of 3 months, the normal term for forward contracts. Mostly the market was used by business to hedge foreign sales and purchases against exchange risks. It became, however, also a short-term credit market. If the interest-rate differential between two major currencies did not correspond to the difference between the spot and the forward exchange rate – of course over the same time horizon – there would be a "currency preference" for the one that was chosen despite indications. But forward rates were obviously not precise predictors.

The sixties preference for the dollar was developing in an awkward way around different interest rates. The Eurodollar market developed, not only because rates were higher in Europe than in the United States but because, even though the rates on the British pound were higher, yet there was no flight into the pound. Therefore, one has to agree with the minority view that the emergence of the Eurodollar market showed the strength of the dollar. In the heyday of the Eurodollar reign, the difference between the spot and forward rates and the short-term interest rate differentials would be erased for the dollar, if it were accepted that the Eurodollar interest rates were those prevailing for the dollar. In a sense, therefore, gold was thrown out as an active player when other factors became more interesting, and that was first of all the interest rates. The classical gold standard had no inhibitions on exchange-rate changes between paper currencies. The grand old differences between the new interest-rate significance and the pre-WWI days was that interest rates then referred predominantly to trade differences and not to investments. Not that outward-bound investments did not take place but these were so long term that they had little market significance.

By having both different short interest rates and variable exchange rates, the system became more indeterminate.[14] Once the forward market had developed after the breakdown of Bretton Woods, these differentials could enforce devaluation in partial fixed-rate systems as happened in the later pound crisis (1992) where George Soros played a prominent role by dumping pounds, putting Great Britain in the dilemma whether it should defend the pound or leave the European Exchange Rate Mechanism. It chose the latter.

Economic textbooks continue to have a predilection for the contention that the determinants of flexible exchange rates are price levels or perhaps changes in price levels (inflation) or even related to the "law of one price," documented by such as the Big Mac index. However, even if prices were uniform at given exchange rates or moved uniformly, this might be based on internal differentials in factor costs and productivity. For example, poor countries have very low labor costs but also low productivity. The same wholesale price of a product across the world may thus reflect differences that are in no way developing uniformly. Over long stretches of time the differentials can be hidden, but eventually they will come unstuck and the "equilibrium" be unhinged. This is another version of Marx's statement that surplus value is lower but profits higher in the poorer parts of the world, with the disclaimer that profits nowadays have to be higher because otherwise investments will not take place. Marx obviously thought that investment costs for fixed capital and intermediate products would be lower in poor countries, but this is not necessarily the case in today's world. Intermediate goods may be more expensive in poor countries. On the other hand, there is less overall investment in equipment and, notably, a lot of ancillary costs are lower or inexistent (safety, cleanliness, environment). The point here is that behind identical prices a lot of differences can be hidden, at least if you do not assume that which should be proven.

The contention that massive capital flows determine currency directions rather than price movements or levels is supported by the fact that there is no uniform price level or movements of prices. Commodities do not have the same price in different countries when translated at the daily exchange rates (incidentally not even in the euro area of a uniform currency). Even commodities traded on the world market will have different mark-ups or additional costs so that "one price" becomes an illusion. Consumers cannot arbitrage freely either.

It stands to reason that the movements initiated by capital to exploit differentials in production and financial markets, are the most weighty determinants and that exchange rates are now determined in the complex game between interest rates and capital yields in developed markets whereas those of underdeveloped markets are determined by the variety of reasons for flows of foreign currencies.

8. THE NEW YORK STOCK EXCHANGE GETTING A NEW ROLE

With the demise of the Eurodollar as an important phenomenon and flexible exchange rates accepted, something else happened, again based on capital markets. The United States had regained its competitiveness or, rather, Europe had lost momentum. The flow was henceforth reversed, and massive funds found their way to the principal US Stock Exchange. Wall Street became the main attraction. This caused another observation: there was an interaction between share prices and exchange rates, not necessarily as a one-way street as there were observations of both increasing and lower stock prices with the same direction of exchange rates. But foreign buy orders increased. In the first quarter of 1978 foreign investors purchased $670 million of American stocks, which was 25% above the inflows during the same three months of the year before. The absolute amount may not seem overwhelming, but relatively foreigners accounted for 36.5% of all net purchases of stocks in 1977 (Arenson, 1978). The dollar depreciated so large foreign equity investments and increase in stock prices accompanied declines in the dollar exchange rate, but at times the two went in the same direction. Both the dollar and the stock market fared better in the beginning of 1979. Information from NYSE indicates that trades in US shares constituted 44% of world trades in 1980, a height it has not reached since. This excludes NASDAQ, which took off in a major way around 1990. The market capitalization of equities, again excluding NASDAQ, compared with the rest of the world, was 41% in both 1980 and 2001, but was lower in all other years. In 2005 it was 33%, and at the end of 2006 it was down to 30%. Including NASDAQ the market capitalization reached a maximum so far of nearly 52% of world shares in 2001, but was down to 41.3% in 2005.[15] At the end of 2007 NYSE was about 35% of the total, 44% with NASDAQ. It is now becoming more difficult to separate the New York Stock Exchange from Western Europe with the creation of the integrated Euronext.

The observed relation between currency rates and the stock market does not mean that the stock market started to determine the exchange rate. It might, however, be true that the stock market summed up part of the relevant information for determining the exchange rate although in an interaction with the classical interest-rate or bond-rate mechanism (Elliott Wave International, 2009).[16] If interest rates/bond rates increase, and the bond market is dominating, then share prices will fall but the currency may be strengthened. The new development was that sometimes the stock market strengthened and so did the currency (Petersen, 1979).

The end seventies and beginning of the eighties were confusing times. The eighties have been called the lost decade. Capital was ample, not least because of the sums accumulated in western banks due to the oil revenues that Arab countries had procured for themselves. Capital was lent to Asia, Latin America, and even Africa. But interest rates were high and the returns on the invested capital often disappointing. The money could not but boomerang back to Wall St. immediately because profitable investments were not really found abroad. These phenomena have hurt countries and people enormously, but will not be discussed here because they do not represent new form developments or mechanisms. This money ping-pong helped Wall St. until it crashed in 1987, simply because there was no real surplus value creation behind the figures. However, the fall on Wall St. in 1987 was but a downward blip in an otherwise upward direction. The nineties started to find the new forms, but the Asian crisis 1997–98 may be seen as another example of money flowing around aimlessly without being based on real value creation.

9. THE EURO

The euro was created in part to overcome internal differences and jealousies and to facilitate the internal market of the European Communities countries when they were in the process of transforming themselves into a union.

The lack of currency market stability in the seventies led to attempts at aligning European currencies in the snake (1972) and later the European Monetary System (EMS) in 1979. It aimed at fixed exchange rates through the Exchange Rate Mechanism. Deviations triggered consultations among central banks, not exactly a dramatic response. *The Economist* gave vent to economists trying to change the course of economic history when it published the so-called "All Saints' Day Manifesto" on November 1, 1975 (Basevi et al., 1975). Here the Europa was trumpeted. It should have constant purchasing power (i.e., using a questionable theoretical concept for actual currency creation) and should coexist with national currencies.

The work toward an Economic and Monetary Union was furthered in 1988 by the creation of the Delors Committee preparing the Maastricht Treaty, which was adopted in 1992. In the eighties exchange rates had stabilized and nominal interest rate differentials narrowed in Europe. The emphasis on price stability and zero or very low inflation was overwhelming, bolstered by fiscal policy restraints. The advantages of a common exchange rate were seen to lead to much more predictability in economic relations, with lower transaction costs and better economic and financial market integration. Also it was supposed to be beneficial at an overall level as it had been an experience with flexible rates that nominal exchange rate changes did not soften external shocks. The emphasis for the EMU was – again-on price stability plus convergence criteria (limits on fiscal deficits and debt ratios) and the creation of the European Central Bank (ECB). Mechanisms to ensure financial stability (capital market stability) were not included in the eventual euro set-up (Sørensen, 2004). Coincidentally with the Maastricht Treaty, in 1992 the pound was forced to exit from the Exchange Rate Mechanism through speculation against it while the Swedish krone and Italian lira got into serious trouble. Going forward to create the euro can be seen as daring, and its technical success surprising.

The euro is not entirely monetarist in a narrow sense as it is also surrounded by restrictive fiscal policies, cemented in the Growth and Stability Pact that imposed limits on government deficits (less than 3% of GDP) and debt levels (less than 60% of GDP), reinforced by institutional emphasis. A stable price level (rising less than 2% annually) was and is the overriding issue, however, although this is only the so-called second pillar, the first being an indicator of the growth of monetary aggregates in the form of announcement of the desired path of M_3 (von Hagen & Matthias, 2001). The euro has been able to keep an exchange rate vis-à-vis the dollar that has mostly been higher in a value sense (i.e., fewer euros for one dollar) than it was when it started. It can be discussed whether Euroland ever was an "optimum currency area" according to the criteria defined in 1961 by the 1999 Economics Nobel Prize winner, Robert Mundell, involving the degree of integration of the various markets, including the labor market (McKinnon, 2000).[17] However, here it is the monetary mechanism and international significance that is of interest.

The euro is fundamentally different from the dollar. Its creators were not concerned about a large reserve base. The ECB's reserves or paid-up capital were just € 4 billion. However, the total asset base was about € 40 billion, 15% in gold and 85% in US dollars and yen. The National Central Banks (NCBs) can claim equivalent amounts in euros. Downstream, its backing consists of assets that are pledged against the purchase of euros on auctions/tenders. Thus the euro is asset-backed but in a diffuse fashion. Various instruments are offered by the ECB, from short to longer-term euro securities. Its weakness is that it is not backed by past state deficits materialized in outstanding government bonds where mature states have to honor their debts, which, paradoxically, provides a guarantee for the future. In this case it is the contrary. The ECB tenders are not based on debt and it imposes on states not to have too high debts. It is as if ECB does not really want to get involved in IFI and has shown itself very restrictive and promoting disinflationary measures. At various points the ECB has been criticized for not lowering interest rates sufficiently to get economies started. This criticism abated after the serious increase in oil prices and the beginning turn-around in euro economies after the US Fed started its series of rate increases in 2004 where ECB stayed put for a long time. After the 2007 credit crunch the ECB also retained its rate, not lowering it when the Fed and the Bank of England did. But the ECB tried to assist during the beginning crisis by pumping out liquidity/overnight funds. Later on panic struck and it lowered its benchmark.

The euro is very much a unifying "policy" instrument. It is thus rather the articulation of a common monetary policy than a truly common currency as it just tries to harmonize the different tendencies. To note that all – now 27 – EU central banks are part of the European System of Central Banks (ESCB), which is in charge of the common monetary policy executed by ECB. In addition there is some confusion if it is the NCBs of the Eurosystem (the 16 countries that have so far adopted the euro as currency) or the ECB itself that determines the direction. It is perhaps logical that it must be one or two-stringed as it would otherwise end in confusion, but its single-mindedness has caused problems, too. As a currency unifier, it has been a success, as a means of promoting what could be defined as common European economic goals it has been a fiasco. Take your pick. An absurd juxtaposition of phenomena is that Europe became less of a unity after the currency unified. European businesses were basically, like others in the rich part of the world, leaving Europe.

In its mode of operation the euro is managed predominantly through the central banks that make up the system. Open-market operations are performed with refinancing operations, mostly reverse transactions where a transaction is evened out after a certain time or covered by assets. The open-market operations are executed through tender, either with a fixed interest rate and variable volume or fixed volume and variable interest rate. Counterparties, commercial banks registered with Euroland NCBs, can bid. The winners are determined by auctions comparing the bids as per the cut-off points. Also swap operations in foreign currency can be performed (ECB, 2004). There is no need to further detail the way in which the euro is operated. No doubt it is done very skillfully, but this should not deter one from criticism of its economic base and interaction patterns as its shakiness has become clear for all to see from the beginning of 2010.

In a way it is not so strange that monetary rates could be held low in the Eurosystem. The ECB does not need a high rate in order to cash in "seignorage" because its own debt is low. This also shows that it is not fully integrated in capital markets in the way the dollar is. The dollar responds to and expresses first of all capital markets in the United States and those which respond to the US markets in other parts of the world. The euro for the first many years of its existence has nearly lived up to the Europa economists' dream of a yawningly stable price level guarantor while surreptitiously letting capital markets on the loose. But obviously it is the contention of this work that the ECB cannot determine price increases and worrying signs occurred in 2008. The supposedly uniform interest rates on participating countries' bonds began to diverge in unsustainable fashion, and an outright euro crisis started in 2010 through the joint effect of internal misalignments and outward attacks. The talk about the euro replacing the dollar abated.

The combined stock market capitalization of the EMU countries was 28% of the United States in 1998, already in 2000 it was 38% of that of the United States.

Denmark voted on the euro in 2000 and said no. However, the Danish policy has been to maintain a pegged rate toward the euro with a small margin, managed through monetary policy instruments, trying to keep the interest rate very close to the euro rate and having a restrictive fiscal policy, especially through the freezing of taxes and thereby declaring that expenditures must be limited too. The outcome was low-interest rates and high house prices and an economy praised for its dynamism, whether there was a connection or not to the euro tie. In no way could anybody claim with a shadow of verisimilitude that the Danish economy suffered from not being member of the Eurosystem. However, in the panic of 2008 the Danish Central Bank raised its lending rate by 0.4 percentage points to 5.0 to defend the Danish krone the day before the ECB lowered its key rate by 0.5 percentage points to 3.75%. Later in October the Danish Central Bank increased this rate further to 5.5%. Given that the market rates do not necessarily follow, or rather, that the central banks have limited power over market rates, it did not make that much difference.

Maybe this rather shows something else, viz. the prior contention that the Eurosystem is a coordinating mechanism with some random common paper, which countries could adopt as a currency or not, at least when they are at the margin. It is the coordinating mechanism that counts, and Denmark is obviously part of ESCB. Differences remain, but are patched over on the surface. It could perhaps be claimed that Denmark has a double advantage: benefiting from the existence of the euro and not having adopted it officially.

Some bright economists have now noticed that a stable consumer price level of commodities is not enough. They have discovered that there are more price levels than one and that asset prices can diverge from consumer price levels even more when the focus is on the latter. This was exacerbated when cheap goods started entering from the east in a massive way. Distinctions are made between headline inflation and core inflation, though. The latter excludes food and energy prices.[18] There would be some sense in taking housing out also as it, like food and energy, is influenced by rent phenomena. Then core inflation should be negative (=deflation) even before headline inflation went down in the latter half of 2008 with the spectacular fall in oil, housing and to some extent agricultural prices.

If there are core price increases in Euroland and its satellites, it is a sign that inflation, if anything, is even higher as prices or rather, values, of a lot of goods have decreased in real terms. This is another sign that inflation is in practice extremely ambiguous, that is, even if prices are stable, they should perhaps be decreasing. Conversely, there will be huge internal redistribution among different elements or toward middlemen. Even *The Economist* (2002) started to see the difference between deflation and price decreases due to productivity growth. Whereas the latter is acceptable, the former, associated with output and demand weakness, may be blurred by the resistance of some prices to downward pressure. The article blamed central bankers for obsessing with inflation while the opposite was the danger.

When one thinks about the euro and its philosophy, one cannot help exclaiming: economists understand economic laws perfectly – except those governing capitalism. The 2008 panic showed that the ECB was pushed aside when the crisis really hit because of the lack of official financial market integration in Europe. The national governments had to take over, and this despite the fact that many banks reached far beyond national borders.

10. DARK MATTER

"Global imbalances or bad accounting? The missing dark matter[19] in the wealth of nations" by Ricardo Hausmann and Federico Sturzenegger made waves at the end of 2005–beginning of 2006. The paper dealt with the fact that current account statistics do not include the international wealth effects of investing abroad. Note first of all that there is only discussion of current account, which includes interest payments. The below is based primarily on the revised version taking account of early criticisms (September, 2006).

The paper argued that the USD 792 billion current-account deficit that the United States registered in 2005, coming on top of cumulative deficits, was in fact counterbalanced by the difference in service flows between liabilities and assets and adding capital gains and unmeasured asset returns. The interest rates paid on US debt were a lot lower than the earnings on assets invested so even if the flows were not unilateral, there would still be a positive difference in favor of the United States, viz. when capitalized at the same risk-free rate of (in this case) 5%. Therefore, in fact, the low-interest country might be able to borrow a lot more than it invested and still come out with a zero balance.

The authors looked for capital gains or unexplained returns and concluded in three factors, which "… all involve a persistent return differential between assets and liabilities. This difference in returns may originate in three main sources: a return differential for FDI investments, the sale of insurance, and the provision of liquidity services" (Hausmann & Sturzenegger (H&S), 2006, p. 10). The first channel involves FDI investors coming with ideas, a blueprint, a product, and a business know-how that is usually poorly accounted for. Because of the difficulties in tracking the international service operations of corporations it is likely that official numbers underestimate their worth. The second channel may arise because of the capability of an economy to sell some of its stability to the rest of the world, akin to the sale of insurance.[20] The third channel was related to the provision of liquidity services to the rest of the world, basically through the desirability of a currency (read: the dollar) or the lower return on its liquid financial markets.

The authors found an approximation to their FDI hypothesis in the fact that the S&P 500 reflected gains from overseas investments, and if they were included in foreign accounts, the net position of the United States would be even more positive. They attributed them to "the stability of the US economy, its role as a cradle for ideas, or the ability that it commands on liquid assets and prudent macroeconomic policies" (H&S, 2006, p. 21).

The insurance (in a figurative sense) related to US stability may appear a bit strange. In order to bolster this argument, the authors dragged in Nobel laureates Kenneth Arrow and Gerard Debreu merged into the sometimes hyphenated theorem, Arrow-Debreu. Their theorem on contingent securities used to reduce risk was deployed to argue that the United States had a lower risk premium. Since this was what they started out assuming, there is nothing surprising about the result although it required a bit of math. It really says that if there was a higher perceived risk in some countries, this would lead to a risk premium which meant that investments would require a higher rate of return. Whether it is true that the risk was higher in other countries is not examined. At one point the authors seemed to think that the value of insurance not only increased after the Asian crisis but that the "benefit may have further increased after 9/11 as the United States is, ... , still the economy that can better deal with the global implications of such threats" (H&S, 2006, p. 13). This seems to amount to claiming that the United States has become ever safer after it has made the world even less safe since what the authors set out to do was to prove that the United States is the most risk-less and stable country, a somewhat questionable claim, but well in line with mainstream economics that refuses to deal with profits and power. It nearly resembles a slip of the tongue.

Liquidity services could in part yield seignorage, in part reflect the fact that the rate of return on the dollar was lower than equivalent paper in overseas markets (not lower than that of the yen, but let that be). It was lower in the sense that the dollar was accepted abroad. The advantage for the US dollar would consist of people around the world holding US cash at no or lower interest rates than other currencies. Contrary to their original thoughts published at the end of 2005, in the later version the authors found that it was not an important source of dark matter.

At the end of the chapter the authors went on to measure dark matter and came to the conclusion that, "To the extent that FDI assets abroad continue to rise and to generate excess returns then we should expect to measure continued export of dark matter" (H&S, 2006, p. 20). In this way poor China "remains an important importer of dark matter" (H&S, 2006, p. 19), a somewhat strange statement, given that China may well be an importer of foreign capital but to state that it imports others' excess profits, sorry, excess returns, is a bit odd. Wouldn't it be truer to say that China exports excess profits that are generated in China with foreign capital? Of course mainstream economists think that the Chinese just pay back for all the technology so generously and unselfishly put at their disposal.

Dark matter is not one thing for these authors. It is exported, yet it also comes back as returns. It is not an export bought with money, it is an export that only manifests itself through all the matter that oozes back to the United States and other dark matter "exporters" (or, more correctly, importers) and which is not an equivalent amount to anything but the darkest of secrets: high or excess profits as the other side of the capital export coin.

11. DARK MATTER AND THE EURODOLLAR

Despite the critical remarks on the explanations offered by H&S, there is no doubt that they in a way revived questions dealt with in the debate on the Eurodollar above. The asset side in the foreign balance is important and has to do with – not official reserves – but US private investments. At least it springs to mind that part of the overseas investment may be outsourcing so that it is the same firms that got a markup on the US stock markets that dragged huge profits out of the countries to which outsourcing took place. The undervaluing in the current account statistics had the equivalent in the overvaluing on the stock market. But the US stock market valuations do not show up in the current accounts except through foreigners' return on investments.[21] In addition, many US firms investing abroad were not listed on the major exchanges. The huge returns on their investments may be due not to their technological superiority but to their ability to extract surplus labor from workers. Also, the more the US imports from China (just to take this simple case), the more profit is repatriated. However, because of the national bias, a transfer out of the US will be registered, too.

Again a triangular relationship. China has simply replaced Europe in the relationship.

Interpreting this in terms of flow of funds, there was a trade deficit, the United States was buying more than it sold. But those who sold to the United States might actually be an American firm invested abroad that used the proceeds to reinvest locally. And because of the returns implied in the goods sold, they would have earned so much that it about balanced the excess borrowing. A loan might have been taken in the United States and invested in China. In principle it had to be converted to renminbi and the dollars deposited in the Reserve Bank of China (here is a lack of parallelism to the Eurodollar). But afterwards developed new investment came about through excess dollars generated in the process. The relatively low dollar interest rate also made it possible to take market loans on cheap terms. US businesses might borrow in euros too, but there was still an exchange risk to take into account which might make it look unfavorable. As long as US businesses or banks lend (to themselves) in dollars, there will be a constant inflow of short-term dollars. Inflow is the other side of outflows.

Rewriting the balances from the section on balance-of payments concepts:

Exports of goods and services
less imports of goods and services
equals current account balance

To make it more comprehensible, it should be:

Exports of goods and services
less imports of goods and services
plus return on capital and interest earned abroad (inflow)
less return on capital and interest earned by foreigners (outflow)
equals current account balance

where commercial, technological, and professional services enter into the first two lines together with goods and the last two expressions "above the line" are financial service flows. In previous notions the services in current account implicitly also included return on capital (and indirectly, capital gains), but return on capital should be viewed as a special item, particularly if capital flows themselves are ignored. These are truly the "invisible" items.

However, capital flows should be included in the analysis, both capital movements in the form of FDI and short-term flows:

Net outflow of long-term capital
plus net outflow of short-term capital
equals (net inflow of long-term capital *plus*) net inflow of short-term capital

Adding the two we have:

Exports of goods and services
less imports of goods and services
plus return on capital and interest earned abroad (inflow)
less return on capital and interest earned by foreigners (outflow)
- -
equals current balance
less net outflow of long-term capital
less net outflow of short-term capital (foreign private creditors)
equals net inflow of long-term accommodating capital (Treasury bills)
plus net inflow of short-term capital.

This is in fact an attempt at a reconstruction of the BOP measures, just including the return on capital explicitly. If these returns are very positive, then in fact there may be a "balance of payments" surplus. As it is, normally the current account balance is mixed up with capital flows; therefore current account balance is not as negative as is assumed, it is rather that capital is flowing out and the net inflow of short-term capital that is equal to the so-called deficit is nothing more than the capital abundance of the dominant economy. The net inflow of short-term capital below the line thus has to do with the net money creation when money is an asset that is also the reserve currency whose central bank (The Federal Reserve) issues it as a liability. Notice also that the net outflow of short-term capital above the line was credited as a positive item in the official settlements balance. This would suppose, however, that the short-term money should be deposited in the US banking system abroad, which is not what seems to happen today.

That the US money is in fact a liability that can come back to haunt the dominant economy means that the Fed has to keep interest rates low in order not to have to pay too much on its own debt, and for a long time this worked successfully, stimulating markets at home at the same time as capital flowed out. But this does incur the risk that the bills will be exchanged for higher-interest-bearing securities in another currency denomination, especially when the currency – the dollar – is appreciating but perhaps expected to depreciate. Therefore the US interest in keeping the dollar low, urging the Chinese to revalue. But if the dollar is kept low, the Chinese would require higher remuneration in the United States or would move their funds elsewhere, thus an insolvable dilemma, which was for a long time resolved through the conservatism of the Chinese.

Looking at the capital flows alone, assuming that there is no inflow of long-term capital to the United States, US outflow of long-term and short-term capital is equal to net inflow of short-term capital. This is exactly how it works: long and short-term capital is exported from the United States to fund investments and goods. The net inflow is simply the holding of Treasury bills by the central bank of the capital-importing country. However, the current account does not account correctly for the remuneration of investments (or rather, the capital flows stemming from the service flow, viz. profits that are reinvested as new capital) and thereby China can hold huge reserves of Treasury bills and at the same time this is not necessarily a deficit problem for the United States.

As can be seen above, if read above the dotted line, the current balance could be positive, except that the "return on capital" is not really recorded.

When the crisis struck, H&S were seen as having been too positive. A writer in the *Financial Times* mentioned the dark matter theory as one of those which had erred on the optimistic side. "Academics and the Fed also fell into the trap of rationalizing unsustainable features of the global economy. In 2005 a paper by Ricardo Hausmann and Federico Sturzenegger of Harvard caused excitement about the possibility that financial 'dark matter' would prevent a big bang in the world economy. The failure to believe in this dark stuff, the authors concluded, made 'analysts predict crises that, for good reason, remain elusive' " (Giles, 2008).

True, but the question here is if the meltdown had its reason in the financial imbalances that Hausmann and Sturzenegger did not think were real. The problem may well lie in the fact that the United States did not find sufficiently profitable investments at home in a "productive" sense, which helps explain the employment losses in the United States. The high return on capital abroad supported the exaggerated financialization of the United States and led to its eventual meltdown.

12. THE EMERGENCE OF THE "SINODOLLAR"

Other countries also import from China and similarly export capital to it. Reinvestments develop China's internal economy. One could ask why China itself could experience a boom when it imports–exports so much dark matter? This has to do with the structure of the Chinese economy that is based on subcontracting where Chinese entrepreneurs extract their own profits at the behest of low-paid workers. There is enough for everyone, even if the resulting goods come out at the cheaper end. Despite having modernized its views on the world a bit by for example admitting that profits are increasing relative to wages worldwide, the ever-vigilant *Economist* persists in the erroneous notion that China, by having a current-account surplus vis-à-vis the United States, does not also import capital. In fact, *The Economist* occasionally thinks that China is hoarding its surplus (2006). This view of Chinese hoarding became patently absurd in 2008 where it was realized that the economy had rather been overheating before it sank down and needed stimulus.

International financial intermediation has to do with one "real" asset as the foundation of different financial instruments (long and short lending and short borrowing), or rather, the long lending creates an asset through direct investment. The money returns to the banking system as short lending for the private capital market (US and international investment banks and funds operating in Hong Kong and Shanghai) that can be the basis of short borrowing or converted to reserves and thus to Treasury bills as a way of getting remuneration on this extra money.

There is here a major difference between China now and Europe after the Second World War. The Eurodollar came after the liberalization of capital account but with some banking restrictions at work. China still has restrictions on capital account, which means that the excess dollars cannot easily be held privately and if they have nothing to do (are not invested overseas) they will tend to be hoarded by the Reserve Bank of China in the form of US Treasury bills. However, Mainland Chinese have been allowed to invest in Hong Kong. New firms are entering all the time. They come in with foreign currency that should be converted to renminbi.

Ere long, the firms will have exported and bring in new currency for the part that is registered locally as exports. The part that is registered externally of course does not enter Chinese accounts. To be fair, some foreign companies also source and sell in China. Despite the fact that they should probably be much higher, enormous exports are still recorded. The market for those dollars that are converted to short-term deposits in commercial banks (over and above those that come into the coffers of the China Reserve Bank) are the Sinodollars, which have taken on a life of their own despite restrictions. They are "hot money" (Martin & Morrison, 2008), but not all hot money in China is Sinodollars. Remember that the Eurodollar market was made up of the dollars that had exited the US money supply without entering the European coffers. The same is the case now, there is a float that represents excess newly created dollars. It is the triangulation that makes them Sinodollars. This shows among others that in developed capitalism the ways of finding an outlet cannot be regulated for ever. When long-term capital investments are allowed, short-term flows will follow and these will enforce either liberalization or a persistent gray market.

The enormous profits that are extracted by foreign firms in China are not necessarily registered as external and therefore not entering the service account. Or rather, China exports commodities that are not split up in components of domestic and foreign provenance and ultimate destination. Therefore it will also "export" the profits as if they were homegrown when measured in commodities. But when it comes to the final day of reckoning, all of this should be split into the different categories of profits, wages, raw materials and other costs, homegrown and outward bound. And it is difficult to reconcile. Add to this the tax interests of firms in obscuring matters, that is, pretending that costs (production prices) in China are higher than they are.[22]

This will also make China vulnerable. The fist sign was in March 2007 when the Shanghai stock exchange fell dramatically in just one day. Commentators were bewildered and hurried to say that there was no connection to the US market. There was. This happened when the housing market in the US weakened. One large subprime mortgage company went belly-up based on increasing default rates in the underlying housing market. Later on China fared better as the financial meltdown in the west barely touched it because Chinese banks had not invested extensively in strange derivative vehicles. China only started to suffer in a real sense in the last part of 2008 through the US consumer's purse and his/her influence on markets.

13. CONCLUSION

The dollar overcame the breakdown of Bretton Woods and flourished in the 1980s through investments in the United States while being used as a vehicle of international short-term flows in the 1990s. This led to the Asian crisis but not to a serious attack on the dollar. The advent of the euro has perhaps been beneficial as it created two large currency areas. However, despite voices to the effect that the euro would take over, this has not happened. The recent euro crisis has on the contrary strengthened the dollar. The dollar detractors thought that it would be punished through the excessive holdings of US short-term funds and treasury bills by China (estimated at more than USD 800 billion), Japan and India, but this has not happened. In fact, US officials' request that the renminbi revalue have largely gone unheeded. Net FDI into China is undiminished and the Chinese authorities are trying to curb bank lending through increased reserve requirements. China today is as much dependent on the United States as vice versa. However, China's strength is being reinforced through the build-up of its industry through investments, and it is going in the direction of autonomy.

It is the hypothesis of this chapter, which the author sees confirmed in the movements taking place, that international money continues to be created in private markets and that the dollar has a superior role in IFI that cannot be assumed by any other currency at this time. This does not mean that there is no evolution, but the discussion about competition from the euro has abated through revelations of the latter's obvious architectural weaknesses. The dollar can survive the US current account deficit – in that sense the author agrees with the dark matter theorists – but the United States may in the longer run lose power through the overall loss of domestic industry whose attempted remedy, financial market innovation and abuse has created bubbles and instability.

NOTES

1. The distinction sometimes drawn concerns the variations around par, for example, "managed float" or completely flexible rates without any anchor.
2. It can be argued whether the persistence of gold in reserves is a remnant or inherent feature of the monetary base. Despite the obvious ability of gold to store value, literally, and, notably in a crisis, to serve as a private store of wealth gold has ceased to have official monetary functions but central banks still have gold reserves that serve as a buffer.
3. "The major confusion here (…), i.e. that value as such (interest) comes to be the use-value of capital, is something that Tooke does not see" (Marx, 1991, p. 476).
4. Believe it or not, the Marshall Plan money is still around (Hundley, 2004), "Marshall Plan Still at Work in Germany." This *Chicago Tribune* article recorded that the $1.4 billion for West Germany had grown to $12 billion. West Germany paid back one third of the original money and kept investing the proceeds in, for example, low-interest loans to industries. Other countries assumed they did not have to pay back and did not do so either.
5. The conclusion of de Long and Eichengreen (1991) was that it was the reduction of controls that mattered.
6. See Chapter 1, "Challenges to Capital," (Glyn, 2006) about "real" economic events after World War II.
7. In developing countries, particularly Africa, the conversion of short borrowing to long lending seems to be onerous and difficult. Bankers are prone to tell an

inquirer that, since they have very little long-term deposits, they are not able to lend, as if maturities between lending and borrowing should match 1 to 1. Others contend that long-term lending prospects are not sufficiently profitable. So they finance the large commercial houses. A factual reason is that those who lend long for foreign direct investment (FDI) tend to come with their own cheaper money from home.

8. This is one step away from Keynes who thought very literally about liquidity as cash. Maybe it is better to think of liquidity preference not from the asset but from the liability side, the one with high liquidity preference will only borrow if rates are low.

9. The graph is from Kindleberger (1966, p. 7).

10. Author's graph (Petersen, 1976).

11. Ragnar Nurkse, Estonia-born economist, 1907–1959. Was prominent in the interwar years for his work on capital movements and sometimes termed a pre-Keynesian. He was the main author of *International Currency Experience – Lessons of the Inter-War Period*, League of Nations, 1944.

12. Lederer was director of the balance of payments division of the US Commerce Department from 1954 to 1969.

13. The reader may wonder that net *inflow* of gold was at first listed as the balancing item and then it was changed to net *outflow*. This is not to be taken too seriously but depends on the fact that Kindleberger sometimes assumes that the balance is zero, and then the above and below the items will have to equal zero each of them. The important point is that net inflow of short-term capital and net outflow of gold are listed in parallel below the line. It means that if there is a deficit, then in order to have a balance, gold should be moving out – as presumably happened in the good old days – or there must be inflow of short-term funds, otherwise it will not be tenable. So therefore, obviously, the current wailing about the US deficit is a bit pathetic. It is in the nature of the animal. This will be looked at from another angle in the section on dark matter below.

14. Any observer knows that, for example, sometimes raising central bank rates will make the domestic currency appreciate, sometimes not. Economists are prone to exclaim that the information was already internalized or the rate should have been raised by more points or inflationary expectations were already out of control or other such highfaluting hogwash if the classical Bank-rate style reaction of appreciating exchange rates does not ensue when rates are raised.

15. Based on data from the NYSE official website, www.nyse.com (www.nyxdata.com/nysedata).

16. According to this source the Dow Jones Industrial Average and the US dollar index both rallied from 1995 to August 2000, then fell together from March 2002 to early 2003 and since then have traded opposite each other. In a later publication (April 2, 2010), EWI states that from July 2007 to June 2008 the stock market and the dollar both declined (S&P500 vs. US dollar index). The author of this chapter thinks that the reason that no two markets will stay positively or negatively correlated all the time is the change in their relative weight (e.g. stock market vs. bond market dominance) vis-à-vis other markets, such as the one for foreign exchange.

17. Mundell, skeptical at first, later on came to defend monetary integration in Europe.

18. One explanation is that these prices are "volatile." Taking certain goods and services out, makes the indexes less of an indicator of inflation according to the classical definition of 'general price rises' and simply means that the standard notion of inflation. The Economist (2008), says "Ultimately, inflation is a monetary phenomenon, so responsibility lies with central bankers." Agreed that inflation is a "monetary" phenomenon, but not that this necessarily places its causes in central bank action, let alone makes it possible for central banks to control it. But secondly, prices may well increase without it being a monetary phenomenon.

19. The authors specify the use of the term 'dark matter' in finance as the difference between their own measure of net foreign assets and that given by official statistics (H&S, p. 1). This seems a weak explanation. The interest is rather whether or not official statistics capture important phenomena.

20. In their revision, the authors have toned down the insistence on the United States and made the propositions more generic.

21. The authors note that capital gains are not treated in the same way for all countries in balance-of-payments statistics. In a sense the authors tried to estimate how much the capital gains should be if correctly reflected in asset prices and then incorporated this capitalization in their current account revision. However, "capital gains" is a capital account phenomenon so the complaint should be about the treatment of capital account/balance. The problem occurs because capital account is not fully published.

22. To their home governments. In China they would do the reverse, that is, pretend that profits were low.

REFERENCES

Aliber, R. Z. (1974). Attributes of national monies and the interdependence of national monetary policies. In: R. Z. Aliber (Ed.), *National monetary policies and the international financial system*. Chicago and London: Chicago University Press.

Arenson, K. W. (1978). New life invades the equity market. *The New York Times*, August 7, Section Business & Finance, p. D1.

Basevi, G., Fratianni, M., Giersch, H., Korteweg, P., O'Mahony, D., Parkin, M., Pieters, T., Salin, P., & Thygesen, N. (1975). A currency for Europe: (All Saints' Day) Manifesto for European Monetary Union. *The Economist*, November 1, pp. 33–38.

de Long, J. B., & Eichengreen, B. (1991). The Marshall plan: History's Most Successful Structural Adjustment Program, October. Prepared for the Centre for Economic Performance and Landeszentralbank Hamburg conference on Post-World War II European Reconstruction, Hamburg, September 5–7, 1991. Available at http://www.j-bradford-delong.net/pdf_files/marshall_large.pdf

Elliott Wave International. (2009). U.S. dollar and the DJIA: How can one get stronger if the other falls? Available at http://www.elliottwave.com. Retrieved on 7th December.

European Central Bank. (2004). The implementation of monetary policy in the Euro area. General Documentation on Eurosystem Monetary Policy Instruments and Procedures.

Gilbert, M. (1968). *The gold-dollar system: Conditions of equilibrium and the price of gold.* Princeton University: Essays in International Finance, #70.

Giles, C. (2008). The vision thing. *Financial Times*, November 26, p. 9.

Glyn, A. (2006). *Capitalism unleashed: Finance, globalization and welfare*. Oxford: Oxford University Press.

Hausmann, R., & Sturzenegger, F. (2006). *Global imbalances or bad accounting? The missing dark matter in the wealth of nations*. CID Working Paper no. 124. Harvard University, Revised version. September.

Hundley, T. (2004). Marshall plan still at work in Germany. *Chicago Tribune* (online edition), October 12.

Johnson, H. (1969). Theoretical problems in the international monetary system. In: R. N. Cooper (Ed.), *International Finance*. Harmondsworth: Penguin.

Keynes, J. M. (1970). *The general theory of employment, interest and money* (First published in 1936). London: Macmillan St Martin's Press.

Keynes, J. M. (2000). *A tract on monetary reform* (First published in 1923). New York: Great Minds Series, Prometheus Books.

Kindleberger, C. P. (1966). Balance-of-payments deficits and the international market for liquidity. Chapter 1. *Europe and the dollar*. Cambridge, Massachusetts, London: MIT.

Kuwayama, P. (1975). Measuring the United States balance of payments. *Federal Reserve Bank of New York Monthly Review*, August 1, 183–194.

Lederer, W. (1963). *The balance on foreign transactions: Problems of definition and measurement*. Princeton, NJ: International Finance Section, Department of Economics, Princeton University.

Martin, M. F., & Morrison, W. W. (2008). China's "Hot Money" problems. *CRS Report for Congress*, July 21.

Marx, K. (1976). *Capital* (Vol. I). (First published in 1867). Penguin Classics, Penguin Books.

Marx, K. (1991). *Capital* (Vol. 3). (First published in 1894) Penguin Classics, Penguin Books.

Mayer, H. W. (1970). *Some theoretical problems relating to the Euro-Dollar market*. Princeton University: Essays in International Finance, #79.

McKinnon, R. I. (1974). *A new Tripartite Monetary Agreement or a limping dollar standard?* Princeton University: Essays in International Finance, #106.

McKinnon, R. I. (2000). Mundell, the Euro and optimum currency areas. Stanford Economics Department Faculty Papers 00-009. Available at http://www-siepr.stanford.edu/workp/swp00009.html

Meulendyke, A-M. (1998). *U.S. monetary policy and financial markets*. New York: Federal Reserve Bank of New York.

Petersen, K. H. (1976). *International Financial Intermediation and Money Creation* (mimeographed). New York: SUNY Stony Brook.

Petersen, K. H. (1979). *An asset market model of exchange rate determination: Capital market – Exchange rate interactions*. Ph.D. Thesis. SUNY Stony Brook (mimeographed), New York. (available in electronic format).

Sørensen, P. B. (2004). Niels Thygesen and European monetary integration. In: P. B. Sørensen (Ed.), *Monetary union in Europe. Historical perspectives and prospects for the future – essays in honour of Niels Thygesen*. Copenhagen: DJØF Publishing.

The Economist. (2002). Of debt, deflation and denial. October 12, pp. 95–96. Available at http://www.economist.com/node/1382605. Accessed on October 2010.

The Economist. (2006). *Economics focus: On the hiking trail*. September 2, p. 66.

The Economist. (2008). *A delicate condition*. January 19. Available at http://www.economist.com/node/10534662. Accessed on January 17.

von Hagen, J., & Matthias, B. (2001). *Monetary policy in unknown territory: The European central bank in the early years*. ZEI Working Paper B18-2001. Revised Version, Zentrum für Europäische Integrationsforschung (Center for European Integration Studies), Rheinische Friedrich-Wilhelms-Universität, Bonn, August.

Yeager, L. (1966). *International monetary relations*. Particularly pp. 467–471, "Pyramiding and "Eurodollars"," New York.

CRISIS AND "LAW OF MOTION" IN ECONOMICS: A CRITIQUE OF POSITIVIST MARXISM

Alan Freeman

ABSTRACT

This chapter restores the concepts of freedom, consciousness, and choice to our understanding of "economic laws," so we may discuss how to respond to economic crisis. These are absent from orthodox economics that presents "globalization" or "the markets" as the outcome of unstoppable forces outside human control.

They were integral to the emancipatory political economy of Karl Marx but have been lost to Marxism, which appears as the inspiration for mechanical, fatalistic determinism. This confusion arises from Marxism's absorption of the idea, originating in French positivism, that social laws are automatic and inevitable.

The chapter contests the organizing principle of this view: that economic laws are predictive, telling us what must happen. Marx's laws are relational, not predictive, laying bare the connection between two apparently distinct forms of appearance of the same thing, such as labor and price. Such laws open the door to democracy and choice, but do not unambiguously predict the future because what happens depends on our actions.

The National Question and the Question of Crisis
Research in Political Economy, Volume 26, 211–250

ISSN: 0161-7230/doi:10.1108/S0161-7230(2010)0000026008

The commodity form conceals these laws, disguising the true social and class relations of society. Accumulation, however, undermines the circumstances that permit the commodity to play this role. The result is crisis, defined in this chapter as the point when the blind laws of the commodity form are suspended and open political forces come into play.

In past crises, capitalism has restored the rate of profit through such destructive interventions as imperialism, war, and fascism. Economic laws, properly defined, offer society the real choice of alternative outcomes from crisis.

1. INTRODUCTION

This chapter seeks to restore the notions of freedom, consciousness, and choice to our understanding of "economic laws," placing discussion about responses to economic crisis on a rigorous foundation. These concepts were integral to the emancipatory political economy of Karl Marx. They have been lost, I will argue, to mainstream political economy and also to Marxism, which is, with great irony, cast as the originator of the opposed notion of mechanical or fatalistic determination.

This is the result of two substitutions for Marx's own ideas. As TSSI scholars (Freeman, 2010; Kliman, 2007) have established, modern academic Marxism has replaced Marx's value theory with a reinterpretation casting it as a variant of general economic equilibrium. This misuse, I suggest, accompanies an even broader misreading of his concept of economic law, imported from *French positivism*. The idea at stake is that society is governed by deterministic laws in which the actions of humans, and above all the collective choices of society, do not figure.

To clarify the extent of this misreading, I will distinguish a "relational" law, for example that the magnitude of value is equal to the time of labor, or that profit is equal to surplus value, from a "predictive law," for example that the crisis will end next year. The law most widely associated with Marx – the tendency of the rate of profit to fall – is widely read by Marxist scholars as predictive. I will argue that it expresses a relation in time instead: the rate of profit will fall for as long as capitalism accumulates value. It yields no prediction independent of what classes, states, and nations *do*. This explains why it has been reversed several times, and also why the human cost has been so great; since accumulation is the means by which capitalism exists, when it is suspended, society can only be kept in existence by suppression or transition to something else. It took fascism and war to recover from 1929; recovery from the Great Depression of 1873–1893 and the crash of 1893 was achieved by imperialism. This law, hence, expresses a relation between action and outcome. It permits us to identify actions that can avoid the destructiveness of the last two "solutions."

Marx's signal achievement was to make transparent the central relational laws of our economy – such as those relating price to labor, and income to property – allowing society to grasp the link between what it chooses to do, and what happens as a result. This is a deeply emancipatory project: knowledge, for Marx along with the enlightenment tradition, is the means to freedom. Capitalism however conceals the true relation between our actions and their outcomes within the commodity form. The systemic consequences of individual decisions therefore take the illusory form of automatic laws which Marx sought, in his own words, to "lay bare."

This endeavor stands in diametric opposition to the *Weltanschauung* that dominates modern thought and particularly neoliberal and even liberal thinking that view the workings of the economy as inevitable and outside human control – paradoxically in view of their nominal emphasis on freedom, to which we shall return. The best-known modern expression of this outlook is the portrayal of "globalization" as an unstoppable process driven by the growth of trade, communication, and travel. Its distinctive feature is inevitability. Its apostles discuss only whether it is good or bad; opponents are cast not just as morally wrong but *illogical*. Since it is going to happen in any case, it "makes no sense" to oppose it: it would be like calling for the repeal of the law of gravity.

Two options are excluded. I will show they are two sides of the same coin. The first is the possibility of *endogenous self-contradiction*: that "globalization" – or capitalism, or indeed, accumulation – may damage the conditions for its own existence, hence containing the seeds of its own destruction. The second is the possibility that human agency may alter anything significant. Though communication, trade, and travel are all peculiarly human and social by their very nature, their history is presented as an alien, inhuman force. These two failures are coupled in the analysis – or rather, lack of analysis – of *crisis*, which is the moment at which self-contradiction creates both the necessity for, and possibility of, a transition to something else.

Above all else, this idea dominates modern thinking about the economy. With the crisis, discussion on the joys of globalization seamlessly gave way to a moral panic about government spending. Country after country fell victim to a régime of retrenchment whose burden fell on working and above all poor people.[1] At first sight the grounds of the discussion had shifted.

Following globalization's unexpected but not unforeseen (Freeman, 2004) demise, government and even nations re-entered, stage right. Yet a shadowy figure stalks the corridors of power. True, it is said, we may be foolish enough to give destitute people a place to live, or let workers retire with 15 entire years of life ahead of them – but, if we do, we will be punished. By whom? The markets. So, it appears, there never was a choice – the "markets" have already decided what must be done.

A deep, persistent intellectual flaw, perhaps the most characteristic of the new Spenglerian age, underlies both discourses. We, the people, made the institutions that are said to rule us. They are a product of our consciousness. It is literally absurd to assert that we cannot consciously shape or override them. It violates rational use of the word "conscious." Yet society has lost the intellectual capacity to think in any other way. "Economic necessity" is like a construction of Orwell's Ministry of Truth, in whose invented language "Newspeak" the very notion of social change could not be stated in words.

This flaw was concealed, but never really overcome, by positivism's Austrian descendants like Hayek, who posed as champions of freedom by defining economics as the science of individual choice. It appears paradoxical that they were so often found on the side of tyrannical practices such as Pinochet dictatorship. But it is no paradox; their device leaves no place for *collective* freedom – the action of classes, states, nationalities, social movements, in fact any agency through which individual freedoms are actually realized. Hayek articulates the ideological opposition of wealth-owners to all forms of collective power other than their own. The market is "theirs" and neither the rigid hierarchies of the corporation, nor the power of finance, is seen as an intrusion on freedom. Hostility is reserved for the state, the trade unions, and all forms of class organization except those which uphold property and "order." The laws that still lie at the heart of the mythical world of neoliberal theory live outside the reach of collective intervention, that is to say, democracy. In this mythical world, it is anathema that people may choose to implement universal social rights; the market is the only permissible expression of collective will. So that a privileged half billion can afford health, food, and security, 12 times their number go sick, hungry, and fearful. This, our world calls "freedom."

Marx made rigorous the enlightenment intuition that individual freedom rests on democracy, Marxism then evolved the different, alien notion that freedom means submission to "laws of history." Defending neither collective, nor individual freedom, nor even their mutual dependence, it has written itself into history as a champion of abstract necessity against free human action.

2. POSITIVIST MARXISM'S POISONED CHALICE

The appearance of determinism in Marx's theory is reinforced, superficially, by his own writings. Is not the very notion of "economic law" Marx's own? Did he not write (1992, p. 92) that

> when a society has got upon the right track for the discovery of the natural laws of its movement – and it is the ultimate aim of this work, to lay bare the economic law of motion of modern society – it can neither clear by bold leaps, nor remove by legal enactments, the obstacles offered by the successive phases of its normal development. But it can shorten and lessen the birth-pangs.

Is not his value theory "all about" the "determination" of prices and values? So, is his message not that we must recognize the forces shaping our destiny, embrace them, and obey them? Is freedom not, as Engels famously wrote, the "recognition of necessity" – and nothing more? This fatalistic reading makes nonsense of both thinkers' passionate involvement in the First International, his writings on politics and history and above all the equally famous Eleventh Thesis on Feuerbach (Marx, 1972): "Philosophers have hitherto only interpreted the world in various ways. The point is to change it." Consciousness, and human action, are integral to Marx's concept of historical determination, springing from the Hegelian discourse on freedom and necessity which was the starting and end point of his philosophical journey.

The idea of "iron" or "inevitable" economic and social laws came into Marxism by a different route; via the rationalist tradition of the French revolution which transmitted itself into national workers' movements through leaders like Lassalle. It then evolved into what is variously called technical determinism or mechanical materialism (Coletti, 1985; Labriola, 1970; Lukacs, 2000).

This doctrine was articulated quite late in the history of the enlightenment by Auguste Comte (1798–1857), who named it positivism. Confusion surrounds this word nowadays, which is why I refer specifically to "French" positivism. It is reduced to the idea of using numbers or mathematics or even being exact. It gets confused with the logical positivism of the Vienna Circle (Stadler, 1998), to which "positive economics" can be traced. It is neither. Reduced to its essentials it is the notion that human life is governed by *externally defined abstract law*, as Comte (1856) explains with admirable clarity:

> To understand this economy aright, we must remember that it embraces not merely the inorganic world, but also the phenomena of human life, [which] though more modifiable than any others, are yet equally subject to invariable laws; laws which form the principal objects of Positive speculation. Now the benevolent affections, which themselves act in harmony with the laws of social development incline us to submit to all other laws, as soon as the intellect has discovered their existence. The possibility of moral unity depends, therefore, even in the case of the individual, but still more in that of society, upon the necessity of recognising our subjection to an external power. By this means our self-regarding instincts are rendered susceptible of discipline. In themselves they are strong enough to neutralise all sympathetic tendencies, were it not for the support that the latter find in this External Order. Its discovery is due to the intellect; which is thus enlisted in the service of feeling, with the ultimate purpose of regulating action.

Since our actions are all completely determined, all "bad" things that occur can only be the result of our ignorance of the true laws of our destiny. Therefore, our task is to discover what those laws are, and obey them. This is explicit: Comte, above, states that the task is to "recognize[e] our subjection to an *external power*." [my emphasis – AF] He was equally explicit on the religious subtext, founding a "religion of humanity" (Comte, 1851–1854).[2]

Though Comte's direct influence has faded, such ideas are among the most influential of our age: How many victims have been claimed by the god of "progress" and its cousins, the Civilizing mission of Imperialism, the superiority of the Western Way of Life, and our general contempt for any who do not fit modernity's arrogant self-image? "Development," given birth in the archetypal vision of Walt Whitman Rostow's (1960) *Stages of Economic Growth*, exacts an equally high price, reducing the economic choices facing poor countries to a preordained course of historical development whose exemplars are the very countries that produce and maintain their misery.

Bourgeois enthusiasm for such ideas should come as no surprise. More surprising is the position of Marxism, which appears as the inspiration and origin of what can only be described as morbidly technicist fantasies. Its fatalism extends, in a different direction, to many leftists, in the idea that capitalism has no way out of crisis. However, its dominant expression is Marxism's most characteristic positivist product: the academic current I term "Marxism without Marx" (Freeman, 2010). Within the general equilibrium interpretation it has foisted on Marx, it is impossible to formulate the idea that capitalism generates contradictions from within itself; that the rate of profit may fall, that the market may increase inequality between nations (Freeman, 2009b), that capitalism may fail to generate sufficient demand to call forth the continuation of accumulation (see Desai, 2010, this volume), or even that circulation may be interrupted by hoarding money.

This gives rise to a further paralysis. Unable to diagnose how capitalism can generate crisis, Marxist discussion is almost devoid of ideas on what to do about it. There is, virtually, no such thing as a "Marxist response to the crisis." I have suggested such responses elsewhere (Freeman, 2009a) but it is not the purpose of this chapter to repeat them. Here, I wish to show that by reclaiming Marx's theory, recognizing choice within it as an irreducible element, society may choose between all possible responses, identifying those actions whose outcomes are demonstrably consonant with their intentions. I claim, in short, that Marx, properly understood, offers an economically rational theory of political action. This is the most consistent interpretation of the famous dictum that opened this section.

3. THE OBJECT OF STUDY: SOCIETY IN CRISIS

I do not claim that this project is simple. The difficulty lies in a contradictory fact at the centre of the problem that (present-day) Marxism fails to address: capitalism's inner laws express themselves in two apparently different ways during booms, and during crisis.

In the run-up to a major crisis, for periods lasting years and sometimes decades, the contradictions of capitalism express themselves as blind laws of motion, outwith human control. They *take the form* of apparently natural laws – a long, slow decline in the rate of profit, the inexorable separation of rich from poor nations, the apparently limitless growth of inequality of all types, and so on. But at the point of crisis, and after, these accumulated failures burst out into the open and the very failure of the market brings explicit, conscious class action into play, creating the conditions to overcome these accumulated contradictions, whether using the retrograde measures of the capitalists, or by opting for superior ways to organize society. Class interests then come out into the open. Savage attacks on working and poor people in austerity budgets contrast with refusals to exact any price from the bankers and investors who caused crisis. Classes and nations are drawn into a maelstrom of ever more open political conflicts – as in Greece, for example – involving all the institutions they create or rest on, be they states, banks, corporations, armies, social movements, or indeed, riots. Capitalism's laws take the form of a battle of class forces. The meaning of "law" mutates into its legal, juridical sense of laws passed by a government or imposed by a people.[3]

I previously (Freeman, 2003) approached this with the idea that crisis is "endogenous" – caused by factors internal to the workings of capitalism – but that exit from crisis is "exogenous," depending on conscious action. Political economy itself establishes this very division in counterposing the "political" to the "economic" sphere or indeed to "civil society."

Should we then suppose that capitalism has two sets of laws, the one blind and economic, the other conscious and political? I wish to argue for a dialectical approach: for an *Aufhebung*, a synthesis, of two ideas of "law" whose opposition, from a higher conceptual standpoint, arises from the one-sided understanding they offer when isolated from each other. This is not out of fanciful notions that it sounds erudite or looks good in a seminar, but because the object of study is the same: namely, capitalist society; specifically, capitalist crisis. Moreover, as this object evolves, the two aspects of economic law do not separate out neatly like magnetism and gravity so that each can be studied in isolation, "government" on the left and "markets" on the right. In a certain sense, the positivist error consists in the illusion that this separation is possible. Its illusory character is, I think, a key point in Marx's own critical understanding: capitalism's nature is to conceal its own operation from its agents. The very notion of an "invisible hand" perfectly expresses this idea. Let us interrogate it, since it is the key to the synthesis we require.

Marx characterizes capitalism from the outset as *Eine ungeheure Warensammlung* – a monstrous collection of commodities. Mandel (1974) specifies capitalism as "generalized commodity production" – a society which organizes all, or nearly all, social relations through commodities. Marx's analysis of alienation and fetishization focuses on the fact that in the commodity, the true nature of social relations is concealed, or rather, appears in an illusory form. It appears that I exchange an egg for a piece of paper; actually, I am taking part in an association of labor and gratification linking me to the farmer, the drivers, the retailers and indeed, the hens, every bit as material as when my family sent me to the backyard to collect the material product of the domestic labor of chickendom.

Society's laws of motion become the laws of motion of the commodity form. But precisely because that form conceals these laws, they appear as blind and external. For this same reason, it is in crisis that this concealment falls away, not only in perception but also in practice. Because, and to the extent that, the commodity fails to organize social life, overt class agencies take its place.

These are not two different laws. The object of study – society – is a single entity, and cannot be split into two "parts," one conscious of itself and the other inaccessible to that same consciousness. A concept of the "laws of economic movement" has to subsume both the blind workings of the commodity form and the explicit action of class, nation, and state. I will argue that this renders, far more accurately than any positivist interpretation, Marx's own idea of "law".

Moreover, crisis itself is an object of study. It is a regularly recurring moment of accumulation. It is not an accident, a "deviation" or a surprise; it is constitutive of capitalism. I will criticize the popular notion that crisis is abnormal or unrepresentative of capitalism. After 40 years of more or less continual decline, we have every right to conclude that the reverse is the case. An integrated conception of the law of accumulation must therefore apply at times of crisis as well as boom. Crisis is a specific phase of accumulation when relations between action and outcome become transparent and political action becomes a primary determinant of economic movement. This is, in fact, the most appropriate and rigorous way to define a "capitalist" crisis. It is not just a monstrous collection of problems; it is that point when capitalism's normal mode of existence as a "purely economic" means of reproducing society gives rise to intractable failures of governance.

This is of course an oversimplification; capitalism can be understood during booms, though less people do so, and they have less influence. During crisis, truth always remains to some degree concealed. However, in crisis, class relations are *clarified.* Choice is then posed in the following sense: its outcome depends not only on who takes the streets with greatest determination and force but on how well the actors formulate, and understand, the true choices before them. In crisis, above all, *consciousness* rises; this is the soil in which the seed of freedom can be planted. We need a concept of "law" that can water that parched flower.

4. DOES CAPITALISM HAVE LAWS?

Does capitalism have any laws at all? I will briefly summarize the empirical evidence that it exhibits the two main features just described – endogenous, concealed, but self-contradictory decline, alternating with exogenous and explicit political reconstruction. The most recent "long boom," widely recognized in the literature, originated with the phenomenal resurgence of the US economy during and after the war, following the prolonged depression of 1929–1941. Both the depression, and the boom, were worldwide phenomena.

It is more controversial, although widely recognized, that this boom ended around the end of the 1960s with no comparable resumption of growth. Since then, the overall movement of the world economy, particularly the US economy, has seen a more or less protracted decline with lower growth rates, increasingly explosive financial crises, decreasing capacity utilization, and rising unemployment.

Chart 1 illustrates the basic point, showing the long-run trend of growth in world GDP since the war. Chart 2 presents the same indicator for the US economy, for which longer run figures are available. Cyclic variations can obscure the overall downward trend; however, two facts make it reasonably difficult to claim it is absent. First, each successive major peak of the long-run moving average is lower than the last. Second, average growth over the business cycle, as defined by the National Bureau for Economic Research (NBER), has been systematically lower since 1970. It is just possible to interpret this, with Duménil and Levy (2004), as a double boom with a trough in 1974 and a new peak in the neoliberal years. But this stretches the

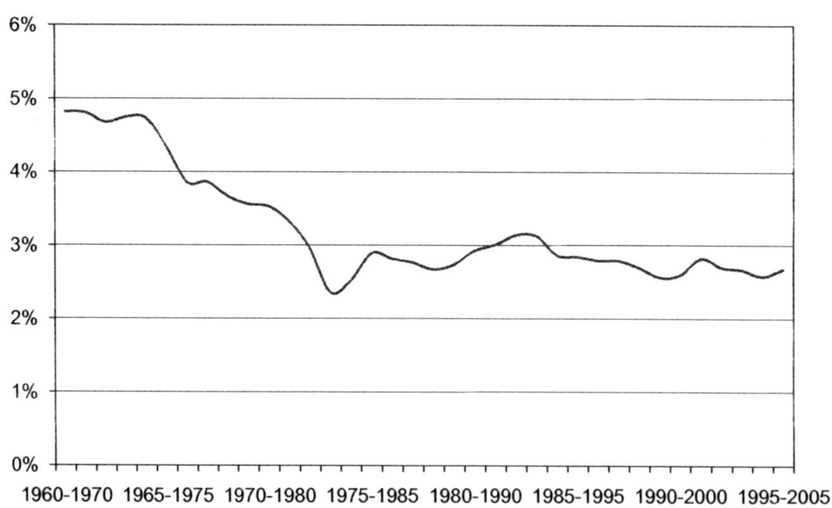

Chart 1. 10-Year Average Real GDP Growth of the World Economy. *Source:* IMF (World Economic Outlook); Groeningen RuG project, German national accounts, author's calculations.

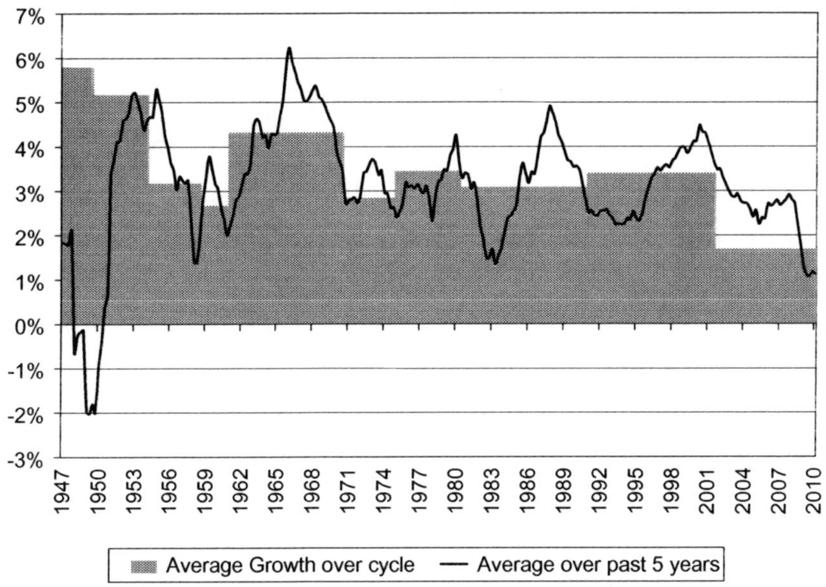

Chart 2. Growth Rate of US Real GDP. *Source:* US Bureau of Economic Affairs NIPA table 1.1.6 US GDP in chained 2005 USD.

fabric of evidence close to tearing point: in no cycle since 1961–1968 has growth risen above the average of the whole of previous period; and growth before 1968 only briefly, between 1953 and 1961, fell below the highest post-1968 point.

The pattern of decline becomes even clearer when the picture is completed with further evidence. Chart 3 shows the long-term decline in industrial capacity in the United States since at least 1973. Chart 4 illustrates the relentless growth in unemployment, most critically long-term unemployment – the best indicator of the reserve army of labor – which is now nearly twice the rate of any other postwar year and significantly higher than the 1974 peak.

Finally Chart 5 from Kliman (2010a) shows that the profit rate of the US economy, in both value and price terms, has trended downwards since the war, at no point returning to anything remotely resembling its postwar peak.

Is this decline a unique event? Have similar things happened before? Most certainly. Long declines follow every expansive boom like the *Belle Époque* of 1893–1914 (C. Freeman, 1995) and the Golden Age of 1942–1968. They have a lawlike character; they last a long time covering at least two industrial

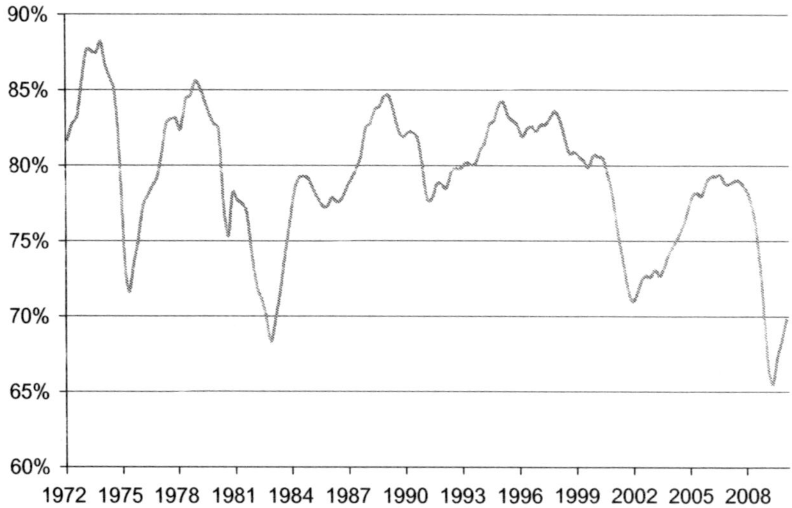

Chart 3. US Manufacturing Industrial Capacity. *Source:* US Bureau of Economic Affairs, series CUPM, quarterly, seasonally adjusted.

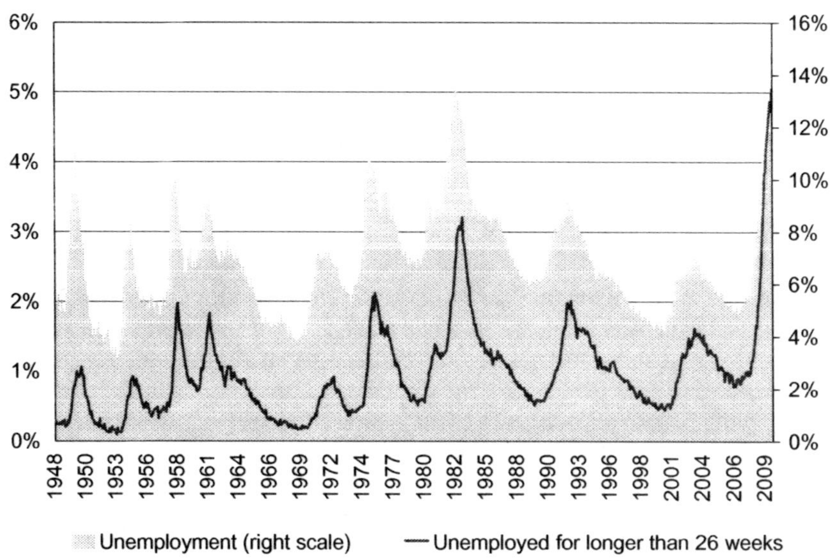

Chart 4. US Long-Term Unemployment. *Source:* US Bureau of Labour Statistics, CPS (household) unemployment monthly, seasonally adjusted.

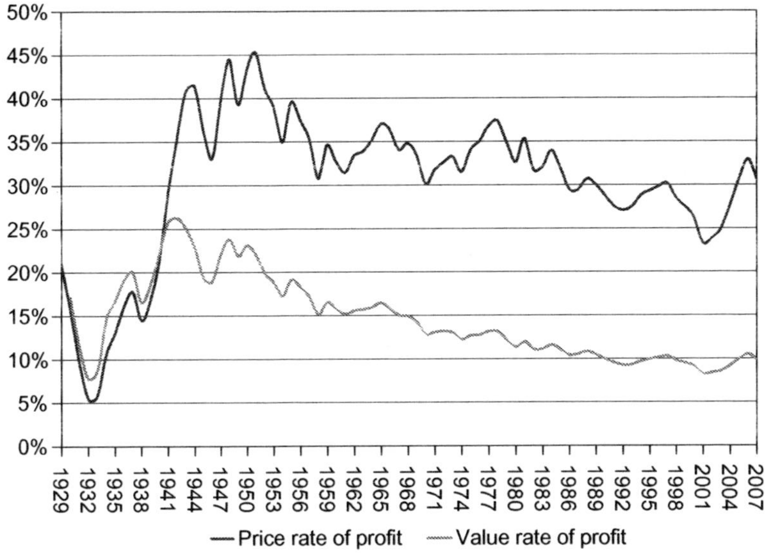

Chart 5. US Profit Rate. *Source:* Kliman (2010a).

cycles, during which they show no serious sign of stable or permanent reversal. Each such crisis exhibits a long period of depressed growth, high unemployment and falling prices affecting the whole capitalist world. 1873–1893 was widely referred to (Krugman, 2010) as "The Long Depression."

Their endogenous nature is almost undeniable. The very fact that they happen regularly – at least four times since the industrial revolution – suggests they share some common feature. This makes it hard to blame the crisis on allegedly new phenomena like "financialization" and exposes the difficulty facing Brenner (1998): having ruled out Marx's "Malthusian" explanation, he has to resort to behavioral explanations, for example, some special form of competition after the war. This may or may not explain the present decline. Does it explain 1929? Or 1873? Similar problems beset Krugman's (2010) diagnosis that "this third depression will be primarily a failure of policy." When a historical event of this scale repeats itself three times, under entirely different circumstances, something beyond policy is at work.

It is also hard to sustain that this common feature is political or governmental, precisely because of the immense variety of political circumstances involved. The very longevity of these declines means that such "exogenous circumstances" change repeatedly. And finally, the depth of those measures that do finally bring them to an end, suggests that the forces producing them are deeply embedded in the nature of capitalism – that, in Marx's (1991, p. 350) words, capital "comes up against a barrier to the development of the productive forces which has nothing to two with the production of wealth" which "comes into a conflict at a certain stage with the latter's further development."

5. HOW DO CRISES END?

Must such declines go on forever? A significant left Marxist trend held this view and still does. The theory of *Zusammenbruch* or inevitable collapse, associated (probably unjustifiably; see Zarembka, 2002; Kuhn, 2007) with the work of Luxemburg and Grossman, was endorsed by a significant section of the left Russian workers' movement, and strongly influenced Council Communism. The tendency to predict crisis as inevitable and unstoppable persists today. I think it is however mistaken.

The residual positivist influence it expresses is nevertheless decisively different from both neoliberal positivism and that of Marxism Without Marx. The latter are celebratory and apologetic, ascribing to capitalism miraculous powers it does not have. Left positivism overstates capitalism's difficulties. The main political risk is fatalism – since capitalism is in such an awful mess, the conclusion is easily drawn that it will collapse of its own and we can build socialism on its bitter ashes. There has never been an unstoppable crisis, and there are no historical or rational grounds for supposing that one will occur in the future. The profit rate *was* restored, and the Great Depression *did* come to an end. Given the havoc this "restoration" inflicted, the idea that one should do nothing except prepare for socialism comes suspiciously close to consent to its barbarism.

However – and this is a very big however – recovery is not automatic. Even a cursory study shows that reversals from major crises are achieved by conscious and, indeed, brutal political intervention. The recovery of 1893 was the product of imperialism. It would have been inconceivable without it. The recovery of 1942 was the outcome of fascism, world war, and the twin, but opposed, world victories of the United States and the Communist Powers (Chart 6).

The postwar boom was launched neither by the New Deal nor the Great Depression, but by World War II. US unemployment never really got below 15 percent until 1940 – after which it sank to a little over 1 percent – and

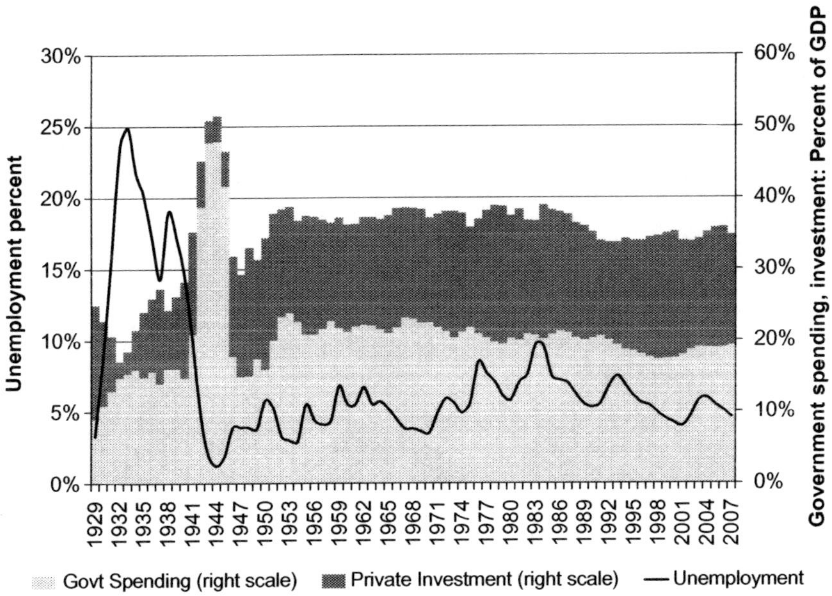

Chart 6. Unemployment, Investment and Government Spending in the US Economy 1929–2007. *Sources:* US Bureau of Economic Analysis NIPA tables; VanGiezen and Schwenk (2002).

never rose above 5 percent until the 1970s. Output growth rose by 1942 to an all-time high of 18 percent.

The background was a level of state involvement in the economy never since seen – reaching nearly half of GDP by 1943. The threat of communism spurred not only German and Japanese reconstruction but the Welfare State itself, while war completely reorganized the map of the world, breaking the colonial domination of the European powers and opening the world to US exports, whilst tooling up US productivity, reportedly, to three times that of Britain. The postwar boom was, in short, exogenous.

Any conception of "economic" law as purely mechanical is, hence, not merely theoretically misguided but directly contradicts the facts. Mainstream theory and Marxism are, I believe, looking through the telescope from the wrong end. The issue is neither "Will the crisis go on forever?" (it won't) nor "Will it end on its own?" (it won't) but "what ways out are there, and what is their price?"

6. PREDICTIVE AND RELATIONAL LAWS IN ECONOMIC THEORY

To answer to the questions just posed, we must return to theory. I begin by distinguishing between "relational" and "predictive" laws. These correspond approximately to the two main headings under which economics studies regularity, though I will attempt more precision in their definition.

Relational laws are usually termed "identities," of which the most famous is the national accounting identity $Y = C+G+I+(X-M)$. It is drummed into undergraduate macro students that this does not tell us whether society will invest, consume, import, or export. It simply asserts an arithmetic identity: the value created each year is equal to the total usages made of that value. Relational laws may be false, for example, Say's law, usually formulated as "supply creates its own demand." This shows a relational law is not void of content, nor even in the strict sense a tautology. If identities were tautological by nature, there could be no such thing as a false identity.

Predictive laws are sometimes discussed as behavioral laws and sometimes as laws of motion. In either case they are called on to calculate the future state of the economy. To many, forecasting is the true arcane business of economists, whose job is to tell us how much wealth and employment the economy will create, just as a weatherman is supposed to tell us when it will rain.

To most Marxists, Marx's "law of motion" is predictive: it tells us what will happen next. This is what I wish to challenge. To get at the problem, I will interrogate the notion of "automatic" recovery, beginning from the surprisingly modern subject of cycle theory. This little-known branch of mainstream thinking, integral to the way it neutralized the concept of crisis, has occasioned little Marxist critique.

Until really quite late in the nineteenth century, all interruptions to economic growth were perceived as a crisis – anomalous, threatening, and unexpected. Marx, in moving from *Grundrisse* to *Capital,* began speaking of the "industrial cycle" (Chapter 15, vol. 1, p. 283) where he had previously spoken only of "commercial crisis" or "money crisis." At the same time, the French Economist Clément Juglar (1862, 1915, see also Besomi, 2005) wrote what has since become, more or less, the definitive account of what is now called the business or trade cycle. Research culminated in the work of Wesley Mitchell (1927), founder of the NBER, and was marked by a wide-ranging interwar debate involving Hayek (1933), Keynes, and many Russian Marxists (Day, 1981) such as Maksakovsky (2004) whose work has only recently become known in the West.

Marx and Juglar are often credited with the contemporaneous "discovery" of the business cycle; yet their concepts of it diverge markedly. For Marx, the cycle, though regular, nevertheless manifests itself in crisis:

> The life of modern industry becomes a series of periods of moderate activity, prosperity, over-production, crisis and stagnation. The uncertainty and instability to which machinery subjects the employment, and consequently the conditions of existence, of the operatives become normal, owing to these periodic changes of the industrial cycle. Except in the periods of prosperity, there rages between the capitalists the most furious combat for the share of each in the markets. This share is directly proportional to the cheapness of the product. Besides the rivalry that this struggle begets in the application of improved machinery for replacing labour-power, and of new methods of production, there also comes a time in every industrial cycle, when a forcible reduction of wages beneath the value of labour-power, is attempted for the purpose of cheapening commodities. (Marx, *op. cit.*)

This cyclic movement is therefore an expression of a more intractable problem: capitalism undermines the conditions for its own existence. The overarching, primary cause is capitalism's persistent tendency, most clearly manifested in the falling profit rate, to accumulate without reproducing the social and economic conditions required for it to function as capital. This produces a series of more or less serious, and never entirely predictable, explosions. During this process, the conditions for supersession by a new state of society mature and accumulate, bursting out eventually in social and political convulsions – for which the working class must prepare by developing organizations capable of taking over society and transforming it.

From Juglar a rather different idea emerged: the cycle was a natural and even desirable feature of capitalism. An important adaptation of the rather implausible "laws of evolutionary motion" sought by the classical economists took place. "Clément Juglar's contribution on periodical crises is often credited with having marked the definite transition from the theories of crises to the theories of business cycles," writes Besomi (2005, p. 1) "The champion of this view is, as is well known, Schumpeter, who propagated it on several occasions."

Cycle theories became particularly attractive, above all in times of economic crisis, because crisis is empirically difficult to reconcile with the notion of unilateral progress. Evolutionary laws by their nature encounter crisis as an interruption. They assert a continued and unidirectional movement; for example the long-run trend of world population growth, or that capitalism indefinitely raises productivity. Yet any allegedly evolutionary law may be interrupted. The Black Death, it is generally accepted, set back European population growth by over a century. In a recession, output growth halts. Has the potter's hand then shaken?

Economists at least are not in the habit of reporting that any such law is untrue. They tend to say is that it has been interrupted, as one would say about gravity, when a falling object hits the ground. What excites their interest is, however, the reason for the interruption. If one is predisposed, not to say funded, to report that the capitalist economy is the highest state of nature, it is irksome when the glorious march of progress grinds to a halt. Economic thought, until the late 1870s, tended to regard its periodic crises as serious, mysterious, and threatening occurrences, portents of significant and unknown danger, much as early civilizations greeted comets and eclipses. As the economic journalists have discovered (although the academic economists are still thinking about it) large crises do not sit very well with fairytale theories of market perfection.

Two basic explanations can be offered. The most common is *exogenous interference*: something was "done to" the economy – bad banking, Napoleon, greedy workers, communists, state interference, 9/11 – the list has not stopped growing. But the recessions of the industrial cycle are repeated and somewhat frequent, and have gone on throughout history. Excuses based on external interference wear thin. Cycle theory provides a get-out, not dissimilar to some Christian explanations of evil: imperfection is the means to perfection. The cycle is a "natural" manifestation of capitalism which cleans out inefficiencies and restores balance. Provided we do not enquire too deeply how a perfect system produced these inefficiencies in the first place, the notion of natural order can be restored. Schumpeter commends Marx for discovering the underlying cyclical process:

> He [Marx] aptly says that "the superficiality of Political Economy shows itself in the fact that it looks upon expansion and contraction of credit, which is a mere symptom of the periodic changes of the industrial cycle, as their cause." ... We find practically all the elements that ever entered into any serious analysis of business cycles, and on the whole very little error. Moreover, it must not be forgotten that the mere perception of the existence of cyclical movements was a great achievement of the time. Many economists who went before him had an inkling of it. In the main, however, they focussed their attention on the spectacular breakdowns that came to be referred to as "crises." *And these crises they failed to see in their true light, that is today, in the light of the cyclical processes of which they are mere incidents.* (Schumpeter, 1965, p. 41, emphasis added)

Schumpeter grasped that if crisis is a phase in a regular movement, it can be repackaged as a reversal. Damage has occurred: hardship and discontent ensure. Society asks "how can this damage be undone?" Cycle theory allows the economist to claim that "natural" market processes will correct the collateral damage inflicted by these same market processes. The best policy is then to do nothing, or merely "work with" the forces that produced the crisis in the first place. Such ideas lie behind the bankers' consensus that informed poststimulus European responses to the crash. Yes, markets caused the problem. What is the answer? More markets. The arsonists have taken over the fire station.

Economic theory thus came to resemble a man who jumps off a cliff supposing he can fly and, on finding that he cannot, concludes that it does not matter because he will bounce. Cycle theory in this sense incarnates a quietist exhaustion of the progressive potential of liberal theory; it asks only how society may return to where it was, and ceases to consider the opportunity for, or even the necessity of, doing anything new. The insatiable quest for security extinguishes all critical capacity.

This culminated in Schumpeter's popularization of Kondratieff's theories of "Long Waves." His aim was to address the biggest problem facing simple Juglarian theories of the cycle: namely the convulsive and protracted crises described in the last section, which cannot be explained as a short-term periodic bounce. Schumpeter was one of the few mainstream figures to take this problem seriously, which is probably why, though few economists explicitly endorse his ideas, many quietly defer to them. He adapted Kondratieff's statistical discovery that long periods of rising prices alternate with long periods of falling prices, constructing a highly original if ultimately apologetic theory. Crisis, for Schumpeter, becomes an expression of regularity. Past economists, he says above "failed to see [crises] in their true light, that is today, in the light of the cyclical processes *of which they are merely incidents*." Crisis is back in Pandora's box as a "natural" law – a repetitive, and above all automatic process, requiring only a little bit of creative destruction before normal service is resumed.

This manifests itself in the disputed concept of *endogenous* recovery of which Schumpeter's theory of Creative Destruction is the progenitor. The market itself establishes the conditions, after a long period of decline, for a long period of growth – a long boom. Thus, Schumpeter acknowledges (without much analysis, it is often said) endogenous causes of decline, suggesting that capitalism does have some serious problems – but counters by asserting that capitalism *itself* can solve these problems, if left to its own devices, that is, endogenously.

7. DETERMINISM AND ENDOGENOUS RECOVERY WITHIN THE MARXIST TRADITION

To what extent does Marxism distinguish itself from this view? Not far below the surface lurks the idea of *natural restoration*. It is almost commonplace in Marxist theory to assert that the role of crisis is the "restoration" of the profit rate. The notion is as follows: capital stock rises during normal accumulation, and must then be reduced. In crisis; this is achieved by simply not producing. The crisis thus "automatically" restores the profit rate.

I have two problems with this idea. First, it is deeply fatalistic. Marxists, according to this notion, need do nothing except proselytize and wait. Second, it is empirically untrue. The great crises did *not* automatically restore the profit rate, even when – as in the case of the New Deal – they were accompanied by considerable government intervention. It took more.

A different, but classical, Marxist approach was introduced by Leon Trotsky in the course (Day, 1981) of the seminal Russian crisis debates of the interwar years:

> One can reject in advance the attempts by Professor Kontrad'ev to assign to the epochs that he calls long cycles the same 'strict rhythm' that is observed in short cycles. This attempt is a clearly mistaken generalisation based on a formal analogy. The periodicity of short cycles is conditioned by the internal dynamic of capitalist forces, which manifests itself whenever and wherever there is a market. As for these long (fifty-year) intervals that Professor Kontrad'ev hastily proposes also to call cycles, their character and duration is determined not by the internal play of capitalist forces, but by the external conditions in which capitalist development occurs. The absorption by capitalism of new countries and continents, the discovery of new natural resources, and, in addition, significant factors of a "superstructural" order, such as wars and revolutions, determine the character and alteration of expansive, stagnating, or declining epochs in capitalist development. (Trotsky, 1923, p. 9, cited in Day, 1981, p. 8)

Trotsky does not dispute that boom and declines alternate. He asks "in what circumstances are they reversed?" The difference between the two concepts is further clarified if we interrogate the word "recovery" itself. This suggests that boom is in some sense the natural state of capitalism, which it achieves with little conscious effort by just being the capitalist system, whereas the declines are an unfortunate interruption. This idea is prevalent among Marxists, giving rise to a phenomenon I term "Capital Worship" – a belief in the almost unlimited power of capitalist productivity to advance and improve without impediment. In this mindset, booms are achieved automatically with no special effort or political intervention. This view was most strongly asserted in Brenner's (1977) famous debate with the dependency school:

> To take the view that development and underdevelopment are *directly* dependent upon, caused by, one another, Wallerstein resorts to the position that both development in the core and underdevelopment in the periphery are essentially the result of a process of transfer of surplus from periphery to core. He must thus end up by essentially ignoring any *inherent tendency* of capitalism to develop the productive forces through the accumulation of capital. (Brenner, 1977, pp. 60–61; see also Gunder Frank, 1978; Emmanuel, 1972; Palloix, 1970)

Capitalism's inherent tendencies to develop productive forces were never really in dispute. However, what sets them going? Persuasive evidence from Bagchi (1982) and Patnaik (2006) shows that the extended and continual application of political force accompanied, and facilitated, an immense mobilization of superprofits from around the world on which accumulation then, as now, depended. Marx studied this particular boom at some length, and his opinion contrasts with Brenner's:

> [The] [c]olonial system, public debts, heavy taxes, protection, commercial wars, &c., these *children of the true manufacturing period, increase gigantically during the infancy of Modern Industry* ... Whilst the cotton industry introduced child-slavery in England, it gave in the United States a stimulus to the transformation of the earlier, more or less patriarchal slavery, into a system of commercial exploitation. *In fact, the veiled slavery of the wage-workers in Europe needed, for its pedestal, slavery pure and simple in the new world.* (*Capital*, Vol. 31, p. 915, emphasis added)

Real booms – prolonged periods of expansion – are rare, not at all a natural state of capitalist affairs. The present decline, on Brenner's (1998) own recent testimony, has been under way for over 40 years, much longer than any known boom. Much closer to reality than the theory of long waves would be a theory of long declines. Capitalist history makes a lot more sense, if we think of booms as politically launched events that punctuate an inherently problematic process of development, instead of the natural form of its existence.

All major booms followed a concentration of great amounts of value in one or two geographical locations, achieved by the forceful political mobilization of resources, value, and hence labour throughout the world. This is achieved in part through the market itself, which both reproduces and extends existing inequalities (Freeman, 2009b) but depends critically on direct political intervention by the powers which function as geographical centers of each new phase of accelerated growth. If the US economy does not need its armed forces, what are they there for? Why did the postwar boom start in the war? If the industrial revolution had no need of Britain's colonial enterprises, what were the King's troops and merchants doing abroad and why was it so difficult to dislodge them? If the "inherent tendencies" of Germany's industrialists were solely responsible for its spectacular rise, what was the function of Prussian Junkerdom, the "National Economy," the arms race, World War I, and fascism?

If Trotsky is right, periodic and often forceful political action is integral to accumulation. A concept of economic law which comprehends this is absent from nearly all modern economic thinking. Almost the only place we find it is in Keynes's writings, not uninterestingly because of his focus on policy. Yet a concept of 'law' which synthesises the blind laws of the commodity form with the conscious, laws of explicit class, state, and national action, is explicit in, and integral to, Marx's own thinking.

8. WAS MARX A DETERMINIST?

Marx's most famous allegedly "determinist" remark appears in the preface to the first German edition of *Capital*, where he writes

> Intrinsically, it is not a question of the higher or lower degree of development of the social antagonisms that result from the natural laws of capitalist production. It is a question of these laws themselves, of these tendencies working with iron necessity towards inevitable results. The country that is more developed industrially only shows, to the less developed, the image of its own future.

However his discussions with the Russian Marxists exposed a far more nuanced approach, as evidenced by his correspondence with Vera Zasulich (Shanin, 1984):

> In dealing with the genesis of capitalist production I stated that it is founded on "the complete separation of the producer from the means of production" ... I thus expressly limited the "historical inevitability" of this process to the countries of Western Europe. And why? Be so kind as to compare Chapter XXXII, where it says:
>
> The "process of elimination transforming individualised and scattered means of production into socially concentrated means of production, of the pigmy property of the many into the huge property of the few, this painful and fearful expropriation of the working people, forms the origin, the genesis of capital ... Private property, based on personal labour ... will be supplanted by capitalist private property, based on the exploitation of the labour of others, on wage labour". (p. 341, column II)
>
> Thus, in the final analysis, it is a question of the transformation of one form of private property into another form of private property. Since the land in the hands of the Russian peasants has never been their private property, how could this development be applicable?

In a draft of this letter he states that if Russia continues along the capitalist road "it will lose the finest chance ever offered by history to a people and undergo all the fateful vicissitudes of the capitalist regime." Losing a chance is a long way from a fatalistic recognition of inevitable necessity.

This restatement was not casual. Marx's prolonged battle with Lassalle over the direction of the German Social Democrats centered on the latter's "iron law" of wages:

> The restriction of the average wage to the minimum that a people customarily requires, to reproduce and eke out a living is, I repeat, the iron and cruel law which governs the wages under present conditions.
>
> This law may be disputed by no one ... This iron and cruel law, gentlemen, you must above all stamp deep, deep in your soul and all your thinking must start from this point.
>
> In these circumstances I can give you and the whole working class an infallible method, which will free you of illusions and deceptions. To anyone who speaks to you about improving the condition of the working class, you must first and foremost submit the following question: does he, or does he not, recognise this law. (Lassalle, 1863 [my translation – AF])

Marx remained indignantly opposed to Lassalle on this precise point throughout his life, referring to him amongst his circle as "the iron man." Engels wrote of this to Bebel thus (March, 18–28, 1875):

> our people have allowed themselves to be saddled with the Lassallean "iron law of wages" ... in *Capital* Marx has amply demonstrated that the laws governing wages are very complex, that, according to circumstances, now this law, now that, holds sway, that they are therefore by no means iron but are, on the contrary, exceedingly elastic, and that the subject really cannot be dismissed in a few words, as Lassalle imagined.

Marx's conception of social change was never fatalistic nor mechanical, being posed in terms of complexities, indeterminacies, historical branch points and above all choices, in which the outcome was determined by the actions of the participants. What is the economic foundation of this historical, political, and ethical vision? We noted in Freeman (2010) that in the "cultural turn" a significant section of Marxism Without Marx, led by the Frankfurt School, abandoned interest in Marx's economic theories. Retreating into the cultural, social, and ethical dimensions of his analysis, they lost sight of the fact that in capitalist society, all such relations are organized by the commodity – the "cell form" of the economy. It makes nonsense of Marx's endeavor to divorce these two aspects of his analysis. It also makes no sense to suppose that he grounded an emancipatory, choice-centered theory of history on a deterministic, positivist analysis of the economy.

9. POSITIVISM, RATIONALISM, AND THE ORIGINS OF MODERN DETERMINISM

Where did we get the idea that economist's "job" is to predict, to calculate the economy's future position like an alien external object, as astronomers forecast eclipses? As indicated, the answer lies in the early history of French rationalism. Philosophy struggled to free itself from the religious dogmas permeating the corrupt, intertwined layers of petty aristocracy and venal clergy, buttressed by, and maintaining in power, the decadent absolutist monarchy which was to provoke the Mother of Revolutions – 1789. The emerging enlightenment sought an alternative morality grounded in the human condition. Catholicism, for which Galileo's ideas remained as much an anathema as Darwin's were to become for Protestantism, deduced the necessity, duties, and rights of the social order, true to its neoplatonic roots, from the perfection of the heavens, whilst the doctrine of the divine right of kings, established by the "Sun King" Louis XIV, excused him all restraints of law. In absolutist France, revolutionary philosophy had to ground itself in *physics*, in mechanics. The simple fact that heavenly movements were ordained by nature was a mortal danger to the monarchy's pretensions. If reason regulated the universe, should it not govern society?

The most characteristic formulation of this mathematical determinism comes from the great mathematician and astronomer Pierre-Simon Laplace (1951 [1820], p. 4), arguably the true father of mathematical positivism. Laplace, it should be recalled, when asked by Napoleon what place God occupied in his system, famously replied "I had no need of this hypothesis." He formulated the "billiard-ball determinist" principle that, once the initial position and momentum of every particle in the universe was given, all its subsequent motion was completely determined by their laws of motion. Since "every particle" includes the atoms that make up our bodies, this includes our own actions:

> An intellect which at a certain moment would know all forces that set nature in motion, and all positions of all items of which nature is composed, if this intellect were also vast enough to submit these data to analysis, it would embrace in a single formula the movements of the greatest bodies of the universe and those of the tiniest atom; for such an intellect nothing would be uncertain and the future just like the past would be present before its eyes.

Laplace was deeply involved in social questions, providing early inspiration to the Comte's generation of moral reformers (Laplace, 1951 [1820], 1836). This paragraph, however, establishes the critical weakness of his argument. Who is this "intellect"? Is He the same as Comte's "external power"? Does He hold court on some distant frozen planet? Does He read his e-mails? His reluctance to intervene is commendable, but has He fully considered the advantages of endowing a few large prizes?

The "external power" does not exist – any more than the God he was supposed to replace. The positivist formulation erects "natural law" into a governing principle of the ruling order every bit as tyrannical as the old absolutist monarchy, with the disconcerting difficulty that, owing to the ruling power's unfortunate incorporeality, His head cannot be cut off. The construction is also intellectually holed below the waterline, though this was not really understood until quantum physics forced the natural sciences to recognize that an experiment's observer cannot actually stand outside the experiment that there can be no such thing as an "external power" in a universe that by definition includes everything.

Laplace's all-encompassing determinism collapses once we ask: *which intellect*? If this intellect were human or indeed, material, it must itself be subject to the laws it is supposed merely to describe. But in that case, it cannot be a conscious intellect in any meaningful sense, since it would be deprived of any capacity to decide on its own actions. But if it is not human – or, in more general terms, if it is not part of the universe of materially determined consciousness – it cannot exist. It is as otherworldly as the eternal "good" (Lovejoy, 1990) of the Neoplatonists. The entire project of constructing a theory of the universe which contains conscious beings, from which conscious action is excluded as a causal factor, is self-contradictory. It is on this contradiction that physics was to shipwreck early in the twentieth century. By a supreme irony, Laplacian positivism lives on only in the social sciences and in fact almost exclusively in economics. Why?

It is not difficult to understand why positivism appealed to the property-owning classes. Catholic support for the landowning classes was an irritant to the rising revolutionary bourgeoisie of the eighteenth century, driving it to seek materialist theories of the cosmos. With the rise of mass labour organizations, and the onset of purely capitalist crises, further dangers surfaced. Darwinism began pushing back the boundaries of faith beyond what was comfortable even for a resolutely nonconformist populace. The most thoughtful section of the working class movement was resolutely atheistic, anticlericalism becoming the hallmark of its revolutionary wing.

Even merely protestant logic, in millenarian forms, could be appropriated by the working class as easily as by any god-fearing protestant industrialist. The notion that "divine justice," administered by revolutionary propertyless classes, implied an end to property and the installation of a collectivist order, was the inspiration for numerous European revolts dating back to the Levellers, the Hussites and indeed, the millenarian tradition (Cohn, 1970) in general. A late nineteenth century rise in fundamentalist movements, often among the very poorest sections of society, placed further strains on traditional alliances between religion and power.

The centre of gravity of capitalist ideology shifted onto the new terrain of natural order. Social Darwinism – the survival of the fittest applied to human society – gained ground. Evolution furnished a useful rationalization of imperialism's "civilizing mission," with primitive peoples presented as closer to apes than humans, justifying all and every act of barbarism against them (Carpentier, 2001). The notion that the capitalist economy *itself* was a creation of nature became more and more attractive, the more the market extended, the globe fell under its sway, and the more striking – in the West – its achievements became. "Positive economics" consummated the urge to free the market from the pernicious influence of ethics, by presenting it as the ultimate in ethics. Theorems of optimality such as Pareto's, and the convivial marriage of marginalism with utilitarianism, provided a new answer to all ethical questions: there is no need to ask whether a given policy is bad or good because the market *itself* is good; nothing better exists. And why does nothing else exist? Because nothing else is *possible*. The market, in and of itself, requires no further justification. It is the natural order of things.

10. WHY DID MARXISM BECOME POSITIVIST?

Positivism's attraction to the bourgeoisie is understandable. But what was its appeal to the working class? A simplistic Laplacian determinism was extremely influential within the Marxism of the late nineteenth and early twentieth century. More work is needed to understand how this came to be, but it had reasonably clear material roots. For workers laboring under great privation, often suffering heavy losses, it was a source of almost religious solace, with a close affinity to Millenarianism, to think of themselves as taking part in some inevitable working out of history, humbling mighty despots and raising up the downtrodden. Progress, the

Second International's Marxism proclaimed, was *inevitable*. The working class was the instrument of its destiny.

Lassalle's "iron and cruel law" offers a further clue. As Marx ironically notes in his *Critique of the Gotha Programme*, what Lassalle actually deduces from this law is the role of the state. If capitalism can only drive down wages, the state must act to keep them up. In elucidating his own very different conception of the state, Marx sourly notes that Lassalle conveniently omits the trade unions along with all vehicles of working class action except the German Social Democratic Party. Beneath the Second International's mechanical materialism lurked the underpinnings of class compromises that heralded its subsequent decline: the idea of a passive and compliant people surrendering to necessity, entrusting their future to a powerful and wise state machine,[4] where its unruly elements could be exclusively represented by sagacious leaders. Lassalle indeed entered a pact with Bismarck, supporting the annexation of Schleswig-Holstein in return for universal suffrage (Marx to Kugelman February 23, 1865; see Riazanov, 1928). The notion of a different type of state based on a different type of economy, the outcome of the conscious choices of an active working class, slipped away.

The language of inevitability, of the necessity of progress, and crucially of the "external" nature of social laws, was taken over almost unmodified into Soviet orthodoxy (Labica, 1984), notwithstanding its revolutionary origins. The conception of a "state safe for capital" took the form of a promise that the regime would not pursue revolutionary ambitious beyond its frontiers, becoming a fixed feature of soviet policy after 1936. The notion of "progress" became identified with the soviet state itself, projected as the incarnation of the next stage of historical progress. This took powerful hold on the minds of a generation locked in battle against fascism. The struggle for progress took on a concrete national form, the Manichean gods of good and evil personified in the heads of state of the two greatest powers in the conflict.

It is easy to pass judgment. One should not forget that all this was very much the spirit of the age, the *Zeitgeist* of all classes. It was the *Leitmotif* of twentieth century US culture portraying America, just like the USSR, as the incarnation of human destiny, the pinnacle of progress to which others could but dream to aspire. Indeed this idea is all too evident in much American Marxism, which in accepting and even promoting the myth of their own country as the "highest form" of social progress, often does little more than place a Marxist veneer over its civilizing mission.

When we, comfortably distant from events, weigh up the intellectual deficiencies of this idea against the sacrifices of a generation to which we owe freedom from fascism, we should refrain from finding too much fault. It is an entirely different matter when the spiritual energy of a dead generation is prostituted to the intellectual pretensions of a live one. Following the prolonged defeats that culminated in the collapse of the USSR and the disintegration of the mass Western and Soviet communist parties, the theoretical heritage of Marxism fell into the near-exclusive possession of academia. The mantle of deterministic positivism settled comfortably on the shoulders of a social caste freed of accountability to, or responsibilities for, the great mass of those on whose behalf they claimed to speak. It put them, effectively, in the position of a priesthood – of securing a living – as experts in, and interpreters of, the inevitable but impenetrable laws of the economy. We now turn to this ideological evolution and its consequences.

11. GENERAL EQUILIBRIUM MARXISM: A POSITIVIST SUBSTITUTION

Freeman (2010) and Kliman (2010b) argued that Marxism, as we today find it, no longer bears any serious relation to Marx's economic theory. Marxism Without Marx adopted a substitute, originated by Austrian economist Ladislaw von Bortkiewicz (1952), in which Marx's theory of value is presented as a variant of general equilibrium. I now explore the tight theoretical relation between this interpretation and the positivist notion of economics as prediction, before showing how a temporalist interpretation leads in a very different direction.

The academic presentation of Marx as a general equilibrium theorist begins with Sweezy (1968, p. 53) who writes, in a formulation virtually unchallenged by Marxists since then, that

> The law of value is essentially a theory of general equilibrium developed in the first instance with reference to simple commodity production.

Morishima (1973, p. 2) openly celebrates Marx as a founder of equilibrium theory, on hermeneutic grounds at which we can only marvel:

> Marx's theory of reproduction and Walras's theory of capital accumulation should be honoured together as the parents of the modern, dynamic theory of general equilibrium.

This is the universally adopted assumption of modern Marxist academic economics and the principal cause of Marxism's present paralysis. This is clarified by the specific role of equilibrium – which now dominates and overshadows almost the whole of mainstream economics and many of its heterodoxies – in the theory of crisis, making it *par excellence* the ideological expression of capitalism triumphant. General equilibrium theories, whether marginalist, physicalist, or even ISLM "Keynesian," have a property which makes them extremely attractive from an apologetic point if view: they *logically* exclude endogenous crisis. Breakdown arising from the market's internal laws of motion cannot be deduced from an equilibrium theory (Freeman, 2003, 2007).

The reason is not difficult to understand. The premise of equilibrium is that the market will reproduce itself without change. The equilibrium theorist writes down a number of "simultaneous" equations and solves them, to "predict" prices and quantities produced and sold, given only some externally given magnitudes – consumer preferences in marginalist economics, production functions in Sraffa (1962), propensity to consume, and liquidity preference in ISLM Keynesianism.

But because the equilibrium theorist assumes from the outset that the market reproduces perfectly, nothing within this market can cause any of these variables to change between one period and another. There is no reason for any price to rise or fall, or for anyone to consume or produce more or less. Such a system *must* continue in the same state without change except and unless an external change disturbs it. What happens after a disturbance? Does the disturbance not contradict the initial assumption? The equilibrium answer, termed "comparative statics," is to suppose the market moves from one perfect state to another. It adjusts from the equilibrium state uniquely determined by the old conditions, to a new state uniquely determined by the new conditions. The theory does not deny that in theory the economy is, for a time, in an "imperfect" state corresponding to neither set of external conditions. It however holds that such disturbances or "adjustments" can be discounted. The economy can be analyzed *as if* it consisted of a sequence of perfect states, none of which diverges from market perfection. Any "law of motion" is then entirely governed by exogenous variables. In no case can anything from within the market itself affect its motion. If any forces do arise from its process of "adjustment," the theory discounts them. Indeed this is why the variables considered by any such theory are partitioned into two categories, explicitly named "endogenous" and "exogenous."

General equilibrium is hence a mathematically pure presentation of the positivist view of a capitalist economy, whose trajectory is given entirely, with no additional determinations, by the exogenous variables. The predictions that arise are 100 percent determinate. They eliminate not just crisis, but humans. Walras' players are so constrained that they have no means of actually reaching the prices his system decrees for them, leading him to invoke the mysterious "auctioneer" – a figure remarkably similar to Laplace's "external power" – to get them there. The determinacy of general equilibrium is a primal requirement, and its absence in temporal interpretations of Marx engenders a near pathological fear. Thus Mongiovi (2002, p. 22)

> Temporal Single System models avoid the appearance of inconsistency by introducing so many degrees of freedom that Marx's invariance postulates cannot possibly be violated: the models are so open-ended that they explain nothing at all.

For Mongiovi, as for "long-run" economic theory on whose behalf he speaks, the "problem" is to secure a fully determinate prediction of the relation between prices, profits, wages, and value. Actually, this is impossible. Prices, profits, and wages must be indeterminate in any realistic theory because the real world is itself indeterminate. The intrusive degrees of freedom of which Mongiovi complains are known as "people." It is only *because* temporal formulations of Marx's theory are open-ended that they can explain anything other than some hypothetical mathematical world masquerading as a society.

This makes the copious body of work on a "statistically determinate" correlation between values and prices (Ochoa, 1984; Shaikh, 1998; Cockshott & Cottrell, 1998, 2005; Tsoulfidis & Maniatis, 2002), apart from its statistical flaws (Kliman, 2002, 2005; Freeman, 1998) particularly misconceived. The most interesting things in a capitalist economy occur not when prices are close to values but when they are distant. The driving force of productivity is the *excess profit* which a new invention yields, for the whole period in which it coexists with old and less productive techniques. In contrast, the driving forces of financialization are profits with no remaining connection to underlying values. Not least, imperialism is driven by the North's self-reinforcing monopoly of productive advantage, by gerrymandered commerce, and by plain robbery, its mobilization of resource rents showing up in world oil prices surpassing values by factors approaching 30. *Superprofits* are described by Marx in many places as the actual driver of capitalist motion. Every divergences of price from value expresses a social relation, laying bare the source of the political power of the banker, the oil major, and the imperialist. The purpose of an "economic law" is to identify and account for these social relations, which, actually, run our world.

An enterprise dedicated to proving them statistically insignificant merits a special Marxist place in the circle outside hell which Dante reserved for the Futile.

A more thoughtful observation comes from Foley (1997), who objects to the temporal formulation of Marx's theory as follows:

> Accounting identities ... cannot by themselves constitute a predictive or explanatory theory, so that Freeman's discussion is inevitably only the first step toward the development of the type of theory he calls for.

The striking point of this criticism is the very fact that "prediction" and "explanation" appear, for Foley, to be synonyms. His criticism would be legitimate, if this were so. But for a temporalist, an "explanation" means something that lays bare the relations, concealed within the commodity form, between real, human, social magnitudes such as labor, culture, care, love, or spiritual being, and the alienated, fetishized, dead symbols we call "money" on the other. It is thus the very opposite of a prediction.

What did Marx think? A growing body of TSSI research (Freeman & Carchedi, 1995; Kliman, 2007; Potts, 2009) has established that his theory was *temporalist* or as sometimes designated, *successivist*. The issue of determinism begins at this precise point. Within a successivist derivation, values at any given time depend on values at some previous time, and the labor performed since then. Prices are not "determined" at all. They simply exist: they are *data*. This is why the "transformation problem" does not really exist. It arises from the positivist notion that Marx's value theory "determines" prices and "determines" values, in the sense of predicting what they must be. The temporalist to the contrary seeks to establish the concealed relation between values, given by labor time, and prices, given by the real world, thus revealing what the prices actually consist of. The temporalist does not seek to predict what prices must be. She seeks to reveal what their actual magnitudes tell us.

Most of the "laws" we find in Marx's work are clearly relational. The law of value itself states that the amount of value produced by any capital – and by society as a whole – is equal to the time of labor it employs. It thus relates the two central categories of price and labor. The second such law connects source of income to property; workers, who sell only their own labor, receive wages; capitalists, who employ this labor, receive the rest. This expresses two social relations constitutive of capitalism – both value, and profit, are created by, and only by, the labour of workers hired by capitalists to produce commodities for those same capitalists to sell.

Note that relational laws are *exact*. A modern confusion identifies positivism with exactness, and the positivists own identification of exactness with prediction blinds them to the exactness of relational laws. This exactness must hold, because such laws express *qualitative* relations of identity: for example, that price is a *form* of value. The statement "only labour can create value" could not hold if any such relation was in error by even 0.0001 percent. There would then be a source of value other than labour.

Therein lies the importance of the transformation of values into prices, which is not a prediction at all, further underlining the futility of "proving it empirically." Moreover, it is false if it is not exact, so that it confirms nothing to show it is "97 percent true." It demonstrates that the social and class relations established under the simplifying assumption that goods sell at their value,[5] are not modified when this simplification is relaxed.

The notion that "mere identities" are devoid of content is seriously misinformed. Almost all physical laws are relational. As soon as astronomy got beyond Copernicus, it could no longer simply forecast planetary movements but had to asked why they happened. Newton's laws of motion are all relational. The best-known relational law in physics, Einstein's famous $e = mc^2$, gave us nuclear weapons. It would take a bold economist to claim it added nothing to knowledge. It is a relation between two forms of appearance – matter and energy – of the same thing, showing that two phenomena which appear distinct are actually related. This offers a more than superficial parallel to Marx's theory of value, whose power lies precisely the relations it establishes between quantities of labour and magnitudes of money.

These magnitudes become crucial precisely when we need to exercise collective choice, changing the social relations they express. Economists have so far only predicted the future in various ways. The point is to make it. Because we live in a commodity economy, many magnitudes present themselves as "purely" economic. Universal health requires hospitals, doctors, drugs, not to mention health education. At first sight this is a money question – the "cost" of the system. But, actually, it is a labour question: the time spent by the builders, doctors, nurses, medicine-makers, educators, and indeed, patients. How may the most desirable use of social labour time be ascertained? The result could be achieved by various means: free agreement, state direction, or some hitherto-unknown system of servitude. The point is this: whatever solution is contemplated, the changes really required will remain mysterious until money is understood to be a symbolic representative of labour.

We get a glimpse of this underlying reality when it is revealed, for example, that 12 percent of all UK pensions are financed by the oil revenues of one single company. Why did we have to wait until the Gulf of Mexico got poisoned to find that out? A liberatory political economy would make all such relations transparent at all times and in all spheres of society. Society can then choose whether it wishes to tie the future of its elderly to the destruction of the flora and fauna of a large part of the Ocean, or to some more healthy and commendable activity.

12. THE RATE OF PROFIT: A TEMPORAL RELATIONAL LAW

In the light of the above, what is the function of the law for which Marx is perhaps most famous, and which is almost universally viewed – whether to proclaim or dismiss it – as a predictive law of economic motion – the "law of the tendential fall of the profit rate?" In this final section, I will argue that it should be understood as a *temporal relational law*. It has, however, the peculiar characteristic that when the commodity relation is functioning, as during booms, its form of appearance is blind, automatic, and therefore, has predictive power. Its automatism arises precisely because the measures required to overcome it are abnormal to capitalism; it is, therefore, in a profound sense, a law *of* capitalism – it holds sway as long as capitalism functions as such.

First, what does Marx's own derivation establish? He occasionally employs the emphatic language of inevitability. However, his many careful qualifications make it clear that something quite different is intended. What is required in all such cases is to examine the logic of the argument, as expressed by its author. What does Marx's reasoning achieve, in its own terms? It demonstrates that the rate of profit will continue to fall for as long as accumulation continues. Again we must note that this differs from such vaguenesses as "it sometimes rises and sometimes falls." It is an *exact* statement; its exactness may be appreciated only when its *qualitative* nature is grasped. The law, Marx says, is "the expression, peculiar to the capitalist mode of production, of the progressive development of the productivity of labour" (Marx, 1991, p. 319). That is, "crisis is the result of accumulation."

We can turn this statement around. The rate of profit will be restored if, and only if, accumulation *goes into reverse*. Stated this way, its superiority becomes clear. For orthodoxy, crisis is overcome naturally, as part of the functioning of capitalism. For Marx, it is overcome only if capitalism ceases to function naturally. Disaccumulation – the destruction of previously advanced value – is an enormously disruptive process. It can be achieved, theoretically, in one of two ways; if a long depression deprives large numbers of people (including many capitalists) of their living, or if the state, which produces use-value without producing value, steps in and replaces the private investor, as in war or developmental states.

The law establishes two political and social facts. Accumulation undermines the circumstances which enable people to take part in it; and the consequence is large-scale social and political disruption. The law of the tendency of the rate of profit to fall is, in short, an explanation of crisis. Yet such an interpretation demonstrates where Marx stands in relation to many one-sided, partial, or monocausal theories of crisis. An account based on the TRPF is not *counterposed* to any particular explanation of capitalist crisis (underconsumption, overproduction, overaccumulation, social structures of accumulation, financialization, etc.). Each is a particular expression of the general law, and occurs to some degree in every real crisis. Marx (1991, p. 350) saw no contradiction in the almost casual assertion that the fall "promotes overproduction, speculation and crises, and leads to the existence of excess capital alongside a surplus population", bringing together most monocausal explanations in one short bracketed subclause as mere expressions of the general law.

The real issues arise when one asks what can be done. Like the clown's car, no "solution" to crisis may be arrived at by addressing only one, or a few, or even all of these tendencies. Before launching a boom, capitalism has to stop accumulating, which is to say in some very basic sense, it has to stop being capitalism as we know it. Needless complexity, arising from the peculiarities of a theory Marx never held, have obscured the simplicity of Marx's reasoning. In the alien interpretation foisted upon him, "value" is identified not with labour but with physical products. Capital is seen as a mass of objects: machines, food, raw materials, and so on. When Marx presents his own law in terms of quantities of labour, the logic is clear:

> it is a self-evident necessity, deriving from the nature of the capitalist mode of production, that as it advances the general average rate of surplus-value must be expressed in a falling general rate of profit. Since the mass of *living labour* applied continuously declines in relation to the *mass of objectified labour* that it sets in motion, i.e., the productively consumed means of production, the *part of this living labour that is* unpaid and objectified in surplus-value must also stand in an ever-decreasing ratio to the

> *value of by the total capital applied.* But this ratio between the mass of surplus-value to the value and the total capital applied in fact constitutes the rate of profit, which must therefore steadily fall. (Marx, 1991, p. 319, emphasis added)

This is every bit as relational as the transformation of values into prices; the only difference is that the relations exist in time. Each year, a certain amount of value is produced, equal to the total expended labour of that year. Each year a certain amount is consumed by workers. Each year, a certain further amount is unproductively consumed. What remains is invested. Time arises because the value cannot be invested before it is produced.

Time then enters in a second way: this investment grows as long as, each year, a part of the produced value is added to the advanced capital of society. Literally and almost by definition, the mass of advanced capital will rise until and unless this stops.

The confusion of the equilibrium, physicalist presentations arises because they suppose that this past advanced value can be "wiped out" by technical change. This is not so. It occurred in the past, before the technical change, and cannot be wiped off the balance sheets of the capitalists who spent the money. Nor can this value be destroyed in mere circulation. This is why the crisis is protracted. The initial, financial crisis simply brings prices into line with underlying values. Fictitious assets, based on the capitalization of income streams, fall towards the underlying value of the assets – in some cases, zero.

This is not enough, which is why "financialization" is an insufficient account of the process. Even such a dramatic adjustment does not eliminate underlying past values. The destruction of *value* requires much more; it calls for the transfer of the accumulated value back into society, by "disaccumulation" in which capitalists use up what they have stockpiled, either by wasting it or by converting it into new products without replacing it. In short, to restore the rate of profit, net private investment must sink below zero. But capitalism's *raison d'être* is to invest. That's how it reproduces. When the private investor leaves the field, society can no longer reproduce, rapidly descending into political crisis.

So why cannot this impasse be overcome tomorrow? The obstacles are not economic but political. The investing class may withdraw from the economy, but not from society. Any measures to relieve the billions falling under the hammer of the crisis, or place their destinies in their own hands, attacks wealthy people who resist, but cannot restore. An effective programme is little more than a statement of how this resistance may be overcome.

In pure economic terms, remedies are not hard to find.[6] The Third Depression has a unique feature: with an average real GDP of $6,000, equal to that of a US citizen of the 1950s, the world can for the first time produces enough for everyone. The *only* limit on using it wisely is social. Any reasonably rich country can secure a decent future and a prosperous and equal citizenry by suspending all dividend payments, compelling its bankers to cease dealing in speculation and commit to a long programme of productive investment, by winding up all overseas armed activities, and by making arrangements for large programmes of investment in education, information, culture, infrastructure, and a sustainable way of life, all financed by large taxes reducing personal wealth to the minimum required for a comfortable lifestyle for immediate family. The rapid growth of China and India shows moreover that contagion from the rich countries' failure to undertake these measures can be corralled and limited and directed to the benefit of various classes within the nations, as the national polity determines by a sufficiently energetic developmental state.

These calculations are a no-brainer. The real problem is the present class balance of material interests above all in the rich countries. The problem is, hence, to enable those who choose so to do, irreversibly to alter this balance. The corresponding theoretical problem is to translate between quantities of money and classes of people so as to reveal the likely political consequences of the measures proposed – be they universal rights, an associative economy tomorrow, or just plain higher taxes and more spending. The point is this: but such laws are not those the positivist economics is accustomed to. Such laws will not say how long the crisis will last or how deep it will go. They will tell us what we must do, in order to shorten it and above all, exit from it without the social costs of the previous such crisis. The bottom line is this: social justice, organized through economic democracy, is the only lasting way for humanity finally to free itself from crises which, for the first time in history, are entirely of its own making. This, the true road to freedom, is what Marx, I am fully convinced, really intended.

NOTES

1. The UK coalition government, in its June 2010 budget, wheeled out the magical "80/20" rule according to which 20 percent of the deficit would be made good through tax rises and 80 percent through welfare cuts.

2. As did John Stuart Mill. The positivist religion was particularly influential in the Latin America where there are positivist temples to this day. The slogan "Ordem e Progresso" on the Brazilian flag is a positivist nostrum.

3. The depth and perhaps antiquity of this ambiguity is reflected in language; "law; can mean either 'natural law' or 'law of the land'" in a large number of languages.
4. The very term "state machine" gives the game away.
5. The Bortkiewicz–Sweezy–Morishima interpretation is so universally taken for granted that Marxists almost everywhere assert that, in Volume I of *Capital*, goods are purchased at their value. This is not true. Marx's abstraction, showing surplus value cannot arise from circulation, applies to the sale price at the end of the period. not the purchase price at the beginning.
6. The *Communist Manifesto*'s one-page economic programme offers a surprisingly modern-sounding package of measures would certainly overcome today's crisis, if implemented.

ACKNOWLEDGMENT

I am indebted to Julian Wells who drew my attention in conversation and in his seminal PhD (Wells, 2009) to many of the ideas in this chapter, and to my other fellow TSSI scholars. All mistakes are of course my own.

REFERENCES

Bagchi, A. K. (1982). *The political economy of underdevelopment (Modern Cambridge Economics)*. Cambridge University Press.

Besomi, D. (2005). Clément Juglar and the transition from crises theory to business cycle theories. Paper prepared for a conference on the occasion of the centenary of the death of Clément Juglar, Paris, 2 December 2005. Available at: www.unil.ch/webdav/site/cwp/users/neyguesi/public/D._Besomi_. Accessed on 14 May 2010.

Bortkiewicz, L. von (1952). Value and price in the Marxian system (part I). *International Economic Papers, 1952*(2), 5–60.

Brenner, R. (1977). The origins of capitalist development: A critique of Neo-Smithian Marxism. *New Left Review, I*(104), 25–92.

Brenner, R. (1998). The economics of global turbulence. *New Left Review, I*(229), 1–266.

Carpentier, A. (2001). *Explosion in a Cathedral*. University of Minnesota Press.

Cockshott, P., & Cottrell, A. (1998). Does Marx need to transform? In: R. Bellofiore (Ed.), *Marxian economics A reappraisal. Vol. 2: Essays on volume III of "Capital": Profit, prices and dynamics* (pp. 70–85). London: Macmillan.

Cockshott, P., & Cottrell, A. (2005). Robust correlations between sectoral prices and labour values: A comment. *Cambridge Journal of Economics, 29*(2), 309–316.

Cohn, N. (1970). *The pursuit of the millenium*. Oxford: OUP.

Coletti, L. (1985). Bernstein and the Marxism of the second international. In: L. Coletti (Ed.), *From Rousseau to Lenin. Studies in ideology and society* (pp. 45–108). New York: Monthly Review Press.

Comte, A. (1851–1854). System of positive polity, or treatise on sociology, Instituting the Religion of Humanity (1851–1854, four volumes).

Comte, A. (1957 [1856]). *A general view of positivism* (J. H. Bridges, Trans.). Robert Speller and Sons.

Day, R. B. (1981). *Crisis and the crash: Soviet studies of the West, 1917–1939*. New Left Books.

Desai, R. (2010). Consumption demand in Marx and in the current crisis. In: P. Zarembka (Ed.), *The national question and the question of crisis* (Vol. 26, pp. 101–143). Bingley, UK: Emerald.

Duménil, G., & Levy, D. (2004). *Capitalism resurgent*. Harvard University Press.

Emmanuel, A. (1972). *Unequal exchange: A study of the imperialism of trade*. T(B. Pearce, Trans.). New York: Monthly Review Press.

Foley, D. (1997). Review of Marx and non-equilibrium economics. *Eastern Economic Journal*, *23*(4), 493–496.

Freeman, A. (1998). The indeterminacy of price–value correlations: A comment on papers by Simon Mohun and Anwar Shaikh. In: R. Bellofiore (Ed.), *Marxian economics. A reappraisal. Vol. 2: Essays on volume III of "Capital": profit, prices and dynamics* (pp. 225–251). London: Macmillan. http://mpra.ub.uni-muenchen.de/2040/1/MPRA_paper_2040.pdf

Freeman, A. (2003). When things go wrong: The political economy of market breakdown. In: R. Westra & A. Zuege (Eds), *Value and the world economy today: Production; finance and globalization* (pp. 91–118). London: MacMillan. Prepublication version available at http://ideas.repec.org/p/pra/mprapa/5586.html

Freeman, A. (2004). 'World empire or a world of empires?' In: A. Freeman & B. Kagarlitsky (Eds), *The politics of empire: Globalisation in crisis*. London: Pluto.

Freeman, A. (2007). Heavens above: What equilibrium means for economics. In: V. Mosini (Ed.), *Equilibrium in economics: Scope and limists* (pp. 240–260). London: Routledge.

Freeman, A. (2009a). Investing in civilization. In: J. Guard & W. Anthony (Eds), *Bailouts and bankruptcies*. Winnipeg: Fernwood Press.

Freeman, A. (2009b). The poverty of statistics. *Third World Quarterly*, *30*(8), 1427–1448.

Freeman, A. (2010). Marxism Without Marx. *Capital and Class*, *34*(1).

Freeman, A., & Carchedi, G. (1995). *Marx and non-equilibrium economics*. Edward Elgar.

Freeman, C. (1995). *The third Kondratieff wave: The age of steel, electrification and imperialism*. Sussex: SPRU.

Gunder Frank, A. (1978). Dependent accumulation and underdevelopment. New York: Monthly Review Press.

Hayek, F. (1933). *Monetary theory and the trade cycle*. New York: Harcourt Brace.

Juglar, C. (1862). *Des Crises commerciales et leur retour periodique en France, en Angleterre, et aux Etats-Unis*. Paris: Guillaumin.

Juglar, C. (1915). A brief history of panics and their periodical occurrence in the United States. Available at http://manybooks.net/titles/juglarcletext05panic10.html

Kliman, A. (2002). The law of value and laws of statistics: Sectoral values and prices in the US economy, 1977–97. *Cambridge Journal of Economics*, *26*(3), 299–311.

Kliman, A. (2005). Reply to Cockshott and Cottrell. *Cambridge Journal of Economics*, *29*(2), 317–323.

Kliman, A. (2007). *Reclaiming Marx's capital: A refutation of the myth of inconsistency*. Lanham, MD: Lexington Books.

Kliman, A. (2010a). *The persistent fall in profitability underlying the current crisis*. New York: Marxist-Humanist Initiative.

Kliman, A. (2010b). The disintegration of the Marxian school. *Capital and Class*, *34*(1).

Krugman, P. (2010) 'The third depression' *New York Times*, (June 27), 2010. <dealbook.blogs.nytimes.com/2010/06/28/Krugman-the-third-depression> Accessed on 4 October 2010.

Kuhn, R. (2007). *Henryk Grossman and the recovery of Marxism*. University of Illinois Press.

Labica, G. (1984). *Der Marxismus–Leninismus: Elemente einer Kritik*. Berlin: Argument.

Labriola (1970 [1897]). *La concepcion materialista de la historia*. La Habana.

Laplace, P. S. (1836). *Exposition de systeme du monde*. Paris: Bachelier.

Laplace, P. S. (1951 [1820]). *A philosophical essay on probabilities*, translated from the 6th French edition by Frederick Wilson Truscott and Frederick Lincoln Emory. New York: Dover Publications. French edition Laplace, P. S. (1820). *Theorie analytique des probabilites*. Volume VI of complete works, Paris: Gauthier-Villars.

Lassalle, F. (1863). Offenes Antwortschreiben Available at http://www.marxists.org/deutsch/referenz/lassalle/1863/03/antwortschreiben.htm

Lovejoy, A. O. (1990). *The great chain of being: A study of the history of an idea*. Harvard University Press.

Lukacs, G. (2000). *Tailism and the dialectics* (German original Lukacs, G. (1996). Chvostisms tendus und Dialektik, Budapest, Aron Verlag). London: Verso.

Maksakovsky, P. (2004). *The capitalist cycle*. Brill.

Mandel. (1974). *Late capitalism*. London: Verso.

Marx, K. (1972). *Feuerbach. Opposition of the materialist and idealist outlooks*. Moscow: Progress Publishers.

Marx, K. (1991). *Capital* (Vol. III). Penguin Classics.

Marx, K. (1992). *Capital* (Vol. I). Penguin Classics.

Mitchell, W. C. (1927). *Business cycles: The problem and its setting*. New York: McGraw-Hill.

Mongiovi, G. (2002). Vulgar economy in Marxian garb: A critique of temporal single system Marxism. *Review of Radical Political Economics (RRPE)*, *34*(4), 393–416.

Morishima, M. (1973). *Marx's economics: A dual theory of value and growth*. Cambridge: CUP.

Ochoa, E. M. (1984). *Labor-values and prices of production: An interindustry study of the United States economy, 1947–1972*. Ph.D. dissertation, Department of Economics, New School for Social Research, New York.

Palloix, C. (1970). 'Inégalité des échanges mondiaux ou inégalité du développement des forces productives à l'échelle mondiale'. *La Pensée*, no. 150, mars-avril 1970.

Patnaik, U. (2006). The free lunch: Transfers from tropical countries and their role in capital formation in Britain during the industrial revolution. In: K. S. Jomo (Ed.), *Globalization under hegemony: The changing world economy*. New Delhi: Oxford University Press.

Potts, N. (2009). Trying to help rescue value for everyone. *Critique*, *37*(2).

Riazanov, D. (1928). 'Lassalle and Bismarck', Pravda 14 July 1928, translated in *Labour Monthly*, February and March 1929. http://www.marxists.org/archive/riazanov/1928/07/lassalle.htm

Rostow, W. W. (1960). *The stages of economic growth: A non-communist Manifesto*. Cambridge: CUP.

Schumpeter, J. A. (1965). *Capitalism, socialism and democracy*. London: Unwin.

Shaikh, A. M. (1998). The empirical strength of the labour theory of value. In: R. Bellofiore (Ed.), *Marxian economics. A reappraisal. Vol. 2: Essays on volume III of "Capital": Profit, prices and dynamics* (pp. 225–251). London: Macmillan.

Shanin, T. (1984). *The late Marx and the Russian road*. Monthly Review Press; First edition (March 1, 1984).

Sraffa, P. (1962). *Production of commodities by means of commodities*. Cambridge University Press.

Stadler, F. (1998). The Vienna circle. In: E. Craig (Ed.), *Routledge encyclopedia of philosophy* (Vol. 9, pp. 606–616). London: Routledge.

Sweezy, P. M. (1968). *Theory of capitalist development: Principles of Marxian political economy*. Modern Reader Paperbacks.

Trotsky (1923). 'O Krivoi Kapitalisticheskovo Razvitiya' ('The Curve of capitalist Development'), Vestnik Sotsialisticheskoi Akademii, 4, April–July. Cited in Day (*op. cit.*).

Tsoulfidis, L., & Maniatis, T. (2002). Value, prices of production and market prices: Some more evidence from the Greek economy. *Cambridge Journal of Economics, 26*(3), 359–369.

VanGiezen, R., & Schwenk, A. E. (2002). *'Compensation from before World War I through the Great Depression'*. New York: BLS.

Wells, J. (2009). PhD Thesis, Kingston University. <staffnet.kingston.ac.uk/~ku32530/phdindex.html> Accessed on 30 October 2010.

Zarembka, P. (2002). Rosa Luxemburg's *accumulation of capital*: Critics try to bury the Message. In: L. Jennifer (Ed.), *Bringing capitalism back for critique by social theory, current perspectives in social theory* (Vol. 21, pp. 3–45). New York: JAI/Elsevier Press.

PART III
A SCIENCE OF CAPITAL

FUNDAMENTALS OF A SCIENCE OF CAPITAL AND BOURGEOIS SOCIETY: MARXIAN NOTIONS OF VALUE, PRICES, AND THE STRUCTURE OF TIME

Jørgen Sandemose

ABSTRACT

This chapter gives an interpretation of basic elements of Marx's scientific method, focusing on his exposition in the first edition of the first chapter of Capital I. *It can be shown that Marx's critique of political economy rests on fundamentals that are traceable in many a philosophical endeavor. This goes especially for categories and concepts relating to the theory of science and epistemology formulated in earlier German philosophy dating back to Kant. I try to demonstrate that such fundamental categories, expressed through our basic thought determinations – universality, particularity, and individuality – are developed through the judgmental and syllogistic forms of logic common to Marx and his immediate predecessors inside philosophy – thinkers as relevant in the modern world as they were in the adolescence of capitalism. Furthermore, I want to show how the concept of time is crucial in uniting the thought-determinations in question. The investigation tries to make it*

The National Question and the Question of Crisis
Research in Political Economy, Volume 26, 253–299

ISSN: 0161-7230/doi:10.1108/S0161-7230(2010)0000026009

clear that the scrutiny of social forms of thought pursued by Marx amounts to a valid, immanent criticism of all the fundamentals of traditional bourgeois theory of science and economics. To this effect, the chapter evaluates some characteristics of the philosophies of Kant and Hegel. Also, to clarify the profundity of Marx's thinking and the thoroughness of his analysis, I go back to some of the philosophical ideas which were starting points for men like Kant and Hegel, especially in the form that we meet them in the classical political philosophy of Hobbes.

1. INTRODUCTORY REMARKS

Referring to the first volume of *Capital*, Marx once remarked that "the method of investigation" employed had "not previously been applied to economic matters," and that this, inter alia, would render "the reading of the first chapters pretty difficult." He added that "there is no royal road for science, and only those who do not dread the fatiguing climb of its steep paths have a chance of gaining its luminous summits" (Marx, 1966b, p. 434).

Probably, by "the first chapters," Marx meant the three first ones, that is, the whole content of the "first part," entitled "Commodity and Money." The titles of the chapters in question are (1) "The Commodity," (2) "The Exchange Process," and (3) "Money, or the Circulation of Commodities." While no one can seriously contend that Marx makes an outright identification of these chapters with all the "steep paths" of his main work, he seems to imply that an understanding of them is a condition for any understanding of his "critique of political economy" as a whole.

Indeed, it is a thesis of this essay that from these texts one can decipher the whole of the Marxian model of investigation of capitalist production and society.

My own exposition of the basics of Marx's theory will focus on the content of the first edition of the chapter on the commodity. It should be anticipated that in this version, Marx's strategy is to show that in a logical analysis, the very *immediate form* of the commodity will abolish (*aufheben*) itself.[1] Since a commodity is a product seen as *value*, which according to Marx has the form of *exchange* value, this implies that the analysis is meant to show that commodity *exchange* is abolished, in the very process that constitutes "capital," the main object of the investigation.

The abolition takes the immediate form of a passage to commodity *circulation*. In this essay, I concentrate on that passage. The further movements into developed capitalist forms are just being hinted at. On the other hand, it is underlined how these last can be understood only on a basis of the logic of the exchange–circulation relation, and on an adequate notion of the structure of time which comes to the fore inside it.

As will be substantiated below, the immediate benefit of this kind of analysis is to make transparent the *logical* relation between *exchange* of commodities and their *circulation*. The movement of circulation – as depicted in Chapter 3 – then stands forward as a clear-cut alternative to a process of exchange – depicted in Chapter 2. Also, the alternative will be seen to be a cogent one, since the *process* of exchange will lose the logical basis for its existence and consequently yield to circulation.[2]

Now, in the analysis in question Marx is operating with four value expressions or "value forms." It will be shown below that they should be read as variants (and extensions) of the "judgments of necessity" of traditional logic such as they are interpreted in the main works of Kant and Hegel. There, they are made up by the categorical, the hypothetical, and the disjunctive judgments, all of which we shall investigate further on. In Hegel, they are analyzed in "The subjective logic or the theory of the concept" in his *Science of Logic*, while Kant introduces them in his "Analytic of concepts" early in the *Critique of Pure Reason* (Kant, 1996, B 95–B 101).

The point of making such a reference to the logics of Kant and Hegel has to do with the fact that both are concentrating on – and synthesizing – general epistemology and theory of science. Thus, both thinkers were engaged in a project which must also be Marx's, given his notions of the fundamental significance of economic relations for philosophy, science, and the human condition in general. Moreover, as concerns the development of the most important categories, their main works express the same will to depict the inner connections between materiality and conceptual thought, and their living totality.

When it is possible to point out very clear parallels in exposition, in employment of categories, and in actual content of the concept determinations used in the works of different thinkers, it becomes fair to presuppose that there exist a mutual interest and communality of outlook between them. The presupposition made in this case is that the progressive bourgeois interests apparent in German idealism to a significant degree coalesced with the class interests expressed in Marx's theory in *Capital*. The exposition below will – hopefully – demonstrate that there are also significant divergencies of interest. Indeed, such divergencies are seen to lie at the root of Marx's approach to logical problems, building up an immanent criticism of the theories of Kant and Hegel.

The dominating motive of this essay is the need to demonstrate the existence of precisely such an immanent criticism. If it cannot be identified, we would be confronted by a lacuna in any argument which aims at justifying the Marxian theory as revolutionary, that is, as constructing a totality of argument, fit to overcome the whole of bourgeois philosophy. The need for such an overcoming follows from the elevated position of this bourgeois philosophy itself. In what follows, I hope to succeed in demonstrating its own luminous summits, and consequently the true quality of Marx's thinking. To characterize – as it is often done – the Marxian science and method as a true heir of German idealism may be justified, but all too often, it remains a contention unsupported by argument.

2. RELATIONS OF VALUE AND OF EQUALITY: A JUDGMENTAL FORM

As pointed out, Marx's analysis of the commodity includes four value forms.

Let us duly start with his "Form I," the "First or simple form of relative value," that is (cf. Marx, 1966a, p. 226):

$$20 \text{ yards of linen} = 1 \text{ coat}$$

or more in general

$$x \text{ commodity } A = y \text{ commodity } B$$

The sign of equality may here immediately be understood as a judgmental copula, the conjunction "is," which can be taken as signifying "is worth." Marx says explicitly that the form can be expressed as "20 yards of linen is worth 1 coat" (Marx, 1968a, p. 63). The subject matter of the predication is a quantity of linen which in the expression refers to a quantity of coat as to something equal to itself:

> it posits itself as *qualitatively* identical (*gleich*) to the coat, in relating itself to it as *objectivation of equal human labor, that is, of its own substance of value*. (Marx, 1966a, p. 226)

We shall return to the question of the character of this "substance," and now concentrate on the thesis that we have to do with a substantial identity between a subject and a predicate. This would simultaneously imply that a given *quantitative* relation is ascribed to the subject. The identity in question must have a quality that has already made it meaningful to formulate it in quantitative terms.

If we pass on to the appendix "The form of value," which Marx added to the first chapter of the first edition of the work, we find that he makes a distinction inside the analysis of the simple value form. He separates the "relation of equality," which appears in the conjunctional "is" as soon as the expression is understood as a statement of substantial identity, from a "relation of value," expressed through the "worth," that is, the copula-related contention that the substantial equality has a value character. Concerning the equality relation, Marx says:

> The basis for the expression 20 yards of linen = 1 coat is in reality linen = coat, which expressed in words simply means: the commodity species coat is of equal nature, equal substance with the commodity species linen, which is different from itself. (Marx, 1955, p. 265)

The equality relation is the same as that which we meet as a categorical relation between genus and species in the "judgment of necessity" as it is presented by the German idealists from Kant on. As regards the value relation, Marx goes on to say that "the coat is only the same as the linen if they both are values." And in the same way in which a judgment form in Hegel as a rule is the truth of the previous one, in this "only if" we find embedded an *hypothetical* relation:

> The relation *of equality* is consequently *value* relation, but the value relation is first and foremost expression *of the value* or of the *value existence* (*Wertsein*) pertaining to the commodity which expresses its value. (Marx, 1955, p. 266)

In other words, the relation of equality is *conditioned*, and the same is the case in the categorical judgment as developed by Hegel; for an expression like (e.g.) "the rose is a plant" must imply that the copula represents a substantial unity (here: a vegetable nature), which unites the concepts in thought.

However, Hegel contends that such a form is not in accordance with the actual content of the copula, that is, with the *universality* which we have in mind when we connect a singular plant with the vegetable kingdom. For the species which is given (the rose) does not appear with *necessity* from the universality which is also given, since "plant" can signify many other species than "rose." The necessity at hand is consequently *conditioned*: It appears only because a specific species has been *selected*. In fact, we could compare this situation with a commodity owner selecting a certain commodity, and thereby a certain species of commodity, to exchange against his own. He chooses any product having a use value for him; that done – but *only* when it is actually done – he is forced to treat it as a *commodity*, that is, an individual of a species of a genus, an exemplar subsumed under a substantial identity.

Hegel chose to show this kind of conditioning in an explicit way, producing a hypothetical form of the judgment, that is, in the expression "if rose, then plant," or "if A, then B."

In interpreting such a necessity as a fundamental value form, and granting that the analysis has a bearing on full-fledged capitalist relations, we are consequently approaching the kind of coercion in which the commodity owner in bourgeois society finds himself or herself – whether he or she is an owner of means of production or simply of labor power. Equations like "linen = coat," which immediately speak out a blatant lack of sense, take on a true social existence.

Thus, a parallel could be drawn from here to the sociohistorical analyses made by, for example, Robert Brenner and Ellen Meiksins Wood, on the specific kind of logic that must be present in a society as soon as it is characterized as capitalist. Such a logic is a kind of coercion in itself, a special "imperative" forcing men to adhere to certain "laws" concerning markets, without necessitating apparent extraeconomic force. In Wood's work, we find the logical expression of "disjunction" aptly used to denote such a human condition of social separation and coercive thought (cf. Wood, 2002, especially pp. 178, 181). As we shall see in a moment, the relations she is pointing out, *appear* in the *disjunctive* logical form, understood as the unity of the categorical and the hypothetical ones.

Just as Kant did before him, Hegel took it for granted that the categorical form (which in Kant's ethics took the form of an "imperative") refers to the category of *substance*. This is precisely the substantiality that is thought to lie in the copula. Both thinkers go on to imply that the hypothetical form corresponds to a possible causality, a relation of cause and effect, in the outer world. This means that, insofar as the outer world is seen as a mass of substance, any physical movement is interpreted as an instance of causality having its origin in the structure of substance. This way of inference corresponds to our inferring the hypothetical judgment from the categorical.

When something determined follows from another determined entity in thought, Kant calls it a relation of ground and consequence, which, applied to external appearances, turns into Leibniz' proposition of the sufficient reason – that is, that everything that begins to exist does so for a reason which, if absent, would have implied that the thing could not exist (Leibniz, 1999, § 44). Taken concretely, this is the schematized category of causality of Kant, that is, a rule for necessary sequence *in time*.

These relations are, in Hegel as well as in Kant, constitutive in transforming the categorical/hypothetical proposition into a *disjunctive* judgment, like "A is either B or C (etc.)." And in fact, such a structure is immediately present in Marx's development of the value form, which he calls an "expanded value form," such as

> 20 yards of linen = 1 coat *or* = u coffee *or* = v tea *or* = x iron *or* = y wheat *or* = etc., etc. (Marx, 1966a, p. 232; cf. 1968, p. 77)

It will now be necessary to investigate more of the background for such parallels. They invite us to make an in-depth scrutiny of the kind of scientific methodology present in Marx, and to investigate to which extent he accepts basic categories of German idealism as cornerstones for an economic science.

3. EPISTEMOLOGY: POINT OF DEPARTURE FOR A SCIENTIFIC METHODOLOGY

It follows from Marx's exposition up to now that for something to be an economic category, it must be a form of thought. Such a form must be socially valid, that is, it must actually be *used* in any human cognition *and construction* of the subject matter of economics, as well as being a category adopted by the corresponding science. Furthermore, it must be exclusive, in the sense that it does not allow alternatives in its kind: The basic scientific method pertaining to a certain object should be one, and one only. That is not all: The cognition must be a basic one, starting with material objects, which then are classified. As such, it points "backwards" to a materialist theory of knowledge. As we shall see, Marx's investigation includes the quest for the very *possibility* of such elements of cognition, and also demonstrates their necessity in economic science.

To specify, let us look at the epistemological status of Kant's categorical judgment, and consequently of substance, and of the causal relation. The aim of such a scrutiny is to check the relation between Marx's concept of labor and the concept of causality in German idealism.

As we have said, the relation in question points to external appearances. Incidentally, Kant tells us that causality, as it appears in an event, *forces* us to perceive two or more states in a bound sequence (we cannot change the sequence at will), something which demonstrates for us the existence of things in space, that is, *objects*, things encountering us, in a certain *given* time order (cf. Kant, 1996, p. B 242). In compelling us to perceive in a certain given order, it affirms that empirical objects in fact are external and independent of us.

This implies that the categorical judgment, a proposition of substantial identity between entities, is where the crucial point in Kant's theory of cognition is vindicated. Presently, we shall make a general summary of the theory, with the aim of pointing out its relevance for Marx's analysis.

The theory is originally presented in the well-known "transcendental deduction of the categories" (Kant, 1996, p. B 129–169). Here, it is shown that my perceptions cannot have any other common, unifying characteristic than precisely their being *mine*.[3] In themselves, they are utterly different from each other. It is only the cognizing subject who brings unity and order to the world of such appearances. But here lies a problem, for while I am receiving the sense impressions inside perceptions in a passive manner, it is impossible that such a passivity should unite them. The uniting factor thus has to be the *opposite*, that is, an activity, and Kant concludes that the "I" in question is the *spontaneous* subject, not the same subject taken as passive. He refers to it as "the presentation *I think* that must be capable of accompanying all other presentations" (Kant, 1996, p. B 132).[4]

As anticipated above, this reasoning is vindicated in the categorical judgment. Through the latter's relation to causality (cf. its connection to the hypothetical judgment), it is shown that the perceptions in question may refer to factual, time-determined *external presentations*.

Now, if we take as a starting point the specific Marxian version of the categorical judgment, the simple value expression, then the "deduction" of a unifying principle, perceived as a scientific problem, must take the form of a search for a third, comparing factor, a *tertium comparationis* (*TC*) between products, "things" called "commodities." Marx takes a surprisingly light-handed approach to this, simply stating that *TC* is "labor." However, it is clear that if we are thinking of the labor that already is embedded in each product, the weavers in the linen, the tailors in the coat, then these are qualities-in-perceptions that we may receive as passively as we receive other characteristics of the products, like the pale color of the linen and the coat's hairy surface. Furthermore, as such qualities, they are as internally different as are hairs and colors. So, again, we must seek the *TC* in an *opposite* – not in coagulated, "dead" labor, but in the spontaneous activity that is human labor in its original form. The parallel to Kant is clear, in that labor, taken *as such*, and regarded as "abstract labor," is the only possible common denominator.

It seems possible that one reason that Marx in fact renounced on giving such a decisive argument for the "labor theory of value" is that he thought that the logical form of the exposition simply would indicate the true relation to the reader. We shall return to this.

Marx's *de facto* argument here implies that the empirical nature of the commodities in question can be abstracted from, while their common substance is all-important. Hegel's analysis of the causality which appears in the hypothetical judgment ("if A, then B") is closely related, and even offers an interesting interpretation of Kantian judgment theory, since it implies that subject and predicate are taken to be unessential in themselves; what is being focused on is rather the relation between two external entities. The *necessary* relation between them (which Kant took to be the *category of causality*) is all that is *said* to be present. What is at stake, is not the existence of specific material things, but only the nature of the copula.

For such reasons, Hegel contends that the hypothetical judgment is "a proposition of empty form" (Hegel, 1970b, p. 337). Also, he finds that this is the place to stop using empirical subjects or predicates, and to replace them with symbols. It is interesting to note that when Kant argued for the transcendental validity of causality and substantial identity, he did so through an "*analogy* of experience," where he abstracted from concrete, empirical causes (and effects) and restricted himself to stress that one cause (or an effect) or other must be present in external events, in which *time determination* is generated for us (Kant, 1996, pp. B 218–B 265, especially B 233–B 256).

The general train of thought present here, starting from a given form of judgment and passing on the (causal) *activity* behind it, gives us a model for the Marxian analysis of living labor in a capitalist production process as the origin of the value relation between commodities. As we shall see, this matches a theory of substance and causality of labor that was developed in *Grundrisse*, ten years prior to the publication of the analysis of the commodity.

Before passing on to such themes, however, it is fair to critically consider Hegel's way of exposing the judgment in its totality. It will appear that Hegel's conception of the *disjunctive* judgment has weaknesses that make his exposition inferior to Marx's logical analysis of the commodity. Also, it will be demonstrated that Marx's analysis has the form of a conscious *criticism* of Hegel's construction. The scrutiny of Hegel's thought that follows below should, then, be considered important for an adequate understanding of the form of the commodity.

4. HEGELIAN INCONSISTENCIES

In this section, I start with sketching the problem, as one meets it in Hegel's text (*A*). I then try to demonstrate how he handles it in his analysis of disjunction (*B*). Thirdly, I point out that he is not capable of reconciling the concept of free, human individuality with the disjuncted structure, nor – consequently – with a society built on disjunctions (*C*).

4.1. Concerning a Riddle

The issue has to do with a basic duality in Hegel's exposition: On the one hand, he holds the judgment (in general) to be the first appearance-form of the concept, so that the *further* development of logical categories, especially the syllogistic forms, should end up by giving us the final unity of subject and object and the culmination in "the absolute idea," the idealist final aim of the *Science of Logic*. On the other hand, Hegel does *not* start the exposition of the concept with this elementary form, but with a long introduction in which he analyses conceptual *determinations* – universality, particularity, and individuality. He then tries to show that these have an internal logic which leads the concept so to speak to divide itself, so that it "*sich urteilt*." Consequently, *the judgments* now suddenly appear *as a result* in his exposition. Hegel here makes use of the etymology for "*Urteil*" ("judgment") which was recommended by Hölderlin, who argued that the term did refer to an "*ursprüngliche Teilung des ursprünglich Einen*" – an original partition of an original One (cf. Hölderlin, 1962, pp. 226–228).

This implies that an inner dialectic in the "concept" leads to a division which produces the judgment, while on the other hand we have started from the contention that the judgment is the first form of this concept. This is unreasonable, and the kind of "transition" which Hegel introduces on this occasion, indeed is not paralleled by any of the others that we meet in his system.[5]

Hegel's exposition of the concept thus actually starts with a riddle. The culmination of the exposition of "Essence" lies in the theory of necessity, causality, and substance. Consequently, one might have expected the exposition of the "Concept" to start with judgments of *necessity*, presenting us with a transition matching the dynamics of the principles now reached inside the sphere of essence. We shall now consider whether such a starting point is consistent with Hegelian premises. This will be done through a critique of Hegel's thought, which in its turn will demonstrate how Marx's version of the dialectic method supersedes the Hegelian one, and abolishes it. This, furthermore, may be taken as an indication that the whole bourgeois method in philosophy and social science loses its *raison d'être*.

4.2. The Disjunction: An Achilles' Heel in Hegel's System

To take on this task, we first have to return to the situation in the hypothetical judgment ("if A, then B"), and the specific kind of necessity which appears there.

It is clear that an *unconditioned* necessity is not present, so it is an open question if the "judgment of necessity" deserves its name at all. This can only be shown through a possible further development of the proposition, and it is imperative that this is done, since otherwise it is not shown that the necessity in question is capable of creating an immanent force, a coercion of thought, motoring the logical process.

And in fact, it is at the point of transition between the hypothetical form and the following type, namely, the *disjunctive* one (which, like traditional logicians, Hegel takes to form a unity of categorical and hypothetical features) that Hegel makes the decisive step towards *absolute* necessity. The point in question can be seen already in any trivial variant of that judgment, as for instance

> The plant is either a rose or an anemone or an oak etc.

where the "etc." denotes the total number of species inside a genus. For here, the contingency of subject and predicate(s) visible in the hypothetical form has disappeared. Whatever the predicate (any species of plant whatsoever), it belongs necessarily to the subject, and the subject itself is taken as existing. What is even more compelling: One cannot select a subject (a plant-species) without having to count the selected entity as a member of a given genus.

This is not all. Actually, for the first time in the whole of his analysis of the judgment form – which encompasses six types prior to the categorical one – Hegel points to the forms which really separate the *concept* determinations (individuality, particularity, and universality) from the determinations that correspond to them in the *earlier spheres* of the *Science of Logic*. Once more he underlines how the hypothetical judgment has an undetermined form, since its content is not related as subject to predicate. However, he claims that this makes it all the easier to find the mark of universality and particularity in its subject. He says of the subject (A) that "in itself it is the being of the other" (namely, B): The judgment itself makes B into an inherent element of A, which in this manner acquires the character of universality, having a particular in it (cf. Hegel, 1970b, p. 338).

In other words, the universal, as a thought-determination, is latently in place already in the hypothetic form. When one passes to the disjunctive judgment, the genus, for example, "plant," is then naturally the subject to start with. We discover that to tell what the plant is, we can enumerate all the species and presuppose that they make up a totality that describes all the vegetable nature(s) in which the plant can present itself.

Evidently, such a totality of species is not sufficient, since "plant," though being a universal, *appears* just as one species at a time, to the exclusion of all the others.

The genus is thus a unity of integration and exclusion, of simple totality of the species, and a negative principle excluding all but one species.

To underline these points, Hegel chooses to express the disjunctive judgment through symbols, in the form

A is *either* B or C.

One reason for this is that there is no absolute necessity in *empirical* science, since one can never be sure that one has reached to a complete enumeration of all species. The necessity in question cannot be shown directly: "An empirical disjunctive judgment is without necessity" (Hegel, 1970b, p. 340). This indicates a dilemma, and Hegel thinks his point has to be demonstrated by describing the operation of the *conceptual activity* of the thinking subject in any disjunction, be it empirical or not.

In the formula, one symbol stands for the totality of species which form the genus, while the other stands for the negative principle in the genus that splits the species from each other. The disjunctive judgment consequently says that thinking a genus is a unity of totality and negation, and that it is at the same time *either* the one *or* the other.

Thus, since Hegel supposes this is sufficient to show as well the integrating ("A is as well B as C") as the repulsing ("A is B only in so far as it is not C, etc.") function of this judgment, the formula tells all that is essential. Accordingly, the archetypical disjunctive form has got *only two* disjuncts in the predicate. The very proposition: "the genus is what is itself in being something else" signifies precisely that an A is a B, but also that it has something outside itself that is not referred to as B.

Let us look somewhat more in detail at this way of thinking. The very sentence "A is not C" is a determined content which tells something of A (namely, "A might be C, but isn't"), just as much as "A is B" tells us something of A. There is no barren speculation in this, for it is clear (to take an example) that it tells us something meaningful of any cloven-footed animal that it is not horse, that is, is separated off from the order of horses.

On the other hand, it says nothing of the same individual of the genus "cloven-footed animal" that it is not a sea lion (etc.), and this points to a defect which cannot be expressed inside the judgment in question. Consequently: "A is not C" (or better, "A is not-C") has a significance which amounts to "not-C is something else than the genus, but is included in the genus."

Consequently,	(1) "A is either B or C, and in this case is B"
is an interpretation of	(2) "the genus is that which is itself in being something else."

We are approaching a critical point in Hegel's exposition of the judgment. It concerns his view of the disjunction "A is either B or C." In line with the expressions above he interprets it as "The universal is *either* universal *or* particular," where "particular" is what the universal is not, that is, the contrast to the universal. This is consistent, but it raises a new problem when Hegel goes on in the following way:

> In the judgment we have been considering, the disjunction of the concept is in fact itself posited through the concept's own further determination; that which is posited, is what appeared as the *determination being in itself and for itself,* its differentiation in determinate concepts. (Hegel, 1970b, p. 342)

In fact, this is a correction of the whole analysis. Here it appears that the specific *Ur-teilung* of the concept, its diremption, is a *result* of the judgment, and Hegel now says of the concept inside the disjunctive judgment:

> Since it [the concept] now is the universal, the positive as well as the negative totality of the particular, it is *itself* thereby precisely even immediately *one of its disjunctive parts.* (Hegel, 1970b, p. 342)

Apparently, this means: The judging mind *is* the positive totality of its objects, in a manner that to some extent can be compared to Kant's consciousness, in the moment that it defines itself through thinking its many different perceptions as belonging to itself. It *thinks* them, and consequently *is* them, since thinking is nothing but its own activity. The same goes for the fact that to think entities as *entities*, it is presupposed that thinking excludes any one of them from the others. So consequently, since the form of the thinking has to exist as one of the forms mentioned (either-or), consciousness is disjuncted in itself.

This development points to the existence of a *disjunction that is prior* to the logical one, and which may be its socioeconomic condition. If so, the world of commodities with all its spell, fetishism and material coercion now seems to appear as such a form. Marx's version of the disjunction is then a main presupposition for discursive thought and philosophy in general. The case in question amounts to no less.

4.3. On individuality and Freedom in a "Disjuncted" Society

If we go back to Hegel's notion of the "dialectic" of the concept determinations, we have seen that the universal is said to be "the particular," in its two different totalities. This means that the determination of *individuality* is missing from the judgment. This is a point that can be illustrated by the empirical version of the disjunction: To say that

> The plant is either a rose or an anemone or an oak etc.

is the same as saying that something universal consists of particulars, but it leaves out any reference to individuals, since the individual oaks (e.g.) of any given type differ in an infinite number of ways that cannot be covered by empirical laws.

Now, it is clear that such an individual (*either* of the species oak, *or* of the species anemone, etc.) would only *represent* "individuality." For as pointed out, since there is no necessity in the empirical disjunctive judgment, we are searching only for the *concept determination* of individuality. On the other hand, Hegel originally approached the disjunction through empirical examples, because its provenance from empirical reasoning cannot be doubted. Also, it is an implicit presupposition in his thinking, most clearly developed in the *Phenomenology of Mind*, that the cognition of an individual thing implies the original cognition of one's own individual consciousness, that is, individuality.

When there is no apparent individuality in the disjunctive judgment, how can we reach the individual, cognizing subject? How can it appear conceptually? It is a central question whether it will show up in course of Hegel's developing the judgments. If it does not, he has a problem, since it will seem impossible for him to "deduce" the existence of a living, individual subject inside his logic. In that case, he will be without the free entity that *thinks* the philosopher's whole setup.

What Hegel now does is to contend that the individuality will emerge in a transition to the highest type of judgment, which he calls judgments of *the concept*, which break with the sphere of necessity. Their character may be hinted at through examples of the highest form of its kind, the apodictic judgment: "The house which is *constituted* in this special way, is *good*," "the action which is *constituted* in this special way, is *correct*" (Hegel, 1970b, p. 349). Individual objects with a specific peculiarity fulfill our real, universal claims: The determinations of the concept are united to the best for humanity and consequently in style with the teleological aims of Hegel's philosophy.

If one is right in holding that the objective determinations of Hegel's concept are not there prior to the disjunctive judgment, it is, however, erroneous to develop the individuality in the way he does. If it is produced immanently, it has to appear inside of the movement of thought which is composed of the disjunctive form. For the disjunctive judgment demonstrates the universal dissolved in all its particular determinations. For example, a *group* is here demonstrating all its family determinations. The odd-toed hoofed animal is either horse or donkey or zebra. If we take one of the disjuncts and make it the subject in a new disjunctive judgment, we get nearer to grasping the individuality in question. Figuratively speaking, we would get a form like "*This* horse is either Kertag or Arab," and these predicates would correspond to the thought determination which the individuality makes up: A negation of particularity, i.e., of the species, i.e., of the first negation of universality. Therefore, an apodictic judgment is a confirmation of this whole negative content of the judgment, for in such a sentence we describe the Kertag and the Arab in a way that explains why they are distinct from each other, in the same way as we point out the differences between a good and a bad house.

Hegel says of the construction of the judgment of the concept (assertoric, problematic, apodictic) that it is the remaining unity from the judgment of necessity (namely, the one determination not yet investigated), and that consequently,

> [i]t is only this *one* determination, which now has to *posit* its negativity, divide itself in the *extremes* (*sich … dirimieren*) and in this way develop itself completely *to syllogism*. (Hegel, 1970c, p. 345)

However, it is clear that this is not the same as a diremption inside the disjunction itself. Perhaps one could say that Hegel's sentence reflects such a diremption of the particular joints in the original disjunctive expression, and this is in fact a thesis put forward by an outstanding commentator, Leo Lugarini:

> [the division] must repeat itself also in their case; and by the fact that they constitute similar particularities, their differentiation will give room to a mass of individualities,

> whose relations, again, will take the form of community (*comunanza*) and mutual disjunction. (Lugarini, 1957, p. 243)

And this is in fact, Lugarini contended,

> ... *the individual*, which the disjunctive judgment itself points out when one develops it in a consequent manner, taking one of the particularities residing in its predicate as subject in still another disjunctive judgment. (Lugarini, 1957, p. 245, italics added)

5. VALUE FORMS AS THE GENESIS OF PRICE

As anticipated above, the investigation will show that Marx's analysis of the commodity contains an immanent criticism of Hegel's exposition of the judgments, and consequently a realization of Lugarini's logical criticism. That we have to study a critical political economist instead of a logician to this end should surprise nobody, since Marx makes a point of this parallelism:

> It is scarcely a wonder that the economists, totally subsumed under material interests, have overlooked the formal content (*Formgehalt*) of the relative value expression, when the professional logicians prior to *Hegel* did overlook even the formal content (*Forminhalt*) of the judgment and syllogism paradigms. (Marx, 1966a, p. 274)

5.1. The Second Value Form in General

Let us evaluate this criticism, returning to Marx's analysis. As pointed out, he treats Form I as a unity of categorical and hypothetical expressions. He lets it be followed by a disjunctive expression, which he calls "Form II," and which is written as follows (Marx, 1966a, p. 232):

II. Second or expanded form of relative value:

20 yards of linen = 1 coat *or* = u coffee *or* = v tea *or* = x iron *or* = y wheat *or* = etc., etc.
z commodity A = u commodity B *or* = v commodity C *or* = w commodity D *or* x commodity E *or* = y commodity F *or* = etc.

This "total or expanded value form," as Marx also calls it (Marx, 1968a, p. 77) is described much more accurately in the first version of the chapter on the commodity than in later ones. In these versions (the second German edition, the English, and the first French one, where the internal textual differences are negligible) a main argument is that as a form, it is unsatisfactory, since the row of possible equivalents for the linen is unending and not definite. In the first edition, Marx concentrates just as much on describing the form in positive terms, and as a specific transcending of the simple value expression:

> ... this second form is an essential further development, for its content tells us not only that the linen expresses its value contingently, now in coats, then in coffee etc., but also that it expresses it in coats *as well as* in coffee etc., *either* in *this* commodity *or* in that one, *or* in a third, etc. (1966, p. 232)

Here the subject in fact *is* (in the copulative meaning "is worth") the one commodity as well as the other in unending series, and at the same time is equal only to any single of them, since they exclude each other mutually in an *Either–Or* relationship. This means that it is not only the predicate that is disjointed; the whole expression is disjointed in what might be called two different principles. Precisely as Hegel would have it, it appears as a unity-in-difference of the forms *As Well As* and *Either–Or*.

In Marx's exposition, too, the disjunction must be abolished in one way or another. Now, of course his motive is not to let a concept liberate itself from its own more immediate inner differences or contradictions, so that thought – taken as a form, if not as content – can move omnipotently inside an "absolute idea." But he tries to disjoint the contradictions of the value forms in order to show to which extent bourgeois society can function in a free form on the basis of its historical conditions and limitations. With this aim he investigates the possible dissolution of the disjunction in question. This is a discussion that takes place through analysis of two more value forms. Let us now follow that development.

In discussing Form II, Marx in fact presents two separate investigations, namely, one of each of the two true parts in the disjunction, *As Well As* and *Either-Or*. Still, this cannot be carried to an end if it does not take place in accordance with a tendency to dissolution which is already present in the development of the value forms themselves. Let us look at this double analysis.

5.2. First Variant of the Second Value Form: Form III

The principle of *As Well As* gets a chronological priority in the discussion, since it is logically the basic one: concepts of species cannot be disjuncted at all if they are not originally to be found inside a common genus. This genus is their substantial identity. The genus encompasses *as well* the one species *as* the other, *as* all other species.

The ensuing discussion takes place within the value expression which Marx calls Form III – a form which is embedded in Form II, and thereby "dissolves itself retroactively (*rückbezüglich*)" in Form II. It is generated on the background of what we may call the disjunctive value expression, since this one can be said to consist of a "sum" of equations of the type we find in Form I (1966a, p. 233):

> Each and every of these equations, like 20 yards of linen = 1 coat, also includes … the retroactive movement (*die Rückbeziehung*): 1 coat = 20 yards of linen, where the coat expresses its value in the linen and, precisely through this operation, lets the linen appear as equivalent. Since this now goes for each of the countless relative value expressions of the linen, we get:

III. Third, inverted or retroactive second form of relative value:

20 yards of linen = 1 coat *or* = *u* coffee *or* = *v* tea *or* = *x* iron *or* = *y* wheat *or* = osv.
1 coat = 20 yards of linen *or* = *u* coffee *or* = *v* tea *or* = *x* iron *or* = *y* wheat *or* = etc.
u coffee = 20 yards of linen *or* = 1 coat *or* = *v* tea *or* = *x* iron *or* = *y* wheat *or* = etc.
v tea = etc.

As we have seen from the categorical/hypothetical value expression (Form I) the extremes of these forms are externally existing, contingent commodities. The relation of equality between them implies that subject and predicate can change positions in an immediate way, and it is grounded in the substantial relation of equality between commodity *owners*, whose form of appearance is precisely that their different products can be *exchanged* against each other. This imagined exchange implies in its turn that the products can always change their positions, externally as well as conceptually. This is a relation that is not changed in Form II, but as it is seen in Form III (considered as an analysis of Form II) the linen appears as what Marx calls "universal equivalent"; it has been developed from being just an individual relative value form opposing an "individual equivalent" in Form I. In Form II it is *de facto* equivalent for all other commodities, and this relation is explicated, liberated so to speak, in Form III.

As regards the literature on Marx's work, it is as good as unanimous in considering his third form *not* as implied by his second, but as a real, progressive development, a functional, partial abolition of the contradictions of commodity exchange, and consequently as an important step towards what in the second edition is called *the money form*, the construction of a conventional, socially established, *real* universal equivalent in the process of exchanges of commodities. This view has dominated simply because Marx's exposition is radically changed in the second edition.

In the 1873 edition, Marx continues to operate with four forms. Here they are called A, B, C, and D. C and D are completely new. The first (C) depicts the linen as a universal equivalent, but gives up the exposition in the first edition, where the linen is presented in a series of equations (illustrating all the different joints of the disjunction). The second (D) simply replaces the linen with gold, ending up with naming it "Money form" – something one would expect to be a result of Chapter 2, "The exchange process." No logical development whatsoever is traceable. Confusion is added by the fact that pieces of texts fairly similar to paragraphs found in the first edition are spread around in the exposition of (C) and (D), without any clear setup.

What Marx is in fact showing us in the first edition, to the contrary, is precisely the opposite of any linear development like the one hinted at in the 1873 edition: Namely, that an abolition of the basic commodity form, transforming it into money form, is impossible on the basis of Form II alone. If one had been conscious of the disjunction described in this chapter, misunderstandings might have been avoided, for in that case it must come into view that Marx had a need to analyze the aspects of such a disjunction, that is, investigate something present instead of immediately showing a progressive development.[6] The strongest criticism, however, has to be directed against Marx himself, since he scrapped the original setup without compelling reasons.

Let us go back to Form III, which accentuates the relation *As Well As*, to the extent that it places a whole circle of commodities as equal and conjoined vis-à-vis one exclusive commodity:

> Through their common value expression in the material of linen, all commodities do consequently *separate* themselves qua exchange values from their own *use values* and at the same time relate themselves to each other as *value magnitudes*; they posit themselves as *qualitatively equal* and *compare* each other quantitatively. (1966, p. 234)

Seen from the viewpoint of bourgeois liberty and equality, this is a welcome result. But it is far from any social reality, it just describes a possible reality, which is, furthermore, nonviable on the said basis. What we have before us is only an analytical implication of a situation (Form II), where the linen is not universal equivalent, and nothing more than a potential individual equivalent, placed in relative value form. Thus, if Form III does show that any other commodity is such an individual equivalent (even in relative value form) for the linen, it also demonstrates that any commodity whatsoever can take the place as an equivalent form for the linen. This means that "each and every other commodity-body is here equivalent" for the linen, "so that it is immediately exchangeable with it."

5.3. Second Variant of the Second Value Form: Form IV

Consequently, we get (cf. Marx, 1966a, p. 239):[7]

IV. The specific relative value form of the universal equivalent:

20 yards of linen = 1 coat *or* = *u* coffee *or* = v tea *or* = x iron *or* = y wheat *or* = etc.
1 coat = 20 yards of linen *or* = *u* coffee *or* = v tea *or* = x iron *or* = y wheat *or* = etc.
u coffee = 20 yards of linen *or* 1 coat *or* = v tea *or* = x iron *or* = y wheat *or* = etc.
v tea = etc.

We have before us a potentially unending series of disjunctive value expressions, as a consequence of the fact that any commodity in principle is equivalent for every other commodity, and consequently is not only liable to be exchanged with it, but also to be conceptually determined in the same way as it is. We are inside the chapter "Die Ware"; what is analyzed is the commodity in general, the determinations belonging to each and every commodity. In this original first chapter, Marx is, then, in no way focusing on the concept of money, that is, a commodity standing in a specific opposition to all others. Such an analysis is reserved for the chapters that are to follow – "The exchange process" and thereupon "Money or the circulation of commodities." What is at stake here in the chapter on the value form[8] is a demonstration that the value expressions, in the logical (judgmental) form they now have, must be abolished to yield new results. The basis of the abolition is given through the value expressions themselves, since they dissolve the specific genus, namely, the field of *As Well As*, which the analysis has ascribed to it. Consequently, we can say we have passed over into the analysis of the negative principle, the *Either–Or*.

With reference to the unending series of disjunctive expressions in Form IV, Marx notes:

> But *retroactively* (*rückbezogen*) each of these equations gives coat, coffee, tea, etc. as universal equivalent; consequently, they give the value expression in coat, coffee, tea, etc.,

> as a universal relative value form for all other commodities. The form of universal equivalent always belongs to only one commodity in contrast to all other commodities; but it belongs to each and every commodity in contrast to all others. But if each and every commodity is positing its own nature form (*Naturalform*) in front of all other commodities as form of universal equivalent, then all commodities are excluding all [commodities] from the form of universal equivalent, and through this they exclude themselves from the social valid exposition of their value magnitudes. (Marx, 1966a, p. 240)

But the exclusion from such a "valid exposition" means that the actual *commodity* form of all products is abolished. It is a condition for being a commodity that the product in question *appears* as such. In the analysis of the commodity it is presupposed from the beginning that the products *are* commodities. It is also presupposed that they at least have value magnitudes which *are capable of* being exposed as socially valid: The proof of this is the development from Form II to Form IV, where the *value magnitude* of a commodity at every moment comes to the fore in an unending circuit of specific spatial or intensive magnitudes of other commodities. To the extent that this kind of appearance seems instantly to disappear for one specific commodity (namely, for the linen as "universal equivalent" in Form III, since *qua* equivalent an equivalent does not measure its own value, i.e., is *excluded* from that function), it is all the more forcefully reinstituted in Form IV, where each equivalent appears as a relative value form. But precisely in this restoration the reciprocal validity of all value magnitudes is being abolished, and consequently the products are formally being abolished as commodities. Or, "the form of the judgment has perished," as Hegel says when he shows how the form of the syllogism has to take over in the development of the concept.

5.4. Result of the Complete Disjunction: Price Form and Money

It will take us too far to investigate the common structure of Hegel's syllogism and Marx's model for circulation of commodities. In Marx's published works, it is mentioned as such only (and briefly) in the second chapter of the *Critique* from 1859 (1972, p. 76). (In *Grundrisse*, it appears on several occasions.) Suffice it here to point out explicitly that "Form IV" is the link which Lugarini's analysis showed to be missing: The definite partition of the species of the original disjunction.

In the philosophical tradition, the syllogism is the construction of a firm and common *universal* presupposition for thought, producing a middle (*medius terminus*) that is present in different, diverging premises or judgments.

It so to speak stabilizes the contingency of the judgment forms, showing their common basis. Similarly, in Marx, the circulation movement Commodity–Money–Commodity (C–M–C) is not to be taken as a conglomerate of judgments, but as a new, superseding, and encompassing conceptual form.

Let us now presuppose that the *débâcle* depicted by Marx in his second chapter, "The exchange process," has led to the exclusion of a precious metal, the *gold* commodity, positing it as universal equivalent, and consequently has provided the kind of equivalent that, for technical reasons, was destined to win this first agonizing competition among commodities. In that case, looking at things as they appear when we step out of Form IV, *all* other commodities have the same relation to gold, *versus* what would be the case in exchange. The form of circulation is not x commodity A = y commodity B, but instead x commodity *A*–Money–y commodity B, or better C–M–C.

Let us turn for a moment from Marx's relation to Hegel to his main criticism of the approach of the classical political economists: He focuses on their treatment of the first of the categories which are developed from the universal equivalent – the *measure of value*. Here, the labor time producing a given weight of gold is used as a measure of a given quantity of a commodity x, whose value is compared to a commodity y through the gold, while the gold in its turn (that is the next step in the movement) takes the form of *standard of prices* (*numéraire*) where other specified quantities of x or y, or of every other commodity, can be reciprocally compared on the physical rod of gold.

When gold (as money) and commodity change hands in circulation, we have what Marx calls an *Austauschen*, an "*exchanging*," between the two (Marx, 1972, p. 70) which is quite another thing than a commodity exchange. However, it *does seem* to be such an exchange, and the reason for this is simply

> that in the prices a certain quantity of commodity is already posited as equal to a certain quantity of gold, i.e. is already related to gold as money, universal equivalent, and *therefore* is immediately exchangeable with it. (Marx, 1972, p. 72)

According to Marx's theory, then, what separates a commodity exchange from an "exchanging" of gold and commodity is that in the latter, there is present a measuring of value in a *universal* medium (here: universal equivalent). *De facto*, this amounts to saying that a misunderstanding of the gold's function as measure of value coincides with the belief that money and commodity are exchanged as two commodities, which, again, means that circulation is confused with "immediate exchange between gold and commodity" (Marx, 1972, p. 72) – a howler which has had disastrous consequences in the literature, transforming potential Marxist analyses into clumsy, Marxisant misapprehensions.[9]

In *Theories of Surplus-Value*, we find an excellent exemplar of Marx's argument: He criticizes Ricardo's theory that the relation between profits and wages in an industry is dependent on the composition of capital in that industry as compared with the composition in gold-producing mines. Marx argues as follows:

> ... here we have got to do with Ricardo's *false presupposition* that money, inasmuch as it serves as means of circulation, is exchanged as commodity against commodity. [On the contrary:] The commodities are evaluated in it before they circulate. (Marx, 1968b, p. 198)

The abolition of Form IV has resulted in circulation. But this abolition cannot mean the disappearance of each and every "relative value form of the universal equivalent." On the contrary, the existence of the form C–M–C just means that no commodity, with the exclusion of one, retains this immediate specific form. This last commodity, the gold, will have no price in the accurate meaning:

> The *price* of the commodity serving as measure of value and consequently as money does not exist at all. ... The relative value of money is expressed in the innumerable prices of all commodities; for in each of these prices, where the exchange value of the commodity is expressed in money, the exchange value of money is expressed in the use value [= the material] of the commodity. (Marx, 1968b, p. 198)

Thus, for instance, I can speak of a "wheat price of money" (1968b, p. 198) or of money-expressions in all other extant use values (less the gold), but the word "price" is here used analogically – something which, on the other hand, does not mean that it is unreal.

This means that, in the midst of circulation, and despite the fact that circulation can correctly be called an abolition of the contradictions of the exchange process, there remains an immediate "judgmental form" in the disjunctive expression of the universal equivalent. The whole price system, and consequently the developed capitalist system, is manifestly dependent on a *real* disjunction, which in its turn can be logically expressed. This disjunction rides the thoughts of men as a dominating coercive power, reminding us of the meaning of the social basis of concepts like the Hobbesian "fear," and described by a modern historian:

> ... while the scope of capitalist economic imperatives can far outreach direct political rule and legal authority, the same disjunction that makes this possible is the root of an irreducible contradiction. (Wood, 2002, p. 178)

Thus, it turns out that Marx criticizes Hegel in the appropriate way, pointing out that a disjunction has to have its cause in finite forms of thought, that in turn have their background in production relations – relations between subjects mediated through their relation to material entities. This gives a hint that in the *Science of Logic*, the only acceptable passage from the sphere of "necessity" to that of the "concept" goes through a finite disjunction. Since this would imply a diremption that has a disjunctive form *prior to* the concept, whose first disjunction has the form of a judgment, we are left with the supposition that Hegel's "original partition of the original One" goes back to a diremption in the category of causality, that is, *die Ursache*, which Hegel takes to represent the "Ursprüngliche Sache," the "original entity" (cf. Sandemose, 1973, p. 229).

5.5. Summing up the Joints

To sum up: Hegel's dialectic goes astray because it cannot reconcile the structure of empirical (disjunctive) judgments with a theory of concept determinations. Since he could find no *necessity* in an empirical judgment on species in nature, the connecting link between sensory experience and thought disappeared out of sight. The necessity Hegel expected to find in the concept did not show up, because it had no empirical counterpart matching it.

In Marx, on the other hand, this gap is bridged, since the empirical entities in question are *material things produced* by men. In principle, the number and totality of species of commodities are known by the subject who *creates* them. Furthermore, since Marx's general view is that man cognizes through the social process of production, we may well suppose that he thinks that a disjunctive structure among produced things mediates our cognizing of genus, species, and laws in the natural world.

Actually, in the "Chapter of Capital" in *Grundrisse*, Marx prepares us for such a solution. He *de facto* takes up Hegel's category of substance, which in *Science of Logic* is developed as an immanent critique of Spinoza's substance and its aspects *natura naturans* and *natura naturata*. Hegel's parallel categories, active and passive substance, Marx interprets as capital, as far as it is consisting of both itself and the conscious labor power, and he regards the worker as active causality (Marx, 1953, 205 sq, 1973, 297 sq, cf. Hegel, 1970b, pp. 217–240; Sandemose, 1973; Part II, *passim*, Sandemose, 2007, pp. 159–183). The forms presented in the first chapter of *Capital* are reasonably understood as the immediate products of such a capitalist production, based as it is on a diremption between active worker and passive, "congealed" labor. Especially the "value relation" in that chapter, pointing back to Hegel's pure causality relation in the hypothetical judgment, and consequently to the pure active causality of industrial work, seems rooted in those passages of *Grundrisse*.

It should be noted that "*Diremtion*," a classical expression in German idealism, was also used as a clue concept by Marx in the same passages.

> The only diremption posited by the process of production itself is the original diremption, that posited by the difference between objective labor and living labor itself, that is, that between *raw material* and *instrument of labor* (Marx, 1953, p. 207, 1973, p. 300).

The case in question concerns the kind of splitting-up of the categories of the worker's thinking activity in the labor process, and shows that what stands forth simply as differences in the technical process has the potential to develop into inimical relations as soon as capital steers the process. The differentiation (or diremption, *ursprüngliche Diremtion*, as Marx says in the original) between *objective* and *subjective* labor can posit a diremption only between two *objective* modes (raw material and instrument). This exclusive diremption in the objective process takes on a living and contradictory form because the results of the "splitting," the "division," are conceptually constructed by a worker who is placed as an *alienated* subject inside a *capitalist* process.

This structure is underlined later in the chapter, where the author describes the necessary alienation of the worker, and (*apparently*) writes:

> Thus labour capacity's own labour is as alien to it – and it really is, as regards its diremption etc. – as are material and instrument. (Marx, 1953, p. 366; 1973, p. 462)[10]

This is of course a version of the structure pointed out in the third main section above. Any economic category must, as such, have the form of a *thought*, with a general valid form and a necessary structure, warranting its universality in the society in question. Such a thought is a way of cognizing a relation, and thus of *acknowledging* this same relation *as* universal and necessary. *Ipso facto*, the thought actually *is* in itself the category that is being thought.

Simultaneously, what we have before us is the adequate description of the category of "abstract labor." On the one hand, Marx is depicting the abstract common feature of the physical process of labor (using instruments on materials), on the other the mental aspect of the same process, where the worker conceptualizes it as something alien and as an object of "diremption."

6. TRANSCENDING CLASSICAL PHILOSOPHY: A CONCEPT OF TIME

Marx's way of presentation takes the form of an immanent critique of Hegel's conceptual idealism. Still, in Marx's setting there remains a factor of central importance which is not to be found in Hegel's *Science of Logic*, namely, *time*, here in the form of labor time, functioning as the substantial identity between empirical entities in the judgments. This category, originally presented as the "measure of magnitude" of labor, is closely related to abstract labor.

Of course, since the unveiling of the value forms as forms of judgment has been so conspicuously absent in the literature, so has also any thorough understanding of the concept of time that we meet in Marx's work. In some recent literature, misunderstandings have got disturbing proportions.[11] These have a background in a simplification of his notion of time, reducing it to a concept of succession and extension.

For the sake of clarity, we shall look at the subject matter in three subsections. First, there follows an interpretation of Marx's time-concept in light of Kant's "analogies of experience"; second, of the relation between intensivity and extensivity of time; third, of the category of value-producing labor, which it measures.

6.1. Value Forms as Time-Analogies

The concept of time calls to mind the philosophy of Kant, and (indirectly) Hegel's attempts to overcome it, in claiming that time (which in Kant is the primary form of intuition, being the form of both the outer and the inner sense) is something that can be *getilgt*, "destroyed," by human experience *in actu* (Hegel, 1970a, p. 584).

It is fairly certain that Marx did not read Kant after finishing his university studies (1841). However, he had a critical attitude to what was *de facto* Hegel's criticism of Kant, and the idea that Kant's revolutionizing view of human sensibility in some way could take part in a materialist alternative to Hegel cannot have been far away.

In all events, the overshadowing philosophical problem in the first chapters of *Capital* is the same as that which meets us in Kant's analogies – the core of his treatment of time as well as of causality. The problem has to do with the fact that we can only *deduce* that time is the form of all our sensuous experience, since time in itself is both *a priori* given and impossible to perceive in itself. The fundamental structures of time, Kant contends, can only appear indirectly, through perceivable relations between things ("appearances"). It is in this context that the logic of the transcendental deduction comes to concrete reality, as we have seen.

In Marx, the problem is that since labor time is not a tangible entity, albeit it can be deduced as the substance of value, it can *appear* only in material use values, which will be standing in special definite relations to each other. These relations are those of necessity, and their forms, as we know, are categorical, hypothetical, and disjunctive.

In Kant, the corresponding relations are substance (or substantiality), causality, and interaction – all similar to the categories which mark the closure of Hegel's logic of necessity and essence. Substance, in Kant, is the thought of the totality of the physical world taking the form of, so to speak, an "immense collection" of enduring empirical substances. These combine in *events*, whose relations to each other are causally determined and take the form of bound sequences in time (plain causality) and of simultaneity, with interaction between all substances.

The central thought in Kant's analogies is that when we think substance as a physical totality, we are compelled to presuppose that it is constant in quantity, which means that we are in fact referring to the inchangeability of *time*. The movement of singular substances takes place in empirical time, whose concept is a derivation of the general and abstract time-concept of substance in general. The analogies point to modes of thought pertaining to the intellect and are structuring our capacity to judge in empirical cases. That means that the analogies in question express themselves in empirical judgments of necessity.

Similarly, in Marx we have a concept of abstract universal labor time,[12] which includes references to any extant exemplar of human labor, that is, to every *concrete* labor time. These exemplars of time, the singular commodities, are what correspond to empirical, singular substances in Kant's first analogy. His second analogy, analyzing determined sequence in time, that is, causal sequences, treats the (mental) production of such presentations, a fact that is underlined by the name Kant gave it in its original version: "Principle of production" (Kant, 1996, p. A 91). As for Kant's category of interaction, it presents causality in its general form and as a *totality* of simultaneous presentations or appearances.

As hinted above, these matters may well indicate the reason why Marx does not make any separate argument for the *tertium comparationis* in his chapter on the commodity. For in Kant, the very existence of the (transcendental) judgments in question presupposes "pure" time, outside any presentation; its structure is of such a kind that it is expressed precisely in appearances that combine as they do in the judgments of necessity. A labor theory of value, to the extent that it is a theory of labor *time*, has to imply the types of commodity structure which correspond to (i) a categorical inner substance common to commodities, (ii) the causal relation, which points out that the inner substance is labor time and nothing else, and (iii) the disjunctive and interactive totality, its interactivity including exclusions, implying that the theory holds necessarily in all relations of labor time. These implications also warrant, conversely, that products presented in these forms are *time-entities*, that is, that their material forms are "appearances," forms of presentation. Such a fact may indeed lead commentators to the conclusion that Marx's theory represents an idealist way of thought. Of course, the point is that the material relations of ownership make the world look "ideal," a fact taken all too seriously by German idealism – and by many a bourgeois sycophant.

However, to say that the presentation in question is an appearance-form of labor time pure and simple would be incorrect. There exists, on the contrary, a form of appearance of abstract labor time (i.e., of labor time in so far as it is *abstract*, going on in a labor process whose presupposition is that the worker is expropriated from the means of production), which is the universal equivalent. Here the Marxian scheme transcends that of Kant: The latter thought he had no use for any exclusive material form of presentation – *Erscheinungsform*, "form of appearance," in Marx's vocabulary – since his theme was human experience in general, not just economics.

The best exposition of Marx's theory in the matter is, perhaps, given in his *Critique* from 1859, where he describes how one "cannot recognize in the gold if it is metamorphosed iron or metamorphosed wheat" (Marx, 1972, p. 75), and that consequently gold can represent *any* concrete labor.

In Kant, all time-determinations point back to the analysis of the transcendental judgment forms. The disjunctive form, specifically, where the different disjuncts represent a potentially unending chain of physical substances, is a necessary thought-structure for our conception of a physical totality. It consists of substances, human bodies included, considered as mechanical entities. At first sight, this seems to reactualize the mechanist materialism in Hobbes' theory of the state. However, by presupposing that such a world is a human-produced *appearance*, not a thing in itself, Kant inserts the theme of human dignity into the picture. In this he paves the way for Marx, who constructs a material model of human interaction, whose disjunctive form is confined to the epoch of capitalist commodity production. Thus, as we shall see in the next section, the Hobbesian theory looms in the background.

6.2. *Time as Intensity*

The critical importance of making theoretical use of *all* the concepts of time modes – and, as we shall see in a moment, of their dialectical abolition into certain higher forms – can be induced from the fact that we should expect a correlation between (1) disjunctive form and *simultaneity* in time,[13] (2) hypothetical form and (bound) *succession* in time, and consequently (3) categorical form and *permanence* of time. This last form, through its correlation with the other two, by itself expresses the fact that succession and simultaneity are *permanent* aspects of time, or – more loosely formulated – that there is no radical break between succession and simultaneity, since they are both incorporated in time as such.

However, this "time as such" needs explication.

In Marx's chapter on the commodity, he makes it clear that value-producing activity *appears* as the labor time which is necessary for producing a certain use value under given "socio-normal conditions of production and a given social average degree of skill and intensivity" (cf. Marx, 1966a, p. 218). Value is here tentatively defined as a function of an extensive magnitude of time. However, in the moment that the intensitivity of labor is changing in a part of the economy, we stand before a change in the extensive measure, and "one must consider the reversion of extensive magnitude into intensive, or a magnitude of degree" (Marx, 1968a, p. 431).

If we go to the capitalist mode of production proper, we are confronted with machinery steadily bringing with it an accelerating "speed and thus intensity in the work," and "this condensation of a greater quantity of labor in a given period of time now counts as what it is, as a greater quantity of labor" (Marx, 1968a, p. 432).

Marx's wordage may indicate that he is considering a "Kantian" solution, implying that time is an extensive magnitude. In the original manuscript, he writes something similar, namely, that "*the quantity of labor* in a given time-period is rising." But then this is immediately being explained through a thesis that "the pores of time so to speak are being decreased through compression of the labor" (Marx, 1976, p. 307), something which is to be seen in connection with the fact that in another, contemporary manuscript he implies that the "condensation" is taking place "so to speak through compression of the pores of labor" (Marx, 1968e, p. 302). All in all, the logical consequence is here to consider time as such as possessing an intensive magnitude (insofar as it is a measure of the quantity of labor), since the implication is that "time" is "labor," that is, an expression of human negativity and active working existence. Such a conception of time is to be found at many places in

Grundrisse, as when Marx is implying that the time laid out in one specific branch is "qualitatively" different from the time we find in another (Marx, 1953, p. 313; 1973, p. 408), and as when he is presupposing that a specific historical development is needed to validate "pure" time: " ... the determination of value through the pure labor time takes place only on the basis of production of capital" (1953, p. 701, 1973, p. 797). Another important example lies in his calling labor "the living time" (1953, p. 266, 1973, p. 361) or when he says that capital buys "*living labor time*" (1953, p. 474, 1973, p. 580), paralleling his thesis that it is "labor *time* that stands forth (*erscheint*) as the value-producing activity" (1953, p. 437, 1973, p. 540, italics added).

It is this way of thinking that is expressed in *Capital*, when Marx calls the "condensation of labor" not simply a "higher tension of labor power," but also "a more dense filling-up of the pores of labor time" (1968a, p. 432). Here, condensation of living labor is evidently the same as condensation of labor time.

There is consequently good reason to take Marx to mean that labor time in itself is an intensive magnitude, whose existence lies at the bottom of any calculation of time as extensive. As we have seen from his explanation in the first chapter, a given intensity is a precondition of a measuring of value in extensive time.

Furthermore, this is a theory that, in the midst of the text of *Capital*, points to a dialectical character of the exposition, to an even higher extent than what can be found in the *Grundrisse*, despite the fact that "Hegelian" terms are far more flourishing in the latter work. For to posit labor time as such a quantity is the same as taking it to exist as a "moment" with a certain intensive power. Measuring by degrees means comparing different (intensive) moments in time, not temporal extension. The "intension" at t_0 can be compared only to the intensivity at another point of the working day, t_1 or t_2, etc. These are so to speak different limits, a series of "Nows."

For Kant, it made good sense to make a separation between time and "moment," for in his analysis he is generally presenting time as what is called a "B-series," which, as regards succession, means that the passing of time is taken to be nothing but a sequence of states (with different degrees of permanence). It should be noted that in his discussion of the nature of intensive magnitude, Kant says that our perception of something real (which gives us an impression), "taken as the quantity of something insofar as it fills time is precisely [a] continuous and uniform *production* of reality in time" (Kant, 1996, p. B 183, italics added). Such an idea of production could scarcely occur in philosophy prior to the eve of industrialism. The expression used can be found nearly verbatim in some descriptions of the labor process in Marx. But in Kant, time as *succession* (in bound sequence) is in the picture. What he depicts here is our perceiving the different stages of intensity *as they appear in succession* (production), not the instantaneous perception of a reality. In contradistinction to Marx, Kant does not think of this latter as a basis of time.

However, taking (as Marx does) intensity of time to have priority means a breaking up of the Kantian position. Presenting the concept of time from a "moment" on is in fact something very close to presenting it as an "A-series," that is, as a Now, a limit posited by the active human being (a worker), and implying the relation past–present–future. These are what Hegel calls "the *dimensions* of time" (Hegel, 1970c, p. 47, italics added), superseding the concept of time modes. They are time as thought from the human teleological perspective; they are a consequence of teleological and intentional activity, the foundation of human labor. Marx described the latter in his text on "Labor process and valorization process," the fifth chapter of the original edition of *Capital.*

Such a concept of time implies yet another superseding of German idealism. Above, we saw how Marx abolished Hegel's theory of the judgment from an immanent basis; here, we witness how his superseding of Hegel does not simply lead him back to a Kantian position, but implies the use of a more advanced concept of time, for which Hegel found no serious application. It is also important to note that Hegel's failed attempt to construct a free subject in the process of disjunction implies that he is not capable of rooting out the time-determinations from the world of logic. It seems that even Galileo's theory looms in the background!

6.3. Time as Abstract Labor

The exposition up to this point makes it possible to collect some main points related to a materialist view of time.

As for Marx, it seems that his general theory of labor's constitutive role in human cognition disposes him to say that time is man's general way of conceiving his own productive activity. The possibility of such a conception lies in man's working activity itself, in his psychophysical "intension."

The same general theory seems to lead Marx to suppose that what is spent in production of a certain material thing is a *concrete* time, in contradistinction to other kinds of production and of concrete times. It is fair to think that as regards society in general, independent of its forms, he would call the common time, which allows man to compare distinct activities, a "universal," or perhaps a "time in general." The expression "concrete universal," derived from German idealism, would probably be adequate.

Furthermore, it seems that in capitalist society, these concrete aspects of time are being overdetermined by a time in the abstract, because the products of labor, which in man's natural setting make up the substances which present time-determinations, now persevere as abstracted (expropriated).

Through such a development, capitalism stands forth as a civilizing force, its abstractions showing humanity the true possibilities of time and production. This of course has a coercive background, and takes the form of abstractness. What is in play is *conceptual* understanding, developed by capital. We have seen how it enters the scene. In that way, abstract labor is conceptual labor – physical labor steered by working individuals through *concepts*, not through religious sentiments, ritualistic motives, or idolatry, as in elder societies.

It is clear, then, that "abstract labor" can in no way be taken to be "material" – something which would amount to a contradiction in terms. Still, such a use of the category is not infrequent. It has been brought forward in later years, probably connected with a general crisis among Marxisant intellectuals as regards in-depth understanding of economic categories. It is effectively refuted by the view of the value forms developed above.

The standpoint can, for example, be found in Murray (2000), in Starosta (2009), and in Carchedi (2009a, 2009b). Starosta writes of a "remarkable merit" in Murray's work when it comes to "the importance of highlighting the *materiality* of abstract labor" (Starosta, 2009, p. 307). To underpin, he quotes Marx (cf. 1968a, p. 58), saying that the value-producing labor is "productive expenditure of human brains, muscles, nerves, hands etc."

However, one should keep in mind that by Marx this description is the result of an analytical abstraction that has already explicitly abstracted from utility and thus from commodity materiality (cf. 1968a, p. 58). Furthermore, he has also made it clear that to abstract from all useful labors inherent in commodities leaves *only a natural* "substrate" (cf. 1968a, p. 57). It stands to reason, then, that abstract labor cannot be material (or "natural") – which is precisely the meaning of the word "materiality" as used by the authors in question.[14]

In Carchedi, abstract labor is even called "human metabolism," and it is contended that "[t]he observation of the expenditure of calories during production is the observation of abstract labor" (2009a, 2009b, p. 249).

It is evident, however, that abstract labor cannot possibly be reduced to metabolism. It is a simple fact that labor is labor, a conscious, teleological process performed by a human being. Thought is not material: It is precisely the contrariety to materiality. It is clear, then, that to speak of *abstract* labor, which, in addition, is an abstraction *from* actually *concrete* labors, as "material" indicates confusion.

Labor is a construction of concrete, material substances through concrete syntheses. This construction is of course conceptual as well as material in the stricter sense. This means that if we find that its products are appearing in the form of certain judgments, then these are forms of thought that necessarily are being used in the process itself. They are the workers' own *conceptualizing* of the process – their mental "disjunction" included.[15] Consequently, it is shown once again how a scientific investigation has to use concepts that necessarily are employed in and *by the investigated object itself*. In these relations lies the secret of the appearance of the forms of value. The abstract content of the actual process of production is indeed something very far from "observation of abstract labor." Abstract labor cannot be "observed" at all, and it is still a fact that "to this day no chemist has discovered exchange value in pearls or in diamonds" (1966a, pp. 245–246). What happens in the capitalist labor process is that the kinds of intellectual (judgmental, syllogistic) approach that we can reconstruct through analyzing its *results* (as Marx does in the first chapter of *Capital*) stand forth as *preconditions* of that process. In Marx, the special intellectual character of the thought-activity performed by the worker is a consequence in part (i) of the fact that the capitalist process is a *necessary* one, a result of exigencies of a natural process, and in part (ii) of the fact that the necessity itself has the form of *expropriation*: It is not only a technical necessity, but also an *abstract* one, since it depends on the worker being abstracted from the means of production and thus from the technical process. Since he enters as propertyless in the process, he reflects its abstract character through his work. Just as the result of the process confronts us in the form of commodity fetishism, so the process that shaped the result is dependent on the worker's presupposition that the expropriation of his faculties seem to follow as from a law of nature. In this way, "abstract labor," the view that the work process in some distinct manner is devoid of concreteness, turns into a "popular prejudice," an undisputed condition of labor, pervading all levels of society.

The view that abstract labor is "material" is closely connected with an inability to discover the *conceptual* forms of the *products* of labor – the true content of *Capital*'s first chapter. For it is only in *conceptual* thinking – not in simple "logic of reflection" or "essence," whose categories (appearance, identity, difference, etc.) are so unanimously hailed by Marxisant theoreticians trying to discover the Hegelian heritage in Marx – that *material* things force their way to thought, structuring the latter in determinate forms. As soon as these are discovered, it becomes clear how the thinking in question is tied to material objects – making obsolete the notion of a material human labor abstracted from thinking activity. And as soon as these factors turn out to be united, we have to consider abstract labor as *time*, since the genesis of time is placed in the intentionality of man.

7. CIRCULATION: STATE AND IDEOLOGY

Having pointed out the basic characteristics of the forms of value, that is, their judgment-structures *and* the time-aspects which they express, it is time to focus on some important features of circulation. Through three sub-sections, I try to show (A) the latter's relation to the value forms, (B) the consequence of this relation for a science of society, and (C) that individuals, in their disjunction, are held together by specific illusions which both create and mystify *the state*.

7.1. Circulation and Value Forms

As mentioned above, the theoretical passage from exchange of commodities to their circulation is to be found in the moment that the universal equivalent is used as measure of value *and* as a *numéraire*. In that moment, the total of disjuncted value expressions turn into a system of prices, and commodity circulation becomes a reality.

Bourgeois economics has traditionally identified and/or confused values and prices. At the same time, its so-called theory of prices, which in general terms has remained identical since the time of James Steuart, can be called the center of bourgeois theory of society. To the extent that circulation for Marx must represent the passage to a (societal) *system*, something similar can be said of his theory: The theory of price formation is basic for his model of capitalist society.

Consequently, it is no wonder that these theories collide; they are opposed through the fact that while bourgeois economics thinks it possible to measure the prices of one commodity through the price of another, Marx takes this to be impossible, and wants to measure all prices through division of the *material* of one specific commodity.

It is a spectacular fact that for a century, the Marxisant writers who have taken the matter up, in practice have unanimously tried to "defend" Marx's economics through hailing the *bourgeois* theory of prices, dating back to the age of mercantilism. There seems to be a clear parallel from this to their misunderstanding of the relation between the value forms, especially the disjunctive ones.

When the Marxian value forms are abolished, they persevere as the building stones of the overarching syllogism of circulation. Especially in the two variants of Form II, they determine the forms of value and price on the social surface: On the one hand the circulative movement pertaining to all members of the commodity mob, on the other the disjunctive expression of the universal equivalent. Also, we have seen that Marx takes the *exchangeability* of gold to nourish the belief that circulation consists of conventional acts of *exchange*.

This last fact gives a concrete meaning to a well-known passage in Marx's first chapter, where he characterizes value by stressing that "[i]ts *form*, which turns it into precisely exchange value, must ... be analyzed" (Marx, 1966a, p. 219). Apparently, this might be taken to mean that all value, however much it may be *circulating*, will *appear* as being *exchanged*. For the exposition which Marx then starts ends precisely in Form IV. Since this is absent from later editions, the significance of taking the "exchange value" as "form of appearance" for the value may well have been lost to readers.

It is of interest to note that the *reflection* of the owner of the money commodity must necessarily be a disjunctive syllogism, since he must start by taking a real disjunctive situation as given, as expressed in the judgment. The syllogism will be of this kind:

A is *either B* or *C* or *D*,
A is not *C* or *D*;
A is *B*.

This reflection says that gold can *be*, or be transformed into, certain other commodities, whereupon a specific one is chosen, to the exclusion of others. As Hegel points out, this syllogism has universality as its *medius terminus*. Marx says the same of circulation (cf. Hegel, 1970a, II, p. 398; Marx, 1972, p. 76).

Hegel lets the formal syllogistic thought come to a halt at this point, and declares that it has turned into objectivity. There is no "syllogism of the concept" in Hegel, except the oncoming *objective* "syllogism." This objective aspect of the concept consists of separate chapters on "mechanism," "chemism," and "teleology," which must be regarded as advanced conceptual versions of the categories of essence: Their subsumption under the conscious subject comes to the fore in that the categories pertaining to substance and causality now attain a teleological character. If one searches through *Science of Logic* for the categories most related to Kant's "principles," his analogies specifically, this would be their place. Correspondingly, when we have described the Marxian judgment-value forms as "time-analogies," this should be taken to imply an anticipation of the interpretation of capital as causal and interactive substance, generating the products of capital enclosed in the value forms (cf. again Marx, 1953, p. 205, 1973, p. 297).

Formally, the parallel to Marx's exposition is obvious, since the formal syllogism is sublated in the objective, in the same manner as the productive movement of capital in Marx is a development where mechanical and chemical processes, and their use values, take on the specific form of capitalist subjectivity. However, in Hegel, this process goes on as if the subjectivity inherent in the use values is humanity pure and simple, while by Marx it is the commodity owner. Hegel's viewpoint goes back to the very mistake that made it possible for him to jump to the concept without mediating the analysis of the factors of judgment and causality, thereby presupposing that the process of production goes on without real antagonisms.

If this last critique is correct, we may safely conclude that the analysis of the "judgmental" value forms can give us the arsenal we need to infer which factors are crucial, important, or obsolete for an economic theory, even considered as a model of capitalist society. Let us now look at the "statal" aspect of that society – not with the intention of drawing special consequences regarding state *power*, but with the aim of learning more about the society in question, and of the adequacy of an understanding of the state that consciously accords with the analysis of the forms of value. The motivation is connected with the fact that no analysis of the *society* in which these forms are operative can be completed in isolation from the structure of its *state*. One should keep in mind that the Marxian disjunction (Form IV) presents us with *all* commodity owners as *individual* subjects, and does not take a halt with any "species." It will be substantiated presently that the statal structure is a function of such a value form.

7.2. The Causal Realm. A Base for Contract Theories

The Hobbesian contract, the presupposition of all bourgeois theories of the state (whether they endorse it openly or not) is a covenant between *all individual* members of society, where the primary result is the exclusion of one, whose privilege it is to be subject to no contract (cf. Hobbes, 1973, 90 sqq). This is the sovereign, *de facto* the state, and his exclusivity is mirrored in the status of money, the excluded commodity which, in contradistinction to any member of the "commodity mob" (Marx), has the apparent immediate exchangeability. The legitimacy of money is structured as the legitimacy of the state. Just as each and every commodity upholds the money form, so each and every commodity owner upholds and legitimizes the state.

Furthermore, the fact that the society of commodity owners does also include owners of labor power makes it possible to appreciate the legitimative potential of the state. It is a result of a movement of exclusion in which all members of the working class take part, by the simple fact of being forced to sell their labor power, that is, being points of circulation, or of *money*. The antagonistic character of the state *power* vis-à-vis workers' *class* interest is revealed later – independently of their perennial legitimizing of the state – through the exploitation, based as it is on equal rights in exchange, and on the reversal of these rights, which results from the process of accumulation.

If the Hobbesian theory gives us the adequate picture of the bourgeois state, that fact is visible in the structural similarity between two different, basic models, namely, on the one hand Hobbes' own "state of nature," and on the other Marx's "exchange process." When Marx criticizes the view that commodities are "exchanged" in circulation, he says that such a structure would have meant that "their relative value will be shown (*ermittelt*) from their exchange as commodities pure and simple" (Marx, 1972, p. 72). That is, there would be no measuring of values in a universal and common material, a fact which must imply that we were not yet in a civil society, that is, in what Hobbes calls a "commonwealth." We are in what he calls "the state of nature," where subjects simply are excluded from each other. What Marx shows is that it takes an existence as privately owning commodity producers to make up such a totality of mutual isolation. The relative value magnitudes of commodities will here present themselves through bargaining between different "cells" of the social organism, instead of being socially determined on a manifest, objective scale.

The structural similarity between the situation which in Hobbes leads to the introduction of a commonwealth, and the one which in Marx produces the existence of a bourgeois society, is also shown through the mechanistic character of the settings. In Marx, and effectively in Hegel too, true freedom is not to be obtained here, since it is blocked by a social disjunction.

Consequently, we persevere in the realm of necessity. This realm is pervaded by mechanist causality. In Marx, this causal realm has a double form of appearance: First, it consists of *commodities*, a fact that does not bar its potentialities as a mirror of nature, for in the capitalist system all material things can become commodities. Second, it consists of commodity *owners*, making up the members of some social formation. The upshot is a virtual unification of two seemingly different paradigms in the philosophy of the modern era – paradigms which we may call the one of the *state of nature* and the one of *inertia*.

The theory of *inertia*, developed from Galileo on, holds that it is the natural tendency of an object to move (uniformly) if it is not hampered by another one. Its importance in our context is that it was taken for granted by Kant, who felt it was in accordance with his analogies. The theory of the state of nature, from Hobbes on, is the accurate parallel: It holds that human beings have a natural tendency to move in a way that leads to clashes, unless they are held in check by a superior power. In Hobbes' variant, this power is structured as if it were a transcendent force, in principle identical with the state which one finds by Hegel and Marx, and in a money theory like Marx's.

The important point here is that insofar as Hegel does not manage to construct a transition from causality to freedom, he in fact falls all the way back to Hobbesianism, since the refined character of the human agency in his thought relatively to Hobbes' is not warranted if the subject is not developed to its climax in the "Subjective logic." For parallel reasons, the Marxian diremption indicates a specific Hobbesian world. Marx offers a model where "commonwealth" and "state of nature" *coexist* (as a unity of circulation on the one hand, and disjuncted exchange of gold on the other). This could be taken to be an affirmation of Hobbes' *Leviathan*, for what Hobbes meant was precisely that the state of nature was inherent in the commonwealth, not prior to it.

7.3. The State of Bourgeois Intellectualism

The commodity-analysis describes how *all* members of society basically behave. We are shown that to the extent that they, *viz.*, "we," are *individuals*, we are so through Form IV – as disjuncted entities, *membra disjecta* of an economic relation under the immediate surface of society. The so-called freedom that can be attained in this situation is the one Hobbes assigned to the sovereign. If the sovereign of *Leviathan* is born through exclusion, then he is excluded from a structure that equals Marx's closing value form. But in that case, each and every commodity owner is excluding himself, comparable to the Hobbesian sovereign.

The exclusion in question, which equals the political liberty attainable for any individual, is nothing but the mutual exclusivity of the roles of *citoyen* and of *bourgeois* as opposed to each other in each member of society. The latter is the role of owner, the former the role of political subject. Insofar as money is an excluded commodity, we have got a *society*. But this society consists precisely in the same exclusion, insofar as it pertains to everybody. Every member of society is disjuncted: He is a *citoyen* insofar as he is not a commodity owner, and a *bourgeois* insofar as he is not a *citoyen* (cf. Sandemose, 2008, 274 sq.) Still, he is both. The diremption is being perfected.

All members of capitalist society are to be considered as commodity owners whose mentality is described by "commodity equations" that are abolished into commodity circulation. Any Marxist, then, should acknowledge that the bourgeois state is held together by the workers as well as by the bourgeoisie (and others). Without such a relative unanimity, there would be no true or pervading legitimacy for the power structure in capitalist society. But this power structure, often rendered "Staatsgewalt" by Marx, is (as hinted above) something else than its foundation, the *state* proper, that is, the total relations of circulation. The state *power* is a *concretum*, usually a specific *national* concretum of diverse means of subjugation, whereas the bourgeois *state*, differing from both bourgeois and prebourgeois state power, has quite another transnational uniformity.

What we are actually doing when accepting the confusion of circulation with exchange is contending that to distribute commodities we are bound to return to a kind of society where there exists (at most) a *contingent* relation between the economic sphere and the political structure. But as we just saw, nothing could be less true of capitalist society.

Thus, while the state is made up of a reciprocal structure of consciousnesses, these last tend to be false, reproducing precisely the illusions that brought it into being. In social research and science, the fundamental illusion is the belief, fostered by the mutual exclusion of state and society, that scientific evaluation of social facts can be executed by means of standards indifferent or alien to the social construction itself.

Admittedly, as soon as capitalist crises explode, the logical structure seems to disappear: The nature of the exchangeability of the universal equivalent changes, and the disjunctions seem to let go of their capitalist character. However, the immediate exchangeability of gold is always something *apparent* (it is never guaranteed that an exchange takes place), and the basic thing is to understand how such an appearance is capable of dominating society. What changes in a crisis is the nature of the appearance (for actual exchange can disappear). A more concrete investigation of state and society is precisely the incorporation of such new appearance-forms in the analysis. But if this is done while the original constellation is no longer understood as basic, then the Marxist character of the analysis vanishes. A not too uncommon by-product of such illusions on the part of professional intellectuals is a voluntarism in their approach to science.[16]

In contemporary crisis-ridden Western societies, we are confronted with an ideal situation for aloof ideology-makers, such as, for example, those of the modern, so-called "welfare" state, apt to treat the working class as if it were a mass of nonconscious subjects in need of expert guidance. Historically, this attitude was born with utopian socialism, and was brought to a climax by utilitarian moralists-and-economists, of whom J. M. Keynes was not the least important.

The condescending attitude is part of a mode of "scientific" approach which renounces on immanent analysis and concentrates on finding appropriate "tools" of analysis, instruments that are alien to the economic–political system in question, but all the more fitted to expand the prestige of the user. The debates on the "transformation problem," starting out precisely from the circulation–exchange confusion, bear witness of this (Sandemose, 2004).

The Marxian analysis of the commodity by its very nature tends to block one of the main misapprehensions in that debate: As we can see now, it is, for example, impossible to introduce "labor time" in the way done by Paul M. Sweezy, who, in his vindication of von Bortkiewicz's well-known papers from Bortkiewicz (1907) 1906–07, said that one could solve all measuring problems posed by Marx' analysis of prices by "choosing" the unit "labor time" for both values and prices (cf. Sweezy, 1942, p. 122).

Such a way of thinking has led many a present-day theorist to introduce a category called "monetary expression of labor time" ("MELT"), and to use it directly in economic models with apparent affinity to Marx's.[17] The point with this invention is to link the value produced in a certain time to a form of currency rather than to the money commodity, thereby creating an entity which is not a commodity, and thus immune to price changes. But such changes would represent no problem if Marx's theory of the measure of value had been understood: A foregone measuring of values in a *physical* stuff of course cannot be influenced by changes in the *prices* of that stuff (cf. Sandemose, 2004, 52 sq.) Besides, actual genesis of any money form would invalidate the existence of any "MELT." The latter is thus a phantasm-category; it is unreal and can take no part in the experience of the subjects involved in analysis. It is forgotten that the investigation is about humans and their actual categories, and consequently their *actual thoughts* and logic. It is such social thought-structures that actually reflect and construct "value," which is a mental form, since it is dependent on an *abstraction from* material forms of labor. The "MELT" is thus not only meaningless, but a concept which is contraproductive to social science. It can be compared to certain auxiliary-astronomical "points" in space, "measuring" devices invented by Ptolemeus and his followers, which Kepler found horrendous, since they, as he said, "do not exist in nature."

Another glaring example of theoretical troubles in this field is to be found in Heinrich (2006). The author criticizes Marx's theory of the money commodity (and indeed any extant theory of such an entity). He accepts its necessary existence in a real but transitory historical stage, that is, that it had to be there before one could transcend it and change the money from a commodity to an entity which is a noncommodity, purely a *Repräsentant* of "value as such." He argues for such a possibility by contending that

> [e]ven if the money commodity (*Warengeld*) might be a *historical* starting-point for the genesis of money, its existence does in no way follow logically-conceptually from the commodity form of the product of labor. (Heinrich, 2006, p. 236)

This is true enough. But in fact, inside the economic field there is nothing which follows conceptually, though it may, or must, follow in accordance with concepts. That is precisely what Marx points out in his chapter on the exchange process: In practice, and "in their embarrassment, our commodity owners think as Faust did. In the beginning was the act" (Marx, 1968a, p. 101). They act, and it turns out that they are bound to act within certain structures, corresponding to a mode of rational thought. This mode is depicted in *Capital's* first chapter, first version in particular: It is conceptual. Had they acted in another context, the result would have been of another kind. Here, they act to persevere in a field that may grant them certain use values. Their practical activity results in the exclusion of a material that is the most adequate for storing labor, the value substance. In logical terms, this was anticipated in the expression making the relation of equality into a relation of value.

This may serve to remind us that the "diremptive" exposition in the first chapter of *Capital*, with its disjunctive form, implies a claim that what is a *necessity of thought* is also a necessity of *the real*, that is, of the concrete unity of thought and material structure (to the extent that this last may be separated from thought). The social movement of commodities, from the end of the production period to their sale for individual or productive consumption, is bound to follow rules that are rules of thought, since "value" is itself an extension of thought, the commodity itself being a sensuous–supersensuous thing (cf. Marx, 1968a, p. 85). This theory consequently implies that what is ("economically") real is *necessary*, and that it must be possible to express it as such. The ideas of a "representative," of a "MELT," not to speak of a commodity value measured by means of value – all these presentations are phantasies which cannot even be formulated inside such a frame. They belong to a field of contingency whose horizon is in the head of the theorist.

No doubt, the condescending attitude always has an unconscious component, since it follows from an illusion of one's own intellectual exclusivity that is social through and through. Still, a lack of consciousness does not amend any action. The illusions mentioned here might seem to have their logical summit in the view that a human labor that is abstract is in reality material, and that workers performing it are creatures who can do so without using their wits and concepts.

In fact, if we believe, as do so many benevolent Marxisant authors, that one can discover the form of money and prices through an abstraction from the realities of workers, then we are behaving precisely like aloof sovereigns, who presume they can discover their true selves without acknowledging the trouble of others. We are putting ourselves in the same exclusive situation as is the owner of the money commodity or the alienating state representative.

What is needed now is rather a political movement that makes it possible to recreate Marxism, building on its true sources, abstracting from all the different bourgeois quasi-interpretations that have been mixed up with it for generations, to the detriment of revolutionary thought and action.

NOTES

1. The word "abolition," whether it is a translation or not, is here always to be taken in the significance of the German "aufheben": "Abolished" in the sense of being preserved in a higher form.

2. On the differences between the editions of the first chapter, see H.-G. Backhaus: "Zur Problematik des Verhältnisses von 'Logischem' und 'Historischem' in der Marxschen Kritik der Politischen Ökonomie," in *nueva politica*, Mexico City 1978. I know the article only as translated in Backhaus (1980). For the criticism of Marx referred to, see Backhaus (1980, p. 159). See also Sandemose (1983, p. 63). Also, Backhaus (1997), *passim*.

3. For the connection between this reasoning and categories of bourgeois property relations, see Sandemose (2008, p. 285).

4. The word "presentation" is here a translation of Kant's term "*Vorstellung*." The special kind of *Vorstellung* that Kant specifies as "*Erscheinung*" is a term that denotes actual objects, processes, or substances, in an external world, or the human perception of such objects. Here, such a presentation is called 'appearance." These translations of "*Vorstellung*" and "*Erscheinung*," respectively, are the ones used by Pluhar in the edition of *Critique of Pure Reason* mentioned in the reference list below.

5. For a criticism of Hegel on this point, see Sandemose (1973). Also Hartmann (1999, p. 265).

6. However, it should be stressed that the most important attempt to explore the intentions of Marx in the 1867 version is done by Hans-Georg Backhaus. Sandemose (1983) criticizes Backhaus for not having transcended the limits of a "logic of reflection" (or "logic of essence") in his criticism of Marx's second version. Backhaus, for example, does not point to the judgment forms of the commodities. This also goes for Backhaus (1969, 1997), and it points to a general weakness already in the early *Kommentarliteratur* to Marx's works on political economy in the wake of "1968." even of its best representatives. Examples are Morf (1968), Reichelt (1970), and Krahl (1971). Smith (1990), Arthur (1979, 2002a, 2002b), together with Wolf (2002) are more recent instances. The general problem with this literature is that its ignorance of the provenance of Marx's paradigm in social science is combined with a stern conviction of having grasped the essential features of dialectic method. In this way, much of the potential for a Marxist criticism of modern science and logic evaporates. This was a danger apparent already in the important work of Zeleny (1962).

7. The name here given to Form IV is to be found only a little later in the chapter (p. 240).

8. I use this expression for the chapter, in agreement with Marx's term in the foreword to the first edition, where he says that it is the only text in the volume that might give the reader serious difficulties (Marx 1968, p. 12).

9. The word "Marxisant," indicating a person or a standpoint focusing on themes developed by Karl Marx, is adopted in this chapter, much to replace the often misleading term "Marxist."

10. Note that the editors of *Grundrisse* have "*Direktion*," not "*Diremtion*." It should be checked whether this could be a misreading. The same ("direction") goes for Martin Nicolaus' translation (Marx, 1973). In Dussel (2001, p. 195), "Direktion" is used as a specific Marxian term.

11. An important issue in present debates is a confrontation between "simultaneists" and "temporalists" on Marx's theory of value and prices. Here, especially by certain "temporalists," the basic concepts for any theory of time are hopelessly intermingled or simply left out of consideration. As an example may serve Carchedi (2009a). Here, "time" is reduced to succession alone: He holds that "simultaneism," as an economic theory or model, stands for "a reality without time," simply because it, under specific conditions, abstracts from change (2009, p. 263; also, see Kliman, 2007). The reason for this kind of polemics is of course the basic misunderstanding that time is in some way one-dimensional. In our text above, it will be shown how all time-determinations necessarily are working together in the Marxian setup so that it is fully adequate to concentrate on one or two of them, provided the way of

abstraction follows a specific rule. The basis for the unity of the time-determinations is, as one sees, that labor time by Marx cannot be expressed at all if not through a value expression that contains both permanence (categorical relation), sequence and bound succession (hypothetical relation), and simultaneity (interaction, disjunctive relation).

12. I think this is the full and adequate formulation of the category "abstract universal labor," which is common in *Capital* and *Critique of Political Economy*. In the *Grundrisse*, "time" is often added to such expressions, as, i.e., 1953, p. 701, 1973, p. 797. See also Sandemose (2007, pp. 129–134).

13. Namely, since there are here a plurality of minds measuring time in their interaction.

14. In Carchedi, 2009b, 153sq., it is argued that Marx's *dictum* in the first chapter, to the effect that as exchange value, a product does "not contain an atom of use value," is not the same as saying that we have to do with a non-material entity. This is clearly incorrect. In the chapter in question, Marx operates with several synonyms (no less than 16!) for "use value," among them "*Naturalform*," "*Warenkörper*," and "*unmittelbares Materiatur*." See, for example, 1966a, pp. 216, 226, 228, 229 (where we find the expressions "*Gebrauchswert oder Warenkörper*," while he says that the "*Gebrauchsgestalten*" of the commodities are their "*Naturalformen*"), etc. Let me add here that Carchedi's work is marred by a curious confusion, in that he takes "value substance" to have the same meaning as "value as a substance" (cf. 2009b, p. 149). This leads him to identify value and abstract labor, while for Marx, labor is the *substance of* value.

15. In 2009a, p. 151, Carchedi tries to overcome the difficulty by contending that his concept of abstract labor includes "the working of the brain and thus the production of knowledge. (...) Abstract labour can be expended both in the production of material objects and in the production of knowledge." He then separates these analytically, calling them "*objective and mental transformations*," which "are, respectively, the transformations of the reality outside us and our conceptualisations of that transformed reality, or knowledge." They are "constituent elements of labor in general," and they "take always place contemporaneously." While avoiding to call this abstract labor, and constantly shifting his expressions, Carchedi then tells us that "mental labor" is a "material" process. This result was necessary, since otherwise his main thesis would dissolve itself. Furthermore, it is connected with the fact that Carchedi does not at all describe a conceptualizing process of labor, since he, as we saw, uses the expression "conceptualizations of ... transformed reality," not of active thought employed to transform the physical process into *human labor*. Carchedi seems in fact to propagate a vulgar materialism on level with some modern "neuroscience," where thought is in effect some sort of matter.

16. A remarkable example is, again, Carchedi (2009a), where it is contended that Marx's analysis in *Capital* is "class-determined" from the start (p. 236). However, the existence of classes is, to the contrary, developed only as a result of his fundamental analyses. It cannot surprise that Carchedi tries to analyze society from a set of "Principles" which he does not in the least try to justify as such. Instead, he ought to have seen that in these matters there can be no principles other than those

residing in the "analogies" of the value forms. This view, however, is completely alien to him, since he is confusing time-determinations (cf. footnote 15).

17. See Ramos (1998, pp. 69, 77) and Kliman, 2007 (p. 25 and *passim*), cf. Foley (1986, 20sq). Also, Aglietta (1979; "Monetary expression of labour hours").

ACKNOWLEDGMENT

I want to thank James Lawler and Rolf Wesøe for their many helpful and scholarly suggestions, turning my drafts into a readable essay.

REFERENCES

Aglietta, M. (1979). *A theory of capitalist regulation, the US experience*. London: New Left Books.

Arthur, C. (1979). Dialectic of the value-form. In: D. Elson (Ed.), *Value. The representation of labor in capitalism*. New Jersey: Humanities Press.

Arthur, C. (2002a). Review of dialectics and deconstruction in political economy. In: *Historical materialism* (Vol. 10(1), pp. 251–257). Leiden: Brill.

Arthur, C. (2002b). *The new dialectic and Marx's Capital*. Leiden: Brill.

Backhaus, H.-G. (1969). Zur Dialektik der Wertform. In: A. Schmidt (Ed.), *Beiträge zur marxistischen Erkenntnistheorie* (pp. 128–152). Frankfurt am Main: Suhrkamp.

Backhaus, H.-G. (1980). [Trans] "Zur Problematik des Verhältnisses von 'Logischem' und 'Historischem' in der Marxschen Kritik der Politischen Ökonomie". *Kurasje, 27–28*, 117–160. Copenhagen: Modtryk.

Backhaus, H.-G. (1997). *Dialektik der Wertform. Untersuchungen zur Marxschen Ökonomiekritik*. Freiburg: ca ira.

Bortkiewicz, L. v. (1906–1907). Wertrechnung und Preisrechnung im Marxschen System. *Archiv für Sozialwissenschaft und Sozialpolitik*, Bände XXIII and XXV, J. C. B. Mohr, Tübingen.

Bortkiewicz, L. v. (1907). Zur Berichtigung der grundlegenden theoretischen Konstruktion von Marx im dritten Band des Kapital. *Jahrbücher für Nationalökonomie und Statistik*, Band 89. Stuttgart: Fischer.

Carchedi, G. (2009a). Limits and challenges of the consistency debate in Marxian value theory. *Research in political economy, 25*, 234–275. New York: Emerald.

Carchedi, G. (2009b). The fallacies of 'new dialectics' and value-form theory. In: *Historical materialism* (Vol. 17, pp. 145–169). Leiden: Brill.

Dussel, E. D. (2001). *Towards an unknown Marx: A commentary on the manuscripts of 1861–63*. London: Routledge.

Foley, D. (1986). *Understanding capital. Marx's economic theory*. Cambridge, MA: Harvard University Press.

Hartmann, K. (1999). *Hegels Logik*. Berlin: de Gruyter.

Hegel, G. W. F. (1970a [1806]). *Phänomenologie des Geistes. Werke in zwanzig Bänden* (Vol. 3). Frankfurt am Main: Suhrkamp.
Hegel, G. W. F. (1970b [1815]). *Wissenschaft der Logik II. Werke in zwanzig Bänden* (Vol. 6). Frankfurt am Main: Suhrkamp.
Hegel, G. W. F. (1970c [1830]). *Enzyklopädie der philosophischen Wissenschaften im Grundrisse II. Werke in zwanzig Bänden* (Vol. 9). Frankfurt am Main: Suhrkamp.
Heinrich, M. (2006). *Die Wissenschaft vom Wert.* Münster: Westfälisches dampfboot.
Hobbes, Th. (1973 [1650]). *Leviathan.* London: Dent.
Hölderlin, F. (1962). Urteil und Sein. *Sämtliche Werke*, Band 4, pp. 226–228. Stuttgart: J. B. Metzlersche Verlagsbuchhandlung.
Kant, I. (1996 [1781,1787]). *Critique of pure reason. Unified edition.* (With all variants from the 1781 and 1787 editions.) Translated by W. S. Pluhar, with an introduction by Patricia Kitcher. Indianapolis: Hackett.
Kliman, A. (2007). *Reclaiming Marx's "Capital." A refutation of the myth of inconsistency.* New York: Rowman & Littlefield.
Krahl, H.-J. (1971). *Konstitution und Klassenkampf.* Frankfurt am Main: Verlag Neue Kritik.
Leibniz, G. W. (1999 [1710]). *Theodizee/Théodicée.* Frankfurt: Suhrkamp.
Lugarini, L. (1957). Il giudizio in Hegel. *Il Pensiero, II*, 202–265. Roma: Ateneo.
Marx, K. (1953). *Grundrisse der Kritik der politischen Ökonomie.* Berlin: Dietz.
Marx, K. (1955 [1867]). Die Wertform. In: *Marx/Engels: Kleine ökonomische Schriften.* Berlin: Dietz.
Marx, K. (1966a [1867]). Waare und Geld. In: I. Fetscher (Ed.), *Studienausgabe Politische Ökonomie* (pp. 216–246). Frankfurt: Fischer Bücherei.
Marx, K. (1966b). Marx to Lachâtre, March 18, 1872. *Marx-Engels Werke, 33*, 434. Berlin: Dietz.
Marx, K. (1968a [1867]). *Das Kapital. Erster Band.* Frankfurt: Europäische Verlagsanstalt.
Marx, K. (1968b [1861–63]). *Theorien über den Mehrwert. Zweites Buch.* Frankfurt am Main: Europäische Verlagsanstalt.
Marx, K. (1972 [1859]). *Zur Kritik der politischen Ökonomie.* Berlin: Dietz.
Marx, K. (1973). *Grundrisse.* London: Penguin.
Marx, K. (1976). *Kritik der politischen ökonomie (Manuskript 1861–63), MEGA III/3.1.* Berlin: Dietz.
Morf, O. (1968). *Geschichte und Dialektik in der politischen Ökonomie.* Frankfurt: Suhrkamp.
Murray, P. (2000). Marx's 'truly Social' Labour Theory of Value. *Historical Materialism, 6*, 27–65. Leiden: Brill.
Ramos, A. M. (1998). Value and price of production: New evidence on Marx's transformation procedure. *International Journal of Political Economy, 28*(4), 55–81. Armonk: Sharpe.
Reichelt, H. (1970). *Zur logischen Struktur des Kapitalbegriffs bei Karl Marx.* Frankfurt am Main: Europäische Verlagsanstalt.
Sandemose, J. (1973). *Kapitalbegrep-Begrepsbegrep [Concept of capital-Concept of concept].* Dissertation, University of Oslo, Oslo.
Sandemose, J. (1983). Vareanalyse [*Analysis of the commodity*]. *Kurasje, 32*, 53–76. Copenhagen: Modtryk.
Sandemose, J. (2004). The 'Transformation Problem': Wage form, numéraire, and value transfer. *International Journal of Political Economy, 34*, 41–58. Armonk: Sharpe.
Sandemose, J. (2007). *Totalitet og netode* [*Totality and method*]. Oslo: Spartacus.

Sandemose, J. (2008). Modern Eleusis: Religion and factory. *Science & Society*, *72*(3), 266–294. New York: Guilford Press.

Smith, T. (1990). *The Logic of Marx's Capital.* New York: SUNY.

Starosta, G. (2009). The commodity-form and the dialectical method: On the structure of Marx's exposition in chapter 1 of capital. *Science & Society*, *72*(3), 295–318. New York: Guilford Press.

Sweezy, P. (1942). *The theory of capitalist development.* New York: Monthly Review Press.

Wolf, D. (2002). *Der dialektische Widerspruch im Kapital. Ein Beitrag zur Marxschen Werttheorie.* Hamburg: VSA-Verlag.

Wood, E. M. (2002). *The origin of capitalism. A longer view.* London: Verso.

Zeleny, J. (1962). *Die Wissenschaftslogik und 'Das Kapital'.* Berlin: Akademie-Verlag.